M000288077

PROPERTY RIGHTS
IN POST-SOVIET RUSSIA

The effectiveness of property rights – and the rule of law more broadly – is often depicted as depending primarily on rulers' "supply" of legal institutions. Yet the crucial importance of private sector "demand" for law is frequently overlooked. This book develops a novel framework that unpacks the demand for law in Russia, building on an original enterprise survey as well as extensive interviews with lawyers, firms, and private security agencies. By tracing the evolution of firms' reliance on violence, corruption, and law over the two decades following the Soviet Union's collapse, the book clarifies why firms in various contexts may turn to law for property rights protection, even if legal institutions remain ineffective or corrupt. The author's detailed demand-side analysis of property rights draws attention to the extensive role that law plays in the Russian business world, contrary to frequent depictions of Russia as lawless.

JORDAN GANS-MORSE is an assistant professor of political science at Northwestern University. His articles have appeared in *American Journal of Political Science*, *American Political Science Review*, *Comparative Political Studies*, *Post-Soviet Affairs*, *Problems of Post-Communism*, and *Studies in International Comparative Development*. His research has been funded by the National Science Foundation, the Social Science Research Council, and the American Bar Foundation. He holds a PhD in political science from the University of California, Berkeley.

PROPERTY RIGHTS IN POST-SOVIET RUSSIA

Violence, Corruption, and the Demand for Law

JORDAN GANS-MORSE

Northwestern University, Illinois

CAMBRIDGE
UNIVERSITY PRESS

CAMBRIDGE
UNIVERSITY PRESS

University Printing House, Cambridge CB2 8BS, United Kingdom

One Liberty Plaza, 20th Floor, New York, NY 10006, USA

477 Williamstown Road, Port Melbourne, VIC 3207, Australia

314-321, 3rd Floor, Plot 3, Splendor Forum, Jasola District Centre, New Delhi-110025, India

79 Anson Road, #06-04/06, Singapore 079906

Cambridge University Press is part of the University of Cambridge.

It furthers the University's mission by disseminating knowledge in the pursuit of education, learning and research at the highest international levels of excellence.

www.cambridge.org
Information on this title: www.cambridge.org/9781316607848

© Jordan Gans-Morse 2017

This publication is in copyright. Subject to statutory exception and to the provisions of relevant collective licensing agreements, no reproduction of any part may take place without the written permission of Cambridge University Press.

First published 2017
First paperback edition 2018

A catalogue record for this publication is available from the British Library

ISBN 978-1-107-15396-7 Hardback
ISBN 978-1-316-60784-8 Paperback

Cambridge University Press has no responsibility for the persistence or accuracy of URLs for external or third-party internet websites referred to in this publication, and does not guarantee that any content on such websites is, or will remain, accurate or appropriate.

CONTENTS

*A further Online Appendix can be accessed at http://cambridge.org/
9781107153967.*

TABLES

FIGURES

ACKNOWLEDGMENTS

This book would not have been possible without the support and guidance of many individuals and organizations. At Northwestern University, I have been fortunate enough to find myself surrounded by extraordinary colleagues in the Department of Political Science. Karen Alter, Bill Hurst, Jim Mahoney, Steve Nelson, Wendy Pearlman, Jason Seawright, Jeffrey Winters, Will Reno, Rachel Riedl, and Andrew Roberts offered comments on parts or all of the manuscript, advice about the publishing process, and, perhaps most important, support and encouragement. Meanwhile, the outstanding research assistance of Dong Zhang helped bring the manuscript to completion.

Beyond Northwestern, my good friend and collaborator, Simeon Nichter, provided feedback on countless drafts and helped me brainstorm new paths on the many occasions when I thought I had hit a dead end. Throughout the project, I also received invaluable advice from Tim Frye, Scott Gehlbach, Kathryn Hendley, Stan Markus, Bob Orttung, and Bob Nelson at various critical stages.

I am also grateful to the Northwestern Equality Development & Globalization Studies program and Department of Political Science for funding a book workshop from which this manuscript benefited greatly. At this workshop, Tim Frye, Scott Gehlbach, Anna Grzymala-Busse, and Pauline Jones, along with my Northwestern colleagues Bill Hurst, Jim Mahoney, Jason Seawright, and Jeffrey Winters, graciously offered their time and insights.

This book began as a dissertation in the Department of Political Science at the University of California, Berkeley. I owe a great deal of gratitude to my dissertation committee, Steve Fish, Steve Vogel, Brad DeLong, and, particularly, to my committee chair, John Zysman. Although not officially members of the committee, I also am grateful to Bob Kagan for introducing me to the world of Law and Society scholarship; to Henry Brady for his advice regarding the survey component of my research; to David

Collier for his ongoing support and advice; and to Ned Walker for numerous stimulating intellectual conversations over the years. At Berkeley, I was also part of an exceptional community of graduate students, many of whom directly or indirectly aided me during the formative stages of the project, including (but by no means limited to) Neil Abrams, Sener Akturk, Taylor Boas, Jen Brass, Miguel De Figueiredo, Sam Handlin, Jonathan Hassid, Danny Hidalgo, Diana Kapiszewski, Andrej Krickovic, Ben Lessing, Sebastian Mazzuca, Simeon Nichter, Jody LaPorte, Danielle Lussier, Rachel Stern, Bart Watson, Susanne Wengle, and Kuba Wrzesniewski.

At Cambridge University Press, I'm indebted to my acquisitions editor John Berger, content manager Lisa Sinclair, and the production department led by Velmurugan Inbasigamoni. Their professionalism and advice have been greatly appreciated throughout the many stages of bringing a manuscript to print. Thanks are also owed to Evgeniia Mikriukova, one of Northwestern's many talented graduate students, for her help in designing the cover image for this book.

In Russia, I incurred many debts of gratitude while conducting fieldwork. Andrei Yakovlev and his colleagues at the Institute for Industrial and Market Studies and the International Center for Studies of Institutions and Development, both at the Higher School of Economics in Moscow, provided both helpful insights into the Russian business world and an office out of which to work during several research trips. Peter Skoblikov of the Interior Ministry's Academy of Management patiently introduced me to the details of the Russian legal system. Elena Bashkirova and her colleagues at Bashkirova and Partners conducted the survey component of the project. Maria Ievskaya, Roman Khudaleev, and Dina Balalaeva provided excellent research assistance. I am especially indebted to two good friends with intimate knowledge of the Russian business world, Slava Petrov and Andrei Karapetian, for their insights and support. Most of all I would like to thank the many interview and survey respondents to whom I promised anonymity for taking the time to share their views.

I would also like to acknowledge the generous support of faculty research grants from the Northwestern Equality Development & Globalization Studies program and the Kellogg School of Management Dispute Resolution Research Center; a Eurasia Dissertation Support Fellowship from the Social Science Research Council; a Law and Social Science Doctoral Fellowship from the American Bar Foundation; a Humane Studies

Fellowship from the Institute for Humane Studies; a Fulbright-Hays Doctoral Dissertation Abroad Fellowship; a Jacob K. Javits Fellowship from the US Department of Education; and a Doctoral Dissertation Improvement Grant and a Graduate Research Fellowship from the National Science Foundation. I additionally acknowledge that parts of Chapter 3 draw on materials first used in my article "Threats to Property Rights in Russia: From Private Coercion to State Aggression," published in *Post-Soviet Affairs* volume 28, number 3, 2012, pages 263–295.

My deepest appreciation is reserved, of course, for the encouragement, love, and patience of my family and loved ones, Karen, Larry, Ethan, Bob, who graciously copyedited the entire manuscript, and my daughter Julia and wife Katya, who in addition to love and support kept my theories grounded in the realities of life in Russia.

1

Violence, Corruption, and Demand for Law

Throughout the world, firms employ a variety of strategies to secure property rights. As recognized since Macaulay's (1963) pioneering work, many of these strategies do not rely on formal legal institutions. Firms turn to litigation or law enforcement only as a last resort, preferring instead to resolve conflicts on the basis of personal relationships and informal norms. But under certain conditions, firms eschew formal legal institutions in favor of more nefarious strategies – strategies that utilize violence or corruption.

During the California Gold Rush of 1848, for instance, Umbeck (1981, p. 100) found that "the ability to use violence was the basis for all property rights" and therefore "every miner carried at least one gun." In a more contemporary setting, De Soto (2003, p. 155) documents how many Peruvian firms rely on "the protection that local bullies or mafias are willing to sell them." In Indonesia, private security companies not only fulfill the more prosaic tasks of guarding land and buildings but also offer a wide range of services, including "the intimidation of a client's business rivals" (Wilson, 2010, p. 255). Even in some of the world's most developed economies, firms rely extensively on private coercion. According to Milhaupt and West's (2000, p. 66) analysis of Japan, "the influence of organized crime is readily apparent in bankruptcy and debt collection, property development, dispute settlement, shareholders' rights, and finance." And in post-Soviet Russia, the primary focus of this book, violence in the 1990s reached such proportions that approximately two-fifths of surveyed enterprise managers reported personally facing coercion or threats of physical harm in the course of doing business (Radaev, 1999, pp. 36–40).[1]

In addition to violence, firms frequently rely on corruption to secure property, offering informal payments to state officials in exchange for

---

[1] Further details about this survey are provided in Chapter 3.

protection or for illicit raids against competitors. Wank (2004, p. 113) finds evidence in China of "entire [government] bureaus defining their practical policies and operating procedures to support private firms in ways of varying legality." Meanwhile, in Uganda elected officials serving on Local Councils collect informal fees to resolve property disputes, despite government efforts to move such conflicts into formal adjudicatory institutions provided by the state (Joireman, 2011, pp. 62–66). In Kyrgyzstan, according to one Bishkek-based journalist, "conflicts about property... are impossible to resolve if you do not have contacts with the president or with high-ranking officials" (cited in Spector 2008, p. 163). And in post-Soviet Russia, reliance on corruption, like the use of violence, has been particularly prevalent, with law enforcement and former KGB agents frequently acting "informally as private enforcers" on behalf of firms engaged in business disputes (Volkov, 2002, p. xii).

One might expect that once economies become mired in violence or corruption, these dire circumstances would persist indefinitely, or at best evolve toward formality over many years as societies gradually modernize. Yet in unexpected places and at unexpected times, firms rapidly and dramatically turn from illegal to legal strategies for securing property. Contrary to persistent stereotypes regarding the lawlessness of Russian capitalism, post-Soviet Russia is one of these unexpected places. Between 1994 and 2000, the number of annual court cases initiated by Russian firms increased from around 200,000 to just under 350,000. It then shot up to over one million by 2010 (VAS, 2011). More broadly, based on in-depth interviews with firms, lawyers, and private security agencies, as well as an original survey of enterprises from eight cities, this book demonstrates that many Russian firms substituted mafia enforcers with lawyers and replaced violence with lawsuits beginning in the late 1990s.[2] Whereas surveys of Russian firms from the 1990s indicated that around 40 percent of respondents had suffered from violent incidents (Radaev, 1999, pp. 36–40), the survey I conducted in 2010 (discussed below) found that less than 5 percent of respondents had endured a similar fate. Even fewer respondents had faced encounters with the criminal protection rackets for which Russia became infamous in the early 1990s. By contrast, 46 percent of firms participating in my survey had utilized the court system in the last three years.

---

[2] To be sure, some of firms' use of courts involves abuses of formal legal institutions, but as discussed in Chapter 3, non-corrupt legal strategies have become more prevalent than strategies relying on corruption.

1.1 The Puzzle

Prominent legal scholars have emphasized that firms' use of violence and corruption *undermines* formal legal institutions, whereas firms' use of courts and law enforcement *reinforces* formal institutions' effectiveness and relevance (Pistor, 1996; Hendley, 1997). If this is true, firm strategies for securing property have important ramifications for the development of the rule of law, and identifying the factors that determine whether firms employ illegal or legal strategies is of utmost importance. A tantalizingly simple explanation would suggest that firms rely on violence and corruption when the state is weak and rely on formal legal institutions when state legal capacity improves. But the examples discussed above demonstrate that firms regularly resort to violence and corruption not only in low capacity states but also in states with reasonable levels of capacity. Consequently, state legal capacity can at most serve as a partial explanation.

Even more curious is that in cases such as post-Soviet Russia, firms mobilize legal resources even when the effectiveness of legal institutions is in doubt – and, in fact, even when state officials themselves pose a major threat to property security. Throughout the period in which Russian firms increasingly turned to formal legal institutions, many observers insisted that lawlessness in Russia remained as prevalent as ever. As William Browder, the largest foreign portfolio investor in Russia until government officials attempted to illegally seize his assets, declared, "Property rights no longer exist . . . with the spectacular recent decline in the rule of law, anything is possible in Russia now" (Browder, 2009). Mikhail Khodorkovsky, the richest man in Russia before his politically motivated arrest in 2003, offered a similar assessment in a 2011 interview from his jail cell, proclaiming: "As concerns rule of law, I know only too well that it does not exist in Russia – the judiciary is not independent at all" (*Wall Street Journal*, June 15, 2011). And while few firms in Russia directly face the wrath of Putin or his close associates, they encounter wide-ranging threats to their property rights from lower-level state officials. Rogue law enforcement officers, for instance, frequently arrest businesspeople on false pretenses, seeking to induce informal payments or illicitly acquire entrepreneurs' assets. By some estimates, approximately 100,000 businessmen are either behind bars or have faced criminal prosecution (Yaffa, 2013).

In short, this book centers on a pair of related questions: Why do firms sometimes resort to violence and corruption to secure property, even when formal legal institutions are relatively effective? Why do firms sometimes turn to law even without improvements in the state's legal capacity?

1.2   The Argument

By bringing firms' role in the development of effective institutions to the foreground, this book sets off in a distinctly different direction from most existing studies of property rights. There is broad agreement among policymakers and scholars alike that institutions for protecting property rights are vital for economic development and societal well-being (e.g., North, 1981; Knack and Keefer, 1995; Posner, 1998; Acemoglu et al., 2001; De Soto, 2003; Cooter and Schaefer, 2009). Nearly all prominent studies of property rights, however, seek to understand the security of property by analyzing the conditions under which rulers and governments develop effective institutions (e.g., North, 1981; Olson, 1993; Acemoglu and Robinson, 2006). By contrast, this book demonstrates that state "supply" of formal legal institutions is a necessary but frequently *insufficient* condition for firms to turn from coercion to law. Consequently, a thorough understanding of property rights security also requires a deeper understanding of the conditions under which firms are willing to *use* formal legal institutions, an issue sometimes referred to as private sector "demand" for law (Pistor, 1996; Hendley, 1999).

This book offers a theory of institutional demand and a framework that integrates the supply and demand sides of property security. First, I argue that while a dearth of *state legal capacity* may impede firms' use of law, improved capacity frequently does not increase firms' willingness to utilize formal legal institutions. Institutional supply, in other words, does not automatically create institutional demand. This first component of my argument builds on studies by Pistor (1996) and Hendley (1997, 1999), who lay the groundwork for analysis of why private actors may refrain from using legal institutions.[3] Advancing their foundational work, this book also elaborates the conditions under which firms *do* turn to law. In particular, I emphasize that increasing reliance on formal legal institutions frequently occurs in the absence of heightened state legal capacity. In such cases, two factors other than state legal capacity largely determine whether firms utilize violence and corruption or whether firms

---

[3] See also the insightful discussion about supply and demand for law in Milhaupt and Pistor (2008, 40–44).

turn to law: the prevalence of *demand-side barriers* to using formal legal institutions and the *effectiveness of illegal strategies* for securing property. Demand-side barriers are behaviors or beliefs at the level of firms and individuals that lead these actors to avoid formal legal institutions. As discussed in Chapter 2, prominent barriers include firms' operations in the informal economy, expectations about other firms' reliance on violence or corruption (which lead to collective action problems), and cultural norms. Meanwhile, as with any competing set of services, firms' willingness to use formal legal institutions depends on the effectiveness of alternatives. In the case of illegal strategies, effectiveness largely depends on transaction costs relative to other strategies and the risk of sanctions for illegal activities.

I also demonstrate that to understand institutional demand, it is necessary to develop a more nuanced understanding of institutional supply. The direct supply of institutions is only one way in which the state affects firms' willingness to use law. The state also indirectly – indeed, sometimes even inadvertently – influences firm strategies by altering demand-side barriers or the risks associated with illegal alternatives.

1.3 Contributions

Through empirical analysis of the role of violence, corruption, and law in the protection of property rights in post-Soviet Russia, this book offers broader insights into several pressing lines of inquiry in contemporary comparative politics and political economy.

First, while the importance of the rule of law – and secure property rights in particular – to economic and political development is widely recognized, it remains unclear why institutions for protecting property rights remain ineffective in much of the world. By emphasizing the demand side of institutional development and by analyzing the interaction between institutional supply and demand, this book provides a fresh perspective about the rule of law's institutional underpinnings. Moreover, this book's focus on institutional demand complements but also bridges important gaps left unfilled by existing studies on property rights, which concentrate largely on (1) how states supply institutions or (2) property protection in the absence of effective state institutions.

In contrast to this book's emphasis on how firm strategies for protecting property can hinder or promote institutional effectiveness, the most influential existing studies examine rulers' incentives to facilitate or undermine the security of property rights (e.g., North, 1981; Levi,

1989; Olson, 1993; Acemoglu and Robinson, 2006). These studies find that institutions for protecting property will be more likely to develop when rulers expect to remain in power for the long term, possess effective technologies for monitoring and taxing assets, expect their grip on power to survive destabilization that may accompany economic development, and depend on the skills or resources of private citizens. Yet despite this literature's substantial contribution to our understanding of property rights, the supply-side approach offers incomplete insights because it fails to address the fundamental question of when firms turn to formal legal institutions to protect property rather than resorting to violence and corruption.

The sizable literature on how firms protect property in the absence of effective state institutions, meanwhile, sidesteps altogether the question of when firms use formal institutions (e.g., Greif, 1993; McMillan and Woodruff, 1999; Haber et al., 2003; Markus, 2012, 2015). These studies demonstrate that mechanisms such as repeated interactions between buyers and sellers, private business networks that transmit information about merchants' reputations, and defensive alliances between firms and foreign investors or business associations can help secure property and enforce contracts. While the non-state property rights literature addresses issues of great importance, prominent scholars agree that in complex, modern economies informal institutions can rarely serve as effective substitutes for formal institutions on a large scale (e.g., North, 1990, ch. 6; Ellickson, 1991, pp. 249–254). Unfortunately, the issue of how such formal institutions develop falls outside the research agenda of the non-state literature.

Beyond the rule of law, a study of property rights from the firm's perspective provides distinctive insights into the social and political foundations of state capacity. Following Migdal's (2001) "state-in-society" approach to the study of state building, this book suggests that state capacity – the ability of states to implement policies and enforce rules – depends not only on rulers' policies but also on societal actors' strategies. As noted above, firms' reliance on violence and corruption undermines and destabilizes formal institutions. Their utilization of courts and law enforcement, on the other hand, reinforces the effectiveness and relevance of formal state institutions. Phrased differently, state building is not simply a top-down process of developing and imposing institutional blueprints on society. Rather, it is also a bottom-up, ongoing process involving the daily interactions of numerous "ordinary" social actors both with each other and with representatives of the state.[4] Moreover, while my specific focus is on firms' strategies for securing property, scholars such as Grzymala-Busse (2007, 2010) have demonstrated more broadly that societal actors' strategies have a significant impact on a wide range of formal institutions, including civil service regulations, national auditing offices, and anti-corruption laws. She, too, finds that informal practices have the potential to either replace and undermine formal institutions or, when the conditions are right, to "reify formal rules ... by providing incentives and information to follow formal institutions" (Grzymala-Busse, 2010, p. 311). The demand-side approach developed in this book therefore offers general lessons about the conditions under which formal institutions transcend mere words on paper: Namely, effective formal institutions emerge not simply when states invest in capacity, but also when barriers to citizens' use of formal institutions are removed and steps are taken to diminish the effectiveness of illicit alternatives to formal institutions.

In addition to broader inquiries in comparative politics and political economy, this book contributes to ongoing debates pertaining to the post-communist region. In contrast to the theoretical literature on property rights, scholarship on post-communism has been relatively more attuned to demand-side issues. Key early works by Pistor (1996) and Hendley (1997, 1999) examined firms' use (or lack thereof) of the court system, as well as private sector actors' attitudes toward law more broadly. Shortly thereafter, economists – puzzled by the seeming paradox that many Russian firms appeared *not* to support the development of secure property rights – produced a series of formal models to analyze the issue. For example, Polishchuk and Savvateev (2004) and Sonin (2003) demonstrate that given high levels of economic inequality and weak state institutions, richer and more powerful firms have the incentive to pay for private protection while seeking to maintain the weakness of formal institutions. This environment allows them to guard their own assets while expropriating weaker citizens' wealth. In a related vein, Hoff and Stiglitz (2004) examine how each actor's expectation that other actors will subvert institutions creates further incentives to abandon law and order. They emphasize how factors such as dependence on natural resources and high levels of corruption, which increase individuals' incentives to engage

---

[4] Even in advanced industrial countries, recent studies show that strategies of firms play an important role in shaping state capacity. Hall and Thelen (2009, p. 16) emphasize, for example, that "shifts in firm strategy can erode the viability of some institutions and strengthen others."

in rent-seeking rather than productive investments, can lead countries like Russia to become stuck in an unlawful equilibrium.[5] However, these models are significantly limited by their focus on macro-level explanatory variables. Economic inequality, natural resource dependence, and corruption have become more acute over the last decade and a half, yet during this period Russian firms have increasingly employed legal strategies. Meanwhile, although Pistor (1996) and Hendley (1997, 1999) offer valuable insights regarding potential factors that influence institutional demand, to date there exists no comprehensive empirical treatment of institutional supply and demand in the post-communist region.

Finally, this book seeks to integrate two divergent viewpoints on institutional development in Russia. At one extreme, scholars such as Volkov (2004, 2005) and Ledeneva (2006) perceive nearly all use of formal legal institutions to involve some form of strategic corruption, in which firms use ties with the state to turn formal institutions into private tools rather than neutral enforcers and adjudicators. These scholars therefore are frequently dismissive of claims regarding positive developments with respect to the rule of law in Russia. At the other extreme, scholars such as Solomon (2004, 2008) and Hendley (2006, 2012), while explicitly recognizing the limitations of Russia's legal infrastructure and persistence of illicit practices, paint a much more sanguine picture of the everyday workings of law in Russia. By presenting a unified framework that gives equal emphasis to violence, corruption, and law in Russia, this book provides insights into the conditions under which firms are most likely to turn to each.[6]

1.4 The Case: Post-Soviet Russia

Why focus on Russia during the two decades following the Soviet Union's collapse in the early 1990s? The theory of institutional demand developed in this book offers general insights about the interactions among state legal capacity, demand-side barriers, and the effectiveness of alternatives to formal legal institutions. However, Russia's post-Soviet era, a time

---

[5] It should be noted that these models focus on private actors' influence, either as voters or lobbyists, on the *creation* of formal institutions rather than on firms' *use* of institutions. There also is a small empirical literature on "demand for law" in the form of private sector lobbying for institutional reform in Russia, particularly during the early Putin period of 2000–2003. See, e.g., Jones Luong and Weinthal (2004); Guriev and Rachinsky (2005, pp. 145–148); Markus (2007).

[6] Frye (2017) offers a broad analysis of informal and formal strategies for securing property but focuses on various strategies' effectiveness, rather than on the factors contributing to firms' strategy choices.

period during which Russia was undergoing a dramatic transformation from a socialist command economy to a market economy, offers particularly illuminating insights on institutional demand. Few countries have witnessed such a wide range of firm strategies for securing property, especially in the compact span of two decades. This range of strategies provides fertile material for generating hypotheses about when firms turn to formal legal institutions, and when firms employ violence or corruption.

In all market economies, firms face a variety of challenges related to enforcing contracts and protecting property. Suppliers violate the terms of contracts. Buyers fail to make payments on time. Founding partners of firms engage in ownership disputes. Minority owners in corporations contest violations of their shareholder rights. Tax officials and regulatory authorities issue decrees that infringe on firms' income streams or devalue firms' assets.

But while conflicts related to contracts and property rights are an inevitable part of market transactions, the nature of such disputes often has assumed extreme forms in post-Soviet Russia. In 1994, the Russian Ministry of Internal Affairs recorded more than 500 contract killings, the majority of which involved commercial disputes (Statkus, 1998). In 1996, one survey of Russian shopkeepers revealed that more than half of these respondents had faced recent encounters with mafia extortion rackets (Frye and Zhuravskaya, 2000). Beginning in the late 1990s, Russian firms faced a wave of "illegal corporate raiding" (*reiderstvo*) involving the theft – quite literally – of entire enterprises. Examples included forging a company's shareholder registry or exploiting legislative loopholes to bankrupt financially healthy firms and then loot their assets in the guise of compensating creditors. Meanwhile, from the mid-2000s onward, countless entrepreneurs faced arrest on trumped-up charges as law enforcement officials, acting on their own behalf or on the behalf of paying private clients, sought to acquire firms' assets at below-market rates or eliminate their clients' competition.

Collectively, I refer to firms' efforts to resolve conflicts related to acquiring assets, protecting property, and enforcing contracts as *property security strategies*. I develop this concept more fully in Chapter 2, where I discuss how it relates to common terms such as "property rights" and the "rule of law" and provide a typology of strategies based on the extent to which a strategy is backed by private or state coercion. For the moment, a schematic illustration of the evolution of Russian firms' strategies for securing property offers a starting point for the analysis to come.

At one end of the spectrum are property security strategies that rely on coercion provided by private actors. Russian firms' widespread reliance in the early 1990s on the services provided by organized crime groups and private security agencies – often staffed by former military, law enforcement, or KGB personnel – provides the most clear-cut case of strategies based on private coercion. Private providers of property security offered what the sociologist Vadim Volkov refers to as an "enforcement partnership," or what became known in colloquial Russian as a *krysha* – literally, the Russian word for "roof," in reference to the protection such a relationship afforded to businesspeople. Aside from physical protection, *kryshas* provided an extraordinary range of services: accompanying convoys of physical goods in transit, acquiring information on prospective suppliers or buyers, collecting debts, meeting with the *kryshas* of other firms to resolve – peacefully or otherwise – disputes, and even smoothing out relations with tax or regulatory authorities (Volkov, 2002, pp. 49–53, 139–141). During the heyday of private coercion, criminal elements additionally developed complex adjudication arrangements, creating a system of "shadow justice" (Skoblikov, 2001) in which top-level criminal figures, known as *avtoritety*, served as arbiters for ongoing disputes among businesspeople represented by lower-level criminal protectors.

By the late 1990s and early 2000s, Russian firms were less likely to utilize strategies based on private coercion. Yet the manner in which they engaged state actors and formal state institutions frequently was borderline, if not outrightly, illegal. Because these strategies appropriate state resources for private gain, I refer to them as "corrupt coercion" in the typology elaborated in Chapter 2. A short vignette provided by Andrey, the owner of a small business in Moscow, vividly depicts the nature of such strategies. At the time he was interviewed in 2009, this entrepreneur, an importer of high-end accessories for outfitting luxury automobiles, had been operating his business for nearly a decade. Although he operated without a *krysha* for several years, Andrey sought protection after being physically threatened by an extortionist seeking lavish compensation for a car accident that ostensibly resulted from a defective product purchased at Andrey's shop. At the advice of acquaintances, Andrey turned to a firm specializing in "economic security" (*ekonomicheskaya bezopasnost*), the contemporary variant of the semilegal private security agencies of the early 1990s. The security provider had a flashy office, handed out fancy business cards, worked on the basis of formal contracts, and exhibited all the trappings of a professional consulting firm, but it also made no secret of its ties to powerful state operatives, such as the Federal Security Service, the KGB's successor. The economic security firm at first insisted that the mere mention of his contract for protection would scare away Andrey's extortionists, but when the threats continued, Andrey was invited to accompany the security specialists as they addressed the problem. Having arranged a meeting with his antagonists, Andrey and the manager of the security firm parked across the street from the appointed meeting place. The manager then phoned the extortionists and directed their attention to a military-like personnel transporter parked nearby. The transporter's doors opened, revealing a fully armed and masked elite SWAT team. The security firm's manager said something to the effect of, "Do you now see who protects Andrey?", and hung up the phone. Within minutes, Andrey received an apologetic call from his extortionists, declaring that the matter was now settled. Andrey never saw or heard from his tormentors again (Firm 1, interview, 2009).

From the 1990s onward, however, Russian firms did not merely replace private coercion with strategies based on corrupt coercion. They also increasingly came to rely extensively on formal legal institutions. This trend was already apparent by the late 1990s and continued to build up steam throughout the 2000s. Indeed, firms even came to litigate against state agencies, an endeavor that in many countries elicits trepidation out of the belief that state officials might retaliate against such litigation in unpleasant ways or, at the very least, that judges will favor their colleagues from other state institutions over private actors. Such concerns influence the strategies even of businesspeople with significant means at their disposal, such as Oleg, who built a business empire with one of Russia's first nation-wide car dealerships and then transformed himself into a venture capitalist. When I first interviewed Oleg in 2009, he explained that he had actively relied on lawyers since the 1990s, but that he had never confronted – and hoped he never would confront – the state in court. When I re-interviewed Oleg in 2014, circumstances had forced his hand. But to his pleasant surprise, litigation resulted in a positive outcome even when facing a powerful opponent:

> Oleg: During the 2008 crisis, we entered into some big construction projects in Moscow and St. Petersburg ... In this respect, the legal relations with the government of Moscow were not fully developed. Everyone told us, go and make a deal "under the table." But we said, no, we are going to work with lawyers. And we won a number of cases ... Here's an example: We see that [the government officials] over-calculated the value of [our] land for the property registry, and we are supposed to pay a lot. The lawyers take a look at the legislative framework, figure things out, and

say, no, we should pay less. How can this be proved? Only in court. We file a suit and win at all levels. And the government agencies agreed with this. They didn't start sending inspectors to investigate us, didn't try to, so to say, strangle us. They said, okay, if the court made a decision, then go ahead and pay [this amount].

Interviewer: And you were worried, that possibly the government would start sending inspectors and so on?

Oleg: That's how it used to be. We were always told, what, you are going to sue the Moscow government? How could you! They won't allow you to continue living here (Firm 12, interview, 2014).

As discussed in later chapters, firms' perceptions about the extent to which government agencies seek retribution against those who challenge the state in court most likely have been exaggerated. From the early 2000s onward, firms regularly and successfully litigated against state agencies, the tax authorities in particular. But Oleg's vignette offers a startlingly mundane and legalistic portrait of contemporary property security strategies in Russia, particularly when contrasted with the private coercion underlying property securities of the early 1990s or the corrupt coercion that resolved Andrey's conflict.

This brief discussion of firms' evolving strategies in post-Soviet Russia is by no means intended to convey that such evolution has been all-encompassing, linear, or inevitable. To this day, some degree of private coercion persists, just as some firms in the early 1990s already actively utilized formal legal institutions. Undoubtedly, in the complex and messy world of property security disputes, many firms at times simultaneously employed multiple strategies, some of a more dubious nature than others. But despite fits and starts and the ever-present possibility of reversals, Chapter 3 demonstrates that broad-sweeping trends in Russian firms' property security strategies can be discerned, including a significant decline in reliance on outright violence and a dramatic increase in the use of formal legal institutions.

It is this evolution in Russian firms' strategies over time, as well as the variation in strategies across different types of firms, that facilitates the evaluation of hypotheses about factors underlying institutional demand. In particular, the Russian case vividly demonstrates the central claims of this book: (1) that heightened state legal capacity does not necessarily increase firms' willingness to use formal legal institutions and (2) that even without heightened state legal capacity, firms may increase their reliance on law due to declining demand-side barriers to the use of formal legal institutions or the decreasing effectiveness of illegal strategies.

1.5 Data and Methodology

This book employs multiple methodological approaches. The theory and analytical framework presented in Chapter 2 (and formalized in Appendix D) are evaluated in subsequent chapters using both qualitative and quantitative methods. In line with this multimethod approach, I draw on diverse sources of original data collected during research trips to Russia between 2008 and 2014. First, throughout 2009, I conducted 90 in-depth, semistructured interviews with Russian firms, lawyers, and private security agencies, as well as 35 supplementary interviews with representatives of business and legal associations, business journalists, and Russian academics. In the fall of 2014, I conducted follow-up interviews with 20 businesspeople, lawyers, and security specialists who participated in the 2009 round of interviews. These interviews focused on the ways that firms resolve conflicts with other firms, such as contract and property rights disputes, as well as the ways that firms resolve conflicts with the state, such as tax or regulatory disputes.

Second, in the summer of 2010, I carried out a survey of 301 Russian firms in 8 cities: Moscow, St. Petersburg, Nizhniy Novgorod, Ekaterinburg, Novosibirsk, Rostov-on-Don, Samara, and Kazan. These comprise 8 of the 10 largest Russian cities and provide a geographical reach from northwest Russia (St. Petersburg) to the south of Russia (Rostov-on-Don) and east out to Siberia (Novosibirsk). The sample was split approximately evenly between industrial and service firms and included firms of various sizes, ranging from as small as 3 employees to as large as 9000 employees. State-owned enterprises were intentionally excluded from the sample, although some firms in the sample reported the government as a minority shareholder. The survey questions mirrored the questions posed in the in-depth interviews but were closed-ended to facilitate quantitative analyses. Further details about the interview and survey samples can be found in Appendices A and B.

To supplement the survey findings, I also analyze raw data from surveys of Russian enterprises conducted by the Levada Center, a Russian survey firm; INDEM Foundation, a Russian NGO dedicated to democracy and civil-society promotion; and several rounds of the World Bank – EBRD Business Environment and Enterprise Performance Surveys (BEEPS).

Some of these data are publicly available. Others I attained directly from the source. To further explore themes emerging from interview and survey data, I collected caseload data from the Russian Supreme Commercial Court, crime statistics from the Russian Ministry of Internal Affairs, and relevant reports from the Russian press.

Naturally, research on sensitive topics, such as informal or illegal activities, entails challenges. Firms that are most likely to engage in strategies outside of the law may be less likely to participate in the research. Among participants, there may be hesitancy to provide truthful answers. While these concerns cannot be ignored, they also should not be exaggerated. First, many types of unlawful behavior in countries such as Russia are open secrets that are more freely discussed than outside researchers often recognize. This observation is supported by other analysts. For example, Daniel Kaufmann, formerly one of the World Bank's foremost experts on corruption and the rule of law, argues that "With appropriate survey instruments and interviewing techniques, respondents are willing to discuss corruption with remarkable candor" (Kaufmann et al., 2001). Second, the magnitude of the changes examined in Chapter 3 is overwhelming. For example, more than 40 percent of all firms reported contact with criminal protection rackets in surveys conducted in the 1990s, while fewer than 10 percent report contact in recent surveys. Unless firms have become *dramatically* less inclined to tell the truth over time, a genuine transformation has occurred. Thus, even if rough estimates of difficult-to-measure illegal activities in some cases may be downwardly biased, large changes over time are informative indicators.

Multiple steps nevertheless were taken to ameliorate concerns about the sensitive nature of the research. Following techniques used in World Bank surveys on corruption, interview and survey questions were phrased in an indirect manner designed to elicit information without requiring respondents to incriminate themselves, such as "Can you estimate how frequently a *typical firm* in your line of business makes protection payments?" Additionally, the similar conclusions drawn from multiple and diverse methodological approaches – in-depth interviews, survey research, and the collection of objective data such as court caseload statistics – increase confidence in the validity of the findings.

1.6   Outline of the Book

The remainder of this book is organized as follows: Chapter 2 introduces the study's primary dependent variable – *property security strategies* –

and provides a typology of the strategies that firms use to acquire assets, protect property, and enforce contracts. The chapter then develops a theory of institutional demand and an analytical framework based on three key independent variables: *state legal capacity*, *demand-side barriers*, and the *effectiveness of illegal strategies*.

Chapter 3 turns to the Russian case, analyzing evolution in the dependent variable – firm strategies for securing property – over time. The chapter details three notable trends: (1) the decline of strategies based on private coercion; (2) the replacement of private coercion with strategies based on corruption; and (3) the rise of strategies based on formal legal institutions.

Chapters 4 through 6 are devoted to each of the main variables in the framework and their effects on temporal variation in property security strategies in Russia. Chapter 4 examines changes in the level of Russian *state legal capacity*. It demonstrates that state legal capacity, at least as perceived by firms, has not increased sufficiently to account for the evolution of firms' property security strategies. Chapter 5 examines *demand-side barriers* to firms' use of formal legal institutions, with a specific focus on the effects of firms' operations in the informal economy and collective action problems among firms. Chapter 6 turns to the *effectiveness of illegal strategies*. It traces how factors such as firms' changing time horizons, the development of the financial sector, and Russia's integration into the international economy have affected the transaction costs and risks of sanctions associated with the use of illegal strategies.

Chapter 7 then examines the framework's key variables from another perspective, turning to heterogeneity in property security strategies across different types of firms instead of variation in strategies over time. The chapter identifies factors that differentially shape the demand-side barriers faced by various types of firms, as well as different types of firms' capacity to effectively employ illegal strategies.

Chapter 8, the concluding chapter, steps back and puts the analysis in broader theoretical and comparative perspective. It explores how firm strategies for securing property influence the development of effective state institutions and the rule of law. It then examines the implications of this analysis for the future of the rule of law in Russia. Finally, the chapter draws conclusions about pathways to property security and the rule of law by contrasting transition and developing countries' experiences with the experiences of Western countries.

2

Institutional Supply and Demand

When do firms use violence and corruption, such as mafia protection rackets and illicit government connections, to secure property rights? And when do firms instead turn to formal state legal institutions, such as courts and law enforcement agencies? As discussed in the introductory chapter, firms' reliance on violence and corruption undermines and destabilizes formal legal institutions. Firms' utilization of courts and law enforcement, on the other hand, reinforces formal institutions' effectiveness and relevance. Consequently, the strategies firms use to secure property have important ramifications for the rule of law and, even more broadly, for the state-building prospects of societies seeking to develop effective formal state institutions.

This book offers a theory of institutional demand that offers insights into firm strategies, as well as an analytical framework that integrates the demand and supply sides of property security. To develop this framework, the current chapter first introduces a typology of different types of *property security strategies* employed by firms. The chapter then examines how three key factors affect firms' choice of property security strategies. Existing studies of property rights focus predominantly on the first factor – *state legal capacity* – and suggest that the supply of effective formal legal institutions is the primary determinant of firm strategies. By contrast, the framework advanced here demonstrates that while the absence of state legal capacity impedes firms' use of law, improved capacity frequently does not provide incentives for firms to alter their strategies for securing property. Put differently, institutional supply does not automatically induce institutional demand. Instead, a central argument of this book is that two factors unrelated to state legal capacity often determine the extent to which firms utilize violence and corruption rather than turning to law: the prevalence of *demand-side barriers* to using formal legal institutions and the *effectiveness of illegal strategies* for securing property.[1]

---

[1] The framework's key insights are formalized in the model presented in Appendix D.

After presenting the framework, the chapter provides a preliminary illustration of the theory in the context of post-Soviet Russia. In particular, the Russian experience in the 1990s demonstrates that the development of formal legal institutions does not ensure firms' use of law, particularly when demand-side barriers remain prevalent and illegal strategies remain effective. Meanwhile, the Russian case in the 2000s demonstrates that even without heightened state legal capacity, firms may increase their use of formal legal institutions as demand-side barriers fall or the effectiveness of illegal strategies declines. Finally, the chapter concludes by examining explanatory factors that fall outside of the analytical framework, discussing how these factors interact with the framework's key explanatory variables, and considering the scope and generalizability of the arguments developed in this book.

2.1   The Dependent Variable: Property Security Strategies

The outcome this book seeks to explain is what I refer to as *property security strategies*: firms' efforts to resolve conflicts related to acquiring assets, protecting property, and enforcing contracts. The following discussion defines this concept, clarifies its relationship to other similar concepts, and presents a typology of distinct strategy types. It then offers a brief overview of the evolution of property security strategies in post-Soviet Russia.

The concept of property *security* emphasized here is somewhat broader than the concept of property *rights*, which frequently are defined as the rights to use, derive income from, and transfer an asset to another owner (Hohfeld, 1913; Barzel, 1997, p. 3). Individuals, organizations, and communities throughout history have wielded force to accumulate and protect claims to property. By contrast, the very concept of "rights" presupposes the existence of the modern state, which publicly codifies the law, identifies citizens' privileges and obligations, and establishes the distinction between legitimate and illegitimate ownership (Winters, 2011, p. 7; also see Cole and Grossman, 2002). In modern societies, relying on formal legal institutions to enforce property rights is one possible strategy for securing property. But as discussed in the introductory chapter, firms in modern societies also employ violence and corruption to protect property claims without reference to law. Property security therefore encompasses strategies both for protecting property claims and for enforcing property rights. Meanwhile, although property security is a broader concept than property rights, it is also a more narrow concept than the *rule of law*. Rule of law is frequently presented as a "system in which laws are public knowledge, are clear in meaning, and apply equally to everyone" (Carothers, 1998, p. 96). But given that various understandings of the rule of law encompass wide-ranging concerns such as secure property rights, equality of access to legal institutions, and overall political order and stability (see, e.g., Daniels and Trebilcock, 2004; Hendley, 2006; Haggard et al., 2008), the term hinders rather than facilitates empirical analysis, unlike the more concrete concept of property security strategies. In the book's final chapter, I return to the broader question of how firms' adoption of strategies based on law rather than violence and corruption contributes to rule-of-law development.

Elaboration of the concept of property security strategies additionally requires clarification of two key distinctions in debates over property rights. The first distinction is between *allocation* and *enforcement*. Historical studies of property rights, and many studies of natural resources, focus on the allocation or assignment of this bundle among individuals, the state, or communities (e.g., Demsetz, 1967; Umbeck, 1981; Riker and Sened, 1991; Libecap, 1993). By contrast, throughout much of the contemporary developing world, fundamental conflicts over property more frequently pertain to the enforcement of rights that formally exist at least on paper. This is particularly true in the post-communist region, where large-scale privatization programs of state-owned enterprises established formal property rights in the 1990s. Correspondingly, the focus of this book is on enforcement rather than allocation. In particular, this book examines variation in *how* firms secure property.

The second distinction is between *property rights* and *contracts*. Whereas property rights studies traditionally are preoccupied with the threat of state expropriation of private sector assets (e.g., North and Weingast, 1989), contract enforcement studies more commonly focus on transactions among private actors (e.g., Greif, 1993). These distinctions, however, become arbitrary in transition and developing countries, where private actors coercively acquire assets and state actors frequently participate in negotiations between private entities. The boundary between property rights and contract enforcement becomes even more blurry when one considers ownership and control of modern-day firms rather than land or natural resources, particularly given the influential view of the firm as a "nexus of contracts" (Jensen and Meckling, 1976).[2] Given that this book examines business conflicts involving contemporary firms,

---

[2] Legal scholars continue to debate the distinction between property rights and contracts, but the distinctions they draw have no relation to the private versus state dichotomy common in social science studies. See the discussion in Merrill and Smith (2001).

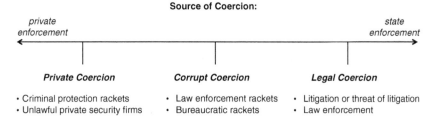

Figure 2.1   Property Security Strategies

both property rights protection and contract enforcement are central concerns. To be more concrete, I am concerned with the variety of disputes over control and ownership of assets that firms face in any modern economy, both with other firms and with government authorities.[3] Although this book does not address disputes related to trademarks, copyright, and other forms of intellectual property, the business conflicts it examines often involve other types of intangible property, such as debts and shares in joint stock companies.[4]

The current section explores three strategies for securing property. Contrary to the seemingly stark delineation between what is legal and illegal, *all* types of property security strategies rely on the threat of physical force (Umbeck 1981, p. 9; Ellickson 1991, p. 175). Even reliance on law does not preclude violence. It only implies that should application of coercion become necessary, it will be coercion legitimatized by formal rules and regulated by the state. Consequently, what distinguishes different types of property security strategies is the underlying *source* of coercion. Broadly speaking, property security strategies fall into three categories, which span a spectrum from private to state sources of coercion (see Figure 2.1):

Private Coercion: Strategies of private coercion rely on private actors with the capacity to wield violence to secure property. As noted above, such strategies are better described as protecting a property claim than enforcing a property right. The classic examples of private coercion are

---

[3] Conflicts among private actors may involve contract violations, disputes over debts, inter-firm conflicts over assets, or conflicts among shareholders of a given firm. Conflicts between firms and the state include tax disputes, problems with licenses and permits, clashes with inspectors and regulators, harassment from law enforcement officials, or outright attempts to expropriate a firm's assets.

[4] This book also does not address conflicts in the agricultural sector. For discussion of the development of agricultural property rights in the post-Soviet world, see Barnes (2006) and Allina-Pisano (2008).

the criminal protection rackets and illicit private security agencies that provided physical protection, debt collection, contract enforcement, and other services in Russia throughout the early 1990s. Private protection providers also have played a similar role in property security in countries such as Italy, Taiwan, and Japan.[5]

Corrupt Coercion: Strategies of corrupt coercion rely on state actors who wield violence without regard to the distinction between legitimate and illegitimate coercion. Throughout transition and developing countries, protection rackets provided by bureaucrats and law enforcement officials use state resources at the behest of private clients to provide security, resolve disputes, and even raid their clients' competitors. A quintessential example of corrupt coercion was offered in the preceding chapter's vignette about the security specialists who helped Andrey, the Moscow businessman specializing in accessories for luxury cars, escape extortionists by demonstrating their ability to mobilize an elite law enforcement SWAT team. A more commonplace example is the straightforward bribing of judges, court officials, or law enforcement agents to obtain a desired outcome. These strategies are corrupt because they appropriate state resources for private gain, and this hybrid of state resources and private interests places such strategies in the middle of the private-state spectrum with respect to sources of coercion.

Legal Coercion: Strategies of legal coercion rely on state actors who resort to coercion primarily in accordance with formal rules. Such strategies entail the (non-corrupt) use of the formal institutions of the state – courts, regulatory officials, and law enforcement agencies – to enforce property rights. They also include a broader set of legalistic strategies that rely directly on the existence of formal legal institutions, even when participants do not actually utilize these institutions. Often referred to as bargaining in the "shadow of the law" (Mnookin and Kornhauser, 1978), examples of such tactics include strategic use of threats to litigate or file complaints with government agencies.

Two additional points of clarification are in order. First, the classification of property security strategies presented in Figure 2.1 naturally refers to ideal types. In reality, the boundaries between illegal and legal coercion may be blurry, particularly in transition periods when laws themselves are changing and the definition of what constitutes criminal activity may be subject to debate (Volkov, 2002, p. xii). Moreover, firms may simultaneously combine multiple strategies, adopt different types of

---

[5] See Winn (1994), Gambetta (1996), Milhaupt and West (2000), and Volkov (2002).

strategies sequentially as a conflict unfolds, or utilize different strategies for different types of disputes. Rather than dividing firms into black-and-white "legal" or "illegal" categories, it is more accurate to conceive of each firm as employing a portfolio of strategies, which for any given firm may be weighted more heavily toward reliance on a specific type of coercion.[6]

Second, the above typology does not incorporate *informal* (as distinct from *illegal*) strategies. Informal strategies are strategies that do not depend directly on formal legal institutions yet also do not inherently violate laws. Examples include reliance on informal norms, repeated interactions, reputational costs, mediation, private arbitration, and sophisticated forms of customized contracting – a set of strategies often referred to under the rubric of "relational contracting" or "private ordering" (e.g., Macaulay, 1963; Williamson, 1985; Ellickson, 1991; Bernstein, 1992).[7] There are stark differences between a firm's choice to utilize informal strategies or illegal strategies. Because informal strategies frequently are not at odds with the law, use of informal strategies does not entail the same risk of sanctions faced by firms employing illegal strategies, a point to which I return in greater detail below. Moreover, when firms rely on violence or corruption, the broader societal consequences can be much more devastating than when firms rely on informal strategies. Whereas informal strategies frequently coexist with *both* illegal and legal strategies, violence and corruption intrinsically pose a challenge to the state's claim to a monopoly on legitimate coercion. Consequently, illegal strategies are a definitive danger that must be addressed if societies are to build effective formal institutions and develop state capacity.

With these clarifications and caveats in mind, this book seeks to explain two key patterns in the Russian context: (1) variation over time in the relative prevalence of firms' use of particular property security strategies and (2) variation in strategies across different types of firms. Contrary to popular perception and a great deal of academic work, there has been a dramatic and extensive transformation in Russian firms' property

---

[6] The extent to which firms combine legal and illegal strategies ultimately is an empirical question. Cluster analyses presented in Appendix F indicate that a firm's propensity to use a specific strategy of private, corrupt, or legal coercion is positively correlated with propensity to use other similar strategies. In other words, firms do tend to rely predominantly on either legal or illegal strategies.

[7] Relational contracting and private ordering have been studied fairly extensively in the post-communist context. See, e.g., Frye (2000), Hendley et al. (2000), Johnson et al. (2002a), Murrell (2003), and Frye (2017).

security strategies. Drawing on original interview and survey evidence, I find that three trends are particularly noteworthy:

The decline of private coercion: In the early to mid-1990s, approximately 40 percent of small businesses in Russia had regular encounters with, or utilized the "services" of, criminal protection rackets (Frye and Zhuravskaya, 2000, pp. 487–493). Many other firms relied on private security agencies to enforce contracts and adjudicate business disputes. By contrast, in my 2010 survey less than 8 percent of small businesses (and less than 5 percent of the overall sample) reported contact with criminal rackets over the last three years. Meanwhile, violent means of resolving business disputes have declined significantly, while the role of private security agencies has been transformed. Security firms in contemporary Russia primarily provide basic physical protection of buildings, cargo, and business executives – much like security firms in the West.

The replacement of private coercion with corrupt coercion: Beginning in the mid-to-late 1990s, Russian firms came to rely on property security strategies that require the corrupt appropriation of state resources, such as protection rackets operated by law enforcement officials. According to the 2010 survey I conducted, approximately one-fifth of firms reported turning to law enforcement or other state officials in an informal or "private" capacity to resolve a security-related issue, while 14 percent of firms admitted using informal connections within the judiciary. These property security strategies involving corrupt force persist to the present day, intermingling with the legitimate use of formal state institutions.

The rise of legal coercion: In the early to mid-1990s, few firms relied on lawyers and the legal system. For example, Russian firms litigated fewer than 200,000 cases in 1994. By contrast, law plays a major role in contemporary Russian business. In 2010, Russian firms initiated over one million court cases, a 400 percent increase compared to the early 1990s (VAS, 2011). Interviews and survey evidence confirm that this increase is due to firms' rising willingness to resolve disputes lawfully, rather than to growing conflict among firms. Meanwhile, the number of lawyers in Russia more than doubled during this period, and lawyers assumed an increasingly important strategic role in Russian firms.

Naturally, the evolution of property security strategies has occurred unevenly across different types of firms. Firm-level characteristics – sector, size, customer and supplier relationships – influence the extent to which a firm faces demand-side barriers to the use of formal legal institutions, as well as the ability of a firm to effectively employ illegal strategies. Such variation across firm types is of great importance: It provides clues

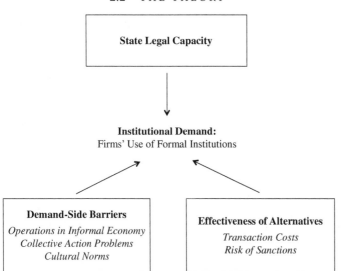

Figure 2.2 Overview of Analytical Framework

as to which actors within the private sector are likely to form a vanguard in the adoption of legal strategies. Chapter 7 is devoted to this issue. The next section introduces a theory of institutional demand that helps make sense of evolving property security strategies in countries such as post-Soviet Russia.

2.2 The Theory

The analytical framework introduced here centers around three key variables: state legal capacity, demand-side barriers, and the effectiveness of illegal strategies (see Figure 2.2). This section analyzes each of these variables in turn, developing a theory of institutional demand that rests on the following propositions: First, state legal capacity is a necessary but frequently insufficient condition for firms to utilize formal legal institutions. Second, firms' increased use of formal legal institutions often occurs even in the absence of heightened state legal capacity. In such cases, demand-side barriers and the effectiveness of illegal strategies play a significant role in shaping firms' property security strategies.

2.2.1 State Legal Capacity

As Douglass North (1981, p. 24) memorably suggested more than three decades ago, "The basic services that the state provides are the underlying rules of the game," including the "fundamental rules of competition and cooperation which will provide a structure of property rights." In this sense, the state is a direct supplier of institutions, the creator and enforcer of property rights. Although few would deny the importance of private or informal institutions for protecting property rights, the comparative advantage of states in providing the foundations for modern market economies has been well recognized. North (1981, p. 24) even goes so far as to claim: "The economies of scale associated with devising a system of law, justice, and defense are the basic underlying source of civilization; and the creation of the state ... the necessary condition for all subsequent economic development."

For the purposes of this study, formal legal institutions include both the formal rules (e.g., laws and government decrees) that shape economic relations and also the state organizations charged with implementing and enforcing these rules.[8] Although courts may be the most obvious institution to fall into this category, law enforcement and specialized regulatory agencies also play essential roles in the rule-of-law regime required for the security of property rights. I refer to the critical "supply-side" variable encapsulating the functioning of these institutions as well as the quality of laws on the books as *state legal capacity*. Measuring state legal capacity presents challenges, but I follow legal scholars in considering metrics, discussed in greater detail in Chapter 4, such as the absence or existence of key laws, codes, and agencies; the financial resources dedicated to upholding the formal legal infrastructure; state officials' competency and independence from political pressure; and the operational capability of legal institutions, including their accessibility, efficiency, and enforcement ability (Hendley, 2006; Solomon, 2008).

The state, of course, is not only the supplier of institutions but also a predatory threat to property security, a fact that has received extensive attention in the literature on property rights. In particular, at least since North and Weingast's (1989) study of the Glorious Revolution in seventeenth-century England, prominent studies of property rights have sought to understand how a ruler with a near monopoly on coercion can credibly commit to respect property rights, given that rulers frequently face incentives to renege on agreements with investors or creditors once investments have been made or loans provided. North and Weingast

---

[8] North (1990, ch. 1) suggests that the rules of the game (i.e., institutions) are distinct from the players in the game (i.e., organizations). For the questions engaged in this study, I find it more tractable to consider rules and organizations in tandem, at least as pertains to rules and organizations tied to the state.

demonstrate how in pre-modern England, the creation of a powerful parliament and the rise of independent courts, backed by the credible threat of forcible dethronement, created self-enforcing checks and balances that limited the king's incentives to violate property rights.[9] Less commonly recognized, however, is that the ability to *constrain* state officials is itself a critical dimension of state legal capacity. As Frye (2004, p. 464) notes, "Analyses of state capacity typically consider what the state can do ... [But] it is also important to consider how constraints on state power influence state capacity. Because providing the public good of secure property rights is a key aspect of state capacity, scholars should devote greater attention to this issue." The fact that constraint on state predation is part of state legal capacity becomes even more apparent in recent analyses demonstrating that for many firms, lower-level predatory bureaucrats pose the greatest threat to property security, not rulers and their coterie at the highest echelons of power (Gans-Morse, 2012; Markus, 2015). When threats to property emanate from lower levels of the state, the creation of effective legal institutions requires some form of institutional constraints preventing state officials from abusing their authority.

It is easy to assume, not without logic, that the extent and quality of state legal capacity are the primary determinants of firms' willingness to use formal legal institutions. This assumption is so strong that few scholars have addressed the issue empirically. To be sure, reasonable evidence supports the proposition that the ineffectiveness of formal legal institutions can impede their use. In the extreme case of Vietnam, there exists "an absence of laws governing property rights," despite the Communist regime's constitutional recognition of private property in 1992. Accordingly, firms not only avoid courts but, more broadly, are forced to "contract without the shadow of the law" (McMillan and Woodruff, 1999, pp. 639–641, 652).[10] In Ghana, firms face a less extreme yet nonetheless serious supply-side barrier in that the court system "remains too costly for most commercial cases." As a consequence, surveys of Ghanian firms

---

[9] Following North and Weingast's (1989) seminal work, numerous scholars have identified other mechanisms that play a role in constraining rulers, ranging from citizen rebellions to defensive alliances of firms and other stakeholders to collective institutions for financing loans to rulers (see, e.g., Root, 1989; Weingast, 1997; Haber et al., 2003).

[10] In surveys of firms carried out between 1995 and 1997 in Vietnam and Eastern Europe, McMillan and Woodruff (2000, p. 2422, fn. 4) note that just 9 percent of Vietnamese respondents believed they could use the courts to enforce contracts with customers or suppliers. In response to the same question, 56 percent of Russian firms replied in the affirmative.

show that "[r]elying on legal sanctions and institutions is not perceived as a practical way of preventing problems." Ghanian firms also rarely turn to the police in times of need, citing, among other factors, law enforcement officials' susceptibility to bribery (Fafchamps, 1996, pp. 441, 443, 446). Similar examples from developing and transition countries abound.

Yet if a lack of state legal capacity serves as an impediment to firms' use of formal legal institutions, the inverse does not automatically follow: Supplying institutions does not necessarily persuade firms to use them. As Pistor et al. (1999, p. 17) note, courts in many fast-growing East Asian countries – countries renowned for high state capacity – for decades were actively engaged in criminal matters but "played a less important role in settling commercial disputes among nonstate parties." Meanwhile, throughout East Asia the adoption of new laws, often modeled after Western best practices, continued in subsequent decades in spheres such as competition policy, consumer protection, intellectual property rights, and securities markets. But once again, despite apparent improvements in state legal capacity, Pistor et al. (1999, p. 41) find that "a striking feature" of these legal innovations "is that most of them were left unenforced for years after they had been enacted."

A similar gap between the development of state legal capacity and the use of formal legal institutions emerged in much of the post-communist world. For example, surveying Russia's legal institutions nearly a decade after the Soviet collapse, Hendley (1999, p. 90) concluded that "Comparing snapshots of the legal landscape in 1985 and 1998 would make immediately apparent the fundamental and far-reaching nature of recent reforms." However, she also emphasized how legal reformers' expectations that increased effectiveness of legal institutions would be followed by private sector reliance on law remained unfulfilled: "Although this connection between supply of and demand for law may have seemed self-evident, it has proven elusive in practice" (Hendley, 1999, p. 89). Pistor's (1996, p. 80) analysis of Russian firms' contract enforcement strategies in the years following the Soviet collapse came to a similar conclusion, noting that "In view of the relatively low and declining numbers of cases referred to [the courts], there seems to be an over-supply of these institutions in relation to the actual demand therefor."

Meanwhile, as the post-communist era unfolded, Russian firms did increasingly adopt legal strategies. With growing frequency, they turned to courts, dispatched lawyers to conduct strategic negotiations, and came to expect that law enforcement or other state officials should help resolve disputes, even without the incentive of bribes. But as discussed in the introductory chapter, it was far from clear that this shift coincided with a significant increase in state legal capacity. To the contrary, Russian firms began to utilize law more extensively *despite* their persistent concerns about the effectiveness of formal legal institutions, and during a period in which their wariness of predatory state officials grew. Nor is Russia simply an isolated case of firms turning to formal legal institutions when the independence and effectiveness of these institutions remain in doubt. In China, for example, the number of economic disputes heard by courts of first instance rose from around 40,000 in 1983 to more than 1.1 million by 2001. Yet as Whiting (2010, p. 183), commenting on the evolution of Chinese firms' strategies, observes, "Courts in the PRC are subordinate to the party, lack competent judges, and have weak enforcement powers. In light of these cultural and institutional features of the Chinese system, the dramatic increase in the litigation of economic disputes appears surprising."

In short, lack of state legal capacity may impede firms' use of formal legal institutions, but the development of legal capacity often does not lead firms to use law. In other words, state legal capacity is necessary but insufficient to induce firms' reliance on legal institutions. Moreover, firms frequently adopt legal strategies even without significant improvements in state legal capacity. To understand institutional demand, two other variables must be taken into account: demand-side barriers to the use of formal legal institutions and the effectiveness of illegal strategies that rely on violence or corruption.

2.2.2 *Demand-Side Barriers to the Use of Legal Strategies*

Barriers to the use of formal legal institutions exist in all countries. Perhaps the most widely examined barrier pertains to legal costs, particularly as they bear on economically disadvantaged groups within a society (Galanter, 1974). For the purpose of this study, I consider these "supply-side" barriers to be part of state legal capacity. *Demand-side barriers*, on the other hand, emanate from outside the legal system. They are behaviors or beliefs at the level of firms and individuals that lead these actors to avoid formal legal institutions.

One prominent demand-side barrier concerns firms' *operations in the informal economy*. In large swaths of Latin America, Africa, and Asia, small firms and individual entrepreneurs conduct business without formal permits and in locales for which they hold no formal property rights. By some accounts, between 40 and 50 percent of the labor force in

Latin America was employed in the informal sector throughout the 1990s (Portes and Hoffman, 2003, p. 50). Meanwhile, De Soto (2003, p. 36) famously calculated the value of informally "owned" property across the developing world in 1997 at over 9 trillion US dollars. Even firms that are formally registered with state authorities may conduct a substantial portion of their operations unofficially. This is the case in many post-Soviet countries, where it is rare for firms to operate without registration but common for firms to use an array of schemes to hide output and wages from the tax authorities. Regardless of the nature of their unofficial operations, firms in the informal economy face formidable demand-side barriers to the use of formal legal institutions. Hay and Shleifer (1998, p. 399), who were foreign advisors during the Russian privatization process, nicely summarized the challenges faced by such firms, noting that one reason "private parties in Russia refuse to use the legal system is that they operate to some extent extralegally to begin with and, hence, do not want to expose themselves to the government."

Another demand-side barrier to firms' use of formal legal institutions results from a *collective action problem* among firms. Law is relatively unique in that it matters most when a sufficient proportion of a society believes that it matters. As Hendley (1999, pp. 92–93) explains, "In economic transactions, the value of law lies in its ability to provide a common language (basic rules and a pre-approved forum for resolving disputes) that need not be contested in every new transaction. If, however, significant numbers of potential users persist in bypassing it, then the law loses this critical virtue." The implications for transition and developing countries of this characteristic of law are grave. Firms' concerns that other firms are not willing to reduce their use of violence and corruption in favor of law hinders the widespread adoption of legal strategies. In Hendley's (1999, pp. 92–93) words, "Managers are understandably reluctant to be the first to make the move [to law], thereby ceding an advantage to law-adverse trading partners who could still appeal to political or other patrons ... In this, we find a classic dilemma of collective action." Consequently, firms' expectations about other firms' strategies can serve as a powerful demand-side barrier, and these expectations must be shifted in order to induce firms to rely more extensively on formal legal institutions.

A third commonly discussed example of a demand-side barrier pertains to *cultural norms*. Cultural explanations have been used, for instance, to account for low reliance on formal legal institutions in Japan, where some scholars perceive "a comfort with particularistic, hierarchically defined roles and relationships" that is "incompatible with judicial decisions based on universal standards of behavior" (see discussion in Ginsburg and Hoetker 2006, pp. 33–34). Winn (1994, p. 200) paints a similar picture of Chinese legal culture, describing a "social order ... anchored in networks of interpersonal relationships rather than founded on ... a central, universal, dominant legal order." And in Madagascar, Fafchamps and Minten (2001, p. 251) find "that coercion is not seen as a common or even correct way of resolving contractual disputes," and consequently "recourse to courts and police is low because traders perceive these institutions to be too antagonistic and conflictual." Hendley (1999, pp. 92–93), too, speculated that Russian firms' hesitancy to use courts in the early 1990s could be attributed to a Soviet legal culture and "a long-standing skepticism of law among Russian citizens," a view she abandoned in later work (see, e.g., Hendley, 2012). Cultural explanations, of course, struggle to account for changes in behavior over time, particularly when changes are rapid. For this reason and others discussed later in this chapter, cultural theories are not a major focus of this book, but a comprehensive framework of institutional supply and demand must at least consider them as a potential explanatory factor.

In summary, demand-side barriers are behaviors and beliefs at the level of firms and individuals which impede economic actors' willingness to utilize formal legal institutions. They may result from firms' operations in the informal economy that make them wary of encounters with the state, from firms' expectations about each other's strategies for securing property, or from cultural predispositions. Regardless of their source, demand-side barriers must be mitigated in order to induce firms to utilize law.

2.2.3 *Effectiveness of Illegal Strategies*

As with any competing set of services, firms' willingness to use formal legal institutions depends in part on the *effectiveness of alternatives*. The effectiveness of illegal strategies, in turn, depends on two factors: *transaction costs* and the *risk of sanctions*.

There is a rich body of literature analyzing transaction costs – costs resulting from acquiring information, negotiating, and enforcing a transaction – and the relative effectiveness of alternatives to formal legal institutions. Although this literature focuses on informal rather than illegal strategies, a distinction introduced in Section 2.1, its insights are broadly applicable for consideration of the relative effectiveness of strategies based on violence or corruption. For example, scholars have come to a near consensus that in small, close-knit communities in which actors engage in repeated exchange with well-known partners, informal arrangements are likely to entail lower transaction costs than formal legal systems. In complex market economies in which large numbers of actors frequently engage in exchanges with strangers and commit to agreements realized over long timespans, formal rules and legal institutions may be a necessity (North, 1990, chs. 5, 7; Ellickson, 1991, pp. 249–258).

It would seem then that the increasing sophistication and complexity of an economy should stimulate the adoption of formal rules and the use of formal legal institutions. But while this to some extent may be true, for several decades scholars also have recognized that even in the most complex and legalistic societies, firms and individuals continue to resolve many disputes without recourse to law (Macaulay, 1963; Williamson, 1985; Bernstein, 1992). Studies of relational contracting and private ordering therefore frequently analyze how the traits of specific goods and services, parties to a transaction, and other aspects of the exchange itself influence the effectiveness of legal strategies relative to alternatives. This literature suggests that legal strategies will be less prevalent when the quality of a good or service is difficult to measure, when assets are produced for specialized purposes and not easily refitted to alternative uses, when frequent market disruptions (e.g., due to weather or transport problems) force regular renegotiation of existing agreements, or when parties engage in long-term interactions rather than infrequent spot transactions (Ellickson, 1991, pp. 256–258; Murrell, 2003, pp. 704–706). These insights inform the analysis in Chapter 7 about which *types* of firms should be more or less likely to effectively employ legal strategies. Transaction costs analysis is, however, less useful for understanding evolution of strategies over time, for the predictions of the relational contracting and private ordering literature pertain more to specific industries or geographic locations than to economy-wide trends.

In addition to relative transaction costs, a firm's consideration of strategies based on private or corrupt coercion also must take into account the risk of significant sanctions. Indeed, such risks often set the use of illegal strategies apart from the use of informal strategies, which do not inherently involve violations of the law. These sanctions come in many forms, ranging from physical harm to criminal prosecution to the loss of funding by investors made wary by a firm's unsavory reputation. Consequently, factors that increase the likelihood or severity of sanctions will lead firms to reduce their reliance on violence and corruption. Clearly, an increase in state legal capacity is one possible source of such sanctions. But Chapter 6 explores a number of less obvious factors that affect the risk of using illegal strategies, such as whether firms have long or short time horizons, the degree to which firms conduct transactions via formal financial institutions, and the extent to which firms are integrated into the international economy.

In summary, the effectiveness of alternatives to legal institutions depends on two factors: transaction costs and the risks of sanctions. Factors that increase transaction costs of illegal strategies relative to the transaction costs of legal strategies provide incentives for firms to utilize formal legal institutions. Factors that increase the probability or impact of sanctions when firms engage in violence or corruption have a similar effect.

2.2.4   Additional Dynamics

The following section applies the analytical framework to the case of post-Soviet Russia. But before considering the framework in the context of a real-world case, two final points deserve further attention. The first concerns the role the state. As noted in the discussion of state legal capacity above, the state simultaneously plays multiple roles in property security. On the one hand, it is the *direct supplier* of institutions, including formal legal institutions. On the other hand, the state poses the most fearsome *predatory threat* to property security, and a key element of state legal capacity is the introduction of constraints on predatory state officials. The state also plays a third role: the *indirect facilitator* of institutional demand, via reforms that intentionally or inadvertently remove demand-side barriers to the use of law.

The state's indirect facilitation of demand can manifest in many forms. One striking example pertains to demand-side barriers resulting from firms' operations in the informal sector – the avoidance of taxes in particular. Firms' level of tax compliance depends on numerous factors, including the current state of the economy, moral considerations, the tax rate, and the quality of tax administration (Levi, 1989; Andreoni et al., 1998). Improved tax compliance may therefore occur independently of reforms initiated by the state. But in the specific case of post-Soviet Russia, tax administration reforms contributed to improved tax compliance, as discussed in Chapter 5. Although considerations of firms' property security strategies were hardly central to tax reformers' goals, these reforms nevertheless played a role in reducing demand-side barriers to firms' use of formal legal institutions.

The second issue that warrants further discussion is the unique nature of demand-side barriers pertaining to firms' expectations about each other's property security strategies. At the most straightforward level of analysis, the collective action problems resulting from firms' expectations affect strategies in the same manner as other types of demand-side barriers. When barriers are high, firms' use of legal strategies will be minimal, and thus expectations must be shifted in order to induce firms to rely more extensively on formal legal institutions. But there is also another aspect to such collective action problems. As discussed more fully in Chapter 5, the interactive effects among firms create a dynamic that resembles the *tipping point* models other scholars have used to analyze revolutions, neighborhood segregation, and the adoption of national languages (Schelling, 1971; Kuran, 1989; Laitin, 1998).

As in such models, the value to using illegal strategies remains higher than the value to using legal strategies until a critical mass of firms comes to use legal strategies, at which point the economy "tips" toward a new equilibrium in which the value of using legal strategies surpasses the value of using illegal strategies. One of the key implications of such dynamics is that the vicious and virtuous cycles resulting from firms' expectations about each other amplify the effects of other trends in an economy. To continue using the above example of tax compliance, consider an economy in which many firms evade taxes, and as a consequence the majority of firms rely on illegal strategies. For one reason or another, tax compliance improves, reducing firms' hesitancy to use formal legal institutions and *directly* leading many firms to expand their reliance on legal strategies. If this initial shift in strategies is sufficiently large to "tip" an economy toward a more lawful equilibrium, then the initial reduction in demand-side barriers will also *indirectly* affect firm strategies, as firms' expectations that other firms are increasingly turning to law encourages even more widespread adoption of legal strategies. Later discussions of coordination problems among firms caution against applying the tipping point metaphor too literally. Among other reasons, when there are firms of different types, it is unlikely that an economy will exhibit a single, unique tipping point. But the tipping point concept usefully draws attention to the unique role that firms' expectations about each other's strategies play in the analytical framework developed in this section: Expectations are both a demand-side barrier that must be overcome and also a mechanism that amplifies the effects of other trends in the economy on firms' willingness to use law.

The analytical framework and theory of institutional demand presented in this section offer insights into the puzzle introduced in the previous chapter: Why do firms in countries such as Russia sometimes resort to violence and corruption to secure property even when relatively effective legal institutions exist, and why do firms sometimes turn to law even without improvements in the state's legal capacity? A significant part of the explanation is that despite the development of formal legal institutions, firms may continue to face significant demand-side barriers or may continue to more effectively employ illegal strategies. Inversely, even without heightened state legal capacity, firms may adopt legal strategies in response to declining demand-side barriers or the falling effectiveness of illegal strategies.

2.3 Institutional Supply and Demand in Russia

The theory of institutional demand introduced above offers general insights about the relationships among state legal capacity, demand-side barriers, the effectiveness of alternatives to formal legal institutions, and firms' property security strategies. Although these insights are broadly applicable to transition and developing countries, this book illustrates the analytical framework through analysis of post-Soviet Russia. As discussed in the introductory chapter, Russia is a particularly well-suited case for theory building, for in few countries can such a wide range of property security strategies be found in the relatively short span of two decades. This evolution in Russian firms' strategies for securing property over time, and the variation in strategies across different types of firms, provides promising material for developing hypotheses about the factors that underlie institutional demand.

The Russian case vividly illustrates the core propositions of the theory introduced above. First, the case of post-Soviet Russia demonstrates how the emergence of state legal capacity does not guarantee that firms will use formal legal institutions. Shortly after the collapse of the Soviet Union at the end of 1991, the newly independent Russian government declared the right of firms and individuals to buy, sell, and trade as they pleased, which for nearly 70 years of Soviet rule had been a crime. The year 1992 also marked the beginning of the largest sell-off of assets in human history. In a span of less than four years, the Russian state transferred approximately

120,000 enterprises to private owners (Blasi et al., 1997, p. 189). After decades of the Soviet command economy, with its strict prohibitions on nearly all forms of private ownership, private property rights were created practically overnight. In 1993, they were enshrined in Article 35 of the new Russian Constitution.

Russia's reformers proposed that once state assets were placed in private hands via a massive privatization program, the new capitalist class would lobby for the development of institutions that protect property rights and then put those institutions to good use (Shleifer and Vishny, 1998, p. 10). After all, such institutions raise the value of assets by ensuring that contracts are binding and property rights are not expropriated. Yet throughout the 1990s, Russian firms routinely ignored formal institutions, relying not on law but on violence and corruption – the most extreme form of which was criminal protection rackets – to accumulate assets, protect claims to property, and enforce contracts (Black et al., 2000; Volkov, 2002). The framework developed here explains why: Even once state legal capacity began to develop, Russian firms still faced extensive demand-side barriers and still possessed the capability to effectively employ illegal alternatives to formal legal institutions.

Second, the Russian cases demonstrates how property security strategies can evolve even in the absence of significant increases in state legal capacity. As the chaos of the 1990s unfolded, many observers came to see Russia's emerging capitalists not as a force promoting secure property rights and orderly transactions but as a fundamental threat to legality and public order (Hellman, 1998; Black et al., 2000; Goldman, 2003). Following a series of seminal articles by Hendley (1997, 1999), other scholars began to question whether Russia was suffering from a deficit in "demand for law" (see, e.g., Hoff and Stiglitz, 2004; Polishchuk and Savvateev, 2004). Yet just as scholars were debating the sources of low institutional demand, major changes in firms' strategies for securing property began to occur. As noted above, the number of court cases filed by Russian firms approximately tripled during the first decade of the twenty-first century, while violent resolution of business conflicts became a rare exception.

Although it is tempting to attribute Russian firms' increasing reliance on formal legal institutions to Putin's rise to power at the end of the 1990s and subsequent efforts to rebuild the Russian state, this book demonstrates the incompleteness of such an explanation. As discussed in Chapter 4, state legal capacity simply did not improve significantly enough to account for the sizable changes in Russian firms' property security strategies. To provide just one example, the World Bank–EBRD Business Environment and Enterprise Performance Survey (BEEPS) has repeatedly asked firms to rate obstacles to doing business on a 1 to 4 scale, where 1 represents "no obstacle" and 4 represents a "major obstacle." In 1999, the average rating for functioning of the judiciary as "problematic for the operation and growth of your business" was 2.1. In 2002, this rating improved slightly to 1.9 before returning to 2.0 in 2005.[11] Enhanced state legal capacity in Russia may have increased the viability of using law, but firms' evaluation of state institutions' effectiveness improved only marginally.

Finally, the Russian case demonstrates how factors such as demand-side barriers and the effectiveness of alternatives to legal institutions can influence the evolution of firms' property security strategies. Chapter 5 analyzes how the mitigation of two prominent demand-side barriers, low tax compliance and collective action problems resulting from firms' expectations about each other's strategies, contributed to an increase in firms' use of formal legal institutions. Chapter 6 then examines how factors such as increasing time horizons, a shift from cash to bank transactions, and integration into the international economy increased the risk of sanctions and thereby lowered the effectiveness of illegal strategies.

In summary, the Russian case illustrates how a framework that integrates analysis of state legal capacity, demand-side barriers, and the effectiveness of illegal strategies can offer a comprehensive approach to property security, combining insights about institutional supply and demand to make sense of property security strategies in the post-communist world and elsewhere.

2.4   Other Explanatory Factors

Numerous factors affect firms' property security strategies, and no single framework can encompass them all. Here I discuss three additional explanatory factors and clarify their relationship to the analysis offered in this book. These factors are (1) transformations in cultural norms, (2) the effects of increasing economic complexity and development, and (3) the strategic role of criminal organizations and oligarchs.

---

[11] Author's calculations based on data from the World Bank–EBRD Business Environment and Enterprise Performance Surveys.

2.4.1 Normative Transformations

As discussed in Section 2.2.2, cultural norms can serve as a powerful demand-side barrier to the use of formal legal institutions. The normative perspective on legal compliance, most strongly associated with the work of social psychologist Tom Tyler (1990, p. 3), "is concerned with the influence of what people regard as just and moral as opposed to what is in their self-interest." People obey the law voluntarily, not out of fear of punishment. Either they believe they have a moral commitment to obey laws, or they believe in the legitimacy of legal authorities' "right to dictate behavior" (Tyler, 1990, p. 4).

With respect to a theory of institutional demand, normative transformations certainly should be considered as a potential explanatory factor. But I devote minimal attention to such explanations in this book, for there is scant evidence that the diversification of Russian firms' property security strategies can be attributed to a normative shift. Throughout multiple fieldwork trips to Russia, including 90 in-depth interviews with firms, lawyers, and private security agencies, not once did a respondent raise the issue of morality in discussions about firms' increased reliance on law. To the contrary, five respondents cited – without my prompting – the same Russian proverb, "Law is like a carriage's steering shaft: You can turn it whichever way you please,"[12] an explicit reference to the instrumental manipulation of law in the Russian context. An American lawyer with more than 15 years of experience in the post-Soviet countries was even more blunt on this point: "Russians view law as a tool. There is no emotional investment as in America. The evolution of the courts is a pure evolution of functionality, of finding new ways to use the [available] tools" (Lawyer 4, interview, 2009).

Nor is there evidence of a sizable shift in the legitimacy of the legal system. According to the 1999 World Bank–EBRD BEEPS survey, only 18 percent of Russian firm managers considered the court system to be "fair and impartial" in resolving business disputes. In the 2002 BEEPS survey, the corresponding figure was 14 percent; in 2005, 21 percent. Similarly, the 1999 BEEPS survey revealed that a mere 15 percent of firm managers considered the court system "honest and uncorrupt" in resolving business disputes. In the 2002 BEEPS survey, the corresponding figure was 14 percent; in 2005, 20 percent.[13] These modest increases can hardly account

---

[12] *Zakon chto dyshlo, kuda povernyesh – tuda i vyshlo.*

[13] Author's calculations based on data from the World Bank–EBRD BEEPS survey. These percentages refer to respondents who "frequently," "usually," or "always" associate the descriptions "fair and impartial" and "honest and uncorrupt" with the court system.

for the significant transformations in firms' property security strategies that have occurred in Russia.

2.4.2   Complexity and Economic Development

A venerable tradition among legal scholars and economic historians sees the emergence of formal legal systems as a necessary result of socioeconomic development and the concomitant challenges of organizing modern, industrialized societies. North (1990, p. 46) puts this position in straightforward terms when he writes: "The move, lengthy and uneven, from unwritten traditions and customs to written laws, has been unidirectional as we have moved from less to more complex societies and is clearly related to the increasing specialization and division of labor associated with more complex societies." Although such arguments are best suited to analyses of long historical epochs, they raise the question of the role of economic development even over shorter spans of time.

In Russia, economic growth averaged approximately 7 percent a year between 1999 and 2008. While many forces contributing to the diversification of property security strategies were already underway before 1999, it is undeniable that during the 2000s the complexity, pace, and volume of economic transactions in Russia significantly increased. Is it possible that Russia's firms simply "outgrew" strategies based on violence and corruption as the economy became more complex?

Explanations related to increased complexity or socioeconomic development suffer from the usual weaknesses of theories based on macro-structural variables, such as the imprecise specification of causal mechanisms. Moreover, notable counterexamples raise questions about such theories, especially Japanese firms' low level of reliance on formal legal institutions during Japan's decades of remarkable economic growth. In fact, until the 1990s, Japanese firms showed a lower propensity to utilize legal strategies than their counterparts in neighboring countries with lower levels of economic development such as South Korea and Taiwan (Pistor et al., 1999, p. 215). Pistor et al. (1999, p. 248), based on cross-national analysis of law in six East Asian countries, therefore conclude that "civil and commercial litigation is a more complex matter than a simple function of the division of labor in society."

The framework presented in this book takes socioeconomic changes seriously. However, rather than treat such changes as an undifferentiated whole, I seek to identify concrete mechanisms and specific processes, such as development of the banking system or foreign direct investment, that affect the transaction costs or risks of using illegal strategies. By changing the level of analysis and taking a more micro-level approach, it becomes possible to trace a clear chain of causal logic and evidence leading from explanatory variables to changes in firm strategies. In short, the argument of this book is fully complementary with explanations based on complexity and economic development. Indeed, by emphasizing specific features of development that may or may not be part of a given country's socioeconomic transformation, the book also sheds light on why economic development only sometimes leads to legal development.

2.4.3   Mafia and Oligarchs

Although this book does not focus on organized crime and the Russian oligarchs, analyses emphasizing these two infamous groups' impact on property security are fully compatible with the framework developed here. In particular, these groups have at various times influenced key variables in the framework, such as the effectiveness of illegal strategies or the level of state legal capacity, thereby shaping property security strategies in the economy as a whole.

Criminal protection rackets receive detailed attention in Chapter 3, but they are introduced as facilitators of firm strategies, rather than as strategic and important actors in their own right. Naturally, the rise and fall of powerful criminal groups involved many factors other than firms' demand for their services, including clashes among criminal factions, pressure from law enforcement, and competition from illicit rackets operated by government officials. Consequently, some scholars see the power and prevalence of criminal organizations as an important explanatory factor contributing to the effectiveness of state institutions. Volkov (2002, p. xii), for example, suggests that "When a high violence potential and high protection costs become burdensome for most participants, the condition for a reassertion of the state emerge. Only then do state laws and their enforcement gradually gain priority." Such an approach parallels the arguments developed in this book, for transformations within the criminal world enter my analysis indirectly by altering firms' costs of using illegal strategies. But given that criminal groups' narrative has been ably and abundantly analyzed (e.g., Skoblikov, 2001; Varese, 2001; Volkov, 2002), this book aims to offer a distinct yet complementary firm-oriented perspective to existing works.

Russia's business tycoons – often referred to as "oligarchs" – also have received extensive attention (e.g., Freeland, 2000; Hoffman, 2002; Guriev and Rachinsky, 2005; Braguinsky, 2009). Their story in many ways parallels the one told here. In the 1990s, they too engaged rampantly in private coercion and corruption. But unlike ordinary, non-oligarchic firms, their choice of property security strategies affected the entire political and economic system given their economic resources and political clout. Instead of utilizing the services of low-level criminal protection rackets, they turned to the top levels of Russia's intelligence and law enforcement agencies for privately provided protection (Volkov, 2002, ch. 5). And rather than hire private security agencies, they built massive internal private security services, creating, as the journalist David Hoffman (1997) observed, "their own private armies of security agents, bodyguards and commercial spies." The oligarchs also pioneered novel ways to use violence and corruption to acquire assets, often undermining the government's intake of revenue that was badly needed for rebuilding state institutions. In the most notorious scheme, known as Loans-for-Shares, oligarch-owned banks received shares in natural resource companies as collateral on loans to the Russian government. When the government defaulted on the debt, the banks auctioned these shares to the oligarchs themselves at rock-bottom prices. Oligarchs additionally invented new forms of illegal corporate raiding, using, for example, corrupt government officials and legal loopholes to secretly force bankruptcy on solvent companies and acquire their assets, helping to undermine the legal system (Volkov, 2004).

Yet by the end of the 1990s, many oligarchs had become advocates of, in the words of the business tycoon Vladimir Potanin (2003), "a new business climate ... based on civilized rules of business and new ethics of relations." Nor was this purely hype. Prior to his arrest, the oil magnate Mikhail Khodorkovsky became a widely-respected advocate for transparency and corporate governance reform. And while not all oligarchs subscribed to this new business philosophy, many analysts noted a broad shift in oligarchs' tactics (Boone and Rodionov, 2002; Zhuravskaya, 2007). Moreover, in the first years of the Putin regime, oligarchs became significant proponents of institutional development, lobbying for – and sometimes participating in drafting – tax, judicial, administrative, and regulatory reforms (Jones Luong and Weinthal, 2004; Guriev and Rachinsky, 2005). Although the oligarchs cared most about reforms that affected their own business empires, not the economy as a whole, these reforms nonetheless affected state legal capacity more broadly. Like organized crime, the oligarchs' story therefore is complementary to the framework developed in this book, entering into the framework by altering the level of state legal capacity.

2.5   Scope of Analysis

Before turning to the case of post-Soviet Russia in subsequent chapters, the final section of this chapter briefly discusses three issues pertaining to the book's scope of analysis: (1) the range of empirical focus, (2) the generalizability of the theory, and (3) the boundaries between exogenous and endogenous variables in the analytical framework.

The empirical analyses in this book examine variation over time and across firms. Although I do not devote extensive attention to regional variation, I do demonstrate that the trends identified in subsequent chapters are by no means limited to Russia's two major cities, Moscow and St. Petersburg. Additionally, as indicated in the previous section, the empirical analyses focus on "ordinary" firms rather than the conglomerates owned by Russia's infamous oligarchs or the state. The rules of the game for such conglomerates – particularly for those in "strategic" sectors such as energy, transportation, or defense – are fundamentally different than for other firms. As Paul Backer (2008), an American lawyer with extensive experience in the post-Soviet region, quipped in reference to the high-profile 2008 conflict between oil behemoths TNK and BP, "gauging the TNK-BP [conflict's] impact on actual business in Russia is like evaluating how a failed NASA space shuttle launch affects commuter flights from NYC to Boston." Moreover, despite the outsized attention to Russia's strategic sectors, "ordinary" firms comprise a broad swath of the Russian economy. Even throughout the oil boom of the 2000s, the natural resource sector's share of GDP was no more than one-third, and as little as one-tenth.[14]

With respect to the generalizability of the analytical framework, a theory of institutional demand is of primary relevance for intermediate-capacity states, a category which encompasses more than 60 percent of the world's countries.[15] Given that state legal capacity is a necessary but

---

[14] See World Bank Country Reports, various years.

[15] I arrive at this figure by excluding failed states and high-income OECD countries. According to the 2010 Failed States Index, 37 countries received a ranking of "alert" or "warning" with respect to "vulnerability to collapse or conflict" (see http://ffp.statesindex.org/). Meanwhile, current OECD membership includes 34 countries. Together, these two groups

insufficient condition for firms to use formal legal institutions, an obvious scope condition is that some modicum of state capacity actually exist. Consequently, in the approximately 20 percent of the world's states that are failed or war torn, the theory put forth in this book likely provides fewer insights into property security. Meanwhile, my arguments are also less likely to apply to the roughly 20 percent of the world's states that are frequently characterized as advanced industrial economies. I have set out to understand why firms in environments where violence or corruption is rife reduce their reliance on illegal strategies in favor of law. I for the most part leave aside the question of whether firms in societies already locked in a lawful equilibrium might abandon formal legal institutions, although in the conclusion I speculate on the theory's applicability to historical cases in Western Europe and North America.

Bearing these scope conditions in mind, the analytical framework developed in this book applies to a wide range of countries with intermediate levels of state legal capacity. The specific examples of demand-side barriers drawn from the Russian case may differ from those in other cases, but whatever these factors may be, they are likely to fall into the categories of operations in the informal economy, collective action problems, or cultural norms. Likewise, the specific mechanisms influencing the effectiveness of illegal strategies may differ from country to country, but the majority of these mechanisms are likely to relate to transaction costs or the risk of sanctions. Accordingly, analysis of how Russian firms choose between violence and corruption or formal legal institutions has the potential to produce important lessons for other developing and transition countries.

Finally, although this book seeks to integrate the demand and supply sides of institutional development, it focuses primarily on demand. The supply-side variable – state legal capacity – is for much of this book's analysis treated as exogenous: I examine how changes in its level affect institutional demand, but I do not seek to fully account for the source of these changes. However, as I emphasize in the concluding chapter, institutional demand does, of course, affect institutional supply. Whether firms use formal institutions or not almost certainly influences the effectiveness and relevance of these institutions. Indeed, this is partly why a better understanding of institutional demand is so important. Although

comprise just under 40 percent of countries in the world. Clearly, this is a rough set of categorizations. In particular, many of the more recent OECD members, such as Mexico or the Czech Republic, could aptly be considered intermediate-capacity states.

a dynamic theory of the ongoing interactions between institutional supply and demand is a worthy goal, my focus on the demand side of analysis is meant to complement existing studies, which overwhelmingly focus on the supply side. Moreover, nearly all existing studies of property rights exhibit the same limitations faced here: They focus on rulers' decisions to engage in institution building while treating demand-side factors, such as a private sector lobbying or firms' use of these institutions, as exogenous. At the end of the book, I return to this issue, both to demonstrate that a more dynamic framework should not influence the validity of this book's main arguments, as well as to lay out a foundation for the development of such a framework.

2.6   Conclusion

The theory of institutional demand presented in this chapter lays the groundwork for the in-depth analysis of post-Soviet Russia to come. The framework integrates the supply and demand sides of institutional demand and offers insights into when firms use violence and corruption, and when firms turn to formal legal institutions. Drawing on three key variables – state legal capacity, demand-side barriers to the use of formal legal institutions, and the effectiveness of illegal strategies – the theory rests on the following propositions. First, the theory emphasizes that state legal capacity is necessary but insufficient to induce firms' reliance on formal legal institutions. Second, the theory makes clear that firms' increased use of legal strategies frequently occurs in the absence of heightened state legal capacity. In such cases, demand-side barriers and the effectiveness of illegal strategies become the primary determinants of firms' willingness to utilize formal legal institutions. In order to more fully analyze these propositions, a more thorough examination of the outcome to be explained is required. The following chapter undertakes this task, providing a detailed portrait of the evolution of Russian firms' strategies for securing property throughout the 1990s and 2000s.

3

The Evolution of Firm Strategies

The Soviet Union's collapse at the end of 1991 initiated a grim period for Russia, with GDP falling approximately 23 percent over the next two years and the annualized inflation rate topping 800 percent in 1993. With respect to property security, Russia resembled few places on earth. During 1993, 61 bombs exploded in Moscow as criminal groups battled for territorial control. In just the first half of 1994, 52 bombs shook the Russian capital (Hoffman, 2002, p. 277). The Ministry of Internal Affairs (MVD) officially catalogued 562 contract killings in 1994, nearly double the official number from the year before, and, naturally, this official figure represented only a fraction of the total (Statkus, 1998, p. 66). Use of the commercial court system, created on the foundations of Soviet institutions in 1992, continued to fall, with firms initiating only about 200,000 cases in 1994 (VAS, 2011). Meanwhile, organized crime crept into nearly all sectors of the economy, extorting firms on the one hand while offering property protection and contract enforcement services on the other (Webster, 1997, p. 2).

Yet by the mid-2000s, a foreign businessperson who had suffered the misfortune of visiting Russia in the early 1990s would not recognize the country that had emerged. The economy was booming, with GDP growing at more than 7 percent in both 2003 and 2004. Inflation was at a manageable 11 percent. If the foreign businessperson were to inquire of Russian business partners about the dangers of mafia rackets, she would have received the same response I did when querying respondents in interviews throughout 2009: a confused and slightly scornful smile, as if to say, "Mafia, please – that was so 1990s!" A more knowledgable foreigner might have possessed the wherewithal to ask business partners about their informal connections with local bureaucrats or law enforcement, who by the mid-to-late 1990s had begun to fulfill the functions of criminal protection rackets. Yet even this inquiry might have elicited disconcerted looks from business partners, many of whom already had come to rely primarily on lawyers and courts. In fact, by the mid-2000s, around two-thirds of larger firms and one-third of smaller firms had sued or been sued (Rimskii, 2009, Table 2.1), and firms' use of the commercial court system had more than doubled since the early 1990s – and was about to double again by 2010 (VAS, 2011). Of course, doing business in Russia still was not devoid of severe and unusual challenges. The Russian business world was still reverberating from the 2003 arrest of Russia's richest tycoon, Mikhail Khodorkovsky, on charges of fraud and money-laundering, an incident that would prove to be a harbinger of an increasingly predatory state, a trend examined in detail in Chapter 4.

Nevertheless, this dramatic transformation in Russian firms' strategies for securing property offers the opportunity to analyze the foundations of institutional demand. In order to lay the groundwork for such analysis, the present chapter investigates the evolution of this book's dependent variable – property security strategies – over the past two decades. To this end, I draw on in-depth interviews with Russian businesspeople, lawyers, and private security agencies, as well an original survey of Russian firms. Three substantial shifts are analyzed. In the terminology of the typology introduced in Chapter 2, this chapter provides evidence of (1) the decline of strategies based on private coercion; (2) the replacement of private coercion with corrupt coercion; and (3) the rise of strategies based on legal coercion.[1]

3.1   The Decline of Private Coercion

In the wake of the Soviet Union's collapse, private coercion came to play a significant role in Russian firms' property security strategies. Business-people frequently settled disputes through threats of violence, eradicated competitors through contract killings, and relied on criminal protection rackets to enforce contracts. Whereas in most countries organized crime is limited to illegal sectors such as prostitution, drugs, arms trafficking, fraud, and money laundering, many otherwise legitimate firms in early post-Soviet Russia relied on criminal protection rackets to provide funda-mental protective and adjudicative functions usually fulfilled by modern states. Yet contrary to popular belief, this era of thuggery peaked before the mid-1990s and then faded in most of Russia's regions by the end

---

[1] Although the focus of this chapter is on broad trends over time, it is important to recognize that these trends occurred unevenly across different types of firms. In Chapter 7, I return to the issue of cross-firm variation in property security strategies associated with firm size, sector, and other key firm-level characteristics.

of the first post-communist decade. Organized crime remains a significant problem, but it is no longer part and parcel of everyday business transactions in Russia. It is instead limited to those illegal sectors "where it belongs," in the words of Elena Panfilova, the then director of the anti-corruption organization Transparency International's Moscow office (author interview, 12 February 2009).

Firms' use of private security agencies was another prominent property security strategy in the 1990s that relied on private coercion. Staffed with former members of law enforcement and national security organs, these private security agencies gradually replaced criminal groups in providing protection, adjudication, and enforcement services. After the end of the wild 1990s, however, demand for the services of private security agencies also evolved. Businesspeople came to rely on security agencies primarily for the same types of security services such agencies provide in Western countries: provision of physical protection for buildings, lots, and transport. Along with these developments, criminal and physical threats gave way to a broader definition of "economic security" (*ekonomicheskaya bezopasnost*) encompassing information security and intelligence gathering, managing relations with government officials, and protecting owners from crimes by employees.

The emergence of private coercion in the Russian world was intimately tied to the creation of private property. The Soviet Union was a socialist command economy.[2] With the exception of personal possessions, all property belonged to the state. The state planning agency, Gosplan, allocated resources to enterprises and set output targets for enterprise directors. Prices existed for administrative purposes, but they bore no relation to the supply and demand of goods and services. The system began to stagnate by the late 1960s but continued to teeter along, in large part due to large oil reserves and high oil prices. When in 1985 Mikhail Gorbachev became general secretary, the leading position in the Soviet power hierarchy, he prioritized the revival of the Soviet economy. In an effort to boost efficiency, Gorbachev decentralized many allocation decisions to the enterprise level, loosening the constraints of the command economy and Soviet totalitarianism. These reforms, known as *perestroika*, or, rebuilding, created some initial operating room for private entrepreneurs – but also for the criminal underworld.

Russian firms' reliance on organized crime had its roots in the criminal subculture that emerged out of the Soviet labor camps. From the

---

[2] For an overview of the Soviet system, see Kornai (1992) and Åslund (1995, ch. 1).

Brezhnev period onward, informal entrepreneurs filled the economic niches created by the inefficiencies of the Soviet command economy. Given that private economic activity was illegal, these early *kommersanty* required sources of protection and arbitration outside of the state. The *vory v zakony*, or "thieves professing the code," who emerged from the labor camps were well-suited for this role. They had developed a complex informal hierarchy for governance of the underworld and had honed skills, such as counterfeiting official documents, essential for moving goods in the Soviet period.[3]

Two early *perestroika* reforms, the 1987 Law on Individual Labor Activity and the 1988 Law on Cooperatives, which legalized small-scale private entrepreneurship, created new fodder for criminal rackets. The rapid emergence of entrepreneurial ventures and open-air markets led to ideal conditions for extortion. In addition to the criminals who earned their underworld laurels in the Soviet penal system, racketeers and thugs, known as *bandity*, emerged from three sources with a comparative advantage in the application of violence: groups of sportsmen, especially boxers, wrestlers, and martial arts specialists; criminal gangs based on ethnic networks from the Northern Caucuses; and veterans returning from the Soviet war in Afghanistan, which after a bloody decade came to a close in 1989.

Gorbachev's reforms stopped short of the creation of full capitalism and democracy, but they entailed enough liberalization to unleash opposition forces that would tear the Soviet Union apart. By the Union's official demise in December 1991, the economy was in free fall. Boris Yeltsin, the new Russian president, took steps to create a full market economy. At the beginning of 1992, nearly all controls on retail prices were abolished. As a result, "Central streets and squares in big Russian cities became crowded with street traders" (Åslund 1995, p. 142). Price liberalization created new victims for the *bandity* who made a living through extortion of kiosks at open-air markets, but by the Yeltsin period protection rackets' relations with Russia's emerging capitalists were already evolving. As open-air markets became crowded with competing rackets, gangs began to offer protection from other *bandity* in exchange for a percentage of entrepreneurs' profits, a service known as providing a "roof" (*krysha*). Soon markets were divided into spheres of influence, with sellers displaying insignia to warn would-be extorters that they were under the protection of a given criminal leader.

---

[3] This section draws on Handelman (1994), Modestov (1996), Skoblikov (1997, 2001), Varese (2001), Volkov (2002), and Shelley (2007).

Yeltsin's reformers next moved to transfer state-owned enterprises to private hands. Privatization re-created the redistribution of property control that had occurred in open-air markets on a massive scale. Suddenly, tens of thousands of shops and small businesses were in private hands and in need of *kryshas*. By 1994, the majority of Soviet firms were privately owned. Many of these enterprises proved to be valuable targets for criminal groups, and simultaneously in desperate need of protection services.

The services for which firms relied on criminal protection rackets continued to evolve. Particularly for smaller firms, *bandity* came to provide contract enforcement, collection of debt, and intelligence gathering on prospective business partners. In the absence of an effective court system, they began to play an adjudicative role. The *krysha* of one firm would meet with the *krysha* of another to negotiate on behalf of their respective clients, or, if need be, to resolve the dispute by force. For long-standing or complex disputes, *bandity* would turn to criminal leaders, known as *avtoritety*, and to *vory v zakone*, who served as arbiters in what became a system of "shadow justice" (Skoblikov, 2001).

Alarming estimates of the influence of organized crime on the Russian economy soon became widespread. An MVD report released in 1994 claimed that up to three-fourths of Russian businesses paid protection money, with the banking sector particularly under the sway of organized crime groups. The Russian Academy of Sciences (RAN) reported in 1995 that criminal groups held 55 percent of capital and 80 percent of voting shares in private enterprises (Webster 1997, pp. 2–3). These studies became the basis for dire assessments of organized crime in Russia by Western analysts (Webster, 1997; Shelley, 2007), although the imprecise distinction among protection, control, and ownership of enterprise assets in these reports complicates assessment of their validity (Volkov, 2002, pp. 97–98). Regardless, the reality of harsh violence during this period was undeniable, including extensive contract killings, car bombs, and all-out gang wars on the streets of cities such as Moscow, Ekaterinburg, and Kazan. Shocking tales emerged. Reputedly, the FBI traced connections of a well-known *vor* directly to the Kremlin (Shelley, 2007), while the journalist Seymour Hersh (1994) reported that criminal rackets even controlled access to the passport line at the US Embassy.

Along with criminal protection rackets, private security agencies played a major role in property security in the early 1990s. These agencies emerged in the aftermath of the collapse of the mammoth Soviet security structures, in particular during the reorganization of the KGB, which created a supply of highly-trained unemployed security specialists. In 1992, the government passed the Law on Private Detective and Protection Activity and issued a concomitant government decree, legalizing the formation of private security structures, a process that was already de facto underway. Private protection enterprises (*chastnoe okhrannoe predpriyatie*), known widely by their Russian acronym as ChOPs, soon became a major facet of the Russian business world. Meanwhile, rather than outsourcing security, larger firms created internal security services. In some cases, such services were enormous: The security department of Russia's natural gas monopoly Gazprom numbered 13,000 employees and was headed by a former KGB colonel (Volkov, 2002, pp. 134–135).

In and of itself, the emergence of a large private security sector was unremarkable. Other countries have private security agencies, including the United States and Britain. But the key difference was that "in Russia, the activity of private protection agencies extended beyond mere physical or informational security and into the sphere of business transactions and civil property relations" (Volkov, 2002, pp. 141). Private security agencies and internal security services offered a long list of services: debt collection, physical protection, collection of data on lawsuits, market research, information on future business partners, protection of trademarks and commercial secrets, and investigations of future or current employees.

The private security sector grew rapidly. By 1993, there were already approximately 5,000 registered private security agencies. This number doubled by the end of the decade, doubled again by 2005, and by the late 2000s was estimated at around 30,000 agencies.[4] Yet despite the growing number of private security agencies, the role of private coercion in the Russian business world has declined dramatically. Evidence that economic conflicts are less likely to be settled by violence appears in the statistics on annual murders of businesspeople, as seen for Russia's Central Federal District in Table 3.1.[5] The numbers remain high by Western standards and indicate that Russia is still a rugged place to do business,

---

[4] Data for up until 1999 are from Volkov (2002, p. 138). Data for the years after 1999 are from Khodorych (2002); Lashkina (2007); Borodkin (2008), and press releases at www.mvd.ru/news.

[5] It should be noted that the secular decline in business-related violence observed in Table 3.1 for the Central Federal District is not necessarily representative of trends in other Russian regions. Based on newspaper reports, for example, Belokurova (2013) identifies a double-peaked distribution of business-related violence, with levels of violence reaching a first peak in the mid-1990s and a second peak in the early 2000s. It is not clear, however, that this bimodal distribution reflects trends in business violence in particular rather than general trends in Russian crime, given that overall homicide rates in Russia show the same

Table 3.1 *Businesspeople Murdered in the Central Federal District of RF, 1997–2005*

	1997	1998	1999	2000	2001	2002	2003	2004	2005
Number of murders	217	170	159	158	110	103	103	55	33

Source: Matveeva (2007), 86.[6]

but they also show a sharp decline compared to Russia's recent bloody past. Meanwhile, most experts concur that reliance on contract killings declined after the early-to-mid 1990s (Skvortsova, 2000; Krylov et al., 2008).[7] Contract killings persist to this day, but observant analysts have recognized that an increasing number of targets are outside the sphere of property disputes. While businessmen, bankers, and bureaucrats with control over valuable licenses or permits are still prevalent among the victims, a rising proportion of contract killing targets are journalists and human rights activists (Skvortsova, 2000; *Kommersant*, 2008; Ram, 2009).

Businesspeople corroborate this decline in physical violence. A survey conducted by Radaev (1999) of 221 enterprise managers across 21 Russian regions in 1997[8] revealed that approximately two out of five respondents reported personally experiencing violent extortion or threats of physical coercion "sometimes" or "often." Businesspeople, however, seemed to be sensing a turning point: Only 14 percent said the risk of threats and extortions was getting worse, whereas 30 percent said it was getting better (Radaev, 1999, pp. 36–40). Indeed, my survey of 301 firms from 8 Russian cities, conducted in June and July of 2010, validates these optimistic prognoses: Less than 5 percent of respondents said they or their employees "sometimes" or "often" had been subjected to threats

---

twin-peaked distribution over time (Lysova et al., 2012). Additionally, there is some evidence that the increase in registered crimes in the early 2000s resulted from heftier penalties against law enforcement agents who fail to register crimes rather than from an increase in crime *per se* (Goble, 2008), and increased newspaper coverage of crime levels quite likely reflects this increase in officially registered crimes.

[6] Matveeva (2007) notes that while these statistics refer to overall murders of businesspeople, her analysis of the data indicates that all but approximately 5 percent of these deaths were related to the victims' business activities.

[7] Contract killings in general are tough to measure, and different sources report drastically varying statistics, not least of all because in the early 2000s the MVD began reporting only the number of solved cases rather than the number of registered contract killings (*Vlast* 2008).

[8] To facilitate comparisons, information about samples for all surveys cited can be found in Appendix C.

or physical coercion. Nor is declining violence limited to Moscow and St. Petersburg. In fact, the average percent of respondents – 4 percent – reporting threats or physical coercion "sometimes" or "often" across the six regional cities in the survey is lower than the average in the full sample.[9]

Survey evidence paints a similar picture with respect to the disappearance of criminal protection rackets. Frye and Zhuravskaya (2000) found in a 1996 survey of 230 small retail shops in Moscow, Ulyanovsk, and Smolensk that over 40 percent of respondents reported having contact with a criminal group in the last six months; a survey of shops conducted in the same three cities two years later found the respective figure to be less than 25 percent (Frye, 2002). Surveys conducted by the Russian business association OPORA (2005, p. 91; 2006, p. 52) in 2004 and 2005 across 80 of Russia's 89 regions found that well under 10 percent of small businesses during these years reported frequent contact (although between 30 and 40 percent reported some "irregular" contact). By contrast, my 2010 survey found that less than 8 percent of 105 small businesses in the sample (and less than 4 percent of the 301 firms in the overall sample) reported contact with criminal protection rackets at any point in the previous three years. Evidence of these trends is again not limited to Moscow and St. Petersburg. Under 7 percent of small businesses (and less than 5 percent of firms of all sizes) in the regional cities included in the survey reported recent contact with rackets.[10]

Most telling in terms of the evolution of property security strategies, firms in the late 1990s were beginning to indicate a clear preference for strategies other than reliance on criminal protection rackets. The survey that Radaev (1999) conducted in 1997 found that in response to

---

[9] The six regional cities in the survey were Nizhniy Novgorod, Samara, Ekaterinburg, Kazan, Rostov-on-Don, and Novosibirsk.

[10] Comparison of surveys over time warrants caution (see Frye 2010, pp. 85–86). First, firms that suffer most from a hostile business environment are more likely to go out of business. Later surveys may disproportionately reflect the views of firms that are least likely to face violence and protection rackets. Such "survivor bias" may lead to inflated assessments of improvements in the business environment. Second, there is the possibility that firms over time have become less inclined to respond truthfully, biasing estimates of the prevalence of illicit activities downward. While these concerns should be acknowledged, it is unlikely that they account for the trends described above given the magnitude of the shift – often 30 or more percentage points – in assessments of violence and organized crime. Moreover, the results of in-depth interviews and analysis of objective indicators, such as murders of businesspeople and caseload statistics, corroborate the survey findings.

threats and extortion, only 15 percent of respondents would turn to criminal groups, while about the same number would turn to the police. The largest category of respondents, 34 percent, said they would rely on themselves to deal with the threat (Radaev, 1999, pp. 42–43). OPORA's 2004 survey similarly found that only 14 percent of small firms reported they would turn to a *krysha* for help should they face a violation of their rights (OPORA, 2005, pp. 70–71). As discussed below in the section on legal institutions, the results of my survey indicate that this trend away from private coercion has only continued.

The extent to which criminal *kryshas* have become a thing of the past is perhaps best summarized by the co-founder of a prominent Moscow private security agency, himself a former Ministry of Internal Affairs agent specializing in fighting organized crime. In the early 1990s, he explained, the majority of his firm's work involved helping clients deal with *bandity*. By 1995, a noticeable shift was occuring: "criminal groups were disappearing to such an extent that they were becoming simply something exotic. If a client came to us and said that some *bandity* from the street had tried to extort him, well, this was for us something exciting. [It gave us a] sort of nostalgia for the old days" (Security 5, interview, 2009). The challenges his security firm faced continued to evolve, and he noted that by the late 2000s it was even more rare to encounter criminal protection rackets.

The shift away from private coercion is also apparent in the private security sector. In the 1990s, the line between private security agencies and criminal groups was often blurry. Some agencies used criminal methods to collect debts and, in some cases, directly extorted businesspeople. In other cases, criminals themselves formed private security agencies in order to legally carry weapons. Some estimates claim that around 15 percent of agencies in the late 1990s had criminal ties (Volkov, 2002, p. 143). Moreover, businesspeople at times turned to private security agencies with explicit demands for illegal activities, including physical attacks and kidnapping (Shebaldin, 2007). The fact that for many years numerous private security agencies, accounting for as many as 150,000 employees, remained unregistered and out of the gaze of the state facilitated the persistence of questionable practices (Pistor, 1996; Khodorych, 2002).

Yet even if firms' shift from criminal protection rackets to private security agencies did not initially entail the complete elimination of criminal elements from the market for private security, it brought about significant changes. Private security agencies were willing to apply force but were more likely than *bandity* to do so only as a last resort. They focused more on conflict prevention and in place of violence often applied pressure to a client's competitors by gathering compromising materials, known in Russian as *kompromat*, which could be used for blackmail. They worked on the basis of formal contracts and usually paid taxes to the state. They had to legally register with the Ministry of Internal Affairs and could have their license revoked if they violated laws and regulations. They encouraged clients to understand and abide by the laws, and they organized business associations to screen out criminal enterprises masquerading as legitimate security agencies (Volkov, 2002, pp. 142–143,147,151–152; Pravotorov, 2006).

As private security agencies brought legitimacy to the market for protection, they simultaneously became more specialized as providers of physical security and less frequently a substitute for state institutions. Today, the Russian acronym for private security agencies introduced above – ChOP – narrowly refers to security guards, whereas the term *krysha* has a clear connotation of criminal connections.[11] Experts estimate that provision of basic physical security accounts for 70 percent of the private security sector's revenues, the rest consisting of information security, legal services, and installment of security systems (cameras, alarms, etc.). Although there has been recognition that profit margins for providing detective services, such as investigating credit histories and locating debtors, are quite high, these services account for a negligible fraction of private security agencies' work (author interview with Ivanchenko[12]; Khodorych, 2002).

Meanwhile, the security concerns of Russian businesspeople have evolved dramatically. Today, "economic security" entails a wide range of threats, including information security, such as computer virus attacks by competitors; espionage by employees with ties to other companies; raids that use complicated legal schemes to acquire assets; and unwarranted inspections (*naezdy*) by government regulators, some of which are instigated by competitors. To address these sophisticated threats, firms specializing in economic security rely far more on lawyers, accountants, IT specialists, and former law enforcement officials than on the application of violence and force.

---

[11] This statement was corroborated without exception in interviews with businesspeople and security specialists. In a typical response regarding the functions of ChOPs, one small businessperson in Moscow explained: "ChOPs? Those are just the guys that stand outside and guard the door" (Firm 1, interview, 2009).

[12] Aleksandr Ivanchenko, Executive Director of the Russian Security Industry Association. Interview conducted on June 8, 2009.

Survey research indicates that this trend toward specialization was already beginning by the late 1990s. A 1997 survey by Hendley et al. (2000, p. 643) of 328 industrial firms from 6 regions found that even though half of the respondents utilized the protective services of a security agency, less than 3 percent of respondents relied on these firms to prevent or resolve problems with suppliers or for evaluating the credit-worthiness of customers. They concluded: "These results suggest that security agencies have the more prosaic mandate of protecting money or property, rather than the task of enforcing contracts through intimidation of trading partners" (Hendley et al., 2000, p. 643). In a 2001 survey of 304 open joint stock companies in Moscow, Tomsk, and Nizhniy Novgorod, Yakovlev et al. (2004, p. 71) reported that only 5 percent of respondents whose legal rights had been violated turned to ChOPs to help resolve the problem. Likewise, in the 2010 survey I conducted, less than 10 percent of respondents reported using the services of a private security agency for any reason in the last three years.

On the other hand, 33 percent of firms in my survey, and approximately 45 percent of firms with over 100 employees, reported using their own internal security service at some point in the last three years to resolve a security issue. However, the reasons firms turn to private security reflect a very different type of threat from the violent disputes of the 1990s. Primarily, firms use private security for dealing with internal problems pertaining to employees and the security of information technology systems. For example, of the 100 firms in the survey sample that report using an internal security service in the last three years, 73 percent used this service to run employee background checks, while 52 percent used the service for issues related to IT security. Such issues as debt collection, contract violations, and property disputes represent a significantly smaller share of the services for which firms turn to private security.

Returning to the typology introduced in Chapter 2, the evidence presented in this section demonstrates the decline of private coercion as firms' primary tool to secure property in Russia. Organized crime today remains a significant problem *in illegal sectors*, but legitimate businesses rely on *bandity* for protection, adjudication, and contract enforcement services almost exclusively in remote and underdeveloped regions (Volkov, 2002, p. 152; Pravotorov, 2006). Analysts sometimes speak of a "criminalized" society in which organized crime groups have established formidable contacts within the Russian bureaucracy and security agencies to protect their illicit activities (Dolgova, 2005; Shelley, 2007). Yet such corruption and crime are fundamentally different from a situation in which criminal groups substitute for state institutions on a massive scale. To the extent that firms continue to rely on illegal property security strategies instead of law, they resort to corrupt coercion – the use of state resources for private purposes – rather than private coercion.

3.2   The Replacement of Private Coercion with Corrupt Coercion

As Russian firms' turned away from private coercion in the mid-to-late 1990s, they began to utilize a host of strategies that relied on corrupt coercion, the intermediate category in the continuum of property security strategies presented in Chapter 2 (see Figure 2.1). Foremost among these were the protection rackets offered by law enforcement officials (known as a *mentovskaya krysha*[13] as opposed to a *banditskaya krysha*, the term for a criminal protection racket). Law enforcement protection rackets offered many of the same services previously provided by criminal protection rackets, such as debt collection, contract enforcement, and adjudication of disputes. Another prominent tool based on the corrupt use of state resources that arose in the mid-to-late 1990s was the "contract inspection" (*zakaznoy naezd*), in which firms paid government bureaucrats and law enforcement officials to selectively conduct tax, fire, sanitation, or even criminal inspections in order to pressure competitors or counterparties in a dispute. Corrupt notaries and judges also figured prominently in these strategies, especially in disputes involving illegal corporate raiding (*reiderstvo*), which became a major source of conflict in the late 1990s and early 2000s in Russia. These property security strategies involving corrupt coercion persist to the present day, intermingling with the legitimate use of formal state institutions.

Law enforcement protection rackets took many forms. The most sought after law enforcement *kryshas* were the MVD's State Directorate for the Struggle with Organized Crime (GUBOP), and its regional branches (RUBOPs), as well as FSB (the KGB successor) units devoted to economic and organized crime. Though these services were semilegal at best, this is not to say that these units were entirely criminalized. For example, GUBOP leaders in part saw provision of private security as a way to finance their unit amid a collapse in state revenues during the 1990s. Reportedly, money earned was put back into the department and used for cars, equipment, and subsidized meals for personnel. Often

---

[13] *Mentovskaya* comes from the term *menty*, which is a common but semi-derogatory term for police.

the charity organizations connected to these security agencies doubled as private security agencies, while simultaneously providing genuine charity for veterans and family members of the security services (Sborov, 2003; Pravotorov, 2006). Lower levels of police also got into the fray. Some estimates suggest that approximately 30 percent of MVD personnel offered some form of *krysha* in the 1990s (Webster, 1997, p. 30).

The line between legitimate and illegitimate use of state resources for the purpose of property security was further obscured by the role of the extra-departmental security division (*vnevedomstvennaya okhrana*) of the MVD, known as the VO. Founded during the Soviet period to guard state property, it received the right to provide commercial services in 1992. While analysts have devoted extensive attention to the role of Russian private security agencies, VO guards have actually formed a larger slice of the private security market, both in terms of personnel and the number of objects guarded (Khodorych, 2002; Lashkina, 2007; Orlov, 2008a,b). This remained true until 2005, when a quasi–state enterprise, FGUP Okhrana, was spun off from the VO. For businesspeople, VO guards were an enticing option, for they had the advantage of wearing police uniforms and being able to carry any type of gun, unlike the limited arsenal allowed to private security agencies (Khodorych, 2002; Orlov, 2008a,b).

By the late 1990s, firms had come to depend almost fully on state officials, or on private security agencies with ties to the state, for protection services – that is, on strategies based on corrupt rather than private coercion. Observers estimated that criminal *kryshas* maintained control of around 10 to 20 percent of the total market for private security, while ChOPs and law enforcement protection services divided up the remaining clients (Skoblikov, 2001; Khodorych, 2002; Volkov, 2002, pp. 169–179; Taylor 2007, p. 45). One journalist summarized the situation as follows: "By the end of the 1990s, the majority of entrepreneurs capable of making money were 'voluntarily' providing support to the law enforcement authorities. It could be said that the country had been divided into zones of 'police patronage' [*militseiskoy otvetstvennosti*]" (Sborov, 2003). Internal cables from the US Embassy in Moscow to the State Department in Washington came to a similar conclusion: "Moscow business owners understand that it is best to get protection from the MVD and FSB (rather than organized crime groups) since they not only have more guns, resources and power than criminal groups, but they are also protected by the law. For this reason, protection from criminal gangs is no longer so high in demand" (Chivers, 2010). Among those using state security services, small firms primarily turned to the MVD, large firms to the

FSB, and the MVD and FSB divided medium-sized clients nearly equally (Pravotorov, 2006).

State protection rackets were not limited to law enforcement agencies. Bureaucrats also proved to be valuable sources of protection, particularly as harassment by state officials came to replace physical threats as a major concern for many firms. As a Moscow lawyer explained, a well-placed bureaucrat (known as a *pokrovitel*, a "protector" or "patron"), sometimes serving as a shareholder on a firm's board of directors, could at times offer better protection from overzealous tax authorities or inspectors than could law enforcement officials (Lawyer 17, interview, 2009; also see Pravotorov, 2006). Describing the diverse mix of "fixers" offering dispute resolution services, a small business owner in Moscow noted that "Today instead of *kryshas* there are police on various levels. And today if you don't turn to the courts, then where can you turn? You know, practically everywhere, close to every case, there are people, intermediaries, former policemen, former judges, or current policemen, who take money and offer their services to resolve all sorts of conflicts" (Firm 21, interview, 2009).

The services which law enforcement and other government officials provided to firms went far beyond mere protection. Businesspeople learned that there were safer, more efficient means than private coercion to undercut competitors or settle disputes – namely, to "order" (*zakazat*) an investigation by a government agency. In the words of one businessperson, "In the past, if someone refused to pay they could damage the shop or just burn it. Now they've understood that it is cheaper and safer to get fire inspection to close it down for a week or two. And the effect is the same" (Volkov, 2002, pp. 50–51; see also Radaev, 1999, p. 48). An even more fearsome tool, experienced personally by several informants, was the "contract investigation" (*zakaznoy naezd*), whereby a competitor or counterparty in a dispute would bribe a prosecutor to open a criminal case.[14] Rather than the loss of financial resources or property, victims of an ordered criminal investigation faced an extreme form of pressure – the threat of a prison sentence. Once the victim agreed to settle a dispute on terms favorable to the attacker, the criminal investigation abruptly would come to an end.

Precise estimates of the use of corrupt coercion are for obvious reasons difficult to obtain. Whereas earlier surveys sought to quantify the extent of criminal protection rackets, much less attention has been paid to

[14] Firms 6, 29, and 30 reported facing contract investigations. Meanwhile, nearly 6 percent of respondents in the 2010 survey I conducted reported having been charged with crimes they did not commit.

firms' corrupt use of state resources. The Hendley et al. (2000, pp. 635–636) survey introduced above found that about 14 percent of purchasing departments reported seeking intervention from government agencies to resolve problems with suppliers, while approximately 22 percent of sales departments turned to government agencies to address disputes with customers. From these figures they concluded that "few enterprises look to the state for help in solving problems with customers and suppliers" (Hendley et al., 2000, p. 643). Yakovlev et al.'s (2004) survey conducted in 2002 found that among the open joint stock companies surveyed, 11 percent would turn to government officials to resolve an economic dispute. The 2004 survey of small businesses conducted by the business association OPORA found that when faced with threats or use of violence, 28 percent of small businesses said that the most common response in their region was to rely on ties with government officials (OPORA, 2005, p. 93). However, in response to a violation of legal rights, a much larger 52 percent of respondents would look to intermediaries with government connections, perhaps indicating a higher reliance on the informal use of state resources (OPORA, 2005, p. 71).

Unlike previous studies, my 2010 survey sought to explicitly distinguish between the legal and illegal use of state resources. The survey indicates that corrupt coercion remains a significant part of property security in contemporary Russia. When respondents were asked about the extent to which their property security strategies rely on law enforcement agencies, members of the judiciary, and government officials (e.g., inspectors, regulators, and other bureaucrats), they were also asked to clarify whether they sought support from these officials in an official capacity or in a private capacity.[15] During the three years prior to the survey, approximately 33 percent of firms reported using bureaucrats, and 27 percent reported using law enforcement agencies, in a formal capacity to address a security issue. Meanwhile, 20 and 17 percent reported

---

[15] The phrasing was formulated based on the author's experience conducting in-depth interviews with Russian businesspeople and private security agencies. The questions were piloted extensively before conducting the actual survey. The goal was to identify phrasing that was not directly incriminating yet was immediately recognizable among Russian businesspeople as an allusion to government protection rackets or similar types of corrupt coercion. For law enforcement officials and bureaucrats, respondents were asked to clarify whether they used these resources in an "official capacity" (*obratitsya kak k dolzhnostnym litsam*) or "unofficial capacity" (*obratitsya kak k chastnym litsam*). For judicial officials, respondents were asked if they went to court fully in a "formal manner" (*v formalnom poryadke*) or whether they also used "informal connections" (*s ispolzavaniem sushchestvyushchich tam svyaziej*).

turning informally to bureaucrats and law enforcement agencies, respectively. Similarly, while 46 percent of all firms reported using the courts in the three years prior to the survey, nearly 14 percent admitted that they also used informal connections within the judicial system. To the extent that respondents may be prone to underreport informal use, these figures should be considered a lower bound and therefore indicate that the corrupt use of state resources is far from insignificant.

Returning again to the continuum of property security strategies introduced in Chapter 2, the evidence presented in this section documents a significant change: firms' substitution of strategies based on private coercion with strategies based on corrupt coercion. Despite the risks that corrupt coercion will subvert formal state institutions, observers of the Russian business world often perceive the abandonment of private coercion to be a positive trend. In the words of one Russian journalist, "the classic *krysha* irreversibly is becoming a thing of the past. In our day 'protection' of businesses appears to be more civilized" (Pravotorov, 2006). The reduction in physical violence is indisputably an encouraging phenomenon. But whether the use of corrupt coercion is a step along the path to legitimate use of state institutions or an occurrence that will mire state institutions in long-term corruption remains to be seen, an issue discussed at greater length in the concluding chapter.

3.3   The Rise of Legal Coercion

This section turns to variation in the third property security strategy that constitutes this book's dependent variable. Whereas Russia experienced declining *private coercion* (replaced in part by *corrupt coercion*) over the last two decades, the nation also experienced a dramatic increase in *legal coercion*. In the early 1990s, Russian businesspeople rarely utilized formal legal institutions. The Soviet Union had little tradition of politically independent courts, and it naturally had no mechanisms for adjudicating disputes among private firms operating in a market economy. Yet since the mid-1990s, significant evolution in demand for formal legal institutions has taken place in Russia. Caseload data, survey data, and in-depth interviews with businesspeople and lawyers indicate a substantial change in firms' willingness to rely on property security strategies based on legal coercion.

At the outset of the 1990s, Russia replaced Soviet institutions with a two-track judicial system. Commercial courts (*arbitrazhnye sudy*) were built on the remnants of the former *gosarbitrazh* system, an administrative dispute resolution forum for Soviet enterprises. These courts were tasked with economic disputes and administrative conflicts between firms and the state.[16] The courts of general jurisdiction (*sudy obshchey yurisdiktsii*) were set up to handle civil litigation and criminal matters. By the mid-1990s, a new Arbitration Procedural Code, Civil Code, Law on Joint-Stock Companies, Law on the Securities Market, and other legislation essential for the functioning of a market economy also had been established.

Despite these institutional reforms, many Western and Russian analysts continue to argue that firms circumvent formal legal institutions, which they perceive as slow, corrupt, or incapable of enforcing court rulings (e.g., Skoblikov, 2001; Volkov, 2002; Tolstych, 2005; Edwards, 2009). Yet, as Hendley and her collaborators have demonstrated, firms' reliance on the commercial courts was already increasing by the mid-1990s.[17] As shown in Figure 3.1, use of these courts had reached significant levels by the early 2000s. Overall, a host of surveys indicates that by the mid-2000s, Russian firms utilized formal legal institutions quite extensively, with about one-third of smaller firms and two-thirds of larger firms having used the commercial courts (Johnson et al., 2002b; Yakovlev et al., 2004, 69; OPORA, 2005, 2006; Yakovlev, 2008; Rimskii 2009, Table 2.1). While a rising number of court cases can result from a growing number of violations of firms' rights rather than increased willingness to rely on legal institutions, survey data suggest this was not the case. For example, Yakovlev (2008) finds that between 2000 and 2007, there was a decline in the extent of legal violations reported by firms. Indeed, it strains credibility to argue that the late 1990s and early 2000s was a period in which firms found themselves more in conflict than in the early-to-mid 1990s.

Moreover, extensive evidence indicates that firms have become more likely to use courts. For example, it is instructive to compare firms' responses to the 1998 and 2008–2009 financial crises. During the latter crisis, inter-enterprise cases skyrocketed as firms turned to the court system to resolve nonpayment disputes. No similar spurt in court usage is apparent during the 1998 crisis, suggesting that firms instead relied on extra-legal forms of dispute resolution. Meanwhile, in the 2010 survey I conducted, 54 percent of respondents reported that in response to violations of their legal rights, they would be more willing or significantly

---

[16] For a detailed analysis of the commercial courts' origins, see Hendley (1998). Note that these courts are state institutions and that the Russian term *arbitrazh* is unrelated to the English term "arbitration."

[17] See, for example, Hendley et al. (2001b) and Hendley (2006).

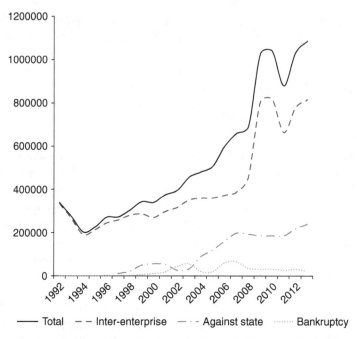

Figure 3.1   Annual Cases Initiated by Firms in Commercial Courts, 1992–2013
Source: Data from reports of the *Vysshyy arbitrazhnyy sud* [Supreme commercial court].[17]

more willing to turn to the courts today as compared to 10 years ago; only 6 percent of respondents replied that they would be less willing. (Thirty-three percent of respondents said that their willingness to use the courts remained unchanged, and 7 percent were unsure.)

An additional indication of the growing reliance on legal institutions is firms' increasing willingness to use legal remedies even in disputes with state authorities. As noted by Hendley (2002, pp. 144–145), turning to

---

[17] Figure 3.1 excludes administrative cases initiated by government authorities, as these cases have little to do with demand for law from the side of firms. For additional information on these cases, see the appendix at the end of this chapter. Data are from reports of the *Vysshyy arbitrazhnyy sud* [Supreme commercial court]: *Svedeniya o rassmotrennykh sporakh s uchastiem nalogovykh organov* [Report on cases with the participation of the tax authorities]; *Spravka osnovnykh pokazateley raboty arbitrazhnykh sudov* RF [Information on the basic indicators of the work of the commercial courts]; *Spravka o rassmotrenii arbitrazhnimi sudami RF del, voznikayushchykh iz administravnykh pravootnoshenii* [Information about cases arising from administrative law considered by the commercial courts]. Recent data are available at www.arbitr.ru; older data were obtained directly from the Supreme Commercial Court (VAS).

formal state institutions when one's adversary is the state itself indicates a significant degree of reliance on law. Between 2000 and 2008, cases against the tax authorities rose from around 13,000 to over 50,000, a 280 percent increase. Cases against other government funds and agencies increased during this period from around 11,000 to 40,000. By 2009, litigation against the state represented nearly 20 percent of all cases initiated by firms, as seen in the rise in cases against the state in Figure 3.1. Nor were these suits hopeless endeavors. Win rates for plaintiffs in cases against tax authorities grew from around 60 percent at the end of the 1990s to above 70 percent in the late 2000s.[19]

Actual litigation rates are, of course, only the tip of the iceberg (Hendley, 2001b). For any dispute that ends up in court, countless others are negotiated in "the shadow of the law," where the threat of litigation shapes negotiations (Mnookin and Kornhauser, 1978). The increased use of the court system thus captures only a fraction of the actual increase in reliance on lawyers, legal strategies, and the legal system. But there is broader evidence that law has come to play an increasingly important role in the Russian business world.

One indicator of the expanding role of law in the Russian business world is the growing population of lawyers (Hendley, 2006, p. 364). The legal community in Russia is divided among *advokaty* and *yuristy*, and only the former are required to take a bar exam and pay bar membership dues.[20] Therefore, only the exact number of *advokaty* is known, even though they represent the minority of all lawyers. Among *advokaty*, there has been a dramatic increase, from 26,300 in 1996 to 63,740 in 2010, a 140 percent change, even though during this period the overall population of Russia was declining.[21] The growing role of lawyers can also be seen in the increased size of legal departments. In Hendley et al.'s 1997 survey, 45 percent of firms had an internal legal department, but their study suggested that these legal departments were largely unreformed from the

---

[19] These data are based on the sources listed in footnote 17.

[20] The distinction is a holdover from Soviet times, during which *advokaty* were the rough equivalent of defense attorneys, and *yuriskonsulty* were the rough equivalent of in-house counsel. Today, the distinction between the two is less clear cut. Only *advokaty* can represent a client in a criminal case, but *advokaty* also regularly serve corporate and business clients. By law, however, they must work for an independent law firm and cannot serve in house. For background on the structure of the Russian legal profession, see Hendley (2010, pp. 8–9).

[21] Biannual data from 1996–2004 on the number of registered *advokaty* can be found in Hendley (2006, 385). For more recent data, see *Federalnaya palata advokatov* [Federal Chamber of Lawyers] (2010, p. 32).

Soviet period and continued to play a routine and insignificant role in Russian business practices. These legal departments ranged in size from 1 to 17 lawyers, with a mean of 2.5 (Hendley et al., 2001b, pp. 690, 693). My 2010 survey similarly found that just over 40 percent of respondents had an internal legal department. Yet despite the fact that the average firm in my sample was smaller than in the Hendley et al. sample, firms reported much larger legal divisions: the size of legal departments in my survey ranged from 1 to 80 lawyers, with a mean of around 6.[22] Clearly, firms with dozens of in-house lawyers consider legal resources to be an important asset.

Lawyers themselves, moreover, see significant changes in their profession and its role in business. As one of Russia's top tax lawyers recalled, today there is booming demand for his services, whereas in the 1990s his "main problem was not winning, but convincing businesspeople that it is worth going to court" (Lawyer 21, interview, 2009). According to a prominent bankruptcy lawyer in Moscow, one of the reasons for this hesitancy was that "lawyers here are part of a very young profession. In the 1990s businesspeople thought of them as con-men (*moshenniki*)." He continued to explain, however, that today the "image of lawyers more broadly has changed. They are like advisors now, not only for legal stuff but more generally in business" (Lawyer 3, interview, 2009). Meanwhile, a young litigator confirms that "Previously, everything was decided with a handshake. Previously, there was no point in signing a contract, because nevertheless no one was going to win anything in court, or enforce a court decision. Now it's not like this ... A court case already means a lot, and it's easy to enforce a decision." This same lawyer also finds evidence of the changing attitudes of businesspeople toward lawyers in more subtle indicators, explaining that "Now people pay [for our time]. Previously, people paid only for a result. They would say, you bring us money [i.e., win the case], and we will pay you for [getting us] the money" (Lawyer 20, interview, 2009). Nor is this development limited to Moscow. When asked

[22] The average legal department size reported here excludes four outliers which reported improbably large legal departments given their overall firm size. Three of these respondents classified their firms as belonging to the food and beverage sector. According to insiders with knowledge of this sector, these firms likely are specialized service centers to whom Russian food and beverage companies outsource their legal and accounting services. If these outliers are included, then the average size of legal departments in the sample increases to approximately 10. With respect to the comparability of the two samples, firm size in the Hendley et al. sample ranged from 30 to 17,000 employees, with a mean of 980 and median of 300. Firm size in my sample ranged from 3 to 9,000 employees, with a mean of 390 and median of 200.

about the extent to which firms now use the court system, a lawyer from the Siberian town of Barnaul observed that "people more or less have come to resolve disputes in a civilized way, by going to court." Indeed, he noted that the courts are so packed with litigants that "to move through the corridors of a courthouse is now impossible" (Lawyer 22, interview, 2009).

Firms' use of law also extends beyond the formal court system, as seen in firms' increasing reliance on private arbitration.[23] Although temporary legislation laid the foundation for private arbitration at the outset of the post-Soviet transition, it was not until the 2002 Law on Private Arbitration that it was fully incorporated into the Russian legal and business worlds. In 2002, experts estimated that there were just over 400 courts of private arbitration. By 2007, similar estimates put this number somewhere between 700 and 1000 (Sevastyanov and Tsyplenkova, 2007, p. 63). A unified source of data on private arbitration courts does not exist, but data from individual courts indicate that demand for private arbitration – although still low – in recent years has been rising, particularly during the economic crisis of 2009. In some cases, this growth has been dramatic: the Federal Court of Private Arbitration (*Federalnyi treteiskii sud*) heard 72 cases in 2008, 364 cases in 2009, and 956 cases in 2010.[24] Further evidence of increased demand for arbitration services can be seen in the data on the number of cases from private arbitration that have been disputed or for which enforcement has been sought via the official commercial court system. Between 2002 and 2009, these cases increased sevenfold, from 672 to 3770, as shown in Table 3.2.[25] Meanwhile, in 2006, the first All-Russian Congress of Private Arbitration Courts took place, and conferences and seminars on arbitration and mediation have become commonplace (Sevastyanov and Tsyplenkova, 2007). Evidence of rising interest in private arbitration can also be seen in the emergence of specialized professional journals such as *Treteiskii Sud*.

---

[23] Although private arbitration often does not directly involve state actors, its success ultimately depends on legal coercion. For example, firms in Russia can turn to the commercial courts to enforce decisions reached in private arbitration.

[24] See http://arbitrage.ru/news/108-Portal-Treteiskii-sud-v-Rossii-podvodit-itogi-2010-goda.html.

[25] Russian legal scholars express confidence that this increase did not result from growing problems with the enforcement of private arbitration decisions but instead reflects a genuine increase in the use of private arbitration (e.g., author interview with Petr Skoblikov, Professor of Law, Ministry of Internal Affairs Academy of Management on November 12, 2009; see also Sevastyanov and Tsyplenkova 2007, p. 65).

Table 3.2 *Number of Cases Related to Private Arbitration Heard by Commercial Courts, 2002–2009*

	2002	2003	2004	2005	2006	2007	2008	2009
Number of cases	672	936	1287	1593	1704	1710	2113	3770

Source: Supreme Commercial Court of the RF. See footnote 17.

The most striking evidence of demand for law, however, is how firms evaluate their reliance on lawyers and courts relative to other property security strategies. Even by the late 1990s, firms seemed to consider use of the courts to be a relatively attractive option when compared with other strategies for resolving conflicts. Hendley et al.'s (2000, pp. 635–636) 1997 study found that with the exception of direct enterprise-to-enterprise formal negotiations, turning to the courts was the most common way of addressing contractual problems with suppliers; likewise, other than stopping trade with a customer, litigation was the most common way of dealing with customer conflicts. Yakovlev et al. (2004, p. 70) found similar results with respect to open joint stock companies' preferred methods of dispute resolution: Turning to the courts was stated as a preferred choice by over half of the respondents, and threatening to turn to the courts by over 20 percent.

My survey indicates that these trends toward reliance on legal coercion have continued, as seen in Table 3.3. When respondents were asked to rank on a 1 to 7 scale how likely a firm like theirs would be to utilize various strategies to resolve an asset dispute (with 7 meaning "very likely" and 1 meaning "very unlikely"), the highest-ranking strategies were the use of lawyers to resolve the conflict out of court (average ranking 6.0) and filing a claim in the commercial courts (5.7). These ranked even higher than direct negotiations with the other firm's management (5.3), which often is considered to be the first step in resolving a conflict and which topped the list of firms' preferred strategies in previous survey research (Hendley et al., 2000; Yakovlev et al., 2004). The high ranking for the use of lawyers out of court is particularly remarkable, providing evidence of the active role lawyers now play in resolving business conflicts. By contrast, the average rankings for the likelihood of turning to a private security firm or criminal protection racket were 2.3 and 1.9, respectively, while the use of strategies involving corrupt coercion fell somewhere in between. A similar question that examined firms' preferred strategies for collecting a debt as opposed to resolving an asset conflict produced nearly identical results.

Table 3.3   *Preferred Property Security Strategies (full sample)*

Respondents were asked the following questions:

Debt Dispute: Let's say that another company owes your firm a significant sum of money for products purchased or services rendered and has not made the payment, even though the agreed upon deadline has passed. To recover the money owed, how likely would a firm like yours be to use each of the following?

Property Dispute: Let's say that a competitor is trying to gain control of some significant physical asset owned by your firm (e.g., office space or a factory). To defend its assets, how likely would a firm like yours be to do each of the following?

Average responses on a scale of 1 to 7, where 1 is "very unlikely" and 7 is "very likely"

Legal Coercion	Debt	Property
Rely on lawyers to resolve the dispute out of court	6.31 (301, 0.07)	6.04 (297, 0.09)
Turn to the commercial courts	5.86 (292, 0.09)	5.69 (293, 0.10)
Seek the help of law enforcement officials acting in their formal capacity	4.83 (298, 0.13)	5.18 (295, 0.12)
Seek the help of government bureaucrats acting in their formal capacity	3.99 (294, 0.13)	4.57 (290, 0.12)
Corrupt Coercion		
Turn to the commercial courts, using informal connections	4.19 (268, 0.14)	4.32 (268, 0.14)
Seek the help of law enforcement officials acting in an informal capacity	3.65 (288, 0.13)	3.78 (280, 0.13)
Seek the help of government bureaucrats acting in an informal capacity	3.37 (286, 0.13)	3.63 (281, 0.13)
Private Coercion		
Rely on an internal security service	3.22 (274, 0.14)	3.29 (272, 0.14)
Seek the help of a private security agency	2.09 (278, 0.10)	2.21 (278, 0.11)
Seek the help of criminal or mafia groups	1.75 (277, 0.08)	1.87 (272, 0.10)

Note: The number of observations and standard errors are in parentheses.

One might question whether firms' increased reliance on legal strategies is limited to Russia's two largest and most economically developed
cities, Moscow and St. Petersburg. But Table 3.4 shows that the trends
examined in this chapter are apparent far outside of Russia's metropolises.
In fact, the differences in the average rankings for firms in regional
cities and average rankings for firms in Moscow and St. Petersburg
are statistically insignificant, with just a handful of exceptions. In the
case of property disputes, regional firms report being *more* likely to use
law enforcement in a *formal* capacity as well as *less* likely to turn to
bureaucrats in an *informal* capacity than firms in Moscow and St. Petersburg. The same pattern holds for debt disputes, although with respect to
debt disputes regional firms also report being more likely to utilize courts.

Nor are firms' relatively high ratings for legal strategies and low ratings
for private coercion attributable to respondents' tendencies to provide
answers that others will view favorably, a phenomenon often referred
to by survey researchers as "social desirability bias." As noted in the
introductory chapter, the role of violence and corruption in the Russian business world are open secrets that are less sensitive to discuss
than outside researchers might imagine. The fact that diverse sources –
survey data, in-depth interviews, and data such as court caseloads – all
point to similar conclusions further casts doubt on the possibility that
the results in Tables 3.3 and 3.4 are simply an artifact of respondents'
dissimulation. Moreover, it should not be assumed that Russian businesspeople have an incentive to overreport their use of the legal system. To the
contrary, Macaulay's (1963) classic study on inter-firm contract disputes
suggests that litigating against business partners breaches social norms,
which might encourage respondents to understate reliance on law.

A final concern raised by some scholars is that Russian firms' use of
legal institutions may reflect increased bribery and exploitation of judicial corruption, rather than increased reliance on law. Volkov (2005),
for example, claims that "Among entrepreneurs, the judicial system has
begun to be used more and more intensively in recent years ... But this
is less related to the rule of law than to the realization of the goals of
groups with administrative and financial resources." Foremost among
these abuses is illegal corporate raiding (*reiderstvo*). While the term is
taken from the American usage, it involves far more than buying up a
company's shares in order to change management. Prior to a 2002 reform
to the Law on Bankruptcy, one common scheme was to acquire a company's debt and then utilize legal loopholes to instigate forced bankruptcy,
despite the firm's sound financial health. Raiders would then bribe a judge
to appoint a loyal bankruptcy trustee, who would facilitate the seizure of

Table 3.4 *Preferred Property Security Strategies (regional cities)*

Respondents were asked the following questions:

Debt Dispute: Let's say that another company owes your firm a significant sum of money for products purchased or services rendered and has not made the payment, even though the agreed upon deadline has passed. To recover the money owed, how likely would a firm like yours be to use each of the following?

Property Dispute: Let's say that a competitor is trying to gain control of some significant physical asset owned by your firm (e.g., office space or a factory). To defend its assets, how likely would a firm like yours be to do each of the following?

Average responses on a scale of 1 to 7, where 1 is "very unlikely" and 7 is "very likely"

Legal Coercion	Debt	Property
Rely on lawyers to resolve the dispute out of court	6.35	6.10
	(125, 0.11)	(124, 0.14)
Turn to the commercial courts	6.12	5.86
	(125, 0.12)	(122, 0.15)
Seek the help of law enforcement officials acting in their formal capacity	5.23	5.45
	(125, 0.20)	(122, 0.17)
Seek the help of government bureaucrats acting in their formal capacity	3.91	4.50
	(125, 0.21)	(117, 0.20)
Corrupt Coercion		
Turn to the commercial courts, using informal connections	4.07	4.21
	(125, 0.22)	(110, 0.22)
Seek the help of law enforcement officials acting in an informal capacity	3.35	3.56
	(125, 0.21)	(113, 0.21)
Seek the help of government bureaucrats acting in an informal capacity	2.81	3.28
	(125, 0.19)	(113, 0.21)
Private Coercion		
Rely on an internal security service	3.35	3.53
	(125, 0.22)	(116, 0.23)
Seek the help of a private security agency	2.29	2.38
	(125, 0.18)	(114, 0.17)
Seek the help of criminal or mafia groups	1.81	1.92
	(125, 0.14)	(106, 0.15)

Note: The number of observations and standard errors are in parentheses. Regional cities included in the survey were Nizhniy Novgorod, Samara, Ekaterinburg, Kazan, Rostov-on-Don, and Novosibirsk.

the firm's assets. Other schemes that continue to be used rely on forgery of internal corporate documents, the creation of a second set of documents by paying corrupt government officials, or the hiring of corrupt law enforcement and tax officials who for a fee initiate criminal cases against target companies, forcing a recalcitrant owner to concede assets to raiders (Volkov, 2004; Firestone, 2008).

The extent of raiding is notoriously hard to pin down, as raiding is difficult to distinguish from legitimate mergers and acquisitions, or in some cases from basic corporate theft and fraud.[26] But even the most shocking estimates do not provide grounds to consider the shift toward legal institutions illusory. Volkov (2004, p. 532) cites figures that as many as a third of bankruptcy cases in 2001 pertained to raiding. Yet, even if this is true, bankruptcy as a whole is a minor fraction of total court usage, as seen in Figure 3.1 above. Although other types of raiding fall into different categories of court cases, nonpayments and unfulfilled contractual obligations have remained the largest class of litigation throughout the 1990s and 2000s, consistently comprising about 60 to 70 percent of annual inter-enterprise cases; cases pertaining to property disputes are a small fraction of total litigation.[27] For many cases, the sum in dispute is relatively small, calling into question the value of investing in connections or bribery. As the founding partner of a Moscow law firm explained, "Connections are probably needed if the case is high-profile, big or political, or if the opponent is a large company. But for middle-sized cases they are not necessary ... and the majority of cases are rather small, and so connections are not needed" (Lawyer 6, interview, 2009). Hendley (2006, p. 351) offers similar conclusions, noting that although "cases that attract the interest of those in power can be manipulated to serve their interests," such concerns do not apply to the bulk of disputes: "mundane cases are handled in accordance with the prevailing law."

In summary, there has been a significant increase in firms' reliance on the third type of property security strategy introduced in the previous chapter: strategies based on legal coercion. Although raiding and corruption within the judicial system are serious threats in the Russian business world, they are not cause to believe that firms turn to formal legal institutions primarily out of corrupt motives. At best, raiding and institutional abuse account for a small fraction of the sizable increase in firms' use of

[26] Approximately 8 percent of the respondents in the survey I conducted reported being the victim of a raid. However, the wide range of raiding tactics makes it difficult to assess the extent to which these raids involved abuses of the judicial system.

[27] For sources see footnote 17.

legal strategies. In contemporary Russia, firms consistently and frequently rely on lawyers, law, and legal institutions.

3.4 Conclusion

This chapter has shown dramatic evolution over time in the outcome – firms' property security strategies – that this book seeks to explain. Following the typology introduced in Chapter 2, property security strategies can be classified by the source of coercion on which they rely: private coercion, corrupt coercion, or legal coercion. With respect to private coercion, Russian firms have significantly reduced their reliance on strategies that involve criminal groups and private security agencies. To the extent that Russian firms continue to rely on illegal strategies, they utilize corrupt coercion – the appropriation of state resources for the purpose of private protection. Most strikingly, Russian firms' reliance on strategies based on legal coercion has increased significantly, with the number of court cases initiated by firms quadrupling since the mid-1990s.

What explains this striking temporal variation in firms' property security strategies in Russia? The following chapters elaborate the argument outlined in Chapter 2, turning consecutively to three key explanatory factors: state legal capacity (Chapter 4), demand-side barriers to the use of formal legal institutions (Chapter 5), and the effectiveness of illegal strategies (Chapter 6).

To be sure, this chapter has employed broad strokes to depict overall trends in Russia over a span of two decades. In reality, these trends occurred unevenly across different types of firms. Chapter 7 returns to the issue of variation in property security strategies across different types of firms, demonstrating how a demand-side approach offers insights not only into changes over time, but also into variation in strategies across different parts of the economy.

Appendix: Understanding Russian Caseload Data

In the section in this chapter devoted to formal legal institutions, the caseload data are analyzed after removing cases initiated by the government authorities. These latter cases, while indicative of the overall use of the court system, pertain to administrative concerns unrelated to firms' willingness to use legal institutions. For example, in the early 2000s there was an effort by the tax authorities to purge shell companies from the official registry of firms (these shell companies were often used for tax evasion purposes or simply left idle due to the hassles and expenses of carrying out an official bankruptcy). Likewise, the introduction of laws regulating the use of cash register machines, an effort to restrict firms from hiding revenues from the state, led to a rash of litigation. The extent of such litigation can be extensive. In 2002, the number of cases the government initiated related to the liquidation of shell companies peaked at 110,000, or nearly 16 percent of total cases in the commercial courts, while in 2001 government-initiated cases related to cash register regulations peaked at around 37,000, or just under 6 percent of total cases.[28]

Another factor contributing to the growth in caseloads in the early 2000s was the sizable number of cases pertaining to the seizure of assets belonging to firms that owed tax penalties or payments to extra-budgetary funds, such as the pension fund. Following earlier declarations by the Constitutional Court of the Russian Federation, changes in the Tax Code that came into force in 1999 mandated judicial approval for such seizures, even when the penalties were undisputed (Hendley 2002, p. 135; Solomon 2004). While this resulted in a barrage of cases, the caseload data show that the Law "On Mandatory Pension Insurance in the Russian Federation," which went into effect in 2002 and included a similar provision, had an even bigger effect. Between 2002 and 2005, the number of administrative cases related to the collection of fees, fines, and payments spiked from approximately 300,000 to more than 950,000. At this peak, these cases accounted for more than 90 percent of administrative cases and 65 percent of total cases. In response to the massive burden this placed on judges, new rules were introduced allowing uncontested cases of minimal monetary sums to be decided in an extra-judicial administrative forum, leading to a dramatic fall in these cases from 2006 onward, particularly from the side of the tax authorities and extra-budgetary funds.

Analyses of Russian caseload data that include all administrative cases thus overstate the extent to which the commercial courts are at the center of business conflicts. Nevertheless, the adjusted data used in Figure 3.1 indicate that reliance on the courts is extensive and continues to grow.

---

[28] See footnote 17 for sources of all caseload statistics presented here.

4

The Role of State Legal Capacity

The preceding chapter examined Russian firms' increasing reliance on formal legal institutions. How can this trend be explained? A temptingly straightforward explanation for the evolution of property security strategies in Russia would be that enterprises increasingly adopted legal strategies in response to rising state legal capacity. After all, Putin assumed the presidency in 2000 pronouncing the goal to build a "dictatorship of the law."[1] The very ambiguity of this phrase, however, speaks volumes about trends in Russian state legal capacity since Putin has assumed power. On the one hand, Putin has sought to improve the effectiveness of courts, law enforcement agencies, and other formal legal institutions. On the other hand, state agencies under Putin, including those responsible for upholding the law, have often arbitrarily persecuted businesses for the sake of government officials' private gain. As this chapter makes clear, rising state legal capacity can at most provide a partial explanation for the evolution of Russian firms' strategies, for it is highly questionable whether Putin succeeded in his efforts to improve the effectiveness of formal legal institutions.

Returning to the analytical framework introduced in Chapter 2, three key explanatory factors influence firms' willingness to use formal legal institutions: state legal capacity, demand-side barriers to the use of legal strategies, and the effectiveness of illegal strategies. The current chapter examines how the first of these explanatory variables – state legal capacity – evolved throughout the 1990s and 2000s, leaving analysis of the other two variables for Chapters 5 and 6. More specifically, this chapter demonstrates the book's key propositions concerning state legal capacity: (1) While a dearth of state legal capacity may impede firms' use of formal legal institutions, improved legal capacity frequently does not induce firms to rely on law; and (2) firms frequently adopt legal strategies even

---

[1] Presidential Address to the Federal Assembly of the RF, July 8, 2000. See kremlin.ru/events/president/transcripts/21480.

when the effectiveness of formal legal institutions remains in doubt. Consequently, the correlation between state legal capacity and firm strategies is weaker than commonly assumed.

Measuring and assessing state legal capacity is, of course, a difficult task. Drawing on the work of legal scholars such as Hendley (2006) and Solomon (2008), I consider five metrics: (1) the *formal legal infrastructure*, including the existence or absence of key laws on the books and the organizations required to implement and enforce these laws; (2) the *operational capability* of formal legal institutions, including their accessibility, efficiency, and enforcement ability; (3) the *financial resources* devoted to developing formal legal institutions; (4) the *competence* of the state officials who staff formal legal institutions; and (5) the *political independence* of formal legal institutions. State *legal* capacity, in turn, constitutes just one dimension of the state's overall ability to implement and enforce policies. As the analyses in Chapters 5 and 6 make evident, other aspects of state capacity, such as tax administration or financial sector regulation, at times *indirectly* influence firms' property security strategies. The ramifications of the state's indirect impact on firm strategies for the book's demand-side analytical framework are examined in more detail in the book's concluding chapter.

This chapter first analyzes the evolution of state legal capacity in post-Soviet Russia through the lens of the five metrics introduced above. This analysis demonstrates that despite the emergence of relatively effective formal legal institutions in the 1990s, firms remained heavily dependent on private and corrupt coercion, as detailed in the previous chapter. It then shows how improvements to state legal capacity were relatively modest and often highly uneven in the late 1990s and early 2000s, a period during which firms increasingly used formal legal institutions. The chapter next considers an additional dimension of state legal capacity: the state's ability to constrain the predatory behavior of government officials. The analysis demonstrates that, somewhat paradoxically, Russian firms turned to state institutions for protection during the very period in which property rights infringements by corrupt bureaucrats and law enforcement agents were on the rise. Finally, the chapter examines developments in state legal capacity from the vantage point of firms, providing evidence of the private sector's persistently critical assessment of state legal capacity in Russia. Regardless of how one interprets objective indicators of state legal capacity, institutional development can only affect firm strategies if owners and managers *perceive* progress. The existing evidence demonstrates that Russian firms' perceptions of state legal capacity have improved even less than an objective appraisal might warrant, making explanations that attribute variation in property security strategies to the effectiveness of formal legal institutions particularly problematic.

4.1 The 1990s: Building the Foundations of State Legal Capacity

This section traces the evolution of Russian state legal capacity over the decade following the Soviet Union's collapse, providing evidence that while state legal capacity is a prerequisite to firms' use of law, heightened state legal capacity does not necessarily increase enterprises' use of formal legal institutions. In the early 1990s, state legal capacity was all but absent. Accordingly, widespread use of formal legal institutions was infeasible. However, this institutional vacuum did not last long. By the mid-1990s, new laws on the books, reformed government agencies, and the other trappings of a formal legal infrastructure had begun to emerge. Yet, as other scholars have noted, the emergence of this legal infrastructure provided insufficient incentives for firms to adopt legal strategies (Pistor, 1996; Hendley, 1997). The lack of financial resources undermining newly formed legal institutions' effectiveness certainly contributed to firms' limited reliance on law. But other factors, particularly the demand-side barriers analyzed in Chapter 5, also played a critical role in discouraging firms' use of legal property security strategies.

The first metric by which the evolution of state legal capacity can be traced is the existence or absence of a *formal legal infrastructure* – the laws essential for a market economy to function as well as the agencies needed to implement and enforce these laws. Modern market economies require a vast institutional underpinning that, among other things, helps keep property secure. Given that all productive assets in the Soviet Union's command economy were state-owned, much of this institutional underpinning had been unnecessary, leaving an institutional void that required time to fill. For example, the massive privatization program of state-owned enterprises created thousands of new private companies and millions of shareholders by 1994, *prior* to the passage of essential commercial and capital market laws. Foreign legal advisors who participated in drafting these laws noted that key concepts such as fiduciary duty and self-dealing did not even exist in the Russian legal lexicon (Black et al., 2000, p. 1752).

Nevertheless, many components of a formal legal infrastructure emerged rapidly. The most consequential development was the formation of commercial courts (*arbitrazhnye sudy*), which, as discussed in the previous chapter, were created in 1992 on the remnants of the Soviet *Gosarbitrazh* system, a bureaucratic dispute resolution institution that settled conflicts among Soviet enterprises. The commercial courts, tasked with hearing cases among firms as well as between firms and state agencies, comprised part of a tripartite judicial system. A Constitutional Court and the courts of general jurisdiction (*sudy obshchey yurisdiktsii*), which hear cases related to noncommercial civil litigation and criminal matters, formed the other two legs of the system. Some specialized regulatory agencies also came into existence early on. For example, the Russian Federal Securities Commission, one of the predecessors to Russia's current Federal Service for Financial Markets, was created in 1994. Meanwhile, a State Committee for Anti-Monopoly Policy that had been created prior to the Soviet Union's collapse continued to function until 1998, when it was replaced by a Ministry of Anti-Monopoly Policy and Support of Entrepreneurship.

A critical step toward developing a formal legal infrastructure was taken in 1993, when Russia ratified its first post-Soviet Constitution, which enshrined the principle of an independent judiciary. By 1996, laws governing bankruptcy, the securities market, and joint stock companies were in place. Meanwhile, Parts I and II of a new Civil Code came into force in 1995 and 1996, respectively, providing a legal basis for contracting between private entities. Throughout the 1990s, efforts to improve the legal infrastructure's effectiveness continued. The *Arbitrazh* Procedural Code, the code regulating the commercial courts, was first produced in the hectic year of 1992 but then amended in 1995. In 1998, the Law on Bankruptcy underwent a complete makeover to facilitate insolvent companies' exit from the marketplace.

Considering the 1990s in broader perspective, significant institutional development took place throughout the decade. Formal legal infrastructure hardly existed in the early 1990s, but just five years after the fall of the Soviet Union, Hendley (1997, p. 236) concluded that "For the most part, the legal infrastructure needed for a market economy has been created – at least on paper. Relatively stable rules exist by which citizens can order their behavior, and institutions have been created that are charged with enforcing those rules. Taken as a whole, the accomplishment is impressive." By 2000, when Yeltsin transferred power to Putin, laws were on the books, a court system was in place, and a rudimentary regulatory apparatus was emerging.

Once a formal legal infrastructure is in place, a second critical metric of state legal capacity pertains to *operational capability*. In the particular case of courts, three issues are of great importance: accessibility, efficiency, and the ability to enforce decisions. Throughout the world, firms consider courts to be too expensive and slow, and Russian firms are no exception. But when objective metrics are considered, the Russian commercial courts have performed well with respect to both cost and speed. Early concerns that filing fees (*gosposhlina*) were dissuading potential litigants led to the introduction of a revised fee system, with a sliding scale that took into account the size of a plaintiff's claim (Hendley, 1998, pp. 96–100). Meanwhile, with respect to efficiency, the Russian courts work under statutorily imposed time constraints, which for the commercial courts during the Yeltsin era required that all cases be decided within two months. Remarkably, judges met the two-month deadline in around 95 percent of all cases, for reputations and promotion decisions were tightly tied to judges' efficiency records (Hendley, 2003, p. 372).

While the commercial courts performed relatively well in terms of accessibility and efficiency, enforcement was, according to many observers, their largest failing. In the 1990s, nonpayments and barter were so extensive that few firms had funds of any significance in their bank accounts. Consequently, those charged with enforcing rulings (known as *sudebnye isponitely* up until 1998) were often tasked with seizing physical assets from debtors, despite the fact that these collectors lacked specialized transport to carry large objects. Even when assets were acquired, challenges persisted. The collectors bore the burden of monetizing confiscated property via auctions, a largely infeasible task given that few of the assets were in demand (Hendley, 1998, pp. 113–114). In recognition of enforcement problems, a new Bailiffs Service was created in 1997, responsible both for enforcing court decisions and protecting courthouses. Unlike their predecessors, the bailiffs (*sudebnye pristavy*) could carry arms and utilize force if necessary. Nevertheless, significant problems persisted. On average, bailiffs faced over 100 new cases per month, a workload that would have required them to enforce a case every two hours in order to keep up (Kahn, 2002, p. 159).

Despite progress in developing a formal legal infrastructure and developing the foundations for operational capability, by other metrics state legal capacity remained limited. A particularly pressing problem was the state's lack of *financial resources*, which hampered the effectiveness of emerging legal institutions. As Solomon (2008, p. 66) explains, "Before and especially during the [1998] financial crisis, courts overall received miserly budgets, and lost parts of those through sequestration. Some courts had no money left after paying salaries ... [T]he courts remained shabby places, as repairs were not undertaken and little automation attempted." If the courts faced a deficit of financial resources, other state bodies found themselves in even worse shape. The regulatory body charged with overseeing security markets, for instance, had a small staff and equally small budget. The journalist David Hoffman vividly captured the weakness of the Federal Commission for the Securities Market with a metaphor in reference to the head of the commission, Dmitry Vasiliev: "I often thought of Vasiliev as the referee at a soccer match, blowing his whistle and waving his arms around wildly as the big muscular players ran roughshod over anything in their way and ignored him" (Hoffman, 2002, p. 452). Law enforcement agencies found themselves even more outgunned – in a literal sense, with smaller weapons, slower cars, and fewer resources than the criminals they chased (Gerber and Mendelson, 2008, p. 10; Favarel-Garrigues, 2011, p. 183).

The effectiveness of formal legal institutions was also hampered with respect to another dimension of state legal capacity: *competence.* Organizations are only as effective as the people who staff them, laws only as influential as the officials who interpret and enforce them. Just as the Soviet legal system itself was ill-suited to a market economy, Soviet-era officials faced the challenge of adapting to a fundamentally different legal environment. Referring to the early 1990s, a commercial real estate executive explained that "If there was a misunderstanding in the business agreement between two commercial parties that are themselves only one, two, three years in business, what do you expect of a judge or court? [Judges were] people who [were] twice my age and didn't understand anything about my market" (Firm 26, interview, 2009).[2] Lack of experienced officials undermined the competence of other institutions to an even greater degree. Law enforcement agencies in particular suffered a "huge exodus of cadres" after the collapse of the Soviet Union. In 1993, less than half of the Ministry for Internal Affair's (MVD) personnel had more than three years of experience (Taylor, 2011, p. 189).

---

[2] Many foreign analysts came to similar conclusions (see, e.g., Black et al., 2000, pp. 1752–1753), but not all observers agree with this assessment. Notably, Hendley (2007a, p. 255), based on a systematic examination of case files, found no evidence to support the claim that "judges were incapable of handling the market-based disputes that began to come before them in the 1990s."

While experience, training, and innate ability shape the competence of state officials, external incentive structures in which government agents work also play a significant role. With respect to formal legal institutions, a particularly pressing issue is the extent to which the judiciary, regulatory apparatus, and law enforcement are subject to political interference. *Political independence* is thus the final metric of state legal capacity considered here. Formally, the 1990s witnessed a historically unprecedented degree of political independence for Russia's judiciary. The 1993 Constitution not only declared the principle of judicial independence (art. 120) but also provided constitutional safeguards against the removal of judges (arts. 121–122). The emergence of judicial qualification commissions (JQCs), which initially were formed in the late 1980s under Gorbachev, helped ensure that independence was more than a mere formality. Staffed fully by judges throughout the 1990s, the JQCs controlled the appointment process, subject to approval by the president, and held sole power over the dismissal of judges. Once appointed, judges in the commercial courts received lifelong tenure, following a three-year probationary period. Additionally, in 1995 a three-level appellate process was created, which increased the likelihood that a corrupt or politically-induced decision would be overturned (Hendley, 2003, p. 365). Meanwhile, by the late 1990s, the judiciary managed to transfer responsibility for administering the court system from the Ministry of Justice – an executive branch agency – to a Judicial Department housed within the Supreme Court (Solomon, 1997, pp. 52–53).

These institutional reforms created considerable *de jure* independence. Unfortunately, *de facto* independence frequently did not live up to the institutional blueprints, in large part because of the lack of financial resources discussed above. Most prominently, the federal government's inability to guarantee sufficient resources forced judges to rely on regional leaders for funding and for benefits such as housing. These ties to local officials created the potential for political interference in cases in which regional leaders held a stake (Hendley 2006, p. 358; Solomon 2008, p. 66).

Overall, following a short period of institutional chaos in the early 1990s, certain aspects of state legal capacity, such as a formal legal infrastructure, emerged relatively quickly. Other aspects of state legal capacity, such as a lack of financial resources and a dearth of state officials with knowledge of a market economy, hampered these emerging institutions' effectiveness. Nevertheless, institutions such as the commercial courts proved relatively accessible and efficient.

Yet despite significant progress in the development of state legal capacity, Russian firms remained more reliant on strategies based on private and corrupt coercion than on law throughout much of the 1990s. As Hendley (1997, p. 246) warned in the middle of the decade, "Russia stands in grave danger of becoming a country with an excellent legal system on paper, but one that remains largely irrelevant for business." Certainly, illegal property security strategies persisted in part because, despite notable improvements, overall levels of state legal capacity remained relatively low. But even in the midst of institutional reforms, observers noted the incompleteness of such "supply-side" explanations. Pistor (1996, p. 87), for example, declared: "In Russia, the early institutional changes aimed at providing a court system for handling commercial disputes have so far proved to be largely ineffective. The main reasons for this appear to lie less in the inefficiency of the system than in the lack of demand for the services that it offers."

In short, a handful of legal scholars clearly recognized that in the Russian case, heightened state legal capacity was insufficient to induce firms to use formal legal institutions. But often overlooked is what came next: Although improvements in state legal capacity were relatively modest and uneven throughout the 2000s, firms significantly increased their use of legal property security strategies.

4.2   The 2000s: The Ambiguous Evolution of State Legal Capacity

This section continues to trace the evolution of state legal capacity in Russia, with a focus on Putin's regime throughout the 2000s. It provides evidence in support of the second claim regarding the weak correlation between levels of state capacity and firms' property security strategies: Even without heightened state legal capacity, firms may increase their use of formal institutions to secure property.

Upon his rise to power, first as prime minister in 1999 and then as president beginning in 2000, Putin pursued an active legislative agenda that continued to improve Russia's formal legal infrastructure. Most critically, state agencies' financial resources dramatically increased under Putin. Yet, as would soon become apparent, Putin's efforts to strengthen the state would have ambiguous effects on state legal capacity. Even as the formal legal infrastructure improved, high-profile political interventions in the judicial system, factional disputes among Putin's ruling circle, and corruption within law enforcement and regulatory agencies undermined other aspects of state legal capacity, such as the independence of formal legal institutions. Given these countervailing trends, improvements in state legal capacity can at best partially explain Russian firms' increasing use of legal property security strategies during the Putin era.

In the first three years of his presidency, Putin continued to promote development of a *formal legal infrastructure*, using his popularity and influence to push through legislation that had fallen prey to political gridlock during the Yeltsin era. During this period, the Russian government brought the Civil Code to completion and introduced new procedural codes for criminal law, civil law, and the administration of the commercial courts. Previously, Russia had operated under a Soviet-era Civil Procedural Code and Criminal Procedural Code, leaving key constitutional rights unenforceable, nearly a decade after the adoption of the Constitution. Among other innovations, these new Putin-era codes shifted the burden of proof in criminal matters to the state and transferred significant elements of authority over arrest and pre-trial detention from the procuracy to the judiciary. They also promoted increased adversarialism, the common law legal approach in which judges serve as neutral arbiters between competing parties as opposed to investigators as in the civil law tradition (Solomon, 2008, pp. 66–67). By the end of Putin's first term in 2004, the laws and codes needed for a market economy to function smoothly were in place, with a handful of exceptions such as a new Law on Competition introduced in 2006. Key legislation such as the Law on Joint Stock Companies and Law on Bankruptcy would continue to undergo revisions throughout the decade, but compared to the first decade and a half of post-communism, the legislative aspect of Russia's legal infrastructure had become relatively stable.

The organizational aspect of Russia's legal infrastructure was less stable. In 2004, Putin shook up the organizations responsible for regulating the economy. The tax police were abolished, the ministries in charge of taxation and competition policy downgraded to the status of agencies and merged into other ministries, and the agencies responsible for matters related to bankruptcy and the securities market renamed (and ostensibly reformed). From the perspective of the business community, abolishment of the tax police was a clear improvement. The tax police, a specialized law enforcement unit authorized to use aggressive tactics to fight tax dodgers, had become notorious for what had become known as "masky shows," in which federal agents in ski masks and armed with automatic weapons raided offices of alleged tax evaders (Easter, 2002b). But the effects of Putin's other organizational changes were more equivocal. On the one hand, many of the new or recently reformed regulatory institutions received authority and status that greatly expanded their influence. As a consequence, Russia's regulatory institutions came to "matter" more, in the sense that private actors could no longer ignore them without consequence. On the other hand, the new institutions came to play a prominent role in politically motivated persecution of targeted businesses, an issue examined in greater detail below. Meanwhile, desperately needed reforms for the Ministry of Internal Affairs, the ministry responsible for law enforcement, were discussed extensively throughout 2002. Despite grand proposals, such as the creation of a Russian equivalent of the FBI and a separate municipal police force, no substantive reforms came to fruition (Solomon, 2005, pp. 234–237).

Operational capability of legal institutions during the Putin era also remained uneven. In many ways, the commercial courts continued to perform well, with their ongoing affordability providing reasonable levels of accessibility. Efficiency proved to be more of a challenge with rapidly rising caseloads. One innovation of the 2002 *Arbitrazh* Procedural Code partially addressed this issue, limiting three-judge panels to bankruptcy cases while ending collegial judging for administrative cases between firms and the state, which freed up badly needed resources (Hendley, 2003, p. 365). Moreover, despite increased caseloads, the judges in the commercial courts continued to work largely within statutorily defined timeframes.[3] Problems with enforcement of court decisions persisted in the Putin era, although the booming economy mitigated some of the troubles prevalent in the 1990s, such as the challenge of trying to collect from penniless debtors. The new *Arbitrazh* Procedural Code also empowered the Bailiffs Service, for example by making court orders (*ispolnitelnyie listy*) to seize funds from debtors' bank accounts valid for three years rather than the previous term of six months, which forced debtors hiding from creditors to avoid using their bank accounts for a much longer period (Hendley, 2003, p. 375). Some evidence began to emerge, moreover, that enforcement problems were not as grave as commonly thought. Hendley (2004) found that in 100 nonpayment cases litigated throughout 2001, at least some debt was collected in nearly two-thirds of the sample.

---

[3] Between 2002 and 2010, the percentage of cases resolved in violation of statutory deadlines ranged from a low of 1.1 percent to a high of 2.8 percent. Data are from various years of the *Tablitsa osnovnykh pokazateley raboty arbitrazhnykh sudov RF* [Table of Basic Indicators on the Work of the Commercial Courts of the RF], a publication of the Supreme Commercial Court of the Russian Federation.

Table 4.1 *Annual Federal Budget for MVD and Judiciary, 1998–2010 (constant 2010 rubles, in billions)*

	1998	1999	2000	2001	2002	2003	2004	2005	2006	2007	2008	2009	2010
Judiciary	32.5	19.0	27.8	30.3	44.1	51.8	61.3	69.9	89.0	107.7	110.9	115.2	109.1
MVD	98.7	68.0	107.8	96.0	102.9	143.4	212.9	240.9	246.6	258.5	290.1	288.9	289.1

Source: Law on Federal Budget of the RF, various years.

Equally striking was an effort by the Russian government to increase transparency by mandating the creation of court websites and public access to online databases of judicial decisions. The need to publicly justify decisions, reformers hoped, would contribute to the quality of judgments and partially act as a safeguard against corruption or political interference (Solomon, 2008, p. 67). By the end of the 2000s, commercial courts were posting the vast majority of decisions online. However, the courts of general jurisdiction lagged far behind in implementing transparency initiatives, and the effectiveness of transparency initiatives remains to be systematically studied.

Putin's foremost contribution to state legal capacity was to significantly increase *financial resources* devoted to funding legal institutions. As seen in Table 4.1, the amount of funding budgeted for the judicial system increased more than fivefold during the first decade of Putin's rule. Increased funding translated into higher salaries, the repair of court buildings, and computerization of court administration (Solomon, 2008, p. 67). Beyond the judicial system, spending on national security and law enforcement tripled between 2000 and 2007, with the largest portion of these resources going to the FSB, MVD, and procuracy (Taylor, 2011, pp. 53–54).[4]

With respect to *competency*, state officials possessed a decade of experience regulating and living within a market-based society by the time the Putin era began. Levels of competency nonetheless remained highly uneven. With increased funding for courts, higher salaries (now paid on time), and improved physical security, incentives to remain within the corps of judges were significantly greater than in the Yeltsin era, although recruitment of judges remained a problem (Hendley, 2007b, p. 108). There also remained a significant gap between the quality of the

---

[4] The figures in Table 4.1 underrepresent the full budget for the MVD, which is partially funded from sub-federal budgets.

commercial courts and the rest of the judiciary. In 2001, one Moscow lawyer described litigating in the general courts as "simply unpleasant," adding: "The qualifications of *arbitrazh* judges with regard to economic disputes is incomparably higher than the qualifications of the judges in the courts of general jurisdiction" (cited in Hendley, 2003, p. 368). Little had changed by 2009, when a partner at a Moscow law firm described the workings of the courts of general jurisdiction as "pure chaos [*bardak*]" (Lawyer 12, interview, 2009). Whatever concerns persisted about the competency of the judiciary, they paled in comparison to concerns regarding the competency of law enforcement officials. Turnover and recruitment problems in the world of law enforcement remained grave. In 2005, the head of the MVD declared the personnel situation at the local level to be "catastrophic," noting that among local-level MVD employees more than half were under-30-year-olds with minimal experience. Well into the 2000s MVD officials faced personnel shortages of up to 50 percent for key positions, such as criminal investigators (Taylor, 2011, p. 190). Citing such problems, Solomon (2005, p. 233) declared that "policing in Russia is less professional now than it was in the late Soviet period."

In addition to lacking qualifications, law enforcement officials continued to engage in supplementary work outside of their official duties, ranging from basic work as security guards to sophisticated protection rackets for private enterprises, as discussed in Chapter 3. In surveys conducted throughout the 2000s, more than one half of law enforcement personnel consistently reported unofficial income streams, often of a magnitude that exceeded their formal salaries (Dubova and Kosals, 2013, pp. 50–51). At higher levels of law enforcement agencies, commercial activities spilled over into intense factional conflicts. The most infamous was the mini-war that broke out among MVD, FSB, and Procuracy officials as a result of the "Three Whales" case, which began when customs and MVD officials stumbled upon an FSB-protected arms smuggling operation operating under the cover of the Three Whales furniture store. Newly created organizations, such as the Investigative Committee, first launched under the aegis of the Procuracy in 2007 and made fully independent in 2011, were ostensibly created to quell corruption within the law enforcement community. Instead, these organizations themselves quickly turned into new pawns in the clashes between factional clans (Burger and Holland, 2008; Taylor, 2011, pp. 172–175). Likewise, police reforms initiated in 2009, despite purging nearly half of the MVD's top leadership, did little to improve the competence of Russia's law enforcement personnel (Taylor, 2014, p. 246).

In addition to questions concerning competence, certain institutional reforms in the Putin era threatened to undermine legal institutions' *political independence*. Particularly controversial were changes to the Law on the Status of Judges that imposed an age limit of 65 on federal judges and allocated to non-judges one-third of the seats on Judicial Qualification Collegia, the sole bodies that could remove tenured judges from the bench. Related reforms also made it easier to open criminal proceedings against judges and impose other forms of disciplinary action. While concerns about judicial independence were not without merit, some of these changes were aimed at improving the accountability of judges and were supported even by liberal pockets within the government, such as the Ministry of Economic Development and Trade (Solomon, 2008, p. 68). Nevertheless, despite the fact that dismissals of judges remained an infrequent occurrence, a handful of high-profile dismissals in the early 2000s created an impression that an independent judiciary was under attack (Hendley, 2005, pp. 356–357). A small but highly visible number of politicized cases against powerful tycoons, the most significant being the attack on the oligarch Mikhail Khodorkovsky, discussed in greater detail below, further contributed to questions about the fate of judicial independence in Russia.

Political interference extended far beyond the judicial system, undermining the effectiveness of numerous regulatory institutions. One glaring example concerns the Financial Monitoring Committee, created in 2001 and renamed the Federal Financial Monitoring Service (*Rosfinmonitoring*) in 2004. Originally formed in response to the International Financial Action Task Force's (FATF) insistence that Russia play a greater role in fighting money laundering and tracking international money flows by criminal organizations, Putin enthusiastically embraced the initiative. In recent years, the FATF has praised *Rosfinmonitoring* as an "exemplary" agency, one of the "best financial-intelligence units in the world." But Gaddy and Partlett (2013) point out that in many ways the agency serves as "Putin's personal surveillance unit," and that rather than successfully fighting financial crime, the agency was created to "ensure [Putin's] control over Russian politics and business." Even when not particularly nefarious, political interference in regulatory activity has frequently led to distorted policy outcomes. Competition policy, for example, played a relatively small role in Russia's regulatory regime until the creation of a new Federal Anti-Monopoly Service (FAS) in 2004 and passage of the new

Law on Competition in 2006. Since then, the number of cases initiated by FAS has skyrocketed. However, Avdasheva and Shastitko (2011) find that over-reliance on anti-trust measures to deal with a broad range of politically significant policy issues, such as rising prices in the food sector, has led to numerous ill-advised prosecutions with the potential to, ironically, decrease competition.

Overall, an evaluation of state legal capacity under Putin produces exceedingly contradictory images. Russia's formal legal infrastructure improved under Putin, particularly in the early 2000s, and the agencies tasked with implementing and enforcing these rules for the first time in the post-Soviet period received the financial resources necessary to fulfill their mandate. The competency of officials staffing legal institutions improved during the Putin era, although competency levels remained highly uneven across different agencies. Operational capability was also highly uneven, with the commercial courts serving as a bright spot with much better performance than the courts of general jurisdiction, regulatory institutions, and law enforcement agencies. Meanwhile, concerns about corruption and about independence from political interference increased significantly.

Brian Taylor (2011, p. 111), in the most comprehensive study by a Western scholar of Russia's law enforcement regime to date, nicely captures the ambiguities of state legal capacity under Putin:

> The achievements of the state-building project were modest and partial, with the greatest gains in capacity taking place in rebuilding a regime of repression to implement extraordinary decisions of the Kremlin. Much less progress was made in coping with the core, routine tasks of the power ministries. Repressing opposition figures and "bad" oligarchs certainly came much more naturally to Russian law enforcement officials than establishing a stable private property rights regime.

Such doubts regarding improvements in state capacity under Putin, despite the trope that he has rebuilt the Russian state, have been echoed in the works of numerous other observers (see, e.g., Hanson, 2007; McFaul and Stoner-Weiss, 2008; Mendras, 2012).

Considering a two-decade span, the picture of state legal capacity in post-Soviet Russia that emerges is one of gradual re-creation of a *necessary* level of capacity, a level that made use of formal legal institutions feasible. Although this capacity in many ways continued to evolve throughout the early Putin era, its development was already well underway by the late 1990s, with a formal legal infrastructure in place, the growing competency of state officials, and the relatively high operational capabilities of one of the most important institutions, the commercial courts. There is not, however, evidence of a sufficiently significant shift in state legal capacity that can account for the diversification of Russian firms' property security strategies away from private and corrupt coercion and in the direction of law. Moreover, when an additional dimension of state legal capacity – the capacity to constrain state officials – is considered, it becomes clear that Russian firms' increasing reliance on formal legal institutions coincided with the emergence of an increasingly predatory state.

4.3   State Legal Capacity's Dark Side: Rise of a Predatory State

In addition to the five metrics of state legal capacity analyzed above, a sixth aspect of legal capacity is important enough to warrant separate discussion. Although state capacity more frequently is conceptualized as the state's ability to implement or enforce, an equally important aspect of capacity – particularly with respect to property security – is the state's ability to *constrain* its own officials (Frye, 2004). Moreover, contrary to the existing property rights literature's focus on the highest levels of the state, the majority of firms face threats not from rulers and their entourages but from lower-level bureaucrats whom even the most powerful dictators often struggle to control (Gans-Morse, 2012; Markus, 2015).

In the case of Russia, the state's capacity to constrain officials from undermining firms' property security declined dramatically as the 2000s proceeded. These threats emanated from at least three distinct sources, including members of Putin's coterie, lower-level bureaucrats, and law enforcement officials. The fact that a key aspect of state legal capacity – the capacity to constrain state officials – declined so dramatically during the same period in which Russian firms increasingly utilized formal legal institutions further demonstrates the incompleteness of explanations that attribute firms' adoption of legal strategies primarily to improved legal capacity.

The most high-profile attack by Russian officials was the arrest of Khodorkovsky for tax evasion and fraud in 2003, an attack orchestrated by members of Putin's inner circle. Khodorkovsky, having amassed a fortune through his exploits in the banking and oil sectors, was at the time Russia's wealthiest man. The charges ultimately led to the bankruptcy of Khodorkovky's oil company, Yukos, whose most lucrative assets ended up in the possession of the state-owned Rosneft oil company after a series of non-transparent auctions.[5]

The Khodorkovsky Affair, however, is not an isolated incident, particularly in the energy sector. Rather than continuing to play a dangerous game, the oligarch Roman Abramovich voluntarily sold his oil company Sibneft to state-owned Gazprom in 2005 (Kramer, 2005). Others were not so fortunate. In 2006, Gazprom acquired a majority stake in the Sakhalin-2 oil and gas project after Royal Dutch Shell, facing legal proceedings for ostensible violations of environmental regulations, agreed to sell some of its assets (Kramer, 2006). In 2007, Mikhail Gutseriev, having fallen out of favor with Kremlin-backed leadership in the Republic of Ingushetia, was charged with tax evasion, fraud, and illegal entrepreneurship. As he fled the country, he sold off his Russneft oil company (not to be confused with the state-owned Rosneft) to Oleg Deripaska, a tycoon known for his friendly relations with the Kremlin (Zarakhovich, 2009).[6] In 2008, a series of office raids, environmental inspections, and back tax claims against TNK-BP raised speculation that Gazprom was seeking to acquire control of yet another oil company (Belton, 2008). TNK-BP, however, managed to remain independent until 2013, when it was subsumed by Rosneft.

These acquisitions transformed the oil sector. In 2000, state-owned companies produced 10 percent of oil output; by 2008, they produced 42 percent (Rutland, 2009, p. 175). The state also has been active in other sectors, although its tactics have not been nearly so coercive. In heavy industry, state-owned corporations throughout the 2000s acquired major firms such as Silovye Mashiny, OMZ, and the auto manufacturer AvtoVAZ. In the financial sector, prominent backers of opposition political parties, such as Igor Linshits and Alexander Lebedev, repeatedly have faced arrest and raids by tax authorities. Meanwhile, the shadow of the Yukos Affair hangs over all major businesses. When in 2008 Putin accused the steel company Mechel of overcharging domestic consumers and issued what appeared to be a personal threat to the company's chief executive, Mechel's shares on the New York Stock Exchange dropped 38 percent for fear of an imminent state attack (Kramer, 2008).[7]

---

[5] The Khodorkovsky Affair has received a great deal of attention. Among other sources, see Goldman (2004) and Sakwa (2014).

[6] Gutseriyev's story ended on a positive note. He regained the Kremlin's favor, his arrest warrant was canceled, and ultimately Deripaska, facing significant debts after the 2008 financial crisis, returned control of Russneft to Gutseriyev.

[7] Putin, speaking at an industry conference, said: "By the way, we invited the owner and director of [Mechel], Igor Vladimirovich Zyusin, to today's meeting, but he suddenly got

For the majority of firms, however, the most pressing concern is not a Yukos-style raid but rather harassment from lower-level officials, whom the top leadership struggles to control in a country as vast as Russia. The harassment and persecution firms face from bureaucrats and law enforcement officials in many ways resembles the property security strategies based on corrupt coercion analyzed in Chapter 3. But there is one fundamental difference: Throughout the 2000s, state officials increasingly came to *initiate* attacks on firms themselves rather than merely offering property security services to private actors.

One key element of a predatory state is that bureaucrats create or maintain excessive regulations, which force firms to pay bribes in order to cut through red tape, acquire necessary permits, or avoid fines and sanctions. Particularly cognizant of the regulatory burden faced by smaller firms, the Russian government initiated significant reforms in the early 2000s. These reforms restricted the frequency of government agencies' inspections, reduced licensing and certification requirements, and sought to accelerate the process of registering a new business (Shetinin et al., 2005).

According to surveys conducted by the Centre for Economic and Financial Research in Moscow (CEFIR), the reforms had a significant one-time effect. But after the initial reduction in regulatory burdens, bureaucrats were able to stall reforms well short of legally mandated goals. Overall, the average number of inspections firms faced in the first half of 2002 was 33 percent lower than the average number faced in the second half of 2001 (Shetinin et al., 2005, p. 5). Progress tapered off thereafter, and the average number of inspections faced by firms remained relatively constant. Moreover, agencies continued to violate the law's ban on repeat inspections during a two-year period. In 2004, of firms inspected by the police, over 40 percent reported a repeat visit; fire inspectors and tax inspectors likewise returned to around 20 percent of firms that had already faced recent inspections (Shetinin et al., 2005, p. 6).

The effects of the laws on licensing and registration were similar. Following the introduction of the licensing law, the share of firms applying for licenses fell from 31 percent in the second half of 2001 to 14 percent by the second half of 2004, showing a reasonable amount of deregulation of economic activity. Yet by the mid-2000s, more than half of all licenses remained illegitimate, in that they were issued for activities which by law do not require licensing (Shetinin et al. 2005, p. 7). More success

sick ... Of course, sickness is sickness, but I think Igor Vladimirovich should get better as quick as possible, otherwise we'll have to send him a doctor" (Kramer, 2008).

was observed with respect to the law on registration. Whereas prior to the new law, a mere 20 percent of firms were able to register in less than a week, by 2004, nearly half of firms managed to do so (Shetinin et al. 2005, p. 9).[8] Yet despite the progress, these figures indicate that half of all firms were still facing delays longer than the legally mandated five-day period. Ultimately, the initial packet of deregulatory laws proved ineffective to such an extent that new laws on inspections and licensing were again introduced – and again had little effect – in the late 2000s (Markus, 2015, ch. 3).

In short, bureaucrats proved resilient against legislation aimed at restraining their influence over business. By maintaining an excessive regulatory burden, bureaucrats have managed to divert a large share of firms' profits to their own pockets by selling illegitimate licenses, collecting bribes from firms seeking to overcome red tape, and forcing firms to pay bribes to avoid inspectors' sanctions.

While regulatory officials can slow a firm's operations or potentially shut down a firm, the most fearsome threats are those posed by law enforcement officials. In such raids, officials usually charge, or threaten to charge, entrepreneurs with criminal prosecution in order to force firms to pay bribes or to sell off assets at below market prices. For cooperative entrepreneurs, the charges may never materialize. For others, the fear of imprisonment may induce cooperation, after which charges are dropped. For the most recalcitrant, the authorities make use of judges' willingness to allow pre-trial detention without bail for extended periods of time, even for non-violent crimes. Although such raids are by no means a new invention, observers widely perceive the aggressiveness of law enforcement officials to have increased after the Yukos Affair, as attacks by Putin's inner circle initiated copycat behavior at lower levels of the bureaucracy. In the words of Yana Yakovleva, the founder of *Biznes Solidarnost*, an association dedicated to aiding entrepreneurs facing persecution by state agencies, every official after 2003 was looking for his "own little Yukos" (author interview, 22 October 2009).

As of 2013, by some estimates approximately 110,000 businesspeople were incarcerated for what in Russia are known as "economic crimes" (*ekonomicheskye prestupleniya*) (Kramer, 2013). Favored charges used to apply pressure on firms include fraud (Article 159 of the Criminal Code), misappropriation or embezzlement (Article 160), and money laundering

---

[8] These figures refer to firms that did not hire a consulting firm or other type of intermediary to help with the registration process.

Table 4.2   *Number of Economic Crimes Reported, 2000–2012 (in thousands)*

	2000	2001	2002	2003	2004	2005	2006	2007	2008	2009	2010	2011	2012
Fraud	47.8	46.2	45.7	47.5	54.1	58.5	66.1	69.5	75.0	78.3	58.2	50.9	52.8
Money laundering	1.8	1.4	1.1	0.6	1.8	7.5	8.0	9.0	8.4	8.8	1.8	0.7	0.6

Source: Rosstat and RF Ministry of Internal Affairs.[9]

(Article 174) (Volkov et al., 2010, pp. 5–6). Unlike crimes such as murder or theft, which are reported to the police by citizens, these economic crimes require proactive investigation by legal authorities, providing officials with significant discretion to probe a wide range of firms. As can be seen in Table 4.2, after 2003, the initial year of the Khodorkovsky Affair, there was a notable increase in the number of economic crimes uncovered by Ministry of Internal Affairs investigators: Between 2003 and 2004, fraud- and embezzlement-related cases, which since the late 1990s had remained relatively constant, increased nearly 15 percent. The number of money-laundering cases nearly doubled and then continued to skyrocket as the decade proceeded.[10]

The range of state agencies that have found legal cover for engaging in raids on private businesses is staggering and includes many of the same government agencies that Putin empowered in his effort to increase state legal capacity, as discussed above. Tax authorities have been

[9] Data for 2000–2002 are from *Prestupnost i pravoporyadok v Rosii: Statisticheskii aspekt* [Crime and Law Enforcement in Russia: Statistical Aspects], Table 7.1. Data for 2003–2012 are from various years of the Ministry of Internal Affairs *Sostoyanie prestupnosti* [Status Report on Crime], available at http://mvd.ru/presscenter/statistics/reports/.

[10] Although an increase in the number of recorded crimes could result from a crime wave or more aggressive policing of genuine criminal activity rather than abuse of the Criminal Code, Volkov et al. (2010) demonstrate that this is not the case. Honest law enforcement officials prefer not to initiate cases with a low likelihood of being prosecuted, for low prosecution rates harm investigators' prospects for promotion. On the other hand, officials seeking to apply pressure on firms are more likely to initiate cases that lack merit, simply as a means of frightening entrepreneurs. In 2007, only 10 to 15 percent of cases relating to fraud and embezzlement resulted in sentencing, in stark contrast to murder and rape, which once initiated, led to sentencing in 90 percent and 75 percent of cases, respectively. While recognizing that the complexity of economic crimes creates legitimate reasons for investigators to drop some cases, Volkov et al. (2010, 15) conclude that the data on economic crimes in Russia indicate that "a significant part of criminal cases related to economic crimes are initiated and carried out in connection with the commercial interests of the law enforcement agencies."

among the most high-profile, playing a key role in raids premised on tax violations, such as the takeover of Yukos. Yet since the abolishment of the Federal Tax Police in 2004, the number of criminal tax proceedings against firms has dropped dramatically (Nazrullaeva et al., 2013, p. 6). However, the Federal Narcotics Control Service (FSKN), which inherited the majority of the Tax Police's personnel and resources, soon found its own ways to pressure firms. In particular, the FSKN lobbied to keep ingredients commonly used by legitimate chemical companies on the list of chemicals deemed illegal due to their potential role in manufacturing narcotics, which allowed the agency to target chemical companies at will. Raiding attacks on chemical companies became so widespread – in Moscow alone the FSKN initiated over 200 such cases between 2004 and 2007 – that the Russian press began referring to the "chemist cases." In another absurd raiding innovation, the FSKN banned even minimal traces of narcotic opium alkaloids in poppy seeds intended for food production and then introduced criminal cases against poppy seed suppliers to Russian bakeries. In yet another common scheme, often referred to as "commodity raids" (*tovarnoe reiderstvo*), police officials or officials from agencies such as the Russian Federal Property Fund charge companies with holding illegally acquired contraband. After confiscating the goods, officials exploit legal loopholes to resell them. In one incident involving a cell phone retailer, state raiders netted an astonishing 50 million USD profit upon the sale of confiscated equipment (Dubova and Kosals 2013, pp. 52–54; Nazrullaeva et al. 2013, p. 7). Still other businesspeople report that state authorities use the pretext of searches for unlicensed or pirated software to raid firms.

The abuse of the criminal code to pressure entrepreneurs became grave enough to attract attention at the highest levels. In April 2010, then president Dmitry Medvedev signed a law prohibiting the pre-trial detention of businesspeople accused of fraud, embezzlement, or the damage of property by deceit or breach of trust. The number of recorded economic crimes subsequently fell, as seen in Table 4.2. But Putin's decision to return to the presidency in 2012, following a four-year hiatus during which he served as prime minister, has raised doubts about the survival of Medvedev's more business-friendly policies. Although Putin created the post of Ombudsmen for Entrepreneurs' Rights in the summer of 2012 and passed an amnesty for some types of economic crimes in 2013, the amnesty ultimately was worded to have limited impact and resulted in the release of fewer than 2000 imprisoned businesspeople (Buckley, 2014).

In summary, examining an additional element of state legal capacity – the state's ability to constrain predatory officials – further demonstrates the inadequacy of explanations that attribute Russian firms' increasing use of formal legal institutions to improved legal capacity. Indeed, Russian firms increasingly adopted legal strategies amidst a growing wave of state predation. However, the most significant evidence of the incompleteness of explanations relying on state legal capacity is that firms' strategies for securing property depend on how firms themselves *perceive* changes in state legal capacity, and these perceptions may or may not converge with objective indicators. In the case of Russia, firms consistently have evaluated state legal capacity even more negatively than objective indicators might warrant.

4.4 State Legal Capacity from the Firm's Perspective

For shifts in state legal capacity to serve as an explanation for the evolution of Russian firms' property security strategies, there must be not only evidence that state legal capacity has increased significantly, but also that firms perceive a significant shift in the level of legal capacity. As noted above, evidence of the former type is relatively weak. Evidence of the latter type, meanwhile, is even weaker.

In order to track firms' perceptions of state legal capacity over time, ideally we would have data based on repeated surveys of the same firms. Given the challenges inherent in firm surveys, such panel data do not exist. The World Bank–EBRD Business Environment and Enterprise Performance Survey (BEEPS) does, however, offer a viable starting point. Although BEEPS does not consist of panel data, the same questions have been asked over multiple rounds on a similar sample of firms. Unfortunately, the first round of BEEPS was not conducted until 1999, preventing analysis of the early years of post-communism. Meanwhile, although BEEPS was carried out in Russia in 2009 and 2012, the format of the questions changed significantly, as did the size and composition for the 2012 sample, making direct comparisons problematic. The analysis presented here focuses therefore on three rounds conducted between 1999 and 2005, a critical period during which property security strategies evolved significantly.

Figure 4.1 shows Russian firms' assessment of the court system on five dimensions. With respect to impartiality, corruption, efficiency, and affordability, firms' assessments of the courts at best improved marginally, and in the case of affordability fell, between 1999 and 2005. Only with respect to the courts' ability to enforce decisions did firms' evaluations

Percentage of firms agreeing that the following descriptions are associated with the court system

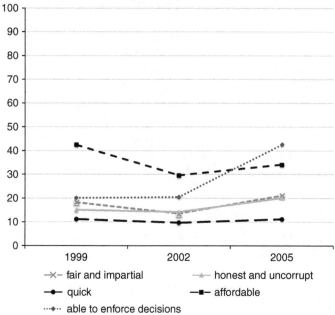

Figure 4.1   Firms' Assessment of Courts
Source: World Bank-EBRD BEEPS survey. These percentages refer to respondents who "frequently," "usually," or "always" associate the descriptions with the court system.

improve during this period, an issue to which I return below. What warrants emphasis is the small percentage of firms throughout this entire period associating positive traits with the courts.

Other indicators from the BEEPS survey paint a similar picture. The survey asked firms to rate on a 1 to 4 scale, where 1 represents "no obstacle" and 4 represents a "major obstacle," the extent to which the functioning of the judiciary is "problematic for the operation and growth of your business." In 1999, the average rating was 2.1. In 2002, this rating improved slightly to 1.9 before returning to 2.0 in 2005. Meanwhile, in the 1999 survey only 27 percent of respondents agreed with the statement "I am confident that the legal system will uphold my contract and property rights in business disputes." This figure increased noticeably but not dramatically to 35 percent in the 2002 survey and leveled off at 36 percent in the 2005 survey.[11]

---

[11] Author's calculations based on data from the World Bank–EBRD BEEPS survey. The percentages of those expressing confidence in the courts refers to those who "tend to agree," "agree in most cases," or "strongly agree" with the statement.

While improvements in firms' assessments of the courts were modest, they were at least headed in a positive direction during the critical period spanning the late Yeltsin and early Putin eras. The same cannot be said of firms' evaluations of other types of formal legal institutions. Yakovlev (2008, p. 222), for example, compared surveys of manufacturing and service firms conducted in the same eight regions in 2000 and 2007. Firms' overall assessment of the commercial courts improved, albeit only among manufacturing firms. But evaluations of the police, which were already negative in 2000, remained unchanged, while evaluations of local regulators and inspectors fell dramatically among both manufacturing and service firms.

Indeed, by the late 2000s, businesspeople, especially owners and managers of small firms, regularly referred to bureaucrats as the primary threat to the security of their assets – a threat more destructive than the *bandity* of the 1990s. In the words of a consultant to small businesses in Moscow: "Who cares about criminals? Inspectors can close you in a matter of seconds. This is in itself a kind of mafia system" (Firm 25, interview, 2009). Or as a small businessman pointed out, "The *bandity* who were here 15 years ago wore a sign that said '*Bandit.*' It was easy to distinguish between *bandity* and non-*bandity* ... Today, in Moscow alone, there are over 50 organizations that have the direct right to inspect and block the work of an enterprise" (Firm 16, interview, 2009). Government agencies' tendency to issue contradictory edicts has been particularly frustrating for firms. In one extreme example, multiple small businessmen in Moscow independently reported a common scheme. First, police inspectors proclaim that a firm's windows must have protective bars in order to be in accordance with safety codes. Then fire inspectors appear to notify the firm that such bars violate a fire safety code (Firms 16 and 42, interviews, 2009).

In short, firms' assessments of formal legal institutions did not improve from the late 1990s to the 2000s. Rather, even as firms' use of property security strategies based on law continued to rise, many firms still believed that the courts were corrupt and suffering from political intervention. The one possible exception concerns the legal system's ability to enforce court decisions, an area in which firms perceived improvement throughout the first years of the Putin era. Yet it is not clear that a lack of enforcement was ever a primary barrier to firms' use of formal legal institutions. Even in the mid-1990s, Hendley (1997, p. 242) found that "rarely do managers cite problems with collection as a reason for bypassing courts." In later work that surveyed in-house lawyers, she furthermore found that while "enterprise lawyers regard the difficulties with implementing judgments as a serious obstacle to using the *arbitrazh* courts ... this feeling does not materially affect their willingness to use these courts" (Hendley, 2001a, p. 39).

Meanwhile, Yakovlev (2008, p. 234) queried firms that faced a legal violation but did not turn to the courts about the reasons underlying their hesitancy. In both 2000 and 2007, the most common reason for not going to court, cited by about two-thirds of these firms, was simply that "there was the possibility to resolve the dispute without going to court." Far fewer of these firms, 12 percent in 2000, indicated that concerns about enforcement issues motivated their decision. This figure actually increased to 30 percent in 2007, despite the fact that firms have become more willing to abide by court decisions. Although the 2010 Levada Center survey found that 56 percent of respondents who received a court judgment in their favor were able to enforce the decision fully, and another 19 percent were able to enforce the decision partially, this did not necessarily reflect state legal capacity. Rather, a striking 75 percent of these cases were executed voluntarily.[12]

The lack of perceived improvement in state legal capacity on the part of firms in and of itself is powerful evidence that "supply" of state legal capacity can at best be a partial factor in the evolution of Russian firms' strategies for securing property. But other evidence additionally indicates that firm strategies are surprisingly insensitive even to firms' own perceptions of the effectiveness of formal legal institutions. Yakovlev (2008, p. 234), for instance, found that firms' concerns about political interference or corruption in the courts played a minimal role in their decisions regarding whether or not to go to court. Only 15 percent of firms in his 2000 survey who faced a legal violation but did not turn to the legal system said they avoided litigation because "there was no hope of an objective look at the case in court," and this number remained at 17 percent in 2007.

A similar disconnect between firms' assessments of formal legal institutions and property security strategies can be seen in regional trends. As Hendley (2012, p. 532) notes, Moscow's commercial courts "enjoy a reputation of being highly capable that is well deserved," suggesting that if state legal capacity is determinative for property security strategies,

---

[12] Author's calculations based on data from the Levada Center's 2010 survey *Otnoshenie predpriyatii k sudebnoy sisteme* [Enterprises' relations with the court system].

Moscow firms should be most likely to use law and least likely to use coercion and corruption. But as discussed in Chapter 3, there are few significant differences between firm strategies in Moscow or St. Petersburg and firm strategies in many of Russia's regions. Even more striking are the results of Hendley's (2012, pp. 554–556) analysis of firms' willingness to litigate, based on data from the 2005 BEEPS survey. She finds that firms' evaluations of such factors as judges' honesty, problems with enforcing court decisions, the legal system's capability to uphold property rights, and the functioning of the courts as an obstacle to doing business are *uncorrelated* with whether a firm chose to litigate during its last dispute. Only firms' concerns about delays or high legal costs seemed to be correlated with lower willingness to use the court system.[13]

In summary, regardless of how one interprets objective indicators of state legal capacity in Russia, there is minimal evidence that Russian firms themselves perceive broad improvements in the effectiveness of formal legal institutions. Moreover, poor perceptions of formal legal institutions do not appear to motivate firms' choices about how to secure property, further bolstering the case that changes in state legal capacity, at least viewed in isolation, cannot offer a compelling explanation for the evolution of Russian firms' property security strategies.

4.5   Conclusion

The Russian case illustrates how the absence of state legal capacity can impede firms' use of formal legal institutions, as evidenced by the widespread use of illegal strategies in early post-Soviet Russia. But once a relatively effective formal legal infrastructure is established, factors other than state legal capacity frequently are determinative of firms' property security strategies. During the period in which Russian firms increasingly replaced strategies based on private or corrupt coercion with strategies based on law, the shifts in Russia's state legal capacity were at best modest and at worst downright ambiguous, due to growing corruption, rising political interference, and increased predation on the part of state officials. More important, beyond objective metrics, firms' assessments

---

[13] In fact, in the case of enforcement, Hendley (2012) finds that firms that perceive enforcement problems to be severe are *more* likely to choose litigation. However, such analyses face endogeneity problems, given that firms' previous interactions with the court system shape their evaluations of the courts at the time of the survey, and therefore should be treated with caution.

of state legal capacity seemed to improve even less than might have been warranted. A comprehensive understanding of institutional demand requires analysis of demand-side barriers and the effectiveness of illegal alternatives to formal legal institutions, the subjects of the next two chapters.

5

Demand-Side Barriers to the Use of Legal Strategies

The previous chapter illustrated the incompleteness of an exclusively supply-side approach to property security. Although a lack of state legal capacity in the early 1990s impeded Russian firms' use of formal legal institutions, a rise in legal capacity can at best account only partially for the evolution in Russian firms' strategies for securing property. This chapter begins the task of analyzing other factors that affect property security strategies. It focuses on *demand-side barriers*: the behaviors or beliefs at the level of firms and individuals that lead these actors to avoid formal legal institutions. Numerous factors can serve as demand-side barriers, but most fall under three categories – firms' operations in the informal economy, collective action dilemmas among firms, and cultural norms.

As discussed in Chapter 2, there is no evidence that cultural norms played a role in the development of firms' property security strategies in Russia. This chapter therefore focuses on firms' activities in the informal economy and collective action dilemmas, analyzing first how these factors served as barriers and then how these barriers declined over time. For example, in the 1990s Russia's informal sector at times constituted more than 40 percent of the overall economy (Johnson et al., 1997, p. 183). But Russia's informal economy differed from that of many other regions, particularly Latin America, where the informal economy consists primarily of micro-enterprises operating outside of the state's purview. Instead, firms in post-Soviet Russia rarely have avoided registration and incorporation, but rather have concealed many aspects of their operations for the purpose of tax evasion.[1] These low levels of tax compliance have had a significant effect on property security strategies. As a Moscow lawyer explained, intuitively capturing the logic of demand-side barriers, "In

---

[1] Even when firms found the registration process to be too burdensome, they often turned to intermediaries who specialized in selling "off-the-shelf" companies (i.e., firms existing only on paper) rather than operating fully outside of the law. Since reforms to the registration process in the early 2000s, registering new companies is rarely a major complaint for firms, reducing demand for such services.

terms of which businesses face problems with bureaucrats and criminal groups, the most vulnerable are those using 'black cash.'[2] They can't turn to the courts or police for help, and everyone knows that" (Lawyer 8, interview, 2009).

As economic growth increased at the end of the 1990s, firms were encouraged to formalize their operations in order to take advantage of emerging opportunities. This, combined with long-delayed tax reforms, led to significantly improved tax compliance, which lowered one of the key hurdles to firms' use of formal legal institutions. Through these reforms, the state *indirectly* contributed to the evolution of Russian firms' property security strategies. It should be noted, however, that in addition to the tax rate and the quality of tax administration, numerous other factors influence levels of tax compliance, including the overall health of the economy, moral considerations, and taxpayers' expectations about other citizens' compliance levels (Levi, 1989; Andreoni et al., 1998). While state-initiated reforms in the Russian case played a role in reducing a prominent demand-side barrier, in other cases reduced tax evasion results from factors unrelated to the state. What is critical for understanding firms' strategies for securing property is that regardless of its source, improved tax compliance – and reduced operations in the informal economy more generally – should induce firms to more broadly utilize formal legal institutions.

A second significant demand-side barrier that impeded firms' willingness to use formal legal institutions throughout the 1990s emerged as a result of firms' expectations about other firms' property security strategies. Several distinct mechanisms combined to create conditions for a classic coordination problem. First, legalizing a firm's operations is a costly process, which may put firms at a disadvantage relative to less scrupulous competitors unless these competitors simultaneously adopt legal practices. Moreover, because law is most effective when a critical mass of actors utilizes formal legal institutions, there are limited benefits to being an earlier adopter of legal strategies in an economy in which illegal strategies are widespread. Finally, the use of violence and corruption often triggers retribution using similarly unsavory tactics, further contributing to a vicious cycle that locks an economy into an unlawful equilibrium in which illegal strategies persist. Consequently, even when the majority of firms would prefer to replace violence and

---

[2] The phrase "black cash" (*chernye nalichnye*) refers to revenues hidden from state authorities.

corruption with law, individual firms may be willing to turn to formal legal institutions only if they are convinced that a significant number of other firms simultaneously will adopt legal strategies.

Russian firms' expectations about each other's willingness to use violence and corruption have nevertheless evolved over time. In part, this evolution has resulted from explicit efforts to overcome coordination problems. Business associations, for example, have helped match lawful firms with likeminded partners and promoted the use of legal strategies through hotlines, educational campaigns, and other similar tactics. But aside from intentional campaigns to change the Russian business environment, the evolution of Russian firms' property security strategies has shifted in a way that resembles the dynamics of *tipping point* games (Schelling, 1971). Just as expectations about other actors' strategies can induce vicious cycles, the interaction of firms' expectations raise the possibility of the opposite: virtuous cycles. As changes such as improved tax compliance (as well as a number of other factors examined in Chapter 6) have shifted the relative effectiveness of illegal and legal strategies in favor of the latter, firms' expectations that other firms are adopting legal strategies have contributed to a self-sustaining trend toward greater reliance on formal legal institutions.

The focus here and in the next chapter is on transformations over time, particularly changes beginning in the late 1990s and continuing through the present day. However, the factors discussed did not affect all types of firms equally. The topic of variation across firms is examined in detail in Chapter 7.

5.1 Tax Compliance and Operations in the Informal Economy

From Peru to Taiwan, scholars have demonstrated how firms with operations in the informal economy face barriers to the use of formal legal institutions (see, e.g., Winn, 1994; De Soto, 2003). Such barriers have been particularly noteworthy in the former Soviet Union, where the Soviet legacy bequeathed to newly independent countries a tax system fundamentally ill-suited for a modern market economy. Consequently, until the late 1990s, avoiding tax violations and informal dealings with tax officials was nearly impossible for Russian firms. As a result, even during times of duress, they hesitated to turn to formal legal institutions for fear of exposing their own legal shortcomings. It was not until the late 1990s and early 2000s, when a new Tax Code and tax administration reform took effect, that firms began to pay taxes and emerge from the shadow economy. This section details these changes in tax compliance in Russia and demonstrates how they affected firms' property security strategies, reducing demand-side barriers and thereby stimulating firms' use of formal legal institutions.

5.1.1   Tax Compliance as a Demand-Side Barrier

In the Soviet command economy, where all productive assets were owned by the state, taxation served as a tool for resource allocation among enterprises and ministries, rather than as a means of extracting revenue from private entities. Consequently, following the collapse of the Soviet Union, Russia's tax administration was underdeveloped and highly dependent on a narrow tax base composed of large, recently privatized firms and the remaining state-owned enterprises. In the mid-1990s, taxes on Russia's 20 most profitable companies accounted for approximately two-thirds of federal government revenues. Regional governments were similarly dependent on tax revenues from one or a handful of large firms (Easter, 2002a, p. 615). Moreover, even well-intentioned tax inspectors lacked basic qualifications. In one illustrative example from the early post-Soviet period, tax authorities were so impressed with the tax forms of a small business owner who recently had studied accounting that they asked him to share his lecture notes (Firm 25, interview, 2009).

Amidst the chaotic rush to liberalize prices and privatize firms during the first years of postcommunism, institutional reforms such as tax administration received secondary attention. Rather than establishing clearly defined and formal rules, the government soon lapsed into Soviet-style tactics of case-by-case negotiations, alternately granting firms exemptions and utilizing threats to coax tax payment. Meanwhile, in an effort to limit secessionism, Yeltsin exempted many regional governors from transferring taxes to the federal government (Easter, 2002a, pp. 614–615). Between 1993 and 1997, Yeltsin also granted regional and local governments the right to implement new taxes (Shleifer and Treisman, 2001, p. 118). By the late 1990s, there were over 200 different taxes, about 170 of them implemented at the subnational level, creating a hodgepodge of tax regulation that was impossible for even well-intentioned firms to untangle (Himes and Milliet-Einbinder, 1999, p. 170). By some accounts, the aggregate tax rate came close to 100 percent of enterprise profits. In response, firms began to conduct many transactions through barter, in part in order to keep assets hidden from tax authorities (Shleifer and Treisman, 2001, pp. 95–97). Firms also developed numerous schemes to reduce their tax burden, such as underreporting sales, number of

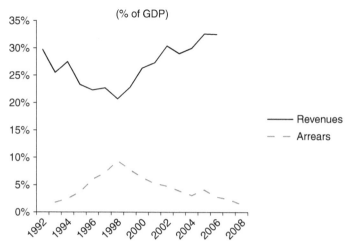

Figure 5.1 Tax Revenues and Arrears to Consolidated Budget of RF, 1992–2008
Sources: Tax revenue data for 1992–1997 from Treisman (1999, p. 148); for 1998–2006 from the Institute for Economic Transition (2006, p. 74). Tax arrears data for 1993–1997 from Treisman (2003, p. 52); for 1998–2008 from Rosstat reports, *Financii Rossii* [Russian Finances], various years.

employees, or amount of wages paid (Yakovlev, 2001). The results were devastating for state finances. As seen in Figure 5.1, tax arrears rose from under 2 percent of GDP in 1993 to 9.4 percent of GDP following the financial crisis of 1998. This amounted to a staggering 46 percent of tax revenues to the consolidated budget (Libman and Feld, 2007, pp. 8).

Legal scholars observing the sorry state of Russia's tax system in the mid-1990s recognized the extent to which low tax compliance served as a demand-side barrier to the use of formal legal institutions. Solomon (1997, p. 54), for instance, noted that "The realities of the tax system and the ways that many firms chose to cope with it (operating partly in the gray economy with two sets of financial records) had the added effect of discouraging those firms from using the courts to resolve disputes." One reason firms avoided courts, he concluded, was because they were "loathe to risk exposing their own illegal practices." Pistor (1996, p. 85) delved deeper into the details of why tax violators hesitated to utilize courts:

> Even where the courts themselves do not inquire into the nature of a transaction, there is a clear danger that cases will come to the attention of other state agencies, such as the Procuracy... [which] still enjoys broad powers to oversee the observance of legality... Tax authorities are also likely to keep an eye on any documentation revealing the volume of transactions or profits of a company.

Furthermore, evidence from in-depth interviews indicates that state authorities themselves do not always have to do the digging. Counterparties in a legal dispute are likely to turn over evidence of suspicious bookkeeping, or as one Moscow lawyer put it, there is "always the risk that somebody who knows about [a company's] 'sins' may whisper [to] the tax authority." Consequently, the existence of tax violations becomes "a weapon which can be used against the company" (Lawyer 8, interview, 2014). In short, due to widespread tax evasion, Russian firms faced a major hurdle to the use of legal property security strategies.

Significant changes finally occurred in the late 1990s. The 1998 financial crisis made restructuring of government finances imperative in order to receive bailouts from international financial institutions, which revitalized tax reform efforts that had been stalled since the mid-1990s. A sharp fall in the ruble's value also stimulated unexpectedly robust economic growth, providing impetus for firms to exit the informal sector in search of suddenly lucrative investment opportunities. More broadly, the crisis rattled the confidence of Russia's private sector actors, raising private sector support for a durable agreement with tax authorities that would produce a more stable and predictable business environment (Jones Luong and Weinthal, 2004).

Tax reforms had a profound impact on the Russian business world. Part I of the new code, which went into effect at the start of 1999, formalized the rights and obligations of taxpayers. It established the presumption of taxpayers' innocence by placing the burden of proof on the state to provide evidence of unpaid taxes. It also created clearer constraints on tax authorities, such as limiting their right to confiscate bank account funds and curbing the number of allowable inspections per tax period. Part II of the Tax Code, which came into effect in stages beginning in 2001, addressed the specifics of tax rates. The reforms aimed to broaden the tax base by collecting from small- and medium-sized enterprises and citizens. The most drastic reform was the establishment of a flat 13 percent tax on personal income. In 2002, a flat tax of 24 percent on corporate profits was also put in place, slashing tax rates for most firms by more than 10 percent. In 2003, a simplified tax system for small businesses was created. Meanwhile, a Unified Social Tax streamlined contributions to extra-budgetary funds for pensions and healthcare; in 2005, the Unified Social Tax was reduced from 35.6 to 24 percent in a further effort to reduce firms' hiding of wages through cash payments – known as paying wages "in an envelope" (v konverte). In essence, the reforms created a new

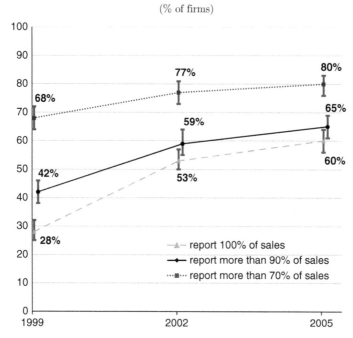

(% of firms)

Figure 5.2   Reporting Sales Revenue for Tax Purposes
Source: Author's calculations based on data from the World Bank–EBRD Business
Environment and Enterprise Performance Surveys. The chart shows the percentage of
firms reporting 70, 90, and 100 percent of sales revenue for tax purposes, along with 95
percent confidence intervals, for the years 1999 (N=552), 2002 (N=506), and 2005
(N=601).

social contract. The state would lower tax rates, consolidate the number
of taxes, and create a more fair and efficient tax administration; in return
firms would pay their dues.

As can be seen in Figure 5.1, tax arrears dropped and tax revenues
rose considerably beginning in the late 1990s. Economic growth played a
major role in reducing arrears and increasing revenue, but most relevant
from the perspective of property security strategies was that more firms
began paying more of their taxes. Figure 5.2 shows data from the Business
Environment and Enterprise Performance Surveys (BEEPS) conducted
by the World Bank and European Bank for Reconstruction and Development. Between 1999 and 2005, the percentage of respondents claiming
that a typical Russian firm pays 70 percent or more of its taxes rose
from 68 percent to 80 percent, a 12 percentage point increase; the change
was even greater with respect to the percentage of respondents claiming

that a typical firm pays 90 percent or more of their taxes – a 23 percentage point increase.[3] These surveys are not panel data, and so some
caution is required in interpreting these changes. But the magnitude of
reported change is striking, and respondents, during in-depth interviews
conducted by the author, consistently indicated that tax compliance has
dramatically improved.

5.1.2 Tax Compliance and Evolving Property Security Strategies

As can be seen in Figure 5.2, tax evasion remains a problem. Even after
significant improvements in tax compliance, a full 35 percent of respondents indicated in 2005 that a typical Russian firm reports less than 90
percent of sales revenues for tax purposes. And as the Moscow lawyer
cited at the outset of this chapter recognized, for firms that continue
to evade taxes, demand-side barriers to the use of formal legal institutions remain in place. However, the overall trend in the Russian economy
has been toward increased tax compliance, and informants specifically
note the effects of these trends on property security strategies. As one
respondent explained in reference to firms' ability to address widespread
concerns about employee theft, firms "have to operate legally (*byt belymi*),
because when they catch a dishonest accountant in the act of stealing,
they explain: *Listen fellow, I pay my taxes . . . so let's go to court.* And they
will not be afraid to go to court, because they know that their books are
clean" (Firm 15, interview, 2009, emphasis added). A founding partner of
a Moscow law firm confirmed these observations, offering similar reasoning: "There are [now] more commercial disputes between legal entities.
That is, *companies have switched, well, are switching, to a legal tax regime
system. Accordingly, they turn to law firms, conclude civil contracts, and
find protection for their contracts in the courts.* Previously, everything was
decided with a handshake . . . Now it's not like this" (Lawyer 20, interview,
2009, emphasis added).

Survey data provide the opportunity to further examine the relationship between tax compliance and property security strategies. In an
ideal world, panel data would facilitate the tracking of individual firms
over time, allowing analysis of how patterns of tax compliance affect a
specific firm's strategies for securing property. Given the relative data
scarcity that characterizes the post-Soviet world, along with the difficulty

[3] Differences between the 1999 and 2005 averages are statistically significant at the 99 percent
level of confidence.

and expense of conducting surveys of firms in general, such analysis is not feasible. However, it is possible to cautiously draw inferences from cross-sectional data. For example, if the hypothesis that improved tax compliance contributes to firms' use of law is correct, then there should be a positive association between tax compliance and legal property security strategies.[4]

In the 2010 survey I conducted, firms were asked, "Approximately what percentage of total annual sales would you estimate the typical firm in your line of business reports for tax purposes?"[5] Sixty-eight percent of those responding to the question stated that a typical firm reports more than 90 percent of sales revenues.[6] A straightforward comparison of firms reporting less than 90 percent of sales revenue for tax purposes with those paying more than 90 percent reveals a stark contrast. Just 37 percent of the former initiated litigation in the three years prior to the survey, compared to 63 percent of the latter. The difference is statistically significant at the 99 percent level of confidence, and persists even when taking into account potentially confounding factors such as firm size, sector, and location.

The distinctly different levels of litigiousness between firms that tend to evade taxes and firms that tend to pay taxes offer initial evidence regarding the relationship between tax compliance and property security strategies. However, comparisons of this type suffer from the challenge of controlling for the nature and extent of threats a firm faces. A firm that faces severe threats naturally will adopt a different strategy profile from a firm that faces moderate threats. Another more compelling approach is

[4] A second data-related concern pertains to the high number of non-responses on a handful of important variables, most likely due to the sensitive nature of some questions (see the descriptive statistics in Appendix E). Given that firms engaging in illicit activities are potentially less likely to respond to these questions, it is implausible that the data are missing completely at random. In such cases, listwise deletion – removing all observations for which data are missing on one or more variables from analyses – can lead to biased inference (King et al., 2001). For the analyses in Chapters 5 through 7, I therefore multiply impute missing data using the AMELIA II package for R (Honaker et al., 2011). (See Appendix G for further details.) I nevertheless find that analyses using listwise deletion produce similar results, as can be seen in the supplementary analyses in the Online Appendix.

[5] The phrasing a "typical firm in your line of business" is intended to elicit information about the respondent without fear of direct incrimination. The World Bank-EBRD BEEPS surveys pioneered this technique.

[6] Respondents were given six choices: less than 10 percent, 10 to 24 percent, 25 to 49 percent, 50 to 74 percent, 75 to 89 percent, more than 90 percent, and "not sure/unwilling to answer." The results shown below are robust if a dichotomous variable with a 75 percent threshold is used in place of the 90 percent cutoff as well as when an ordinal scale of 1 to 6 is used.

to focus analysis on firms' preferred strategies for resolving specific types of hypothetical conflicts. Although respondents admittedly may interpret hypothetical scenarios in differing ways, such scenarios facilitate analysis that to a reasonable degree holds the type of conflict constant. Additionally, respondents have fewer incentives to dissemble when responding to hypothetical scenarios.

Chapter 3 introduced two hypothetical scenarios based on conflicts common to the post-Soviet world. The first concerns a property dispute in which a firm must respond to a hostile attempt to acquire its assets, such as real estate or a factory, a scenario reminiscent of the illegal corporate raiding that plagued Russia in the late 1990s and early-to-mid 2000s. The second concerns a debt dispute in which a customer has a sizable overdue payment and has not been responding to collection attempts. In each case, firms were requested to rate their likeliness of using various strategies to resolve the conflict on a 1 to 7 scale where 1 refers to "highly unlikely" and 7 refers to "highly likely." (For the exact wording of the scenarios and an overview of firms' average responses, see Table 3.3 in Chapter 3.) The analysis spans the range of property security strategies, including strategies based on private coercion (e.g., private security agencies, criminal protection rackets), corrupt coercion (e.g., courts along with informal connections, state officials acting in a private capacity), and legal coercion (e.g, negotiations among lawyers, courts without informal connections, state officials acting in an official capacity).[7]

These ratings of propensities to use distinct property security strategies serve as the dependent variables in the analyses presented in Figure 5.3. These analyses utilize ordinary least squares (OLS) regressions to examine the hypothesis that low tax compliance is associated with a lower willingness to utilize formal legal institutions.[8] The strategies are arrayed along the vertical axis to the left of the figure. The figure shows results from three model specifications. For simple bivariate regressions, the circles represent the difference in average ratings between firms that report less than 90 percent of sales revenue for tax purposes and firms that report more than 90 percent. For regressions including control variables,

[7] As discussed in Chapter 3 (see footnote 15), the strategy descriptions for law enforcement officials and bureaucrats distinguish between using these resources in an "official capacity" (*obratitsya kak k dolzhnostnym litsam*) or "unofficial capacity" (*obratitsya kak k chastnym litsam*). For judicial officials, the strategies distinguish between going to court fully in a "formal manner" (*v formalnom poryadke*) or going to court while also making use of "informal connections" (*s ispolzavaniem sushchestvyushchich tam svyaziey*).

[8] These and other results in this chapter are also robust when using ordered logit regressions in place of OLS. See the Online Appendix.

the circles represent the difference in average ratings holding constant a wide range of firm and respondent-level factors, including the firm's age, number of employees, financial health, sector, city of location, and ownership structure (i.e., whether or not the firm has foreign or government shareholders); the respondent's age, gender, job description, and education; and whether or not the firm had recently faced disputes or engaged in litigation. Finally, the most demanding specifications—which I refer to throughout the book as "saturated models"—include all control variables as well as all variables of interest in Chapters 5 through 7. For all specifications, horizontal lines and vertical tick marks represent 95 percent and 90 percent confidence intervals, respectively. (Regression tables for all analyses conducted in this chapter are included in Appendix G or in the Online Appendix.)

In line with the hypothesis that tax evading firms are less likely to utilize formal legal institutions, firms that report less than 90 percent of revenue (i.e., "tax violators") rate their likeliness of turning to courts to address a property dispute between 0.65 and 0.80 points lower on the 7-point scale than firms that report more than 90 percent (i.e., "tax compliers").[9] The difference is statistically significant at a 95 percent level in all model specifications. When facing property disputes, tax violators also report being less likely than tax compliers to turn to lawyers to settle the conflict prior to court, although the magnitude of the difference is smaller than the coefficient for using courts and in some specifications only on the margins of statistical significance. The results are robust to the inclusion of the wide range of firm and respondent-level control variables listed above. The results are also robust when firms are divided among those that report more or less than 75 percent of sales revenue for tax purposes as well as when an ordinal measure of tax compliance is used.[10]

For resolving a debt dispute, the difference between tax violators' and tax compliers' average ratings of their propensity to use courts is again of a noteworthy magnitude, 0.45 to 0.74, and is statistically significant at a 90 percent level or higher in all specifications. Unlike with property disputes, however, the difference in willingness to turn to lawyers is not apparent in responses to the debt dispute vignette, perhaps because all firms rate the likeliness of using lawyers very highly in this scenario (the average rating is 6.3 out of 7). Overall, firms' responses regarding the use of courts in a

---

[9] Gehlbach (2008, ch. 4) similarly finds that throughout the former Soviet Union, firms hiding a significant proportion of revenue from tax authorities are less likely to report being satisfied with state institutions, including courts and the police.

[10] See the supplementary analyses in the Online Appendix.

The figure below shows the difference between the average responses of firms that report less than 90 percent of sales revenue for tax purposes (i.e., "tax violators") and of firms that report more than 90 percent (i.e., "tax compliers"), on a 1 to 7 scale where 1 is "very unlikely" and 7 is "very likely," holding other factors constant.

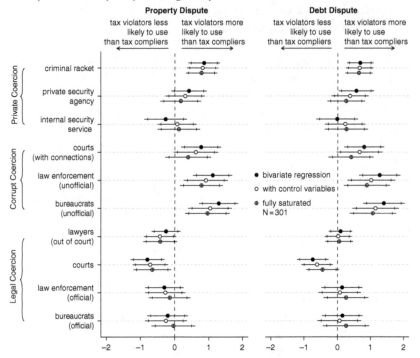

Figure 5.3   Tax Compliance and Propensity to Use Strategies

Note: Circles indicate point estimates from OLS regressions. Horizontal lines represent 95 percent confidence interviews and vertical tick marks represent 90 percent confidence intervals. Control variables include the firm's age, number of employees, financial health, sector, city of location, and ownership structure (i.e., whether or not the firm has foreign or government shareholders); the respondent's age, gender, job description, and education; and dummy variables for recent disputes and litigation experience. See Table 3.3 in Chapter 3 for exact wording of the property dispute and debt dispute scenarios. Missing data have been multiply imputed (see Appendix G for further details).

fully formal manner and, to a lesser extent, responses regarding the use of lawyers out of court are consistent with the claim that tax evasion serves as a demand-side barrier to firms' use of formal legal institutions.[11]

---

[11] For both the property and debt dispute scenarios, there is no statistically significant relationship between tax compliance and firms' likeliness of turning to law enforcement and

Figure 5.3 additionally shows that with respect to both the property and debt dispute scenarios, firms reporting less than 90 percent of sales revenue for tax purposes are more likely to use courts with informal connections, turn to law enforcement or other government officials in an unofficial capacity, involve a private security agency in the dispute, or enlist the help of criminal protection rackets. The magnitude of the difference in the average likeliness ratings between tax violators and tax compliers is particularly large with respect to strategies based on corrupt coercion. For example, tax violators on average rate their likeliness of turning to bureaucrats in an unofficial capacity as much as 1.29 points higher than tax compliers. Nearly all results concerning corrupt coercion are statistically significant at the 90 percent level, and in most specifications the results are significant at the 95 or 99 percent level. With respect to private coercion, tax violators rate their likeliness of engaging a criminal protection racket nearly a full point higher than tax compliers, and these results are statistically significant at the 99 percent level across all model specifications. Tax violators also display a marginally greater propensity to turn to private security agencies.

Two points warrant additional discussion. First, the logic of demand-side barriers clearly predicts that firms with operations in the informal economy will be less likely to use formal legal institutions, but the positive correlation between demand-side barriers and firms' use of private or corrupt coercion would seem to exist only when firms substitute illegal for legal strategies. In the case of tax compliance, there appears to be clear evidence that the substitution effect across strategies is quite significant for tax evaders. Whether this is true more generally requires additional analysis, some of which is conducted in later chapters. Second, as noted at the outset of these analyses, the results of cross-sectional regressions are subject to endogeneity concerns related to reverse causation. Are firms with operations in the informal sector less likely to utilize law, or are firms that perceive little benefit to the use of formal legal institutions more likely to remain in the informal economy?[12] Evidence from

---

bureaucrats in a fully official capacity. One possible explanation is that the dividing line between official and unofficial activities is less stark with respect to law enforcement and bureaucrats, who do not necessarily have an official role to play in either of these disputes.

[12] For example, existing literature on informal economies considers the possibility that low levels of state legal capacity contribute to driving firms underground, but the evidence for this hypothesis comes from the same types of cross-sectional regressions analyzed here (e.g., Johnson et al., 2000).

surveys probing why firms leave the informal economy suggests that concerns about reverse causality should not be overstated. For instance, in a study of small Peruvian apparel firms that recently emerged from the informal sector, only 6 percent suggested that a motivating factor was to be able to "use the justice system to demand contract execution." The top reasons for reducing activities in the shadow economy, cited by a supermajority of firms, were access to more suppliers and customers, the need to obtain credit from formal sources, and the desire to avoid payment of fines (Bruce et al., 2007, p. 46). In the specific case of Russia, moreover, Chapter 4 demonstrated that there has *not* been a significant increase in state legal capacity. It follows that it is much more likely that increased tax compliance has stimulated firms' greater use of formal legal institutions, rather than the other way around.

In summary, there appears to be substantial evidence, drawn from both quantitative and qualitative sources of data, that operations in the informal economy, particularly low levels of tax compliance, create significant demand-side barriers to firms' use of formal legal institutions. Lowering these barriers is therefore essential to creating institutional demand. In the Russian case, tax administration reforms initiated by the state improved tax compliance and thereby indirectly stimulated the evolution of firms' strategies. In other cases, however, improved tax compliance resulting from economic growth, evolving cultural norms, or other factors unrelated to the state should have a similar effect on property security strategies. Moreover, low levels of tax compliance constitute just one example of operations in the informal economy that create demand-side barriers. Chapter 7 examines other examples, such as firms' efforts to bypass import tariffs and customs regulations, that create demand-side barriers for specific sectors or types of firms. More broadly, to the extent that firms engage in activities outside of the formal economy, they will be more prone to rely on private or corrupt coercion. Consequently, any factors that reduce operations in the informal sector will encourage firms to increase reliance on legal property security strategies.

5.2   Firms' Expectations and Collective Action Problems

A second significant demand-side barrier concerns firms' expectations about each other's property security strategies. In environments such as early post-Soviet Russia in which firms come to rely extensively on private and corrupt coercion, many firms may be hesitant to adopt untested strategies – and the very hesitancy of these firms may serve as a barrier to other firms' willingness to utilize formal legal institutions. For example, as a concerned owner of a Siberian import company noted, he would like to operate legally but fears the consequences: If he follows the law while others do not, then the other firm "has an advantage; he gets ahead more quickly" (Firm 51, interview, 2009). The first part of this section analyzes the various mechanisms leading economies to become stuck in unlawful equilibria in which illegal property securities remain predominant.

The second part of this section turns to the question of how economies escape vicious cycles. One way that firms' expectations about each other's strategies evolve is for key actors to explicitly organize in an effort to mitigate coordination problems: for example, by creating business associations. Of course, overt efforts to overcome coordination problems themselves entail significant collective action dilemmas, as all firms want to reap the benefits of an improved business environment but few firms want to shoulder the costs of promoting these improvements (Olson, 1965). As discussed below, there have been notable efforts on the part of Russian business associations to facilitate the transition from illegal to legal property security strategies, although the overall effectiveness of these efforts remains a matter of dispute.

In addition to organized efforts to overcome coordination problems, the same dynamics that contributed to a vicious cycle in the early post-Soviet period contributed to a shift in strategies as firms began to observe other firms' adoption of legal strategies. Like classic analyses of racial segregation, revolutions, and the adoption of national languages (Schelling, 1971; Kuran, 1989; Laitin, 1998), firms' use of property security strategies exhibits a "tipping point" dynamic in which each individual actor's beliefs about other actors' intended actions become self-fulfilling prophecies. When such dynamics are at play, an initial trend set in motion by changes, such as the improved tax compliance discussed above, can gather ongoing momentum. Once a critical mass of actors engages in new practices, firms' expectations about other firms' strategies no longer encourage firms to cling to the status quo but rather become positive forces, motivating additional firms to utilize formal legal institutions.

5.2.1 Collective Action Dilemmas as a Demand-Side Barrier

Once firms have invested in the resources required to utilize illegal strategies, they have strong incentives to continue relying on these resources. For example, in a not uncommon response to government campaigns to root out corrupt bureaucrats, a Moscow small businessmen expressed alarm: "It took me so long to establish my contacts, and I don't want to lose them" (Mereu, 2008). And even when firms have not invested in informal contacts or other similar resources, they may find the process of transitioning from unlawful to lawful practices too imposing. After all, firms may perceive benefits to effective legal institutions in the future, but they must pay the cost of transitioning to lawful practices now. These costs may be prohibitive, especially for smaller companies. They involve educating management and employees about laws, implementing compliance procedures, and, in many cases, changing established business practices.

As illegal strategies become widespread and firms come to expect that other firms will continue using such strategies, a powerful set of demand-side barriers to the use of formal legal institutions arises. Three mechanisms underlie these demand-side barriers: the perception that illegal strategies are more effective when other firms also use illegal strategies, the cost-cutting imperatives of illicit forms of competition, and the logic of retribution that emerges from violent conflicts.

The first mechanism is that of a typical coordination game. Given firms' familiarity with illegal strategies, they may perceive, rightly or wrongly, that legal strategies are not an effective response to other firms' use of corrupt or private coercion. In such circumstances, firms consider illegal strategies a best response to other firms' use of illegal strategies, *even if* they recognize that legal strategies would be a more effective strategy in a world in which the majority of other firms also utilized such strategies.[13] This dynamic was recognized by observers of Russian firms in the 1990s. As Hendley (1997, p. 243) aptly noted:

> Shifting to a reliance on universalistic rules and institutions – submitting disputes to the courts – makes sense only if the shift is made almost simultaneously by a fair majority of economic actors. Absent such a collective shift, a director is naturally reluctant to risk his trading partner going outside the legal system and bringing political pressure to bear, thereby putting the director at a disadvantage. The safer course of action is for the director to forestall that risk by appealing to his patrons. It is a classic dilemma of collective action.

In short, one underlying source of demand-side barriers pertains to firms' perceptions that legal strategies are suboptimal when the probability of facing violence or corruption is high.

---

[13] See the section "Analysis: Demand-Side Barriers and the Effectiveness of Illegal Strategies" in the Appendix D.

The second mechanism locking firms into an unlawful equilibrium takes effect when firms engage in illegal practices to cut costs. As a consequence, other firms are forced to also adopt illicit cost-cutting practices in order to compete. A small businessman and former engineer who began an import business soon after the collapse of the Soviet Union described this conundrum in detail: "I am in general an adherent to living by the law, paying taxes, doing business legally...We started as techies (*tekhnary*)... and when we imported goods, we tried to pay all taxes, and, so to say, all the rest... But as a result, the cost of our goods turned out to be higher than of those goods our competitors were selling on the street – and already making a profit. [This was] because the so-called 'black' imports, 'grey' imports, shuttle traders and so on were flourishing...Therefore, in order to survive, we were forced to also switch to these schemes" (Firm 21, interview, 2009). This downward spiral of cost-cutting has significant implications when firms seek to transition from illegal to legal business practices. A manager of a Moscow consumer electronics company interviewed by Radaev (2002, p. 47) in the early 2000s captured this logic perfectly, explaining that "It's not possible to legalize one's business by oneself. It's necessary that the rest of the market, and maybe even the whole market, be legalized. Because if 90 percent work legally, and 10 percent illegally, then we can't do anything. Everyone [i.e., consumers] will eventually run to the 10 percent, and that's that."

A final mechanism that turns interactions among firms into a powerful demand-side barrier pertains to the vicious cycles unleashed by the use of illegal strategies. Indeed, directors of private security agencies with nearly two decades of experience resolving business disputes indicate that conflicts – especially the most vicious ones – often are driven not by strategic decision making but rather by ego, desire for revenge, or other emotional factors (Security 4, interview, 2009). Along these lines, an expatriate with experience in the Russian steel industry recalled the blunt assessment offered by his firm's general director regarding the use of violence: "We don't send in guys with guns because we don't want guys with guns coming to see us" (Firm 10, interview, 2009). Summarizing results from his study of the consumer electronics sector, Radaev (2002, p. 50) again came to a similar conclusion: "Forceful methods using violence or government regulatory structures already are not considered to be the most effective. For instance, involving 'the boys' (criminal gangs) is a dangerous and expensive matter. And organizing contract inspections[14] by government agencies is of course more reliable, but this also is a double-edge sword. Any rough use of force signifies the beginning of a 'war.'"

Three distinct mechanisms, therefore, foster unlawful equilibria in which interactions among firms create demand-side barriers: the perception that illegal strategies are more effective against illegal strategies, the cost-cutting imperatives of illicit forms of competition, and the eye-for-eye logic inherent in some of the more vicious property security strategies. Survey data provide further evidence of collective action problems creating demand-side barriers. As discussed in the previous section, ideal data would allow for the tracing of firms' beliefs about other firms' strategies over time. But in the absence of ideal data, we should still expect to observe a lower propensity to use formal legal institutions among respondents who perceive that other firms rarely use legal strategies, and vice versa. To this end, the survey I conducted asked the extent to which respondents agreed with the statement: "The majority of firms with whom I conduct business do their best to follow the law." Sixty-six percent of respondents agreed with the statement; thirty-four percent did not.[15]

I again consider firms' preferred property security strategies for responding to hypothetical property and debt disputes, in which respondents rated on a 1 to 7 scale their likeliness of using a strategy. The ratings of firms' propensity to use strategies serve as the dependent variable for the analyses in Figure 5.4. As in the previous section on firms' operations in the informal economy, these analyses utilize OLS regressions. The strategies again are arrayed along the vertical axis to the left of the figure. For simple bivariate regressions, the circles represent the difference in average ratings between firms that disagree and firms that agree with the above statement that the majority of other firms are law-abiding. For model specifications with control variables, the circles represent the difference in average ratings holding constant the wide range of firm and respondent-level factors listed in the note to Figure 5.3. "Saturated"

---

[14] The term "contract inspections" (*zakaznye proverki*) refers to the bribing of government officials in order to instigate an inspection of a competitor or counterparty in a dispute, a practice discussed in Chapter 3.

[15] Respondents could choose to strongly disagree, disagree, neither disagree nor agree, agree, or strongly agree. The analysis here collapses the responses into a binary variable of those who strongly agree or agree versus those who strongly disagree, disagree, and neither disagree nor agree. The results are robust if I use an ordinal variable on a 1 to 5 scale (where 1 is strongly disagree and 5 is strongly agree) instead of the binary variable.

The figure below shows the difference between the average responses of firms which disagree that the majority of other firms are law-abiding (i.e., "pessimists") compared to those which agree (i.e., "optimists"), on a 1 to 7 scale where 1 is "very unlikely" to use a given strategy and 7 is "very likely," holding other factors constant.

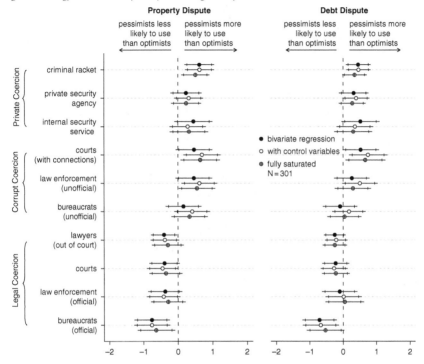

Figure 5.4 Collective Action and Propensity to Use Strategies
Note: Circles indicate point estimates from OLS regressions. Horizontal lines represent 95 percent confidence interviews; vertical tick marks represent 90 percent confidence intervals. For further details on model specifications and the wording of the property and debt dispute scenarios, see the note to Figure 5.3.

models include all control variables as well as all variables of interest in Chapters 5 through 7. For all specifications, the horizontal lines and vertical tick marks represent 95 percent and 90 percent confidence intervals, respectively.

The results are highly consistent with the hypothesis that firms' expectations about other firms' strategies serve as a demand-side barrier to the use of formal legal institutions. Firms that perceive the majority of firms with whom they do business to be lawbreakers (i.e. "pessimists") on average rate their likeliness of using courts, lawyers, or law enforcement officials in an official capacity about 0.35 to 0.45 points lower than firms that perceive their business partners to be law-abiding (i.e., "optimists"). The difference in average ratings is larger – around 0.75 points – for the use of bureaucrats in an official capacity. Just as they are less likely to utilize strategies based on legal coercion, firms that perceive other firms to be lawbreakers rate their likeliness to utilize strategies based on corrupt or private coercion, especially courts with informal connections, law enforcement in an unofficial capacity, or criminal protection rackets approximately 0.50 to 0.70 points higher than other firms. The pattern appears both with respect to the property and debt dispute scenarios, although the results are more robust in the case of the property dispute, where the difference in average ratings is statistically significant at a 90 percent (and in many cases 95 percent) level in all model specifications for 6 out of the 10 strategies.

Naturally, these regression results should be interpreted with caution, perhaps even more so than the analyses of tax compliance earlier in this chapter. In particular, firms that overestimate the lawfulness of others may also be more prone to overestimate their own use of lawful strategies and underestimate their use of strategies based on violence or corruption, a bias that could produce spurious correlations. Yet while concerns about endogeneity and spurious correlation warrant caution, both qualitative and quantitative data indicate that collective action dilemmas serve as a powerful demand-side barrier.

5.2.2 Business Associations and Evolving Property Security Strategies

Despite the powerful mechanisms underlying Russia's unlawful equilibrium in the 1990s, significant changes in firms' property security strategies have occurred. The evolution of these strategies has resulted in part from shifting expectations among firms. As noted above, in the 2010 survey I conducted, 66 percent of respondents agreed with the statement "The majority of firms with whom I conduct business do their best to follow the law." By contrast, only around 31 percent of respondents agreed with the statement "Ten years ago, the majority of firms with whom I conducted business did their best to follow the law."

One possible explanation for the reduction in demand-side barriers related to collective action dilemmas pertains to explicit efforts by firms and individuals to create organizations – business associations in particular – that can facilitate a coordinated transition from illegal to legal strategies. As the owner of a medium-sized Moscow business explained, it was precisely the illicit cost-cutting logic described above that motivated him to form a business association: "I wasn't interested in working, so to say, in an uncivilized market. Therefore, all my efforts, when I understood that due to our principles we were losing income, that we were going to be destroyed, [because] we don't pay bribes and so on, well...The only solution I saw was to try and consolidate entrepreneurs like me...and therefore I tried to do this and I am doing it in different spheres of activity, including in my own market" (Firm 28, interview, 2009). Such associations can shift firms' expectations about other firms' property security strategies in several ways. First, they can offer direct legal and protection services, encouraging members to utilize legal strategies. Second, they can vet members, excluding those with unsavory reputations and transforming business association membership into a signal of a firm's trustworthiness. And third, they can play a significant role in the transmission of information, providing a broader perspective on economy-wide trends to firms that are considering the adoption of legal strategies but that are wary about other firms' ongoing practices.

Following the collapse of the Soviet Union, numerous business associations appeared. However, the vast majority of these associations were created by government officials to maintain control over firms during the process of privatization or to lobby for the interests of firms still owned by the state. With few exceptions, primarily the Union of Russian Industrialists and Entrepreneurs (RSPP), business associations during this period played a minimal role, both with respect to politics and in terms of property security strategies (Hanson and Teague, 2005; Markus, 2007). Hendley's 1997 survey found, for example, that less than 5 percent of firms turned to business associations for help resolving conflicts with suppliers or customers (2000, pp. 635–636); similarly, less than 10 percent of firms in Yakovlev et al.'s (2004, p. 71) 2002 survey had used a business association to help resolve an economic dispute. Nearly a decade later, the findings of my 2010 survey seem – at least at first glance – to indicate that little has changed. Only 12 percent of firms reported using a business association during the previous three years to resolve a security-related problem.

Despite these indicators, there is evidence that the role of business associations is growing. First, beginning in the late 1990s, analysts noted an influx of firms into business associations. Pyle's 2003 survey of 1353 enterprises across 48 regions of Russia found that approximately 35 percent of firms were business association members; in a more detailed follow-up survey of 606 firms, he concluded that the number of firms joining associations in the early Putin period (2000–2003) was nearly twice that of the late Yeltsin period (1996–1999) (Pyle, 2005a, pp. 17, 22–23).[16] The fact that a significant percentage of firms hold membership in business associations indicates that firms see some value in these organizations.

Certainly, larger associations exist primarily as lobbying machines. In the late 1990s, for example, Russia's most powerful business tycoons turned RSPP into a tool for promoting banking, currency, administrative, judicial, and other institutional reforms (Hanson and Teague, 2005). Lobbying, however, is not necessarily the primary goal of associations representing smaller firms. One significant aim of OPORA, the association of small businesses formed in 2001, has been to protect its members' property rights. In 2003, OPORA created a Bureau for the Oversight of Entrepreneurs' Rights, which offers free legal advice and a hotline for firms facing unwarranted inspections by government officials. The head of the Bureau explained that the project was undertaken after OPORA representatives announced in a Moscow newspaper that they would provide several days worth of free legal advice for small businesses by phone. After their phone banks were flooded with calls, OPORA decided that the unexpectedly high demand for such services warranted a permanent Bureau (author interview, 9 April 2008).

OPORA's experience is not an isolated incident. The Center for International Private Enterprises (CIPE) has documented legal service hotlines provided by local and regional business associations throughout Russia, as well as other innovative efforts to thwart legal violations, particularly against state actors. In Krasnodar, for instance, a coalition of business associations set up "quick response teams" consisting of coalition members, lawyers, and representatives of the tax authorities, police, local administration, FSB, and procuracy with the aim of responding to business complaints about illegal actions by state agencies (CIPE, 2006, pp. 7–9). In line with anecdotal evidence, Pyle's 2003 survey discovered that on average, firms' rated the need to receive "informational, legal, and consulting services" as the most important reason to join a business association; they rated "protection from illegitimate government interference" as the third-most-important reason (Pyle, 2011, p. 13).[17]

---

[16] Forty-one percent of respondents in my survey report being a member of a business association.

[17] For a comprehensive analysis of business associations' role in combatting predatory threats from state officials in post-communist countries, see Duvanova (2013).

And as further evidence that business associations play a key role in property security, Pyle (2011) found that business association members are more likely than nonmembers to appeal illegitimate government inspections to a court or another government body. In other work, Pyle (2005b) found also that business associations play a role in information flows, increasing the chance that a firm will learn of disputes in which its suppliers or customers are involved, particularly when these partners are located in other cities. Finally, in addition to providing legal advice and helping members defend property rights, business associations have been one source of private arbitration services (*treteiskii sud*), providing a non-state forum for resolving business conflicts. For example, in 1992 the Chamber of Trade and Industry (TPP) created one of the first courts of private arbitration, which remains active today.[18]

Despite some evidence of success, the extent to which business associations contributed to the evolution of Russian firms' expectations about each other's strategies should not be overstated. The challenges of collective action are well-known. In particular, when the benefits of mobilizing collectively spill over to those who do not actively participate or pay the costs of such mobilization, then firms and individuals will face incentives to reap these benefits without contributing to collective action, a phenomena frequently referred to as "free riding" (Olson, 1965). Accordingly, the effectiveness and influence of business associations face limitations, at least with respect to property security. As noted above, relatively few firms cited the use of business associations to resolve security-related issues even in my 2010 survey. Yakovlev et al. (2014, p. 177) in a recent case study analysis of business associations' efforts to reduce predatory behavior on the part of the state came to a similar conclusion, noting that throughout much of the 2000s "examples of successful collective action of business interests against the predatory state were few and far between." Meanwhile, Markus (2012) found no relationship between business association membership and firms' perceptions of threats to their property rights. In line with the findings of these earlier studies, regression analyses similar to those discussed earlier in this chapter found no systematic correlation between business association membership and firms' propensity to turn to formal legal institutions when facing property and debt disputes. It follows that additional factors must have contributed to the shift in firms' expectations about other firms' strategies.

---

[18] The history of the TPP's private arbitration court can be found at www.tpprf-arb. ru/ru/tsec. For additional examples, see Sevastyanov and Tsyplenkova (2007, p. 65).

5.2.3   Tipping Points and Evolving Property Security Strategies

Both the qualitative and quantitative data discussed above in Section 5.2.1 provide evidence that (1) individual firms in part choose property security strategies based on their expectations of other firms' strategies and (2) many firms consider illegal strategies more effective when a critical mass of other firms also utilizes illegal strategies, just as they consider legal strategies to be more effective when a critical mass of other firms utilizes legal strategies. It follows that while firms' expectations can create a demand-side barrier to the use of formal legal institutions, there is a flip side to the logic of vicious cycles: If an exogenous shock induces a substantial number of firms to adopt legal strategies, then the adoption of legal strategies may become a self-sustaining phenomenon.

The logic of such cycles resembles that of a *tipping point* model. Tipping point logic was famously utilized by Schelling (1971) to elucidate the dynamics of neighborhood segregation. If white residents' willingness to live in a neighborhood depends on a critical mass of other white residents, then once a sufficient number of nonwhite residents purchase homes in the region, white residents' expectations about other residents' plans to leave become self-fulfilling. Kuran (1989) provided another widely cited example of tipping points in his analysis of revolutions. Since the danger of protest in an authoritarian regime declines as the size of the protest increases, protesters' willingness to participate depends critically on other protesters turning out. Once potential protesters observe a critical mass of revolutionaries in the streets, a "cascade" of additional protestors may gather.

The evolution of property security strategies most closely resembles Laitin's (1998) analysis of language identity. Like law, the value of language depends on a critical mass of other actors *using* the language. If a relatively well-assimilated minority group seeks to reestablish national identity through the promotion of a local language, it must somehow convince individuals that a sufficient number of other individuals will also adopt the local language in professional and educational settings. As difficult as it may be to persuade any specific individual to be a first mover, once a critical mass is reached those who have not yet supported the movement face strong incentives to join, or else face the prospects of becoming outsiders unable to take advantage of the local language community. Such systems tend toward two stable equilibria in which all actors speak one language or the other (or for the purposes of the present study, use either illegal or legal strategies), as well as one unstable equilibrium that represents the "tipping point" between the two stable equilibria.

These dynamics of a tipping point game are depicted in Figure 5.5a. On the horizontal axis, the figure shows the percentage of firms utilizing legal strategies. On the vertical axis, it displays the "payoffs" to using legal or illegal strategies. The solid line labeled "legal strategies" depicts the payoffs to using legal strategies as a function of the strategies other firms employ; the dotted line labeled "illegal strategies" depicts the payoffs to using illegal strategies, also as a function of the strategies other firms employ. In accordance with the logic discussed above, if all firms are using illegal strategies, the value of legal strategies is very low, as indicated by the solid line's location far below the dotted line. A few firms adopting legal strategies hardly change the value of using law, as indicated by the fact that the payoff to using legal strategies increases only minimally as additional firms turn to law. Moreover, firms that foolhardily turned to formal legal institutions in such an environment would find themselves consistently at a disadvantage relative to firms employing violence and corruption. They would either go out of business or be forced to turn back to illegal strategies, and the economy would tend back toward an equilibrium in which most firms avoid formal legal institutions.

By contrast, when a large number of firms switch strategies, the value to using legal strategies rises. At the point where the solid and dotted lines intersect, the expected value of using illegal strategies is equal to the expected value of using legal strategies. The percentage of firms using legal strategies such that illegal and legal strategies produce equal payoffs is the critical mass of firms at which the economy "tips." To the right of the tipping point, the expected value of using legal strategies is greater than the expected value of using illegal strategies, as depicted by the solid line's location above the dotted line. Once an economy reaches this point, firms that are still relying on illegal strategies find themselves at a disadvantage. They will either go out of business or adopt legal strategies, and the economy will tend toward a new equilibrium in which nearly all firms utilize formal legal institutions.

Of critical importance for understanding the evolution of property security strategies is how firms react to changes in the relative effectiveness of illegal and legal strategies. Consider the example of increased tax compliance discussed earlier in this chapter. As a prominent demand-side barrier – firms' operations in the informal economy – declines, legal strategies become relatively more effective *regardless* of the number of firms already relying on formal legal institutions. In Figure 5.5b, this

(a) Original Tipping Point

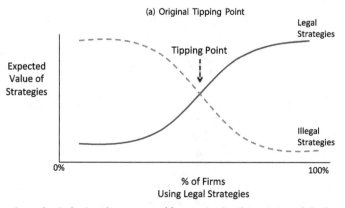

The horizontal axis depicts the percent of firms using legal strategies, while the vertical axis depicts the expected value of each strategy. The solid (dotted) line represents the expected value of using legal (illegal) strategies, as a function of the percent of firms in the economy using legal strategies.

(b) Parameter Shift Creates New Tipping Point

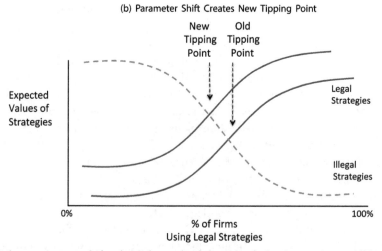

When a parameter shift reduces demand-side barriers, the legal strategies payoff function shifts to the left. A new tipping point appears to the left of the original tipping point, indicating that a smaller critical mass of firms using law is required for the economy to "tip" toward an equilibrium in which all firms use law.

Figure 5.5   Graphical Depiction of Tipping Point Game

change is indicated by the leftward shift of the solid line, the payoff function for using legal strategies. The consequence of this shift is that the new tipping point is to the left of the original tipping point. In substantive terms, the critical mass of firms using law needed to inspire other firms to adopt legal strategies is now smaller. For an economy that was initially short of this critical mass, the removal of a demand-side barrier could potentially set the economy on a virtuous cycle toward greater reliance on formal legal institutions, even if the initial number of firms adopting legal strategies as a result of improved tax compliance is relatively small.

Evidence from in-depth interviews as well as sectoral studies conducted by Russian researchers is consistent with the tipping point interpretation of the evolution of firms' expectations about each other's strategies: Parameter shifts that have reduced demand-side barriers or decreased the relative effectiveness of illegal strategies have induced firms to reevaluate their strategies. The case of the small business owner of a long-running import operation cited in Section 5.2.1 serves as a vivid illustrative example. As described above, this owner fell prey to pressures in the 1990s to adopt illicit practices in order to remain competitive. But over time as illegal strategies' effectiveness declined due to the rising costs of bribery, his willingness to continue relying on corruption evolved: "the costs of these 'gray' [i.e., semilegal] schemes grew, maybe not so much that it became economically profitable, but at least that it was not so harmful to work legally (*vbelyu*). When such an opportunity arose, we started to do this. We switched a large part [of our business] to legal schemes" (Firm 21, interview, 2009). Meanwhile, Radaev's (2002) study of the Russian consumer electronics sector, also cited in Section 5.2.1 above, provides evidence of how initial shifts in strategies can gain momentum, contributing to a virtuous cycle. The analysis earlier in the chapter described consumer electronic firms' unwillingness to legalize operations unless a large segment of their sector abandoned illicit practices simultaneously. Recognizing the demand-side barriers created by this dynamic, Radaev probed further to understand how a widespread shift was occurring despite such barriers. He found that once the process of legalization was underway in the sector, firms were acutely aware of changing tendencies and consistently reconsidered their best choice of strategies in response to a changing environment: "Directors [of firms] know each other, they have followed the activities of their 'neighbors' for many years and, accordingly, they have a good conception of what to expect from them, and what is better to not count on" (Radaev, 2002, p. 48).

To be clear, the tipping point metaphor presented here is a simple heuristic device that abstracts from important real-world considerations. Most notably, in the real world different types of firms employ certain strategies with differing degrees of effectiveness, which is likely to produce multiple tipping points unique to specific sectors, regions, or types of firms. But while leaning too heavily on the tipping point framework is ill-advised, the metaphor nevertheless offers two sets of important insights. First, it helps make sense of how firm by firm, choice by choice, the demand-side barrier formed by firms' expectations of each other's strategies has begun to topple. This evolution was due not only to business associations' coordinated efforts to encourage the adoption of legal strategies, but also to individual firms' reconsideration of their portfolio of property security strategies as the relative effectiveness of these strategies shifted. Second, the framework clarifies the interactive effects between firms' expectations of each other's strategies and exogenous shocks that alter strategies' effectiveness, such as the improvements in tax compliance discussed above and the additional factors that are the subject of Chapter 6. Exogenous shocks have a direct effect on property security strategies, inducing many firms to reconsider their use of illegal strategies. But they also have an indirect and ongoing effect as other firms adapt to the initial wave of changes that such shocks set in motion.

5.3   Conclusion

Returning to the analytical framework developed throughout this book, three variables influence firms' choices about how to secure property: state legal capacity, demand-side barriers, and the effectiveness of illegal strategies. This chapter has examined the ways in which demand-side barriers, the behaviors or beliefs at the level of firms and individuals that lead these actors to avoid formal legal institutions, can significantly impede firms' use of legal strategies. Two types of demand-side barriers are particularly prevalent. First, operations in the informal economy, such as low levels of tax compliance, can reduce firms' willingness to utilize formal legal institutions out of concerns that their own violations of the law will be exposed. Second, firms' expectations about each other's strategies can create demand-side barriers, in part because firms perceive illegal strategies to be a more effective response to other firms' use of illegal strategies. In such circumstances, economies can become locked in vicious cycles in which reliance on violence and corruption persists. In the case of post-Soviet Russia, only once tax compliance improved and firms' expectations about other firms' willingness to use law evolved did the use of formal legal institutions increase. Notably, this decline in demand-side barriers helps explain why Russian firms increasingly adopted legal strategies even in the absence of heightened state legal capacity.

Demand-side barriers are, however, only one of the framework's key variables explaining firms' willingness (or lack thereof) to utilize legal strategies. The effectiveness of illegal alternatives to formal legal institutions also plays a critical role. The next chapter examines several key factors that determine the effectiveness of illegal strategies, thereby influencing firms' choice of property security strategies.

6

The Effectiveness of Illegal Strategies

This chapter examines the final explanatory variable in the framework introduced in Chapter 2: the effectiveness of illegal strategies. Just as the removal of demand-side barriers encourages firms to utilize formal legal institutions, decreasing the effectiveness of illegal strategies provides incentives for firms to reduce reliance on violence and corruption. Underlying the effectiveness of illegal strategies are two key factors. First, the effectiveness of illegal strategies depends on transaction costs – the costs of acquiring information, negotiating, and enforcing a transaction – relative to the transaction costs incurred when using legal strategies. Second, the effectiveness of illegal strategies depends on the risk of sanctions. These sanctions include not only the straightforward risk of physical harm and criminal prosecution but also the risk of lost investment opportunities resulting from a reputation for illicit practices. As the transaction costs or risks of sanctions associated with illegal strategies rise, firms rely less on private or corrupt coercion.

Numerous factors affect transaction costs and the risk of sanctions, but the focus in this chapter is on three particularly key trends: (1) the expansion of firms' time horizons, which limits owners' and managers' willingness to engage in risky strategies; (2) the development of the financial sector, which reduces the size of the cash-based economy and thus increases the transaction costs of illegal strategies; and (3) integration into the international economy, which increases both the transaction costs associated with and the risk of sanctions resulting from illegal strategies.

While the logic underlying each of these mechanisms is applicable to countries throughout the developing world, the specific forms in which trends manifest may differ from country to country. For instance, in the case of Russia, I illustrate how expanding time horizons reduced firms' willingness to utilize risky strategies by analyzing the consolidation of ownership in privatized firms. The process by which Soviet enterprises were privatized created firms with highly dispersed ownership structures, resulting in limited oversight of managers and insufficient protections for minority shareholders. With massive assets up for grabs, the ensuing ownership battles placed a premium on speed and ruthlessness. Under such conditions, managers and owners cared little about a clean reputation or the stability of the investment climate, and therefore willingly incurred the risks associated with illegal strategies. By contrast, once dominant owners emerged and consolidated control over their assets, short-term asset grabs lost their appeal, and long-term investments became lucrative. Accordingly, owners' time horizons expanded, shifting their calculations of risk. Illegal strategies that could destroy a firm's reputation, or potentially destabilize the investment climate as a whole, came to be perceived as unnecessarily risky – and therefore less effective.

While the consolidation of ownership reduced firms' reliance on violence and coercion by extending their time horizons, the development of the Russian financial sector reduced illegal strategies' effectiveness by increasing the transaction costs incurred when using illicit alternatives to formal legal institutions. Throughout the 1990s, firms relied extensively on barter or cash transactions, due in part to a highly underdeveloped banking system. In a typical example, a small business owner in Moscow, an importer of high-end car accessories, related how even in the late 1990s he conducted the majority of transactions not merely in cash – but in US dollars, rather than in Russian rubles. But by the mid-2000s, the situation had changed dramatically. The majority of transactions were now conducted not only in rubles, but via banks. Illegal activities, the business owner explained, depend on access to off-the-books cash. After all, one does not pay a bribe with a bank check (Firm 1, interview, 2009). This is not to say that firms' reliance on the banking system precludes illicit practices. Sophisticated financial schemes involving shell companies, sometimes abetted by the banks themselves, can produce slush funds for financing unsavory tactics. But forcing firms to engage in additional schemes when resorting to violence or corruption raises the transaction costs of utilizing illegal property security strategies, making them less effective.

Finally, the integration of Russian firms into the global economy played an influential role in the evolution of property security strategies. As firms sought foreign investment, they allotted more attention to the risks of illegal strategies, fearing that the use of violence or corruption could undermine their reputations and pose a threat to investment. Concurrently, as multinational corporations bought up Russian firms, new internal regulations imposed constraints on lower-level managers' discretion to use violence or corruption. Integration into the international economy thus had a dual effect, both raising transaction costs and increasing the risks of using illegal strategies.

The focus here, as in the previous chapter, is on transformations over time. The topic of distinctions across firms is then taken up at length in the subsequent chapter.

6.1   Time Horizons and the Consolidation of Ownership

Time horizons play a prominent role in the literature on property rights. But in line with these studies' overall focus on the state, the primary area of concern is with the time horizons of kings, dictators, presidents, and other *rulers*. As Levi (1989, p. 32) writes, rulers with short time horizons "will be less concerned with promoting the conditions of economic growth and increased revenue over time than with extracting available revenue even at the risk of discouraging output" (see also Olson, 1993). Less well-recognized in analyses of property rights is the similar role that time horizons play for firms, particularly in environments in which economic actors face a choice between productive investment and rent-seeking. When engaged in rent-seeking activities such as winning tenders for privatized firms at below market prices, transferring company assets to personal offshore accounts, or speculating on risky government securities, managers of firms place a minimal value on a clean reputation and overall stability in the business world. The goal is to grab as much as possible, as quickly as possible – and if illegal strategies are required to acquire or protect assets, then the risks involved in using such strategies may be worth taking.

By contrast, when seeking longer-term profits through productive investments, a firm's calculus changes. The use of illegal strategies creates the risk of undermining firms' reputations and threatens to destabilize the overall business climate, reducing the value of investments. In short, as firms adopt longer time horizons, the relative effectiveness of using violence and corruption falls.

6.1.1   *Dispersed Ownership and Short Horizons*

The dispersed ownership structures that resulted from the privatization of Soviet industry – the largest reallocation of assets in human history – created incentives for owners and managers to focus on short-term accumulation of assets, using whatever means necessary, legal or otherwise. In the brief four-year span between 1992 and the end of 1995, over 100,000 small enterprises and nearly 18,000 medium and large firms were transferred to private owners (Blasi et al., 1997, p. 189). An asset transfer of such a scale set off a vicious struggle over ownership and control of enterprises. These struggles were exacerbated by the method of privatization used.[1] Reformers aimed to conduct privatization rapidly to make a return to the Soviet command economy impossible, but they faced a population deprived of capital. To address this problem, and to build popular support for reforms, Yeltsin's reform team created a program that would swiftly transfer assets to Russian workers and citizens. Citizens received vouchers exchangeable for shares in privatizing enterprises, and workers received privatization accounts and other means of financial support allowing them to become shareholders in their place of employment.

The privatization program resulted in highly fractured ownership structures that were spread across workers, managers, investment funds, individuals, and firms with cross-holdings. Workers in particular acquired significant shares, leading to widespread *de jure* employee ownership (as seen in Table 6.1). In reality, however, managers pressured workers into selling their shares or turning over *de facto* control rights. Entrenched inside owners further complicated the problem of dispersed ownership, as managers fought to avoid restructuring that could increase outside ownership.

Despite insiders' resistance, the financial crisis of 1998 instigated a significant transformation in ownership structures. Tycoons who weathered the crisis acquired assets from failing enterprises or competing business groups. Shaken by the economic collapse, owners placed increased value on longer-term stability. Meanwhile, the ruble's depreciation made the manufacturing sector competitive for the first time since communism's collapse, increasing the value of investment in productive assets. By the early 2000s, a fundamental ownership shake-up had occurred. Outsiders had on average acquired a majority of shares, while insiders held just over one-third, as seen in Table 6.1. This increase in outside ownership was closely linked to owners' efforts to acquire a dominating share of enterprise assets, in part by reducing the influence of managers, whose average share of ownership dropped significantly by the turn of the decade (Radygin and Arkhipov, 2001, p. 15).

---

[1] For an overview of the privatization process, see Åslund (1995, ch. 7) and Blasi et al. (1997, ch. 1).

Table 6.1   *Ownership Structure of Russian Industrial Firms*

Type of Owner	Avg. Share				
Year	1994	1999a	1999b	2000	2002
Insiders	49.1	44.4	25.0	31.6	36.4
Managers	10.6	14.8	9.4	7.2	17.0
Workers	35.9	29.2	28.5	20.4	15.7
Other	–	–	4.2	4.0	3.7
Outsiders	17.5	32.7	46.5	55.6	55.4
Legal entities	11.1	19.6	21.4	35.7	26.5
Individuals	4.1	9.2	22.2	15.2	27.4
Foreigners	1.5	3.2	2.9	4.7	1.5
State	33.0	22.6	11.4	12.8	8.2

Sources: 1994 and 1999a data from Biletskiy et al. (2001), as cited in Lazareva et al. (2007, p. 5); 1999b and 2002 data from Radygin et al. (2004, p. 290); 2000 data from Radygin and Arkhipov (2001, p. 15).[2]

These efforts to consolidate assets were successful. Table 6.2 vividly depicts the extent of this ownership consolidation. Following privatization, less than 15 percent of Russian industrial firms had a shareholder with a majority stake. By the mid-2000s, approximately three-fourths of firms had such a shareholder.

6.1.2   Consolidated Ownership and Longer Time Horizons

This concentration of ownership transformed owners' incentive structure by increasing the impact of sanctions that could result from using illegal strategies, thereby reducing the effectiveness of property security strategies based on violence or corruption. With undisputed control of enterprises, owners could now reap gains from long-term investments without fear that competing owners or asset-stripping managers would dilute their profits (Boone and Rodionov, 2002; Yakovlev et al., 2004, ch. 3). Longer-term investment required stability and predictability, and

---

[2] Comparison of surveys from different sources requires caution, as there are differences in sample size and composition across the studies. Nevertheless, while these figures should be considered a rough approximation, existing sources are unanimous in their assessment of a significant trend toward outside ownership and ownership concentration in privatized firms from the late 1990s through the early 2000s.

Table 6.2   *Percent of Russian Industrial Firms with Large Shareholder*

Largest Shareholder Owns at Least:	1995	1998a	1998b	2001	2002	2004	2005
25%	44.5	46.8	55.2	67.1	42.0	75.0	83.0
50%	14.8	19.6	32.0	39.5	19.0	48.0	75.0

Sources: Data for 1995 and 1998a are from a Higher School of Economics (HSE) survey conducted in 1999, as cited in Dolgopyatova (2005, p. 7); data for 1998b and 2001 are from an HSE survey conducted in 2002, as cited in Dolgopyatova (2005, p. 7); data for 2002 and 2004 are from IFC, as cited by Lazareva et al. (2007, p. 6); data for 2005 are from Dolgopyatova (2010, pp. 85–86).

owners perceived that violence and corruption could undermine both of these. As Radaev (2002, p. 44) found in his study of the Russian consumer electronics industry in the early 2000s, "Today a definitive reevaluation of risk is occurring among leading players in the market – risk is beginning to be perceived as more painful. The reason is not only possible losses as a consequence of fines and confiscation of goods, and not only entrepreneurs' personal peace of mind ... The fact of the matter is that reducing certain types of risks is necessary in order to increase the general activities and successful promotion of a company's brand. The possible impact in the case of ... inspections threatens the growth strategy [*strategiya razvitiya*] and the reputation of the business."

None other than the tycoon Vladimir Potanin, one of the most prominent Russian oligarchs of the 1990s, expressed similar logic soon after the turn of the century. In 2003 he declared:

> The "corporate wars" had shown that the damage caused by dubious methods in competition exceeded the potential benefits, even for the "winners." ... The positive developments were achieved after most large business groups completed the consolidation of their assets and the owners became interested in improving the quality of management and raising external financing ... Effective Russian companies are interested in having a new business climate in the country, based on civilized rules of business and new ethics of relations (Potanin, 2003).

The extent to which this process of creating "civilized rules of business" altered property security strategies is highly apparent in sectoral studies of the Russian economy. According to Radaev (2002, p. 49), for example, firms in the consumer electronics sector began in the early 2000s to distinguish between business partners that "work according to the rules" (*rabotat po pravilam*) and those that do not. Drawing on interviews with firm managers to parse the meaning behind this phrase, Radaev identified several key components of these emerging rules, two of which directly related to property security strategies. Firms that work according to the rules "reject the use of contract inspections (*zakaznye proverki*) against competitors," a reference to the hiring of state officials to investigate other firms (see Chapter 3), and additionally display a "readiness to resolve problems at the negotiating table." Beyond the direct impact of the rule-building process on property security strategies, Radaev's findings provide additional evidence regarding dominant owners' concerns for stability: A third critical component of "working according to the rules" includes an effort to "'not spoil the market' (*ne portit rynok*), that is, to not destabilize it through one's actions."[3]

Consolidation of ownership also changed owners' incentive structure in another way. Having acquired significant and valuable assets, owners no longer wanted to wage battles using strategies that entailed the risk of physical harm or incarceration. As succinctly stated by a prominent bankruptcy lawyer in Moscow, the mentality of today's businesspeople – in contrast to the 1990s – is that "You can risk in business, but not in life" (Lawyer 3, interview, 2009). Unlike the initial period after the collapse of communism, by the 2000s, businesspeople had significant assets to lose, which reduced their willingness to endure the risk of sanctions associated with illegal strategies. Radaev (2002, p. 44) again came to similar conclusions: "In interviews directors [of firms] frequently talk about how they invested and continue to invest in their business in Russia, how their families are located here, and how they have no intentions of leaving. Therefore there is a more general interest in stability and steady development not only of their firm, but of the Russian economy as a whole."

Survey data provide further evidence of the relationships between ownership consolidation and property security strategies. As discussed in the previous chapter, in an ideal world it would be feasible to trace firms' strategies over time, measuring how these strategies changed as ownership structures evolved. In the absence of such data, cautious inference from cross-sectional data serves as an imperfect substitute. For example, if the hypothesis that consolidation of ownership increases the risks associated with using illegal property security strategies is correct, then

---

[3] Although Radaev suggests that this rule refers primarily to the avoidance of price wars, the formulation of this rule speaks to the logic described above – after consolidation, firms seek stability.

privatized firms with consolidated ownership should be less likely than other privatized firms to use corrupt or private coercion.

In the survey I conducted, respondents were asked, "Does your firm have a single owner or an owner with a controlling packet of shares?" Of the 301 respondent firms, 78 were privatized firms. Of these, 40 – approximately 51 percent – report consolidated ownership. I then reconsidered the data described in Chapter 3 regarding firms' preferred strategies for resolving property and debt disputes (see Table 3.3). Respondents were given two hypothetical scenarios, one in which another firm seeks to acquire control of some of their firms' assets and another in which a business partner refuses to pay an overdue debt. The respondents were then asked to rate on a scale of 1 to 7, where 1 means "very unlikely" and 7 means "very likely," how likely they would be to use each possible strategy to resolve the dispute (e.g., go to court, seek help through informal connections with bureaucrats, hire a private security agency, etc.).

Firms' ratings of their likeliness to use a given strategy to resolve a property or debt dispute serve as the dependent variable in the OLS regression analyses presented in Figure 6.1.[4] The strategies are arrayed along the vertical axis to the left of the figure. The figure shows results from three model specifications. For simple bivariate regressions, the circles represent the difference in average ratings between privatized firms with consolidated ownership and privatized firms without consolidated ownership.[5] For regressions including control variables, the circles represent the difference in average ratings holding constant a wide range of firm and respondent-level factors, including the firm's age, number of employees, financial health, sector, city of location, and ownership structure (i.e., whether or not the firm has foreign or government shareholders); the respondent's age, gender, job description, and education; and whether or not the firm had recently faced disputes or engaged in litigation. Finally, the most demanding specifications—which, as noted in the previous chapter, I refer to as "saturated models"—include all control

---

[4] These and other results in this chapter are also robust when using ordered logit regressions in place of OLS. See the Online Appendix.

[5] More specifically, to assess the effect of consolidated ownership on privatized firms' strategies, I interacted a dummy variable measuring consolidation (with a value of 1 for consolidated ownership and 0 otherwise) with a dummy variable for privatization (1 if privatized, 0 if the firm was created de novo). The point estimates depicted by circles in Figure 6.1 represent the marginal effects of consolidated ownership in privatized firms, calculated as the sum of the coefficients on the consolidation variable and the interaction term. Standard errors are calculated per Brambor et al. (2006).

The figure below shows the difference between the average responses of privatized firms with consolidated ownership and privatized firms without consolidated ownership, on a 1 to 7 scale where 1 is "very unlikely" and 7 is "very likely," holding other factors constant.

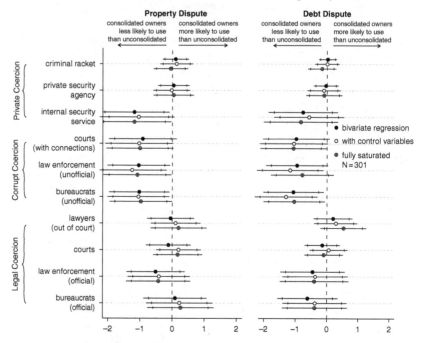

Figure 6.1   Ownership Consolidation and Propensity to Use Strategies
Note: Circles indicate the marginal effect of ownership consolidation in privatized firms, estimated using OLS regressions (see footnote 5 for further details). Horizontal lines represent 95 percent confidence interviews, and vertical tick marks represent 90 percent confidence intervals. For further details on model specifications and the wording of the property and debt dispute scenarios see the note to Figure 5.3.

variables as well as all variables of interest in Chapters 5 through 7. For all specifications, horizontal lines and vertical tick marks represent 95 percent and 90 percent confidence intervals, respectively. (Regression tables for all analyses conducted in this chapter are included in Appendix G or in the Online Appendix.)

Figure 6.1 shows that the analyses produce results consistent with the claim that ownership consolidation in privatized firms provides incentives for these firms to avoid illegal strategies. This is particularly apparent with respect to strategies based on corrupt coercion, such as using informal connections in court or turning to law enforcement or other government officials in a private capacity. With respect to both property and debt disputes, privatized firms with consolidated ownership rate their likeliness of using these strategies approximately a full point lower on the 7-point scale than privatized firms without consolidated ownership. Even controlling for the wide range of firm and respondent-level factors listed above, these estimates are statistically significant at the 90 or 95 percent confidence level in all model specifications involving strategies of corrupt coercion, despite the fact that the estimates are relatively imprecise, perhaps because there are only 78 privatized firms in the sample. In terms of private coercion, the relationship between ownership consolidation and privatized firms' propensity to use internal security services is similar to the relationship between consolidation and privatized firms' reliance on corrupt coercion, although the findings are statistically significant only for the property dispute scenario. While a similar effect is not as apparent for other strategies based on private coercion, such as turning to private security agencies or criminal protection rackets, this most likely is because the ownership consolidation hypothesis pertains specifically to privatized firms. These are larger than other firms in the sample (the average number of employees in privatized firms is 664 compared to a sample average of 390), and larger firms in general are relatively less likely to utilize private security agencies or turn to criminal protection rackets.[6]

In summary, ownership consolidation in privatized firms has lengthened firms' time horizons, as owners have reoriented toward longer-term investment strategies that require a respectable business reputation and a stable business environment. Accordingly, the risks that firms perceive in the use of violence and corruption have risen, reducing the relative effectiveness of illegal property security strategies. Both qualitative and quantitative evidence indicate that as the effectiveness of illegal strategies has declined, firms have become less willing to employ strategies based on private or corrupt coercion.

---

[6] As discussed in Chapter 5, the direct effect of falling demand-side barriers is to make firms more willing to utilize formal legal institutions. By contrast, the direct effect of decreased effectiveness of illegal alternatives is to make firms less likely to utilize illegal strategies. Whether decreased effectiveness of illegal strategies also should make firms more likely to use legal strategies depends, at least in part, on the extent to which illegal and legal strategies are substitutes, which is largely an empirical question. In the case of ownership consolidation presented here, there is no evidence of a substitution effect. Firms with consolidated ownership are neither more nor less likely to utilize legal property security strategies.

6.2   Financial Sector Development

Scholars and policymakers, particularly in recent years, have produced considerable evidence that an effective financial sector contributes to economic development. These studies have focused on factors such as the financial sector's role in providing information about possible investments, improving corporate governance, managing risk, mobilizing savings, and reducing the cost of exchanging goods and services (see, e.g., Levine, 2005). However, the potential impact of financial sector development on firms' propensity to rely on violence and corruption has received minimal attention. This section traces the ways in which Russian firms' growing reliance on the financial sector – and the banking industry in particular – reduced the effectiveness of illegal strategies, both by increasing the risk of sanctions and also by raising the associated transaction costs. In turn, the declining effectiveness of illegal strategies contributed to firms' unwillingness to rely on private or corrupt coercion.

In the 1990s, Russian firms rarely relied on the banking sector. They conducted sales and purchases primarily in cash. To the extent that investment occurred during this recessionary period, firms relied on retained earnings rather than bank financing. It was not until the banking sector developed in the early 2000s that transactions began to flow through the banking system and firms began to seek loans. The switch from cash to bank transactions reduced firms' access to off-the-books cash, which forced firms engaged in illegal activity to develop creative schemes to hide the paper trail that bank transactions leave behind. In other words, as firms increasingly conducted sales and purchases through the banking system, the transaction costs of using illegal strategies multiplied. Meanwhile, the vetting undergone by banks in order to receive loans increased the risks associated with using illegal strategies, which further encouraged firms to avoid violence and corruption.

6.2.1   An Underdeveloped Banking System and the Cash Economy

The banking system that emerged from the Soviet command economy was poorly equipped for financing a modern market economy. As the Soviet Union collapsed and private enterprise became legal, the number of banks skyrocketed, reaching more than 2400 by 1994, far above the OECD average (OECD, 2009, p. 99). Yet few of these banks performed the legitimate role of financial institutions. Banks instead functioned like corporate treasuries for financial industrial groups (FIGs) or other large

Table 6.3 *Bank Transactions, Deposits, and Loans, 1999–2008*

	1999	2000	2001	2002	2003	2004	2005	2006	2007	2008
Number of transactions conducted through the Russian payment system (millions)	–	–	63	738	855	992	1117	1673	2456	2782
Deposits by non-financial enterprises (% of GDP)	1.3	1.6	2.4	2.3	2.1	1.8	2.6	3.5	4.7	8.5
Credits extended to non-financial enterprises (% of GDP)	9.9	11.0	13.7	15.3	18.0	19.2	19.7	–	–	–

Sources: Data for transactions and deposits from Bank of Russia's Bulletin of Bank Statistics, various years. Data on credits for 1998–1999 are from Tompson (2004, p. 6) and for 2000–2005 are from Noel et al. (2006, p. 28).

companies, which in a low-trust environment sought to avoid arm's-length transactions with outside financial institutions. Since banks had the right to deal in foreign exchange, FIGs also valued them as a tool to move capital abroad or launder money. Despite the large number of banks, a handful of institutions dominated the banking system. In the late 1990s, approximately two-thirds of all banking assets belonged to just 30 banks; four-fifths of all banking assets were located in Moscow-based institutions. As seen in Table 6.3, loans to enterprises were almost non-existent, particularly for small businesses. Supervision and regulation of the banking system was highly inadequate and complicated by the continued use of the Russian Accounting System rather than the International Accounting System, with its more rigorous disclosure requirements (Chowdhury, 2003; OECD, 2009, pp. 99–100).

Banks during this period not only failed to serve as intermediaries between holders of capital and enterprises in need of financing, but they also rarely facilitated transactions. The Soviet payment system was woefully slow, posting payment orders by mail. Given the limited role money played in the command economy, this dilatory process was not a major impediment to Soviet enterprises' transactions, but the payment system's inefficiency was a significant problem once a market economy began to emerge. Along with the technical deficiencies of the payment system, banks often intentionally delayed the delivery of payments in transit, profiting from high inflation by holding the payment in a foreign currency (or other assets protected from rapid depreciation) before finally delivering the depreciated nominal payment, sometimes as late as several weeks after the transaction (Poser, 1998, p. 168). Lacking an effective banking system, firms were forced to rely on cash and barter transactions, a tendency compounded by firms' efforts to hide transactions from tax authorities. Some estimates suggest that at its peak, barter accounted for 50 percent of all transactions among industrial firms, and an even higher share of transactions conducted by large firms (Tompson, 1999, p. 259). Meanwhile, surveys conducted in the mid-1990s show that between 25 and 30 percent of payments were conducted in "black cash" – off-the-books funds created through tax evasion schemes – with this cash economy concentrated largely among smaller firms (Yakovlev, 2001, p. 47).

Ultimately, rather than providing loans and facilitating transactions, banks in the early post-Soviet period engaged primarily in speculative activity, including large purchases of short-term government bonds, known as GKOs, the interest on which rose to phenomenal heights – over 250 percent – prior to the 1998 financial crisis. The crisis wreaked havoc on the Russian financial system. At the time of the crisis, one-third of bank assets were tied up in claims on government debt. An additional fifth of liabilities were held in foreign denominations that were inflated away following Russia's currency devaluation. Consequently, many financial institutions were unable to weather the crisis, and the collapse of weaker institutions accelerated the consolidation of the banking sector that was already underway (Barisitz, 2009, p. 48).

In summary, until the late 1990s, firms conducted transactions largely in cash, which facilitated the use of illegal strategies, as discussed in greater detail below. Following the 1998 financial crisis, however, changes occurred that would dramatically reduce firms' reliance on cash in favor of transactions conducted via the formal financial system.

6.2.2   Banking Development and Rising Costs of Illegal Strategies

The economic growth that followed the crisis, the result first of a rise in import-substitution manufacturing and later of rising oil prices, reinvigorated the financial sector. By the early 2000s, capital-starved firms were seeking loans in order to maintain their rapid pace of expansion. At the same time, opportunities for speculative activity based on hyperinflation, short-term bonds, and privatization auctions dried up. Between 2003 and 2005, a series of banking reforms further contributed to the development of the sector. The government created deposit insurance, increased the capital adequacy ratio and minimum capital requirements, introduced a plan for a mandatory transition to the International Accounting Standard, developed a simplified lending system for small businesses, and amended the Law on Banks and Banking Activity and the Law on the Bank of Russia so as to improve the regulatory environment (Chowdury, 2003; Tompson, 2004; Barisitz, 2009, pp. 52–53).

As seen in Table 6.3, firms recognized the growing stability and trustworthiness of the banking system and began to utilize bank transactions and seek bank loans. Simultaneously, the government, in an effort to reduce tax evasion, took steps to require all companies to open bank accounts and introduced mandates that all large transactions take place through the banking system (Yakovlev, 2001, p. 47). During this period, owners of firms began to perceive the unwillingness of a potential business partner to conduct business via bank transactions as a sign of crookedness and to restrict dealings with such firms (Firm 1, interview, 2009). Exclusion of firms preferring to deal only in cash transactions provided additional incentives to rely on the banking system.

Firms' growing reliance on the banking system transformed property security strategies both by increasing the likelihood that illegal strategies would be exposed and by raising the costs of conducting such activities. First, when nearly all transactions were done in cash, it was relatively easy to allocate resources to bribe government officials or pay criminal protection rackets. Indeed, to the extent that cash transactions persist today, businesspeople continue to associate them with illicit behavior. For example, when asked about firms' use of banks in contemporary Russia, a consultant to businesses investing in Russia's regions replied: "[Firms use] only bank transactions – simply now there is practically no cash used. Well, comparably very little is still used. [It is used] for the illicit activities that still are conducted (*v gryaznie veshchi kotorye ostalis*)" (Firm 15, interview, 2009). Similarly, the chief economist for the business group AFK Sistema, Evgeniy Nardorshin, recently remarked: "As the Russian economy is far from being completely transparent, a certain amount of cash is needed by shadow agents (*tenevye agenty*) to service their turnover" (Zhdanova, 2012). By contrast, when transactions are done through the banking system, it leaves a paper trail. It is possible to conceal this trail through front companies, slush funds, and other creative endeavors, but this entails additional time, expenses, and risks of getting caught. These increased costs and risks lower the effectiveness of property security strategies based on violence or coercion.

Second, when firms rely on bank loans, or even seek to open a bank account, an extra system of vetting is introduced that did not exist when the banking system was underdeveloped. For example, a manager at a mail-order business based in Moscow related an incident where a representative of his company who had been sent to open a bank account appeared to be concealing information. His request was denied. Within a short span of time, their company had been blacklisted by banks throughout Moscow (Firm 9, interview, 2009). The possibility that illegal strategies could reduce firms' access to bank loans serves as an additional mechanism increasing the risks of sanctions for firms using illegal strategies.

Survey data again provide evidence of the relationships between the development of the financial sector and property security strategies. In the survey I conducted, respondents were asked: "Approximately what percentage of your firms' transactions are conducted in cash?" Fifty percent of firms responding to the question reported that they conduct less than 10 percent of transactions in cash, while the other half of the sample reported using cash in more than 10 percent of transactions. As in earlier sections of this chapter, firms' ratings of their likeliness to use a given strategy to resolve a property or debt dispute serve as the dependent variable in the analyses presented in Figure 6.2, which use OLS regressions to evaluate the hypothesis that firms with fewer cash transactions are less likely to employ illegal strategies. The strategies are arrayed along the vertical axis to the left of the figure. The figure again shows results from three model specifications. For simple bivariate regressions, the circles represent the difference in average ratings between firms that conduct less than 10 percent of transactions in cash and firms that conduct more than 10 percent. For regressions including control variables, the circles represent the difference in average ratings holding constant the wide range of firm and respondent-level factors listed in Section 6.1.2. "Saturated" models include all control variables as well as all variables of interest in Chapters 5 through 7. For all specifications, horizontal lines and vertical tick marks represent 95 percent and 90 percent confidence intervals, respectively.

Figure 6.2 shows that firms conducting less than 10 percent of transactions in cash (i.e., "low-cash firms") report a lower likeliness of using strategies based on corrupt coercion, and, to a lesser extent, strategies based on private coercion. For example, the average rating for likeliness to turn to courts using informal connections to resolve a property dispute for firms conducting less than 10 percent of transactions in cash is as much as 0.67 points lower than for other firms, depending on the specification. The difference in average ratings between firms that are less reliant on cash transactions and other firms with respect to utilizing law enforcement or bureaucrats in an unofficial capacity or hiring

The figure below shows the difference between the average responses of firms that conduct less than 10 percent of transactions in cash (i.e., "low-cash firms") and firms that conduct more than 10 percent of transactions (i.e., "high-cash firms), on a 1 to 7 scale where 1 is "very unlikely" and 7 is "very likely," holding other factors constant.

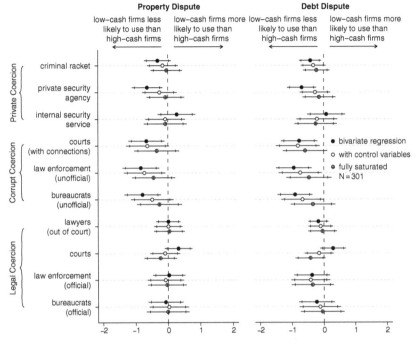

Figure 6.2 Cash Transactions and Propensity to Use Strategies
Note: Circles indicate point estimates from OLS regressions. Horizontal lines represent 95 percent confidence interviews, and vertical tick marks represent 90 percent confidence intervals. For further details on model specifications and the wording of the property and debt dispute scenarios, see the note to Figure 5.3.

a private security agency to resolve a property dispute is of an even greater magnitude – approximately 0.80 points. The differences between low-cash and high-cash firms are often statistically significant at the 95 percent level of confidence for bivariate regressions and for many specifications including control variables. These results remain robust when firms are divided among those that conduct more or less than 25 percent of their transactions in cash as well as when an ordinal variable is used, as shown in the Online Appendix. The coefficients of the "low-cash" variable are not, however, statistically distinguishable from zero in the most demanding model specifications, the "fully saturated" models, most likely because of multi-collinearity with other variables of interest.[7]

In summary, qualitative evidence drawn from in-depth interviews indicates that the development of the banking sector has contributed to the evolution of Russian firms' property security strategies. The results of quantitative analyses also point to the role of financial sector development in reducing firms' reliance on illegal strategies, although these results are less robust than the results of earlier analyses in this and the preceding chapter. Taken as a whole, the existing evidence demonstrates that over time, Russian firms have increasingly conducted transactions through the banking system. Declining cash transactions have reduced the effectiveness of illegal strategies, both due to the increased risk of sanctions and the higher transaction costs incurred when utilizing strategies that skirt the law. Accordingly, Russian firms have reduced their reliance on violence and corruption.

6.3   Integration into the International Economy

A third trend that has increased the transaction costs associated with and the risk of sanctions resulting from illegal strategies is Russia's integration into the international economy. By reducing the effectiveness of private and corrupt coercion, such integration has provided incentives for Russian firms to reduce their reliance on illegal strategies.

Scholars and policymakers continue to vigorously debate the role of multinational companies (MNCs) and international capital flows in facilitating or preventing illicit activities. For example, although some evidence exists that foreign direct investment (FDI) helps reduce corruption (e.g., Larraín and Tavares, 2004; Kwok and Tadesse, 2006; Wang, 2015), other studies suggest that the positive effects of FDI are apparent only in countries already endowed with relatively effective governance institutions. In countries with low levels of governance, MNCs may be more likely than local firms to engage in bribery, kickbacks, and illicit forms of political pressure (Hellman et al., 2002; Pinto and Zhu, 2009).

---

[7] There is also some suggestive evidence that firms conducting fewer transactions in cash are more likely to utilize courts, but the magnitude of the effect is relatively small and not robust to the inclusion of control variables. More broadly, as with the analyses of ownership consolidation earlier in this chapter, there is little evidence of a substitution effect in which firms' decreased use of illegal strategies due to growing reliance on bank transactions corresponds with increased use of legal strategies.

These debates, however, focus on broader conceptions of corruption, often based on measures of bribery or investor perceptions, rather than on the specific question of firm strategies for securing property.[8] The case of Russia illustrates that while foreign investors have at times been willing to countenance low-level bribery, often equated with "grease money" needed to bypass excessive administrative barriers, Russian firms perceive that investors will not tolerate the overt use of property security strategies based on violence or corruption. Consequently, as Russian firms have increasingly sought external finance, both in the form of FDI and initial public offerings (IPOs) on foreign exchanges, the understanding that a reputation for violence or corruption could dissuade potential investors has reduced firms' willingness to use illegal strategies. Meanwhile, MNCs operating within Russia have introduced stricter operating guidelines in the subsidiaries they have acquired, raising the transaction costs of utilizing illegal strategies. MNCs also instilled new business practices in Russian employees, who then spread these practices as they moved on to become managers at large Russian firms or to found start-up companies. Finally, in recent years, Russia's largest firms have expanded into foreign markets, acquiring assets abroad. This has placed an even higher premium on their business reputation and further raised the costs and risks of using illegal property security strategies.

6.3.1 Russian Firms' Turn to Foreign Financing and Investment

As discussed above, in the 1990s managers and owners of Russian firms were primarily focused on short-term control of financial flows, asset stripping, or the rapid acquisition of additional assets via the privatization process or other ties to the state. In this environment, demand for investment capital was limited, and firms were able to satiate what demand there was through retained earnings or government subsidies. Given the rough tactics employed in business, foreign investment was limited to large, powerful players such as McDonald's, Mars, Inc., and ExxonMobil, who believed they had the clout and resources to protect their assets using government connections or private security.

The economic growth unleashed after the 1998 crisis transformed Russian firms' demand for external financing, and they soon exhausted the limits of the domestic financial system. Firms began to seek strategic foreign direct investors. Table 6.4 shows the increase in FDI throughout

---

[8] A notable exception is Wang (2015), who uses a series of innovative measures to show that foreign investment in Chinese regions is associated with lower levels of judicial corruption.

Table 6.4   *Reliance on Foreign Finance*
(in billions of USD)

	1999	2000	2001	2002	2003	2004	2005	2006	2007	2008
Foreign Direct Investment	3.3	2.7	2.7	3.5	8.0	15.4	12.9	29.7	55.1	75.0
PNG* Debt to Foreign Commercial Banks and Other Creditors	20.4	20.4	20.6	24.0	30.3	43.3	82.2	90.1	112.1	166.5
Financing from PNG* Foreign Bonds	2.2	1.4	1.7	4.5	10.9	20.1	33.7	48.7	70.2	78.1
Financing from Initial Public Offerings**	–	0.5	0	0.1	0	0.2	2.9	5.1	12.6	1.5

*PNG = private non-guaranteed
**Includes Russian companies registered offshore

Sources: Data for IPOs provided by Yurii Danilov, director of the Center for Capital Market Development Foundation in Moscow, in response to author's correspondence (see also Danilov and Yakushin, 2008); other data are from the World Bank's World Development Indicators, www.data.worldbank.com.

the 2000s. In 2008, it reached 75 billion dollars – the sixth largest inflow of FDI in the world and second only to China among developing countries.[9] In addition to FDI, Russian firms turned to Eurobonds and loans from foreign banks. By 1998, Russia's private sector had accumulated a larger external debt than that of any other developing country.[10] As the forerunners of bank financing accumulated debt, low-interest loans became harder to acquire, which raised the appeal of IPOs. In 2004, Russian firms conducted only five IPOs, which raised a total of less than one billion dollars. By 2006, Russia was among the top five developing countries in terms of funds raised through IPOs, a trend that continued into 2007. Many of these IPOs occurred on the London Stock Exchange (30 in 2007), and a handful of other firms were listed on the New York Stock Exchange (8 in 2007). Offerings on Russia's domestic exchanges also attracted significant attention from foreign investors (Pappe and Galukhina, 2009, pp. 113–114).

As foreign finance flowed into Russian companies, Russian MNCs also expanded abroad, seeking new markets, access to advanced technology, and international stature. By 2008, Russian companies held the second-largest stock of direct investments abroad among emerging economies,

[9] Data are from the World Bank's World Development Indicators, available at www.data.worldbank.org. For a discussion of different measures of FDI into Russia, see Pappe and Galukhina (2009, pp. 116–117).
[10] This statement refers to private non-guaranteed external debt stocks. Data are from the World Bank World Development Indicators dataset.

significantly more than Brazilian, Chinese, and Indian firms (Filippov, 2010, p. 310). Although a couple dozen companies accounted for a disproportionate share of foreign investment, more than a thousand Russian companies by 2009 were investing abroad. In addition to natural resource enterprises, Russian financial institutions, automakers, metallurgy giants, and telecommunication companies actively engaged in foreign investment strategies (Panibratov and Kalotay, 2009). The former Soviet republics presented a natural target for Russian expansion, but as the 2000s proceeded, Russian companies became increasingly active in European and North American markets. In 2000, Russian companies concluded just six mergers and acquisitions and 25 strategic alliances in Western Europe and North America; by 2007 these figures had grown to 63 and 79, respectively (Filippov, 2010, pp. 317–318). Even as the world financial crisis unfolded in 2008 and 2009, Lukoil continued to invest in Italian oil refineries, Severstal in Canadian coal mines, and NLMK in US steel manufacturers (Panibratov and Kalotay, 2009, pp. 3–4). Overall, throughout the 2000s, Russia became increasingly integrated into the international economy as international firms and capital came to target Russia, while Russian firms expanded their operations and investments beyond Russia's borders.

6.3.2 International Constraints on Property Security Strategies

There are numerous ways in which foreign finance created incentives for firms to change property security strategies. First, the need for external resources increased the risk of sanctions associated with using illegal strategies, because companies seeking financing from abroad recognized that a reputation for illicit behavior could drive away potential investors. This factor is arguably even more pressing for large Russian companies investing abroad than for Russian firms seeking foreign investment, given that an unsavory reputation may make foreign sellers hesitant to conduct business or may lead to objections from host governments. As the head of government relations for the foreign operations of a major Russian metal company explained, "If you're like us, with a headquarters in London, and the only way to expand is by buying companies abroad, then you better focus on your image" (Firm 27, interview, 2009).

Once foreign investment has occurred, the introduction of operating procedures places constraints on cash flows. Like firms' increased reliance on bank transactions described above, these constraints forced managers engaged in illicit activities to exert additional effort to acquire off-the-books cash and to avoid detection, which raised the transaction costs of illegal strategies. For example, when a large Western aluminum company invested in a Russian facility, it learned that the Russian plant had continued to operate a wood chip business inherited from Soviet times, receiving payments in off-the-books cash or barter. Upon acquisition by foreign owners, the side business was immediately shut down (Firm 10, interview, 2009). More broadly, when MNCs invest in assets in countries such as Russia, they seek to limit employee theft, prevent asset stripping, improve top-level executives' authority over lower-level managers, and increase oversight of subsidiaries. Control and oversight of subsidiaries and lower-level managers is particularly important for MNCs subject to anticorruption legislation in their home countries, such as the US Foreign Corrupt Practices Act or the OECD Convention on Combating Bribery of Public Officials in International Business Transactions. Consequently, following investments, large MNCs standardize accounting, human resource, and compliance procedures. In the words of a Russian finance director with experience working in MNCs operating in Russia's pharmaceutical sector, "There are three main reasons why Western companies choose to work legally: (1) the company's image; (2) clearly elaborated procedures; and (3) even if you want to speed up some process, the shareholders don't especially value this, but if there is a [legal] violation, then the penalty is large. There's no sense in risking this" (Firm 41, interview, 2009). These principles limit the discretion of lower-level managers to utilize illegal property security strategies.

Finally, FDI and IPOs require significant legal and accounting services, which attracts international firms with expertise in these spheres. The presence of such firms increases domestic firms' access to the legal and accounting resources needed to conduct audits, carry out due diligence, and adopt best practice corporate governance policies. Already by 2000, before the significant expansion of foreign financing, Moscow had become a major hub for global law firms, nearly on par with major European and Asian capitals (Faulconbridge et al., 2008). These firms trained young Russian lawyers, many of whom by the mid-2000s were working for top Russian firms or starting their own practices. According to a former Russian employee of Ernst & Young, the surge in IPOs had a similar effect on the next generation of Russian accountants and auditors, many of whom found employment with Big Four accounting firms during the height of the IPO period and then moved on to work for domestic companies. Indeed, the informant himself had joined the finance department of a major Russian oligarch's holding company after leaving Ernst & Young (Firm 5, interview, 2009).

Naturally, there are limits to the effect of international financing on property security strategies. Some changes in corporate behavior were largely cosmetic. As a longtime European consultant in Moscow noted, in the early 2000s Russian companies conducted corporate governance reforms "just up to the point needed to get investment" (Firm 11, interview, 2009). Moreover, the direct effect of IPOs and to a lesser extent FDI has been limited to large companies. Nonetheless, the impact of international influences spread beyond the initial recipients of foreign investment via spillover effects. Small businesses working as suppliers to MNCs note fundamental differences between foreign and domestic clients' efforts to comply with laws. For example, a local manufacturer of industrial uniforms in Moscow emphasized that in contrast to many large Russian firms, MNCs do not expect side payments from smaller companies seeking to become part of their supply chain: "[Consider] the mentality of Europeans, of Americans. A manager from TNK-BP, for example, or McDonald's, he won't come to you and say, 'Give me a bribe if you want me to buy from you' ... He always received a good salary, and he didn't have the incentives to also take bribes. He hung onto his job; it was valuable to him ... And so ... in order to survive in this market ... we went to work with international companies [operating in Russia], which allowed us to work honestly, without bribes and kickbacks" (Firm 28, interview, 2009). The scope of MNCs' influence can be extensive. In 2010, McDonald's employed approximately 25,000 residents of Russia, but the Russian companies in its supply chain employed an additional 100,000 people (Kramer, 2010).

Spillover effects also occur as MNCs transform the mentality of Russian employees, producing an additional constraint on the use of violence and corruption. For instance, a 2007 study commissioned by the American Chamber of Commerce in Russia compared the opinions of Russian employees in large American-owned firms to Russian employees in Russian-owned firms. In American-owned firms, 100 percent of respondents agreed with the statement, "The company aims to strictly obey Russian legislation." The corresponding number for Russian-owned companies was 78 percent. As one Russian employee of an American firm explained, "Since the moment I came here, I have never received money in an envelope.[11] I realized what the organization was trying to tell me:

---

[11] The phrase "in an envelope" (*v konverte*) refers to salaries paid in cash for the purpose of avoiding payroll taxes.

'We live according to Russian legislation.' This became crystal clear right away" (American Chamber, 2007). Employees with experience working in MNCs are in high demand, and as they move on to work for Russian firms, they potentially bring along newly ingrained practices and mentalities.

During in-depth interviews, the influence of international investment was the most discussed explanatory factor accounting for the transformation of Russian firms' property security strategies, particularly among representatives of larger enterprises. Of 56 firms interviewed, 17 had over 250 employees. Of these, 9 respondents – without prompting – raised the issue of demand for foreign finance when asked about the factors contributing to the evolution of firms' strategies for securing property. Drawing on industry case studies, Russian analysts also point to the role foreign investment has played in encouraging corporate transparency and reducing illegal practices (e.g., Radaev, 2002, p. 40). Unfortunately, subjecting the hypothesis that demand for foreign finance reduces firms' use of illegal strategies to further testing is challenging due to data limitations. Sample frames for firms with foreign ownership are not readily available, and in my survey only 11 percent of firms reported having a foreign owner with a stake of 10 percent or larger. Only 5 percent of respondents reported having received FDI in the previous three years or expecting to receive FDI in the next three years. Even fewer firms in the sample – 3 percent – had conducted or expected to conduct an IPO. Comparing the property security strategies of firms that rely on FDI or that have conducted an IPO with firms that do not report international ties produces no robust findings, but this may be due to the small number of firms in the sample receiving foreign financing.[12] Other survey samples, including the BEEPS survey conducted by the World Bank and recent surveys by Russian research organizations (e.g., INDEM-CIPE, 2009; Levada Center, 2010), also contain few firms with foreign ownership stakes

---

[12] Other factors might also undermine the expected results. Foreign ownership is usually measured as a foreign shareholder with more than 10 percent of shares, and this is the measure used in my survey. However, some studies of the impact of FDI on enterprise restructuring and productivity find that 10 percent ownership is not sufficient to change firm behavior (Yudaeva et al., 2003). Rather, a majority stake is needed, and a similar ownership stake might be necessary to change firms' behavior with respect to property security strategies as well. A final issue is that data on foreign investment in Russia often include inflows of capital that Russians themselves are reinvesting following the massive capital flight that took place during the chaos of the 1990s. A thorough analysis of the effects of foreign financing on property security strategies may require attention to distinctions between genuine foreign investment and repatriated investment.

and/or do not include suitable variables for examining property security strategies.

While confirmation of the findings from in-depth interviews awaits the collection of additional survey data, the existing evidence indicates that foreign financing has played a significant role in the transformation of property security strategies. Russian firms' reliance on foreign finance has increased considerably, and Russian firms have also begun to invest abroad. This has increased the risk of sanctions associated with using illegal strategies, as the importance of reputation has grown. The integration of Russian firms into MNCs has additionally placed constraints on managers' access to cash flows needed for illicit activities, raising the transaction costs of illegal strategies. Together these factors have reduced the effectiveness of illegal strategies, contributing to firms' decreased use of violence and corruption.

6.4   Conclusion

This chapter has examined the ways in which reduced effectiveness of illegal alternatives to formal legal institutions affects firms' property security strategies. As the risk of using illegal strategies increases, or the transaction costs associated with such strategies rise, firms become less willing to resort to violence and corruption. Firms are particularly less likely to find illegal strategies effective as their time horizons expand, the financial sector develops, and they become more integrated into the international economy. In Russia, consolidation of ownership in privatized firms, the switch from cash to bank transactions, and an inflow of foreign investment combined with an outflow of Russian investment abroad have contributed to illegal property security strategies' declining effectiveness.

Naturally, these broad trends have not affected all firms equally. In addition to the evolution of Russian firms' property security strategies over time, there is significant variation in the barriers faced by different types of firms and the effectiveness with which different types of firms can employ illegal strategies. Variation across firms' property security strategies is the subject of the next chapter.

7

Variation in Strategies across Firms

The previous two chapters offered insights into the factors contributing to the transformation of Russian firms' property security strategies over time. Naturally, this transformation has occurred unevenly. In part, this is because the factors analyzed in Chapters 5 and 6 – tax compliance, coordination dilemmas, ownership consolidation, banking development, and integration into the international economy – affect sectors of the economy, as well as individual firms, to differing degrees. Yet beyond these lines of division, there are also systematic differences across the property security strategies employed by different *types* of firms. This chapter examines the firm-level characteristics that affect the extent of demand-side barriers faced by specific types of firms, or that influence the effectiveness with which certain types of firms can employ illegal strategies.

Examination of variation in property security strategies across different types of firms is important for several reasons. First, variation across firms provides insights into the types of firms that are most likely to be pioneers in adopting legal strategies, which in turn has significant implications for building effective state institutions. As discussed in earlier chapters, firms that use illegal property security strategies undermine and destabilize formal institutions; firms that use legal strategies reinforce the effectiveness and relevance of formal state institutions. But beyond their direct effect on institutional development, property security strategies may also be tied to firms' preferences for legislation and political change. Consequently, variation in strategies offers clues into what types of firms constitute the societal foundation for institution building. Finally, variation across firms bolsters one of the central claims of this book: Changes in the level of state legal capacity offer at best an incomplete explanation for firms' increasing use of legal strategies. Rising legal capacity would presumably affect all firms in a relatively equal manner, meaning that legal capacity cannot account for the types of cross-firm variation analyzed in this chapter. On the other hand, such variation is directly in line with a demand-side analysis: Firms facing distinct types of demand-side barriers or with particularly effective means of using illegal strategies should employ different profiles of property security strategies from their counterparts.

With respect to the *effectiveness of illegal strategies*, the previous chapter focused not only on transaction costs but also on the risks of illicit activity. By contrast, this chapter draws more heavily on the existing literature on relational contracting and private ordering (e.g., Macaulay, 1963; Williamson, 1985; Ellickson, 1991). First, it explores how the type of output a firm produces affects its use of property security strategies. Physical products are often more conducive than services to measurement, verification, and documentation, making the use of law relatively more advantageous for firms with tangible output. As a consequence, service firms should be less likely to use legal and more likely to use illegal strategies than firms in nonservice sectors. Second, it has long been recognized that strategies based on personal connections are most effective in smaller communities. Investment in legal resources, on the other hand, facilitates strategies that (at least theoretically) take advantage of the universal elements of law, and can therefore be employed without concern for local connections. It follows that firms operating in local, as opposed to national markets, should be less likely to use legal and more likely to use illegal strategies. Finally, transaction costs of illegal strategies depend on the types of people and organizations in a firm's informal network. The resources required to use illegal strategies, such as informal connections with government officials, are not equally available to all firms. Providers of illicit services select clients carefully and prefer those with whom trust has been established, either through repeated interaction or personal ties. Consequently, firms that regularly interact with politically powerful customers, suppliers, or government officials should be more likely to effectively employ illegal strategies.

Just as some firms employ illegal strategies more effectively than others, some firms face more extensive *demand-side barriers*, further contributing to variation in property security strategies across different types of firms. Two especially persistent barriers relate to licensing and imports. Permits that are difficult to obtain frequently lead firms to partially conduct business in the informal economy, which then forces firms to avoid formal institutions for fear of exposing their lack of regulatory compliance (Johnson et al., 1997; Frye and Zhuravskaya, 2000). Similarly, imports that cannot be conducted without legal violations limit a firm's range of strategies for addressing conflicts during downstream transactions, for the illegal status of imported merchandise may reduce firms' willingness to use formal legal institutions. It follows that firms struggling to comply with licensing or customs regulations should be less likely to adopt legal strategies.

In addition to factors affecting demand-side barriers and the effectiveness of illegal strategies, *firm size* plays an important role in variation across firm strategies. Small firms face more extensive demand-side barriers than larger firms, which may make them less inclined to utilize formal legal institutions. Large firms also face incentives to circumvent formal legal institutions, but for a very different reason: They have the resources and informal connections to effectively use illegal strategies. Medium-sized firms are capable of overcoming demand-side barriers yet do not enjoy the same level of informal connections as large firms. They are consequently the most likely to employ legal strategies.

These three issues may at times be intertwined. Crucially, in addition to the direct relationship between firm size and property security strategies, firm size interacts with other factors that affect firms' utilization of strategies for securing property. For example, small firms with minimal informal connections may be more sensitive to the presence of informal networks that facilitate strategies based on corrupt coercion. This chapter therefore examines the effectiveness of illegal strategies, demand-side barriers, and firm size both as distinct sources of variation across firms and as interacting phenomena. Finally, it should be noted at the outset that although patterns across firms are consistent with the book's central arguments, the cross-sectional analyses presented in this chapter do not provide a rigorous basis for drawing causal inferences. Nevertheless, results below offer important insights into the relationships between the demand-side barriers firms face, firms' ability to employ illegal strategies, and firms' property security strategies.

7.1   Effectiveness of Illegal Strategies

Classic literature on relational contracting focuses on specific characteristics of transactions that make the use of formal legal institutions relatively efficient or inefficient (Williamson, 1985). These studies offer a set of predictions about when firms should be more or less reliant on legal strategies. All else equal, when transactions are conducted between short-term trading partners and involve standard assets for which quality is observable and verifiable, firms will be more likely to rely on law. When transactions are conducted between frequent and trusted trading partners and involve assets customized to specific firms or for which quality is difficult to verify, law will be more likely to give way to private forms of transactional governance, ranging from long-term contracting to vertical integration.[1]

Two of the firm-level characteristics examined in this section – a firm's type of output and the size of the market in which it operates – build on insights from the relational contracting literature. These two factors affect, respectively, the observability of a firm's product quality and the extent to which a firm is likely to engage in repeat transactions with well-known suppliers and customers. Beyond insights from the relational contracting literature, this section investigates a third factor specifically related to strategies that not only bypass formal legal institutions but that also actively violate the law. Violence and corruption require resources – such as informal connections to government officials – that are not equally available to all firms. Consequently, the informal networks in which a firm is embedded, and the extent to which these networks provide firms with the resources needed to employ private or corrupt coercion, have a significant impact on firms' choice of property security strategies.

7.1.1 Types of Output: Goods versus Services

One particularly important aspect of transactions is whether or not the quality of the assets being exchanged is measurable and verifiable. As Murrell (2003, p. 706) explains, "When quality is easily verifiable, the neutral adjudication provided by the legal system or third parties has advantages over bilateral haggling. When quality is not easily verified by outsiders, the legal system and third parties face difficulties in adjudicating disputes." It follows that there should be observable differences in the strategies of service firms and firms whose primary products are physical goods. Disputes related to physical goods may be more documentable

---

[1] Although there is a vast empirical literature focused on vertical integration (for an overview, see Lafontaine and Slade, 2007), very few empirical studies examine a broader range of strategies. Murrell (2003), a rare exception, considers the impact of asset specificity, measurability of assets, uncertainty, and frequency of trade on Romanian firms' propensity to use the formal legal system relative to bilateral mechanisms, such as reliance on trust and personal relationships. In the context of post-communist transition, he finds little evidence that typical relational contracting variables are correlated with firm strategies. A handful of studies – such as Fafchamps's (1996) analysis of Ghana, Hendley et al.'s (2000) research on Russia, and Whiting's (2010) study of China – report firms' relative reliance on different strategies for contract enforcement, but they do not analyze variation in strategies across different types of firms.

and tangible than disputes concerning the assets of service firms. Consider, for example, the difference between a conflict involving defective auto parts and a conflict over whether a consulting firm fulfilled its obligations to a client. Particularly in a society where reliance on formal legal institutions is relatively new, service firms may be more hesitant to utilize legal strategies.

In the survey I conducted, 44 percent of respondents describe their firm's primary product as a physical good and 56 percent as a service.[2] The extent to which service enterprises perceive less value in formal legal institutions is evident in firms' responses to whether or not they agree with the statements, "An effective legal system makes it easier to do business" and "An effective legal system makes my assets safer." As seen in Table 7.1, approximately 78 percent of service firms expressed agreement with the former statement compared to approximately 89 percent of nonservice firms, while 73 percent of service firms expressed agreement with the second statement compared to approximately 86 percent of firms that produce or distribute a physical product. These distinctions are statistically significant at the 99 and 95 percent levels of confidence, respectively.[3]

It is important to consider, however, that sectoral differences are likely to also affect the extent and types of threats a firm faces. While the characteristics of a service firm may create challenges when using formal legal institutions, service firms' assets also are difficult to expropriate due to the fact that service firms build value through relationships with customers or through high-quality management of employees' skills and knowledge. As the head of a small logistics consulting firm in Moscow explained:

> [Difficulties] also depend a little bit on the industry. For example, the service industry: If these [new entrepreneurs] would set up a small restaurant or a small food production plant or a small "old economy" type of business, they would have much more trouble than if they set up their own small PR agency. There's a big difference. There's no one from the authorities, no one from the fire brigade, no one from the police that is going to come [to my] company and tell me that my fire exit is not all right. Because they don't understand what I'm doing ... Even if I would have a

[2] Respondents were asked to classify their primary product as a physical good, a service, or intellectual property. Given that only 2 percent classified their main product as intellectual property, the analysis here merges the service and intellectual property categories, both of which present more challenges for measurement and observation than do physical goods.

[3] Respondents were given five choices regarding the statement: "strongly disagree," "disagree," "neither agree nor disagree," "agree," and "strongly agree." The percent of firms agreeing with the statement refers to respondents who either agree or strongly agree.

Table 7.1   *Types of Markets and the Effectiveness of Formal Legal Institutions*

	Physical Product	Services	T-Statistic
% of firms agreeing with the statement: "An effective legal system makes it easier to do business"	89.2 (130, 2.73)	77.8 (167, 3.23)	2.70**
% of firms agreeing with the statement: "An effective legal system makes my assets safer"	85.8 (127, 3.11)	74.1 (166, 3.41)	2.54*
Importance of effective commercial courts 1 to 7 scale (1= not important, 7 = very important)	6.12 (132, 0.13)	6.02 (168, 0.12)	0.58
	National Market	Local Market	T-Statistic
% of firms agreeing with the statement: "An effective legal system makes it easier to do business"	88.5 (139, 2.71)	77.8 (158, 3.31)	2.48*
% of firms agreeing with the statement: "An effective legal system makes my assets safer"	82.6 (138, 3.24)	76.1 (155, 3.44)	1.37
Importance of effective commercial courts 1 to 7 scale (1= not important, 7 = very important)	6.28 (139, 0.10)	5.89 (161, 0.14)	2.36*

Note: Number of observations and standard errors in parentheses
$^* p < .05; ^{**} p < .01; ^{***} p < .001$

> raid by the tax police right now, I would say [to my employees], okay guys, we all move to my apartment. [The authorities] would take the computers, well, tough luck. We lose the files, but, okay, what we sell is in here [points to his head]. And that is a big difference (Firm 11, interview, 2009).

Survey data similarly reflect sectoral differences with respect to the number of threats firms face. Of firms whose main product is a physical good, 78 percent report having experienced a violation of their legal rights over the last three years, whereas only 56 percent of firms offering services report such a violation. Correspondingly, 61 percent of nonservice firms have been to court in the past three years compared to 39 percent of service firms. In all cases these differences in means are statistically significant at the 99.9 percent level of confidence.

As discussed in earlier chapters, comparisons of firms' actual use of property security strategies can prove misleading, because firms' strategy profiles depend on the extent and type of threats they encounter. Analyses of firms' preferred strategies for responding to hypothetical property and debt disputes address this issue by holding constant the type of conflict. Figure 7.1a shows variation between service and nonservice firms' propensity to use distinct property security strategies in response to hypothetical scenarios involving property and debt disputes. For each scenario, respondents were requested to rate their likeliness of using various strategies to resolve the conflict on a 1 to 7 scale, where 1 refers to "highly unlikely" and 7 refers to "highly likely." (For the exact wording of the scenarios and an overview of firms' average responses, see Table 3.3 in Chapter 3.) These ratings serve as the dependent variables in the analyses presented in Figure 7.1a, which utilize OLS regressions to examine the hypothesis that service firms exhibit a lower willingness to use formal legal institutions and a greater inclination to resort to illegal strategies.[4] The strategies are arrayed along the vertical axis to the left of the figure. The figure shows results from three model specifications. For simple bivariate regressions, the circles represent the difference in average ratings between service and nonservice firms. For regressions including control variables, the circles represent the difference in average ratings holding constant a wide range of firm and respondent-level factors, including the firm's age, number of employees, financial health, sector, city of location, and ownership structure (i.e., whether or not the firm has foreign or government shareholders); the respondent's age, gender, job description, and education; and whether or not the firm had recently faced disputes or engaged in litigation. Finally, the "saturated" models include all control variables as well as all variables of interest in Chapters 5 through 7. For all specifications, horizontal lines and vertical tick marks represent 95 percent and 90 percent confidence intervals, respectively. (Regression tables for all analyses conducted in this chapter are included in Appendix G or in the Online Appendix.)

In line with the discussion above, service firms report being approximately 0.50 points less likely to turn to the commercial courts than firms whose primary products are physical goods. These results are statistically

[4] These and other results in this chapter are also robust when using ordered logit regressions in place of OLS. See the Online Appendix.

Figure (a) shows the difference between the average responses of service and nonservice firms, on a 1 to 7 scale where 1 is "very unlikely" and 7 is "very likely," holding other factors constant. Figure (b) shows the difference between the average responses of firms operating in local and firms operating in national markets, again holding other factors constant.

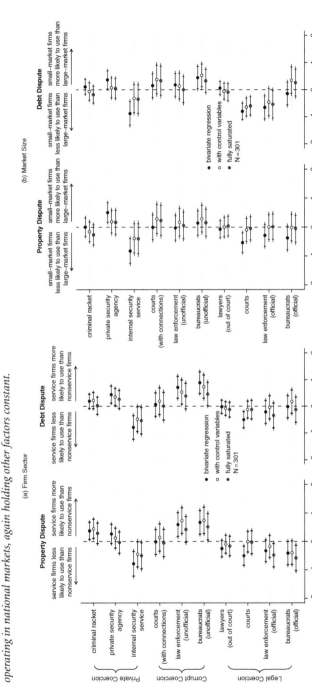

Figure 7.1 Types of Markets and Propensity to Use Strategies

Note: Circles indicate point estimates from OLS regressions. Horizontal lines represent 95 percent confidence intervals; vertical tick marks represent 90 percent confidence intervals. For further details on model specifications and the wording of the property and debt dispute scenarios, see the note to Figure 5.3.

significant at a 95 percent level of confidence for bivariate regressions but are not robust to the inclusion of a full set of control variables. On the other hand, service firms report being more likely to seek the assistance of law enforcement or other government officials acting in a private capacity, as well as being more likely to utilize the services of criminal protection rackets, at least in the case of property disputes. Depending on the model specification, service firms rate their likeliness of turning unofficially to law enforcement or government bureaucrats approximately 0.50 to 0.70 points higher than nonservice firms. These differences are statistically significant at the 90 percent level of confidence or higher in bivariate regressions and in regressions controlling for the wide range of potentially confounding factors listed in the preceding paragraph. The results are not, however, robust in the "saturated" specifications that include all explanatory variables of interest examined in Chapters 5 through 7.[5]

In summary, the analyses provide support for the claim that firms engaging in transactions involving assets whose quality is difficult to observe and verify perceive less value in formal legal institutions. The analyses also offer qualified support for the contention that service firms may be less likely to use courts and more likely to resort to strategies that rely on corrupt coercion.

7.1.2   Market Size

Another distinction among types of transactions that affect a firm's property security strategies pertains to the size of the market in which the firm operates. Just as informal norms are likely to be most effective in smaller communities in which individuals interact regularly with other well-known individuals (Ellickson, 1991, pp. 249–258), firms operating in smaller markets are more likely to conduct transactions with well-known suppliers and customers with whom they have long-standing relationships. Firms in smaller markets also are more likely to be dependent on a handful of customers or suppliers. This dependence increases the risk of hold-up (i.e., that a supplier will seek to renegotiate terms after the buyer has committed to an investment), given the lack of alternative suppliers. Accordingly, firms are more likely to seek the flexibility of relational contracting and less likely to rely on formal legal institutions

---

[5] Service firms also appear less likely to rely on internal security services, although this relationship is less pronounced once control variables for firm size are included in the analyses. The average service firm in the sample has 289 employees compared to a sample average of 390, and internal security services usually exist only in larger firms.

(Murrell, 2003, p. 705). Finally, Black's (1976) classic work on societies' reliance on law suggests that use of informal connections declines in favor of the use of impersonal legal institutions as the geographical distance between interacting parties expands. Personal connections, ties to criminal groups, and protection rackets that depend on local offices of government or law enforcement agencies have a greater impact within a confined environment. By contrast, firms operating throughout a large geographic expanse may find reliance on violence and corruption inefficient, given that they would have to invest separately in the development of informal connections in multiple locations.

In the survey I conducted, 53 percent of respondents report operating in a local market (i.e., a single region, city, or neighborhood), while the remaining 47 percent operate throughout Russia's national market. Table 7.1 offers evidence in favor of the hypothesis that firms operating in smaller markets perceive less value in formal legal institutions. Firms operating in smaller markets are less likely to agree that an effective legal system makes it easier to do business or makes their assets safer compared to firms operating in national markets. Respondents were also asked to rate the importance of effective commercial courts for the success of their business on a 1 to 7 scale, where 1 indicates "not at all important" and 7 indicates "very important." The average rating for firms operating in the national market was about one-third of a point higher than for firms operating in local markets, a difference that is statistically significant at the 95 percent level of confidence.

Figure 7.1b compares the preferred property security strategies for firms operating in markets of various sizes. Firms operating in local markets rate their likeliness of using courts to resolve an asset dispute or debt dispute more than half a point lower than firms operating in national markets, although the distinction is robust to inclusion of control variables only in the case of debt disputes. In the case of debt disputes, firms operating in local markets also report a lower likeliness of turning to law enforcement agencies in a formal capacity.

Although Figure 7.1b offers some suggestive evidence that firms in smaller markets are more likely to utilize strategies based on private or corrupt coercion, such as retaining the services of private security agencies or turning to bureaucrats in a private capacity, these findings are not particularly robust. However, including smaller firms in the analyses to some extent creates an apples-to-oranges comparison, for a disproportionate number of firms operating in national markets are large. Only 20 percent of firms with less than 100 employees and 45 percent of firms with 101 to 250 employees operate nationally, whereas 68 percent of firms with over 251 employees have expanded beyond local markets. Thus, even though they control for firm size, the analyses in Figure 7.1b are primarily comparing large firms operating in national markets with both small and large firms operating in smaller markets.

When the subsample of firms with over 250 employees is considered, the relationships between market size and firms' property security strategies become much more apparent (see Figure 7.2). In particular, larger firms operating in local markets report a significantly higher likeliness, both substantively and statistically, of using corrupt coercion compared to larger firms operating in national markets. In the case of property disputes, large firms serving Russia's local markets rate their likeliness of turning to government officials and law enforcement agencies in an unofficial capacity between 0.75 and 1.15 points higher than large firms operating in national markets, depending on the model specification. For all specifications, these results are statistically significant at the 90 percent level of confidence or higher. Meanwhile, for both property and debt disputes, large firms serving local markets also rate their likeliness of using courts along with informal connections approximately 0.90 points higher than their counterparts with operations in larger markets, and these differences are again statistically significant at the 90 percent level of confidence or higher in all model specifications.[6]

In summary, although the results of cross-sectional analyses should be interpreted with caution – a point to which I return below – the evidence is consistent with the hypothesis that firms operating in smaller markets are less likely to utilize formal legal institutions and more likely to utilize strategies based on corrupt connections, particularly when firm size is taken into account.

7.1.3   Informal Networks

Informal networks – the people and organizations with whom a firm regularly interacts – are a third factor influencing firms' ability to effectively employ illegal strategies. Informal networks have been widely analyzed in studies of contract enforcement. Numerous studies examine how networks disseminate information that helps firms reduce the risk of contract breach, particularly in environments with ineffective

---

[6] The results are similar, although slightly less robust, if only firms with fewer than 100 employees are excluded from the analyses.

The figure below shows the difference between the average responses of firms operating in local and firms operating in national markets, on a 1 to 7 scale where 1 is "very unlikely" and 7 is "very likely."

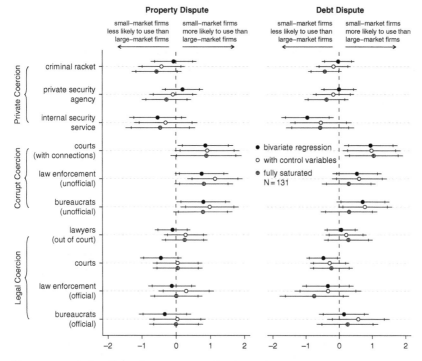

Figure 7.2 Market Size and Propensity to Use Strategies (firms with 250 or more employees)
Note: Circles indicate point estimates from OLS regressions. Horizontal lines represent 95 percent confidence interviews; vertical tick marks represent 90 percent confidence intervals. For further details on model specifications and the wording of the property and debt dispute scenarios see the note to Figure 5.3.

formal institutions (Greif, 1993; Winn, 1994; Brautigam, 1997; McMillan and Woodruff, 1999; Bigsten et al., 2000) but also in developed economies (Uzzi, 1996). Although much of the literature on networks is more closely linked to contract enforcement than property rights protection, recent work by Markus (2012, 2015) finds that in the postcommunist region firms also form alliances with foreign investors and local community organizations as a defensive measure to protect against attacks by other firms or state actors seeking to illegally acquire their assets. For the most part, however, scholars have not identified *which* types of informal networks affect firms' use of distinct property security strategies.[7]

Evidence from interviews with Russian firms indicates that the *types* of clients, suppliers, and government officials with whom a firm regularly comes in contact significantly affect a firm's property security strategies by influencing the resources at a firm's disposal. Naturally, informal networks may contribute to a firm's ability to effectively employ legal strategies, such as when a business manager with an extensive professional network utilizes connections to identify the best lawyers. But informal networks are particularly important for exercising private or corrupt coercion, given that the resources to carry out illegal strategies are often difficult to acquire.

Two examples of networks that offer access to the resources needed for corrupt coercion pertain to state-owned enterprises and wealthy clientele. Private firms that work regularly with state-owned enterprises (SOEs) have a direct source of informal connections with government officials. Despite the massive privatization program Russia conducted in the 1990s, firms with a state ownership stake continued to account for over one-third of all employment as of 2008 (Sprenger, 2010, pp. 72–73). Furthermore, SOEs have extensive contact with fully private firms. In the survey I conducted, firms were asked to describe their primary customers or suppliers. Ninety-one firms in my sample, or nearly one-third, reported that SOEs are among those from whom or to whom they regularly buy or sell. Figure 7.3a indicates that regular transactions with SOEs are associated with the use of property security strategies based on corrupt coercion. For both property and debt disputes, firms with SOE customers or suppliers on average rate their likeliness of using courts with informal connections or law enforcement and other government officials in a private capacity between 0.35 and 1.10 points higher than other firms, and these differences are statistically significant at the 90 or 95 percent level of confidence for nearly all model specifications that include control variables and for all fully saturated models.

Beyond business partnerships with SOEs, a firm's client or supplier base can influence its property security strategies in more subtle ways. Consider, for example, the vignette from the introductory chapter regarding the Moscow small business specializing in high-end accessories for

---

[7] A recent exception is Ang and Jia (2014), who show that Chinese firms with political connections are more likely to use courts, albeit in ways that allow politically connected firms to take advantage of their informal networks to shape courts' decisions (i.e., a form of corrupt coercion).

Figure (a) shows the difference between the average responses of firms with and without state-owned enterprises as clients or suppliers, on a 1 to 7 scale where 1 is "very unlikely" and 7 is "very likely," holding other factors constant. Figure (b) shows the difference between the average responses of firms with and without a wealthy customer base, again holding other factors constant.

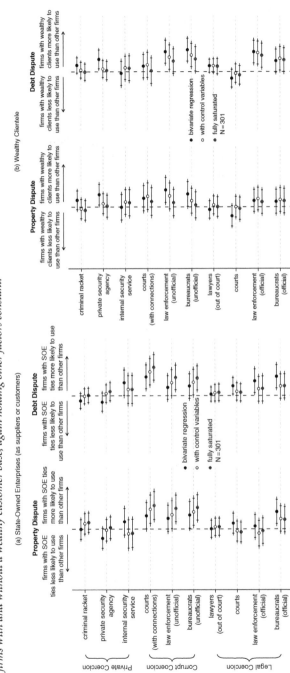

Figure 7.3 Informal Networks and Propensity to Use Strategies

Note: Circles indicate point estimates from OLS regressions. Horizontal lines represent 90 percent confidence intervals; vertical tick marks represent 95 percent confidence intervals. For further details on model specifications and the wording of the property and debt dispute scenarios, see the note to Figure 5.3.

luxury cars, whose security specialists with the ability to mobilize an elite law enforcement SWAT team saved him from would-be extortionists (Firm 1, interview, 2009). For such businesses, nearly all clients are wealthy and many are well-connected. Access to such clients is an important resource, particularly for smaller firms whose networks otherwise might not facilitate access to powerful state officials.

One hundred-twenty respondents in the survey I conducted, or just over 40 percent of the sample, reported a client base composed of individuals with significant wealth. In line with the hypothesis that a firm's type of clients affects its property security strategies, Figure 7.3b provides some evidence that firms with a wealthy customer base are more inclined to use strategies that rely on law enforcement and government bureaucrats, particularly in a private capacity although also in an official capacity. Especially in the case of debt disputes, firms with wealthy clients are around 0.40 to 0.80 points more likely to utilize law enforcement in either an official or unofficial capacity as well as government bureaucrats in an unofficial capacity, depending on the model specification. The distinction is statistically significant at the 90 or 95 percent confidence level in all but one specification. Similar results are not apparent, however, for the property dispute scenario. The evidence further indicates that the importance of informal networks may be particularly pronounced for smaller firms. Arguably, larger firms have multiple sources of access to informal connections with government structures, whereas smaller firms' networks of clients and suppliers may have a disproportionate impact on whether these firms acquire the resources necessary for employing strategies based on corrupt coercion. For firms with under 250 employees, those with wealthy clients on average report being much more likely (as much as a full point on the 7-point scale) to use law enforcement and bureaucrats in a private capacity (see Figure 7.4).

In summary, informal networks are intertwined with firms' property security strategies. The existing evidence indicates that private firms which conduct business with state-owned enterprises or with wealthy clientele are more likely to employ corrupt coercion, although the findings concerning SOEs are more robust than the findings concerning wealthy customers. While it may not be surprising that firms with more informal connections make greater use of such resources, the less recognized finding is that the relatively prosaic issue of whom a firm buys from and sells to can potentially shape the resources at its disposal.

More broadly, the evidence indicates that variation in property security strategies across firms is associated with differences in firms' ability to

The figure shows the difference between the average responses of firms with and without wealthy clientele, on a 1 to 7 scale where 1 is "very unlikely" and 7 is "very likely," holding other factors constant.

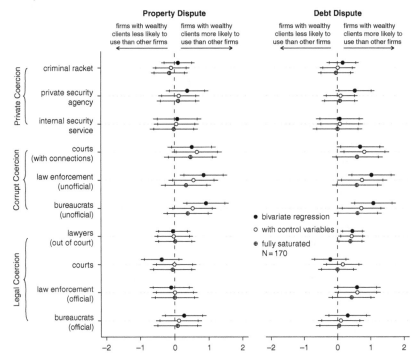

Figure 7.4 Wealthy Clientele and Propensity to Use Strategies (firms with fewer than 250 employees)
Note: Circles indicate point estimates from OLS regressions. Horizontal lines represent 95 percent confidence interviews; vertical tick marks represent 90 percent confidence intervals. For further details on model specifications and the wording of the property and debt dispute scenarios, see the note to Figure 5.3.

effectively employ illegal strategies. As noted at the outset of this chapter, inferences from cross-sectional regressions should be drawn with caution. Such analyses cannot rule out the possibility that an unaccounted-for factor is the simultaneous cause of firms' choices of property security strategies and decisions regarding expansion into larger markets or selection of suppliers and clients, or that the size of a market in which a firm operates conditions its choice of strategies. Nevertheless, the evidence is consistent with the theory that differing capabilities to utilize illegal strategies arise from factors that affect firms' relative transaction costs to using legal or illegal strategies, as well as from firms' access to resources required to engage in violence or corruption. Accordingly, distinct strategy profiles are apparent across service versus nonservice firms, firms operating in small and large markets, and firms with business partners – such as state-owned enterprises or wealthy clientele – that can facilitate strategies utilizing private or corrupt coercion.

7.2   Demand-Side Barriers

In addition to differences in firms' ability to effectively employ illegal strategies, the extent to which specific types of firms face demand-side barriers also contributes to cross-firm variation in property security strategies. This section examines two especially essential sources of demand-side barriers to the use of formal legal institutions: regulatory burdens and illegal imports. Regulatory burdens pose problems for nearly all firms in developing countries, but some firms bear the brunt of these burdens more than others. Excessive regulations can drive firms into the informal economy, creating demand-side barriers that force firms to use private or corrupt coercion and avoid formal legal institutions (Johnson et al., 1997). As Hay and Shleifer (1998, p. 399) explain, firms in the informal economy are nearly always "in violation of some tax, customs, foreign-exchange, or regulatory rules" and consequently cannot "use the official legal system for fear of exposure." Frye and Zhuravskaya (2000) and Frye (2002) additionally demonstrate empirically that, at least among smaller firms, shops that face high levels of regulations and numerous government inspections are more likely to have had encounters with mafia rackets.

Illegal operations that occur at key moments in the life cycle of a firm can have particularly long-lasting effects. Murrell (2003), for example, finds that illegally privatized firms in post-communist Romania are less likely than other firms to utilize legal strategies even years after privatization. In Moscow, a longtime owner of several small businesses related a similar problem. Until the 2000s, it was difficult to lease office space on an official basis, in part because landlords sought to avoid taxation. Yet many other official documents and licenses were unobtainable without documentation of a valid lease, inducing firms to seek further loopholes in laws and regulations in order to continue the process of starting up a business. From the early stage of locating premises for a new business, these challenges forced many firms to operate in semi-legality, making them hesitant to turn to formal legal institutions in times of need for fear that their lack of proper documentation could be revealed in the process (Firm 23, interview, 2009). As elaborated in the discussion below, a similar demand-side barrier emerges when firms rely on illegal import schemes, which then limit their capacity to employ legal strategies when conflicts related to the illicitly imported goods arise.

7.2.1 Regulatory Burdens

At the outset of Russia's transformation to a market economy, regulation for the shops and cooperatives that had appeared during the perestroika era was practically non-existent. Regulatory agencies were highly under-staffed relative to the sudden increase in the number of economic actors, and there were few clear guidelines governing how these agencies should oversee the emerging private sector. Over the course of the 1990s, how-ever, firms would come to face a wave of new regulations. Initially, licensing requirements were set by the federal government, with licenses required for activities subject to regulation in nearly all countries, such as the operation of heavy machinery or the production of pharmaceutical products. But as the state's finances collapsed in the early to mid-1990s, many regulatory agencies were forced to rely on self-financing. As a con-sequence, licenses required by local and regional agencies multiplied, often appearing under the guise of various permits and accreditations (Pryadilnikov, 2009, pp. 67–69, 80).

Seeking to maintain control over the regulatory process, the federal government repeatedly introduced legislation that explicitly identified activities subject to licensing or certification. A 1995 law on licensing limited the number of activities requiring licensing to 495; a 1998 law further reduced the number of activities to 215. Yet despite these legisla-tive efforts, licenses continued to proliferate. By the year 2000, analysts estimated that between 1,500 and 2,000 activities were being subjected to licensing requirements in direct contradiction to the existing legislative framework (Albats, 2004, pp. 287–292; Pryadilnikov 2009, pp. 82–84). Certification requirements exhibited similar trends. Seeking to replace the defunct Soviet system of quality standards, a new legislative framework was introduced in 1993. Soon a veritable industry of special laboratories and agencies, many operating privately or semiprivately, were conducting certification on behalf of the state. According to some estimates, by the early 2000s there were approximately 4,000 certification bodies requir-ing certification on 80 percent of all consumer goods. To put this in perspective, the European Union at the time had 10 agencies managing obligatory certification of a mere 4 percent of consumer goods (Albats, 2004, pp. 281–284).

Due to the avalanche of regulations, many firms found themselves operating extralegally, at least in part, due to the impossibility of fulfilling the ever-changing requirements of the regulatory landscape. Although this regulatory morass affected nearly all firms, certain sectors and industries naturally bore the brunt of the effects. For instance, a small-business owner specializing in bringing gems and valuable metals from Siberia to Moscow contended that the extensive regulation in his line of business meant that violation of some laws was inescapable. This owner furthermore attributed many illicit practices in his industry to excessive regulation (Firm 6, interview, 2009).

Survey data indicate that there is more than anecdotal evidence in support of the claim that firms facing additional licensing burdens are less prone to use legal property security strategies. Firms in the survey I conducted were asked to rate the extent to which obtaining licenses is an obstacle to the success of their business. Forty percent of those responding stated that licensing poses a significant obstacle.[8] As can be seen in Figure 7.5a, firms that consider licensing to be a major obstacle on average rate their likeliness of going to court to resolve a debt dispute as much as 0.45 points lower than other firms, although this difference is not statistically significant in the fully saturated model. In addition to being less likely to utilize formal legal institutions, firms facing problems with licensing report being more likely to utilize strategies based on corrupt coercion. For both property and debt disputes, firms that perceive licensing to be an obstacle on average rate their likeliness of using law enforcement or other government officials in a private capacity as much as a full point higher than other firms, and these differences are statistically significant at the 90 percent (and often at the 95 percent) level of confidence for all but two model specifications. A similar pattern exists between firms' perceived licensing burdens and an increased propensity to utilize informal connections in court, although the results are less robust than for other types of corrupt coercion.

In summary, the evidence provides qualified support for the claim that firms which face excessive licensing burdens, much like firms that do not

---

[8] Firms were asked to rate on a 1 to 7 scale the extent to which licensing is an obstacle to the success of their business, where 1 indicates "no obstacle" and 7 indicates a "major obstacle" (the average rating was 4.04). For ease of interpretation, the analyses in Figure 7.5a collapse the responses into firms with a rating of five or greater versus firms with a rating of four or lower. The results are robust to using a ordinal 1 to 7 scale (see Online Appendix).

Figure (a) shows the difference between the average responses of firms that do and do not consider licensing a major obstacle to doing business, on a 1 to 7 scale where 1 is "very unlikely" and 7 is "very likely," holding other factors constant. Figure (b) shows the difference between the average responses of firms that do and do not consider customs regulations a major obstacle to doing business, again holding other factors constant.

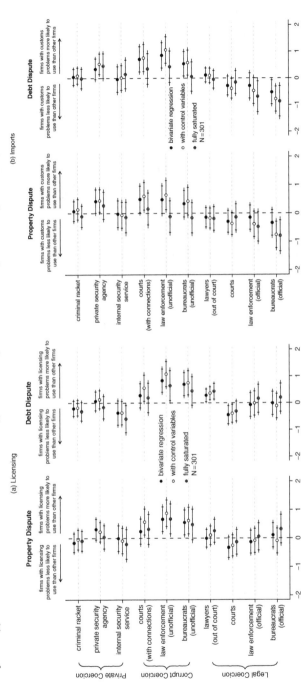

(a) Licensing

(b) Imports

Figure 7.5 Demand-Side Barriers and Propensity to Use Strategies

Note: Circles indicate point estimates from OLS regressions. Horizontal lines represent 95 percent confidence intervals; vertical tick marks represent 90 percent confidence intervals. For further details on model specifications and the wording of the property and debt dispute scenarios, see the note to Figure 5.3.

pay their full share of taxes, are forced to operate extralegally. As a consequence, they become less likely to utilize formal legal institutions and more likely to utilize illegal property security strategies.

7.2.2   Customs Barriers

Similar to the effects of regulations early in a firm's life cycle, burdens at key points in a firm's supply chain can have an ongoing effect on property security strategies, creating long-lasting demand-side barriers. The most pressing example in the Russian context involves imports. Due to corruption, long delays, and a general desire to avoid duties, schemes to bypass customs inspections were rampant in the 1990s. The extent of such schemes was documented by an OECD analysis of Russia's trade with its 15 largest trading partners between 1996 and 2001, which revealed an enormous discrepancy – approximately 50 billion US dollars – between the value of exports to Russia recorded by trading partners and the value of imports recorded by Russian statistics during this period. Estimates suggest that only 20 percent of imported goods during the period in question were fully and properly declared; 70 percent were brought in using "grey" tactics, such as misreporting the product category, price, or quantity; and 10 percent were smuggled in outright (Radaev, 2002, p. 17; OECD, 2005, pp. 33–34).

As with other forms of regulatory burdens, problems with legally importing goods have persisted despite numerous reform efforts. In 2003, Russia introduced a new Customs Code, part of a joint Customs Development Project carried out with the World Bank between 2003 and 2010. Reforms included the implementation of new IT and human resource management systems, as well as the introduction of electronic customs declarations, an approach not only designed to enhance efficiency but also to reduce corruption. Results have been mixed. Surveys of firms conducted by the World Bank and the Russian Federal Customs Service indicate that 50 percent of respondents in 2006 believed the modernization effort had simplified customs procedures. This figure had risen to 61 percent by 2009. Moreover, between 2006 and 2009 the number of respondents reporting that they had encountered "direct or indirect hints about additional payment" – an allusion to bribe requests – had fallen by half. Overall, the percent of import declarations selected for physical inspection reportedly decreased from 30 percent at the outset of the project in 2003 to under 7 percent by 2010 (Johns et al., 2011). However, in direct contradiction to these findings, then Minister of Economic

Development Elvira Nabiullina publicly declared in 2010 that 44 percent of imports were still facing inspections, compared to just 2 to 3 percent in countries such as Germany, Great Britain, and the United States (Tovkailo, 2011).

To the extent that they persist, barriers to legal imports have the potential to influence firms' property security strategies. Without proper documentation, wholesalers, retailers, and traders are forced to partially conduct operations in the informal economy, limiting their ability to turn to formal legal institutions when conflicts arise. As an importer in the consumer electronics sector explained, "The root of all 'dirtiness' in business (*vsya serost biznesa*) goes back to the customs service. All the shady operations (*vsya neprozrachnost*) start at the Russian customs. The products come [to the country] through the customs, and if something shady happens there, or some problems occur there, then everything else goes in the usual (shady) pattern (*idet po tsepochki*)" (interview cited in Radaev, 2002, p. 16).

Survey data offer additional evidence of the link between customs barriers and property security strategies. Firms in the survey I conducted were asked to rate the extent to which customs regulations are an obstacle to the success of their business. Thirty-one percent of those responding stated that these regulations pose a significant obstacle.[9] As can be seen in Figure 7.5b, firms that perceive customs regulations to be an obstacle on average rate their likeliness of turning to courts or to law enforcement and bureaucrats in an official capacity lower than other firms, although these results are not robust across model specifications and pertain primarily to debt rather than property disputes. Firms that face problems with customs regulations, moreover, on average rate their propensity to use strategies of corrupt force, such courts along with informal connections and law enforcement or other state officials in a private capacity, approximately 0.50 to a full point higher than other firms. Nearly all model specifications pertaining to corrupt coercion are statistically significant at the 95 percent level, even when a full set of control variables are included. However, the results are not robust in the most exacting specifications, the

---

[9] Firms were asked to rate on a 1 to 7 scale the extent to which customs regulations are an obstacle to the success of their business, where 1 indicates "no obstacle" and 7 indicates a "major obstacle" (the average rating was 3.35). For ease of interpretation, the analyses in Figure 7.5b collapse the responses into firms with a rating of five or greater versus firms with a rating of four or lower. The results are robust to using a ordinal 1 to 7 scale (see Online Appendix).

fully saturated models that include all variables of interest in Chapters 5 through 7.[10]

In summary, the evidence suggests that demand-side barriers which force certain sectors or types of firms to rely on operations in the informal economy are associated with variation in strategies across different types of firms. When firms are unable to operate legally, formal legal institutions become less accessible, reducing firms' use of legal strategies and sometimes forcing firms to utilize illegal strategies.

7.3   Firm Size

Firm size in many cases mediates the relationships between transaction costs, informal networks, and property security strategies. But firm size also directly shapes firm strategies. Size affects the extent to which a firm finds demand-side barriers imposing as well as the extent to which a firm can effectively employ illegal strategies. This section explores the relationships between firm size and property security strategies in greater detail.

The evidence suggests that both small and large firms face incentives that may reduce their willingness to utilize law, but for very different reasons. While small firms face demand-side barriers to the use of formal legal institutions, large firms have the informal connections to most effectively utilize illegal strategies. Consequently, it is medium-sized firms, which face fewer barriers than small firms but which also haver fewer informal connections than large firms, that face an incentive structure most compatible with legal strategies.

Existing studies have recognized that firms of different sizes are likely to exhibit distinctive approaches to property security, but many of these scholars have drawn attention to the important political and economic roles of *small firms*. For example, Åslund and Johnson (2003) introduce a policy paper on the role of small businesses in post-communist countries as follows:

---

[10] When a dummy variable for whether or not a firm is an importer is used in place of a variable measuring firms' perceptions of customs regulations as an obstacle to doing business, the evidence again shows that importers are less likely to use legal strategies. However, importers are also less likely to utilize corrupt coercion. Given that there may be significant variation among importers with respect to the legality of their import operations, I consider the indicator of customs regulations as an obstacle a more valid measure of a demand-side barrier than the blunt measure of whether or not a firm engages in imports.

Institutions such as strong property rights and the rule of law are important for both long-run economic performance and short-run volatility. Developing good institutions is generally viewed as a desirable goal, but there is no agreed road map for such changes. This paper suggests that, at least for former communist countries, the right way to begin is by lowering the barriers to entry into the formal sector for small-scale entrepreneurs ... These policies have economic advantages, but their most important effect is to change the political equilibrium, creating a powerful force for further institutional improvement.

Jackson et al. (2003) and Frye (2003) similarly suggest that start-up firms are the social foundation of pro-reform constituencies that support the development not only of markets, but also of democracy, in the post-communist region.

For small firms to be the natural constituency for institutional development, it must be the case that smaller firms perceive greater value in formal legal institutions than their larger counterparts. The notion that small firms benefit disproportionately from utilizing formal legal institutions stems from the idea that in a lawless environment, small firms suffer disproportionately because they do not possess the informal networks and financial resources to effectively employ strategies of private or corruption coercion. There certainly is some evidence to support this contention. In the survey I conducted, firms were asked whether they had more, less, or the same level of connections with government officials, law enforcement agencies, and/or courts compared to the companies with which they do business. Twenty-five percent of firms with fewer than 100 employees reported having fewer informal connections. By contrast, only 12 percent of firms with between 101 and 500 employees reported having fewer connections, and a mere 2 percent of companies with over 500 employees perceived themselves at a disadvantage compared to their business partners.[11]

Yet while small firms may struggle to effectively employ illegal strategies, they also face demand-side barriers to the use of formal legal institutions, due to a significant disadvantage in terms of access to lawyers and legal resources. For example, among firms in the 2010 survey I conducted with 100 or fewer employees, 58 percent agreed with the statement, "I am confident the legal system will uphold my legal rights in cases concerning a property dispute with a small or medium-sized private

---

[11] Differences in means between small and medium, medium and large, and large and small firms are statistically significant at the 95 percent confidence level or higher.

firm." The comparable figure for firms with more than 100 employees was approximately 67 percent. The contrast becomes even more stark when firms were asked whether they are confident in the court system when facing a property dispute with a large private firm. For firms with 100 or fewer employees, only 42 percent of firms expressed confidence, whereas 54 percent of firms with more than 100 employees agreed with the statement.[12] Similar disparities across firms of different sizes pertain to confidence in the legal system to resolve contract disputes. The size of firms' legal departments also illustrates the disparity in legal resources available to small and large firms. For firms with more than 100 employees, 53 percent have an internal legal department, and the average size is approximately seven lawyers. Unsurprisingly, only 18 percent of firms with 100 or fewer employees who participated in the survey have an internal legal department, and the average size of these departments is approximately three lawyers. In short, the disadvantages small firms face relative to larger firms when using legal strategies are at least as great as those faced when using illegal strategies, given the significant barriers to small firms' use of formal legal institutions.

By contrast, many scholars have recognized that *large firms* are more capable of protecting themselves using private coercion, and thus may thrive in a lawless environment that allows them to confiscate assets of smaller firms. Sonin (2003, p. 716), for example, notes that "In transition and developing economies ... [E]conomic agents are forced to invest in private protection. Economies of scale in private protection provide rich agents with a significant advantage over poor agents in this environment. Furthermore, the rich agents' ability to gain from redistribution due to improper protection of property rights makes them natural opponents of improvements in public protection" (see also Polishchuk and Savvateev, 2004). Similarly, Shleifer and Treisman (2001, ch. 7) detail how in the 1990s large firms used their informal connections and political clout in disputes with tax authorities, while small firms simply sought to hide from the authorities. Only medium-sized firms, being too large to hide but too small to hold political clout, were forced to comply with laws.

Although large firms can effectively employ illegal strategies, their willingness to do so may be tempered by several factors. First, large firms'

---

[12] For a dispute with a large firm, the difference in means is statistically significant at the 95 percent level of confidence. For a dispute with a small or medium firm, the difference in means falls outside of conventional levels of statistical significance ($p = 0.14$).

resources can be redeployed to effectively utilize legal strategies and create an advantage in court. Indeed, it has long been recognized by scholars of developed countries that large firms are more adept at using the legal system (Galanter, 1974), and existing studies of Russia similarly have found that large firms are more likely than small firms to litigate (Hendley et al., 2001a; Yakovlev et al., 2004; Hendley, 2012). Additionally, the risks associated with using illegal strategies are higher for larger firms. Large firms are both more concerned with building a durable brand and in greater need of international financing, which means they may be wary of using violence and corruption if this risks undermining their reputation or driving away foreign investors (see the discussion in Chapter 6). Nevertheless, though these considerations should be taken into account, the fact remains that larger firms are uniquely situated to employ illegal strategies effectively.

In contrast to small and large firms, *medium-sized firms* face fewer incentives to circumvent formal legal institutions. Relative to small firms, they face fewer demand-side barriers. For example, medium-sized firms express much higher confidence in their ability to fruitfully use the legal system. In fact, the level of middle-sized firms' confidence in the legal system is not statistically distinguishable from that of large firms.[13] Moreover, medium-sized firms have sufficient resources to aim for compliance with laws and regulations, unlike small firms. But while medium-sized firms are, like large firms, less impeded by demand-side barriers, they are less likely to have access to the informal connections or private security options enjoyed by large firms. The consequence is that medium-sized firms are likely to display the highest propensity to utilize legal strategies.

Data on the extent to which firms value formal legal institutions support the hypothesis that medium-sized firms perceive such institutions to be more vital for their business than do smaller or larger firms. In the survey, respondents were requested to rank the importance (on a 1 to 7 scale, where 1 is "not at all important" and 7 is "very important")

---

[13] Sixty-six percent of firms in the 2010 survey I conducted with more than 500 employees expressed confidence the legal system will uphold their rights in cases concerning a property dispute with a small or medium-sized firm. The comparable figure for firms with between 251 and 500 employees was 69 percent; for firms with between 101 and 250 employees, 66 percent. In property disputes with a large firm, levels of confidence across medium-sized and large firms were again nearly identical: 54 percent expressed confidence among firms with more than 500 employees, 56 percent among firms with 251 to 500 employees, and 53 percent among firms with 101 to 250 employees.

of effective and non-corrupt institutions, such as commercial courts and the police, for the success of their business. Unsurprisingly, firms with less than 100 employees ranked the commercial courts' importance lowest, with an average rating of 5.8. The average rating was modestly higher for firms with more than 500 employees – 6.0, a statistically insignificant difference. But the highest rating – 6.4 – was among firms with between 251 and 500 employees, a rating that is statistically distinguishable from the ratings of both small firms and the largest firms.

A similar pattern emerges with respect to firm size and preferred strategies for resolving an asset conflict. Medium-sized firms have a higher reported likeliness of turning to lawyers to resolve the dispute out of court, filing a claim in court, or turning to law enforcement in an official capacity than either small or large firms. Firms' reported likeliness to use strategies based on law rises with firm size, peaks for the firms with between 251 and 500 employees, and then falls again for firms with over 500 employees. In the most pronounced example, firms with 251 to 500 employees rate their likeliness to use courts approximately 0.60 points higher than firms with under 100 employees, but also nearly 1.10 points higher than firms with over 500 employees, distinctions that are both statistically significant at the 95 percent confidence level. The curvilinear relationships between firm size and preferred property security strategies are also apparent when data concerning debt disputes are analyzed in place of data concerning property disputes.[14]

The data thus appear to support the hypothesis that medium-sized firms are the most likely to utilize legal strategies. However, medium-sized firms are also the most likely to use strategies of corrupt coercion. As with firms' reported likeliness to use strategies based on law, firms' reported likeliness of using strategies such as courts with informal connections or law enforcement in a private capacity rises with firm size, peaks for the firms with between 250 and 500 employees, and then falls again for firms with over 500 employees. One possible explanation for this surprising finding is that while mid-sized firms may extensively rely on legal strategies, they are also the most likely to seek expansion, and may be willing to do so using all available tools. While further research is necessary to confirm the mechanisms underlying medium-sized firms' prominent use of corrupt coercion, the existing data support this interpretation. For example, respondents in the survey were asked about the extent to which they

[14] This curvilinear relationship is robust when controlling for firm size, sector, and city of location.

agree that laws and regulations limit their business development strategies (e.g., entering new markets) or the strategies their firm would like to
use for acquiring and protecting assets. Firms with between between 251
and 500 employees were most likely to perceive laws and regulations as
constraining.

In summary, there are distinct patterns of property security strategies across firms of different sizes. Demand-side barriers pose a more
significant problem for small firms than for larger firms, providing a dis-
incentive for small firms to use formal legal institutions. Large firms,
meanwhile, are more likely than smaller firms to possess the resources
and connections to effectively utilize illegal strategies, which also creates
disincentives to use formal legal institutions. Large firms, however, must
also consider reputation costs, which may temper their willingness to use
private or corrupt coercion.

Mid-sized firms, ultimately, appear the most likely to use formal legal
institutions. They are capable of overcoming demand-side barriers, but
they also do not have the same level of connections and resources that
allow large firms to utilize illegal strategies effectively. Both of these factors increase the propensity of medium-sized firms to rely on law. But
medium-sized firms additionally are the most ambitious with respect
to expansion into new markets and the acquisition of new assets. They
therefore appear also to be the most aggressive when it comes to using
strategies of corrupt force.

7.4 Conclusion

Although there is a broad trend toward greater reliance on formal legal
institutions among Russian firms, the evolution of property security
strategies over the past decade and a half has affected firms unevenly.
This chapter has examined the sources of variation in strategies across
different types of firms. While cross-sectional analyses should be interpreted with caution, the existing evidence is consistent with this book's
analytical framework. The findings indicate that to understand variation
in property security strategies across firms, it is essential to consider the
demand-side barriers that different types of firms face, and the ability of
different types of firms to effectively employ illegal strategies. Firms that
face extensive licensing requirements that force parts of their operations
into the informal economy, as well as firms that are forced to engage in
semilegal importation schemes, are less likely to utilize formal legal institutions out of fear that their own illicit activities will be exposed. These

concerns create a formidable demand-side barrier. Meanwhile, factors such as a firm's type of output, the size of the market in which it operates, and the informal networks at its disposal influence a firm's ability to effectively utilize illegal strategies.

Variation in property security strategies across different types of firms is of great importance for the politics of institutional development. Firms that rely on violence and corruption undermine and destabilize formal institutions. Firms that utilize courts and law enforcement, on the other hand, reinforce the effectiveness and relevance of formal state institutions. Firm strategies also may be tied to firms' preferences for legislation and political change, meaning that variation in strategies offers clues into what types of firms are most likely to support institution building in transition and developing countries. Such questions about the broader economic and political effects of property security strategies are addressed in the concluding chapter.

8

Firms, States, and the Rule of Law in Comparative Perspective

This book has introduced a theory of institutional demand and an analytical framework to integrate the demand and supply sides of property security. In contrast to existing studies' focus on the conditions under which *rulers* seek to create effective institutions, this book's framework sets forth a distinctly different approach by emphasizing *firms'* role in the development of effective institutions.

The theory elucidates the relationships between three key explanatory factors and the outcome this book has sought to explain – firms' strategies for securing property. First, *state legal capacity* is necessary but insufficient to induce firms' use of formal legal institutions: While a dearth of state legal capacity impedes firms' use of law, improved capacity frequently does not increase firms' willingness to utilize formal legal institutions. Second, firms' increasing reliance on formal legal institutions frequently occurs in the absence of heightened state legal capacity. In such cases, two factors other than state legal capacity largely determine whether firms utilize violence and corruption or whether firms turn to law: the prevalence of *demand-side barriers* to using formal legal institutions and the *effectiveness of illegal strategies* for securing property.

The first section of this concluding chapter briefly recounts the book's central arguments and summarizes the empirical evidence presented in preceding chapters. The chapter then examines the relationships between firms' property security strategies, the effectiveness of state institutions, and the broader concept of the rule of law. With this broader picture in mind, the chapter turns to the prospects for property security and the rule of law in Russia. Finally, the chapter places the book's central arguments in comparative perspective, considering pathways to the rule of law under various historical and contemporary circumstances.

8.1   The Argument in Brief

Chapter 2 developed the analytical framework described above and introduced the study's dependent variable: firm strategies for resolving conflicts related to acquiring assets, protecting property, and enforcing contracts – a concept I refer to as *property security strategies*. All strategies – legal or illegal – ultimately rely on coercion as a last resort (Umbeck, 1981, p. 9; Ellickson, 1991, p. 175). The only question is whether this coercion is supplied by the state in accordance with formal rules, or whether a strategy relies on coercion supplied by private actors or by state actors illicitly employing state resources. Accordingly, the typology of property security strategies presented in Chapter 2 categorized strategies with reference to their source of underlying coercion. On one end of the spectrum are strategies based on *private coercion*, such as turning to criminal protection rackets or unlawful private security agencies. On the other end of the spectrum are strategies based on *legal coercion*, such as turning to courts and law enforcement agencies. In the middle lies a category of *corrupt coercion*, in which firms utilize the services of state officials and formal state institutions but in a corrupt manner. Examples include bribing judges or utilizing illicit connections to law enforcement agencies or other government officials.

In Chapter 3 the book turned to an analysis of the evolution of property security strategies in Russia throughout the 1990s and 2000s, the two decades following the collapse of the Soviet Union. The chapter presented evidence of three significant trends. First, Russian firms' reliance on private coercion declined significantly over time. Second, to the extent that Russian firms continued to utilize illegal strategies, these strategies took the form of corrupt coercion, such as the illicit protection rackets offered by law enforcement officials. Finally, Russian firms increasingly came to utilize strategies based on legal coercion, relying extensively on courts, formal interactions with state officials, and lawyers who help negotiate in the "shadow of the law" (Mnookin and Kornhauser, 1978).

The remaining chapters applied the analytical framework to develop an explanation of the evolution of property security strategies in Russia, both over time and across different types of firms. Chapter 4 focused on the first variable in the framework – *state legal capacity* – defined as formal laws and regulations as well as the organizations required to implement and enforce these rules. The chapter demonstrated the incompleteness of explanations for firms' use (or disuse) of formal legal institutions that focus primarily on levels of state legal capacity. First, despite significant judicial reforms and other legislation aimed at improving formal legal institutions' effectiveness, Russian firms continued to rely on private and corrupt coercion throughout the early-to-mid 1990s. Second, in the late 1990s and 2000s, a period during which Russian firms increasingly turned to law, the development of state legal capacity was highly uneven. Improvements, such as funding for legal institutions, were often offset by negative trends, such as legal institutions' declining political independence. Moreover, a critical aspect of state legal capacity – the ability of the state to constrain lower-level officials – became particularly problematic: Predatory bureaucrats' expropriation of firms' assets increased throughout the 2000s. Finally, firms themselves frequently failed to recognize the improvements to state legal capacity that did occur during the Putin era, undermining a crucial link in explanations tying property security strategies to levels of legal capacity.

In order to account for the diversification of Russian firms' strategies from a reliance on violence and corruption toward increasing reliance on formal legal institutions, the other two factors in the framework must be considered. Chapter 5 analyzed the first of these factors – the prevalence of *demand-side barriers* – defined as the behaviors or beliefs at the level of firms and individuals that lead these actors to avoid formal legal institutions. In particular, the chapter examined the role of two prominent demand-side barriers: firms' operations in the informal economy and expectations about other firms' reliance on violence or corruption (which lead to collective action problems). Although operations in the informal economy manifest in many forms, in Russia the most prominent issue has been low levels of tax compliance. Throughout the 1990s, firms adapted to unwieldy tax regulations by hiding revenues from the state. They accordingly hesitated to turn to formal legal institutions due to concerns that their illicit tax practices could be unveiled in the process. Consequently, improving firms' tax compliance was an essential step in reducing demand-side barriers and encouraging firms' use of law. Meanwhile, even as Russian firms came to recognize that legal strategies would be more effective (and less dangerous) *if* the majority of other firms would also turn away from private and corrupt coercion, their uncertainty about other firms' willingness to utilize law created a powerful demand-side barrier. To some extent, this collective action problem was mitigated by explicit efforts on the part of business associations to reduce firms' use of illegal strategies. But perhaps more important were the uncoordinated interactions among individual firms. As changes – such as improved tax compliance – induced some firms to adopt legal strategies, a critical mass of firms relying on law accumulated, initiating a classic tipping point process whereby increased use of law stimulated additional reliance on formal legal institutions.

Chapter 6 then analyzed the final explanatory factor in the analytical framework: the *effectiveness of illegal strategies*. This effectiveness largely depends on transaction costs relative to other strategies and the risk of sanctions for illegal activities. In particular, the chapter examined several trends that in the case of Russia contributed to the declining effectiveness of violence and corruption. First, whereas conflicts in the 1990s among multiple shareholders of privatized firms led to fierce battles to acquire assets quickly and using any means possible, ownership consolidation in the 2000s facilitated long-term investment. This shift increased owners' perception of the risk associated with illegal strategies, which could damage firms' reputations and destabilize the overall investment climate. Second, as the financial sector developed, firms increasingly conducted transactions through banks rather than in cash. Given that off-the-books cash is essential for illegal strategies, the transaction costs associated with illegal strategies increased, making them less effective. Third, as Russia became more integrated in the international economy, a number of factors both increased the transaction costs of and the risks associated with illegal strategies. Firms seeking foreign direct investment, for example, became wary of strategies that could harm their reputation. Firms that became subsidiaries of multinational companies, meanwhile, faced new internal constraints that raised the costs of strategies based on corruption or violence.

While Chapters 4 through 6 applied the analytical framework to evolution in property security strategies over time, Chapter 7 demonstrated the framework's applicability to variation across different types of firms. Analysis of cross-firm variation further draws attention to the incompleteness of explanations focused on state legal capacity, for it is unclear how varying levels of legal capacity can account for differences in strategies across firms. By contrast, the fact that different types of firms face distinct demand-side barriers and employ illegal strategies with different degrees of effectiveness serves to illuminate patterns of cross-firm variation in property security strategies. For example, firms subject to extensive regulation related to licensing face higher demand-side barriers than other firms, and accordingly are more prone to use illegal strategies and less prone to use legal ones. Meanwhile, Chapter 7 provided evidence of how a variety of factors that influence transaction costs – a firm's type of output, the size of the market in which it operates, and the informal networks in which it is embedded – affect a firm's ability to effectively employ illegal strategies. Accordingly, firms offering services rather than producing physical products, firms operating in local rather than national markets, and firms with ties to corrupt officials are less likely to turn to formal legal institutions.

Overall, the analytical framework provides insights into variation in Russian firms' property security strategies both over time and across firms. It clarifies the role of "supply-side" variables such as state legal capacity and "demand-side" variables such as barriers to the use of law and the effectiveness of illegal strategies in influencing firms' propensity to use formal legal institutions. But how do property security strategies influence the effectiveness of institutions more broadly? How do strategies affect the prospects of establishing the rule of law? And how does the analytical framework apply to countries beyond Russia? The remainder of this chapter addresses these issues.

8.2 Strategies, Institutional Effectiveness, and the Rule of Law

This book has focused on property security strategies. Firms' choices of strategies have significant implications, for the use of violence or corruption to protect assets clearly has detrimental societal effects. But strategies are also important because they influence the *effectiveness* of state institutions.

One way in which firms affect institutional effectiveness is through lobbying. In the post-communist context, scholars have explored the private sector's role in lobbying for tax reform (Jones Luong and Weinthal, 2004), reform of bankruptcy legislation (Woodruff, 2002), and other institutional reforms ranging from legislation on capital accounts to the judicial system (Guriev and Rachinsky, 2005). These studies have sometimes linked firms' preferences for institutional reforms with some of the phenomena examined in previous chapters. In particular, a popular notion in the early 2000s was that once oligarchs and other powerful private actors consolidated ownership, they no longer benefited from ineffective state institutions and thus sought to transfer the costs of property security to the state (e.g., Boone and Rodionov, 2002; Treisman, 2002; Zhuravskaya, 2007). Lost in these analyses were the distinct incentives faced by different types of firms, as demonstrated by the analysis of cross-firm variation in property security strategies in Chapter 7. An especially fruitful avenue for future research therefore would be to examine the relationship between firm strategies for securing property and their policy preferences for or against institutional reforms.

Lobbying, however, is an activity limited to a relatively small number of larger, more influential firms. Moreover, lobbying provides an *indirect* link between firm strategies and institutional effectiveness: Firms influence legislation, which in turn shapes the course of institutional development. More immediately related to the focus of this book is the *direct* link between firms' *use* (or disuse) of formal institutions and these institutions' effectiveness.

Like prominent studies of property rights, many classic studies of institutional effectiveness and of state capacity approach their subject from the perspective of rulers and state officials (e.g., Zysman, 1983; Evans et al., 1985; Levi, 1989; Geddes, 1994). By contrast, the firm-centered, demand-side approach to property security developed in this book offers a distinctly different perspective on the sources of institutional effectiveness, a perspective more in line with scholars such as Putnam (1994), Evans (1995), and Migdal (1988, 2001), who draw attention to the fact that states' success or failure is not entirely of their own making. Instead, institutional performance depends not only on rulers' policies but also on societal actors' strategies.

Migdal's (2001) "state-in-society" approach is particularly relevant for understanding the influence of firm strategies on institutional effectiveness. Migdal contrasts the *image* of the state with the *practices* of state officials and societal actors interacting with these officials. The image that state builders have sought to create over several centuries, an image reified by many scholarly accounts, is of a unified entity (*the* state) that enforces a singular set of rules (*the* law) and that is clearly demarcated both from other states by territorial boundaries and from private actors by social boundaries. However, practices – "the routine performance of state actors and agencies" – can either "reinforce the image of the state or weaken it; they may bolster the notion of the territorial and public-private boundaries or neutralize them" (Migdal, 2001, p. 18). In other words, state building is not only a top-down process of creating and implementing institutional blueprints, but also a bottom-up, ongoing process involving the daily role of numerous "ordinary" actors in "the ongoing struggles among shifting coalitions over the rules for daily behavior" (Migdal, 2001, p. 10).

From this perspective, the connection between firm strategies and the effectiveness of state institutions becomes clearer. Strategies based on *private coercion* intrinsically *undermine* formal institutions. By avoiding and circumventing state institutions, such strategies contribute to a fundamental divergence between on-the-ground practices and formal rules. Under such circumstances, formal rules come to exist only on paper, what some refer to as "parchment institutions" (Carey, 2000). Others question whether it even makes sense to refer to formal rules that elicit minimal compliance as "institutions" (Levitsky and Slater, 2013). More devastatingly, the very use of private violence weakens the state's claim to a monopoly on legitimate coercion. In this respect, firms' utilization of illegal strategies is fundamentally different from the numerous informal strategies – reliance on informal norms, the expectation of repeated interactions, private arbitration, and so on – that peacefully coexist with formal institutions. As Milhaupt and West (2000, pp. 50–51) explain in their study of organized crime in Japan:

> [P]rivate ordering by organized criminal firms is qualitatively different from conventional private ordering by contract or arbitration. While both avoid resort to governmental institutions, only the latter operates within constraints that are *inherently* legal, because they are legitimized by the same political theory that supports governing generally. Similarly, while the activities of both organized criminal groups and the state are backed by coercive force, only the violence of the legal system is rooted in a deeper conception of public order. The means and ends of organized criminal firms, by contrast, are determined solely in the private interest of the members themselves. Pervasive organized criminal involvement in private ordering thus not only increases the level of violence in society, it is also antithetical to the rule of law (emphasis in original).

In short, when firms' reliance on private coercion is widespread, effective formal legal institutions are unlikely to develop.

If strategies based on private coercion undermine formal institutions, then strategies based on *corrupt coercion* serve to *subvert* formal institutions. The distinction I draw here between undermining and subverting is subtle. The former weakens formal institutions in the sense that they cease to "matter." In other words, institutions come to have a minimal effect on the *de facto* rules governing societal interactions. By contrast, subverted institutions continue to "matter" in that they continue to have a significant effect on the daily interactions of private actors. However, this influence becomes imbued with the logic of private gain rather than public interest. Migdal's state-in-society approach perfectly captures these effects of strategies based on corrupt coercion. As Migdal (2001, p. 20) explains, in many societies "Various parts or fragments of the state have allied with one another, as well as with groups outside, to further their goals. Those practices and alliances have acted to promote a variety of sets of rules, often quite distinct from those set out in the state's own official laws and regulations." These interactions among lower-level state actors and between state officials and private sector actors come to subvert the essential public-private divide upon which contemporary notions such as corrupt versus non-corrupt and legitimate versus illegitimate are based: "These alliances, coalitions, or networks have neutralized the sharp ... social boundary [between public and private] that the first portrayal of the state has acted to establish, as well as the sharp demarcation between the state as the preeminent rule maker and society as the recipient of those rules" (Migdal, 2001, p. 20). Under such conditions, the effectiveness of formal institutions is bound to suffer.

Finally, strategies based on *legal coercion* act to *reinforce* formal institutions. In part, the adoption of legal strategies is similar to Levi's (1989) notion of quasi-voluntary compliance: Firms submit to formal institutions not merely because they fear sanctions that might otherwise result, but also because they view it in their interest to do so. But firms' adoption of legal strategies entails something more than passive compliance with law. It also presupposes an increase in firms' *active* use of formal institutions as a resource. This shift from illegal to legal strategies involves a transformation similar to what Hendley (1996, p. 3) describes as a change from "coercive" law – which consists of laws used by the state to control citizens – to "reciprocal" law, meaning that citizens come to recognize law as a tool for "remedying wrongs and advancing interests." In other words, it is firms' use of formal institutions that imbues these institutions with authority. By using state institutions, societal actors contribute on a micro-level to state-building; by circumventing or subverting state institutions, they contribute to institutional breakdown.

This societal side of institutional effectiveness has implications for nearly all state institutions, but it is especially relevant for institutions related to the *rule of law*. Below I consider rule of law in a broader context. For the moment, my focus is limited to the economic dimensions of rule of law, or what Dam (2006, p. 9) refers to as "rule-of-law issues: the protection of property rights, the enforcement of contracts, and the role of the judiciary in achieving these goals." Most significantly, the effectiveness of legal institutions depends on societal demand to a greater degree than many other types of state institutions. Litigation, after all, is instigated largely by private parties. Moreover, as the discussion of collective action problems in Chapter 5 demonstrated, laws and legal institutions matter only to the extent that private sector actors *believe* law matters to other private sector actors. State-provided legal institutions thus face a greater risk of irrelevance than other types of state institutions. Indeed, commercial courts in early modern Europe often operated entirely outside the auspices of the state. Over time, state courts had to compete with non-state counterparts to convince merchants to settle their disputes in state-provided venues (Berman 1983, pp. 339–355; Benson 1989).

In the following section I build on this discussion of institutional effectiveness to examine more fully the relationships between property security strategies and the rule of law, with specific reference to the Russian case. Before turning to this analysis, however, it is important to recognize one of the implications of linking strategies and the effectiveness of institutions. The fact that strategies influence institutional effectiveness draws attention to one aspect in which the framework developed in this book remains incomplete. State legal capacity enters into the framework as a fully exogenous variable. Its effects are analyzed; its sources are not. But as discussed above, firms' choices of property security strategies affect institutional performance, and a fully comprehensive model would explicitly incorporate what might be described as the effects of institutional demand on institutional supply.

One way to develop a comprehensive framework would be to add a new component to the model in Chapter 2: a strategic state that chooses whether or not to invest in state legal capacity. If one assumes that investment in state legal capacity is costly but that the state benefits when firms use formal institutions (e.g., from taxes and court fees), then a key insight emerges. The state must have some reasonable expectation that firms will respond to investment in legal capacity by increasing their use of formal institutions. Otherwise, the state is better off not investing. Meanwhile, just as the state faces tension between the costs of investing in capacity and the potential benefits, firms face a similar tension. Use of state institutions requires costly tax and fee payments, but given sufficient investment by the state, reliance on formal institutions will be more effective than alternatives. Consequently, firms must have a reasonable expectation that their payments of taxes and fees will lead to a sufficiently large increase in the effectiveness of formal legal institutions. Otherwise, firms are better off avoiding the state and relying on illegal strategies. Although an explicit model must be analyzed to evaluate the implications of introducing a strategic state, similar models, such as Gehlbach's (2007) analysis of "revenue traps," have found that when such strategic complementarities between the state and private actors exist, there are likely to be multiple equilibria. In one type of equilibria, the state invests in capacity, and firms adopt legal strategies; in the other type of equilibria, the state does not invest, and firms utilize illegal strategies. However, given that the model developed in this book already emphasizes strategic complementarities among firms, in that firms become willing to use legal strategies only when they expect other firms to use legal strategies, the simultaneous inclusion of a complementarities between firms and the state is bound to significantly increase the complexity of analysis.

While the addition of a strategic state actor into the framework is a worthy goal for future research, my focus in this book has been on the understudied issue of institutional demand. Whereas existing studies of property rights treat private sector actors' use of institutions as exogenous in their analyses of rulers' willingness to supply institutions, my aim has been to offer a complementary theory. Simplifying the supply side of the story provides for theoretical traction and lays a foundation for the ultimate integration of existing theories into a fully comprehensive framework of institutional supply and demand.

8.3   Prospects for the Rule of Law in Russia

This section turns to the relationships between property security strategies, state legal capacity, and the prospects for the rule of law in contemporary Russia. The rule of law, an ideal that exists nowhere but is better approximated in some countries than others, frequently is defined as a "system in which laws are public knowledge, are clear in meaning, and apply equally to everyone" (Carothers, 1998, p. 96). Many scholars emphasize in particular that the "equal application to all" clause in such definitions implies that rulers, too, are bound by laws and unwilling or unable to engage in the arbitrary exercise of power. However, as noted above, my initial focus is limited to the economic dimensions of the rule of law: the state institutions that provide for property rights protection, contract enforcement, and the resolution of business disputes – what I have referred to throughout this book as "property security." At the end of the section, I return to the question of whether or not progress in the economic sphere of the rule of law spills over into progress in the political and human rights spheres.

Two pivotal insights follow from the analysis in the preceding section. First, because state institutions for property security remain ineffective when private actors' strategies undermine or subvert them, the development of rule of law requires not only constraints on state officials

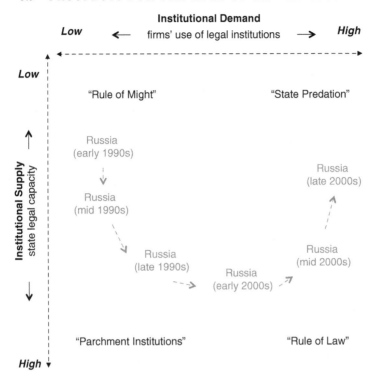

Figure 8.1   States, Firms, and the Rule of Law

but also social actors' adoption of strategies that reinforce state institutions. Second, there are distinct pathways to the rule of law. Societies with ineffective legal institutions and excessive state predation must find a way to bolster state legal capacity and constrain state officials. Societies whose formal institutions fundamentally diverge from de facto social and economic practices must find a way to stimulate institutional demand.

Figure 8.1 illustrates these relationships between firms' property security strategies, supply of legal capacity, and the rule of law. The horizontal axis depicts firms' reliance on formal legal institutions – institutional "demand" – on a continuum from low to high, with movement toward the right side of the figure representing increased use of law. The vertical axis depicts the level of state legal capacity – institutional "supply" – also on a continuum from low to high, with movement toward the bottom of the figure representing increased capacity.

The upper left corner of the figure represents a lack of legal capacity combined with minimal institutional demand from the private sector.

These circumstances – the *rule of might* – create an environment in which those actors, both state or private, who can most effectively wield force triumph. As discussed in Chapters 3 and 4, the "rule of might" moniker aptly describes the chaotic conditions of the early-to-mid 1990s in Russia. State legal capacity was just beginning to emerge during this period. The laws and regulations underpinning a market economy were still being written, the agencies to implement and enforce the rules were still being created or retooled, and state officials were just beginning to adapt to their new roles in the post-Soviet era. Meanwhile, the absence of state legal capacity precluded firms' use of formal legal institutions, leaving Russian firms with few choices other than to rely on criminal protection rackets, private security agencies, and corrupt public officials for property security.

The bottom left corner of the figure represents a high level of state legal capacity combined with minimal institutional demand from societal actors. Following the logic elaborated above, state institutions will remain relatively ineffective regardless of rulers' intentions if firms continue to use illegal strategies that undermine or subvert state institutions. Accordingly, the combination of high legal capacity and low institutional demand will result in the emergence of *parchment institutions*, in the sense that even though an impressive formal legal infrastructure is in place, these formal institutions exist primarily on paper and exert minimal influence over real-world behavior. Russia throughout the 1990s followed a path from the "rule of might" to "parchment institutions." As the decade unfolded, the state made efforts to restore law and order, particularly in the economic sphere, establishing a new Civil Code, passing essential laws on securities and joint stock companies, continuing to reform the commercial courts, and initiating anti–organized crime campaigns. But given that state legal capacity is a necessary yet insufficient condition for firms to use formal legal institutions, institutional demand lagged behind the emerging legal infrastructure. Until the late 1990s, firms continued to rely extensively on violence and corruption.

The bottom right corner of the figure represents the situation in which both state legal capacity and institutional demand are high. This rare combination is the foundation for the *rule of law*, in which state institutions effectively provide property security and firms utilize these formal legal institutions. To be clear, firms' reliance on state institutions does not preclude firms' use of complementary *informal* strategies. But it does require the majority of firms to abandon the use of violent or corrupt *illegal* strategies that undermine or subvert state institutions.

Between 1999 and 2003, a period that began with Putin's rise to power and concluded with the high-profile arrest of the oligarch Mikhail Khodorkovsky, Russia came close to attaining this rule of law ideal, at least in the economic sphere.[1] Putin's foremost priority upon assuming power in 2000 was to rebuild a strong state and restore Russia's geopolitical significance, and he recognized that effective legal institutions could help spur economic growth, which he perceived as a prerequisite for his state-building agenda (Hill and Gaddy, 2013, ch. 3). As detailed in Chapter 4, the development of state legal capacity under Putin was uneven. However, this turn-of-the-century period struck a reasonable balance in which state officials were sufficiently empowered and funded to enforce policies yet simultaneously sufficiently constrained to prevent the state itself from becoming a significant threat to property security.

Russia's business environment changed dramatically following the arrest of Khodorkovsky in 2003, pushing Russia toward the upper right corner of Figure 8.1. This corner depicts the situation in which state legal capacity is low – particularly in the sense of constraining state officials – but firms' use of formal legal institutions remains high. Obviously, at its extreme this situation is unstable, for as legal capacity disappears firms may reduce their use of formal legal institutions. But a society trending in this direction is best described as a *predatory state*. Chapter 4 revealed how after the Khodorkovsky incident, bureaucrats and law enforcement officials of all ranks increased their pressure on firms. These threats included the seizure of firms' assets, facilitation of illegal corporate raiding, extortion, illicit fines, and unlawful arrests of businesspeople.

Whether secure property rights take root in Russia will depend on the outcome of the clash between two countervailing tendencies: the private sector's rising demand for effective state institutions and the increasingly predatory state. In other words, whereas in the late 1990s Russia needed to overcome the divergence between formal institutions and the illegal practices of private actors, in contemporary Russia developing the rule of law will require increased constraints on the arbitrary practices of state officials. Arguably, the massive protests – the largest since the collapse of the Soviet Union – that erupted following fraudulent parliamentary elections in December 2011 were a manifestation of this clash between the expectations of an emerging business class and the practices of state

---

[1] This should not be construed to mean that Russia showed tendencies toward the rule of law more broadly during this period. Even as progress was made in the economic sphere, political and human rights suffered, a trend that would worsen with time under Putin's regime (Fish, 2005; McFaul and Stoner-Weiss, 2008).

officials, as evidenced by the rise of the anticorruption crusader Alexey Navalny as one of the protest movement's most influential leaders.

The extent to which the Russian state's predatory tendencies will wax or wane remains unclear. Following his return to the presidency in March 2012, after four years in the role of prime minister, Putin introduced highly visible anticorruption campaigns and new policies for deregulation in the sphere of small business, but these campaigns were widely dismissed as symbolic. However, some recent policies have suggested cause for optimism. One notable example is Russia's e-government initiative, which, among other things, allows firms and citizens to engage an array of state services, from receiving passports to filing tax claims, through the Internet. Although the initiative had been underway throughout the 2000s, it only recently came to fruition with live websites. Evidence emerging from other countries indicates that e-government initiatives can significantly reduce corruption by limiting the discretion of bureaucrats (Shim and Eom, 2008), and, at least in Moscow, lawyers and businesspeople related – with a sense of unbelieving awe – stories of resolving tax disputes with ease through an Internet portal (Lawyer 10, interview, 2014; Firm 18, interview, 2014).

On the other hand, recent years have served witness to several more ominous harbingers, with the year 2014 arguably marking a turn for the worse. In August 2014, Russia's Supreme Court (*Verkhovnyi sud*), which previously had been the highest instance for the courts of general jurisdiction, subsumed the Supreme Commercial Court (*Vyshhyi arbitrazhniy sud*), which previously had been the highest instance for the commercial courts. As a result, the commercial courts, which since the collapse of the Soviet Union had enjoyed institutional autonomy from the rest of the judicial system, now are subject to the Supreme Court's rulings.[2] As discussed in Chapter 4, for all their faults, the commercial courts were widely viewed as more competent and independent than other institutions within the judiciary, and analysts, both foreign and Russian, have suggested that the end of institutional autonomy will lower the quality of lower courts' rulings in economic disputes (Pomeranz, 2013; Treshchev, 2013). Meanwhile, in September 2014 the oligarch Vladimir Yevtushenkov was arrested on charges of money laundering related to his 2009 purchase of the oil company Bashneft. Although Yevtushenkov was

[2] Appeals of commercial courts' rulings are now heard by an Economic Collegium within the Supreme Court, but this collegium's rulings themselves can be overturned by the Presidium of the Supreme Court. Moreover, very few of the judges from the Supreme Commercial Court were reseated as judges in the reformed Supreme Court.

eventually released, the raid ultimately led to the the acquisition of Bash-neft by the state oil company Rosneft – the same company that acquired many of Yukos's assets following Khodorkovsky's arrest. But what set apart the Yevtushenkov incident from earlier raids by the Russian state was Yevtushenkov's reputation for loyalty to the Kremlin, lack of politi-cal ambitions, and long-standing ties to Russia's security services (Myers and Becker, 2014). To many, the attack on Yevtushenkov appeared to be the collapse of informal rules that previously provided property secu-rity to Russia's most powerful figures in exchange for fealty and political quiescence.

In addition, 2014 was the year in which Russia annexed Crimea from Ukraine, initiating a set of events that in many ways have placed Russia's predatory state at a crossroads. Buffeted by international sanctions and a sharp fall in oil prices, Russia's elite faces a choice between doubling down on grabbing what it can while still firmly in power or constraining preda-tion in an effort to revitalize the private sector. Which path the Russian leadership will choose remains uncertain, though recent signs indicate that the balance is tilting toward predatory tendencies. Particularly note-worthy is the extent to which the Russian state has quietly reclaimed private sector assets in recent years (Mereminskaya, 2016), potentially undermining institutional demand by shrinking the private sector itself.

Even if private sector institutional demand triumphs over state preda-tion, Russia will still face significant challenges. Secure property rights do not guarantee other fundamental aspects of the rule of law, such as human rights, freedom of the press, and the accountability of political leaders. And whether progress in the economic sphere of rule of law can affect the development of rule of law more broadly remains subject to debate. The optimistic view is that the business sector's reliance on formal legal institutions may serve as a stepping stone for broader societal demand for law. Victims of property rights violations have a direct material incen-tive that may provide a stronger stimulus for action than that which results from violations of political, social, or human rights. Moreover, an emerging capitalist class possesses the resources to react to violations of its rights (Hendley, 1996, ch. 7). Once demand for law is established for some spheres of society, this may provide a blueprint for legal action that spreads to other spheres. Spillover scenarios are particularly persuasive in democratic, common law systems, where legal doctrine established in one realm may spread to others. For example, Supreme Court justices in the United States originally applied the due process clauses of the Fifth and Fourteenth Amendments to cases concerning protection of property rights, but the resulting doctrine of substantive due process ultimately came to be used to protect rights as diverse as the right to travel or the right to marry across racial lines (Silverstein, 2003). Yet even in authoritarian regimes, some observers have suggested that the "institutional development and autonomy" required to sustain rule of law in the economic sphere is likely to proliferate. Analyzing rule of law in China in the early 2000s, Peerenboom (2002, p. 134) suggested that "Once institutions gain a certain degree of autonomy and authority and those within the institution achieve a level of professionalism, the institutional actors are likely to pursue further changes to increase their autonomy and authority. As a result, there are likely to be spillover effects from one area of law to another as institutions develop."

In more recent years, however, a relatively pessimistic view has emerged regarding the spillover effects of rule of law in the economic sphere. Drawing on Fraenkel's (1941) work on Nazi-era Germany, scholars such as Hendley (2009, 2011) have recognized the prevalence of "legal dualism," in which legal institutions serve the whims of the state in high-profile, politicized cases yet function in accordance with law in run-of-the-mill cases, particularly those involving economic transactions that pose no threat to the state's power. Singapore in particular has for decades combined legal property rights protection with political repression, and countries such as China seem to be using this approach as an explicit model (Silverstein, 2008; Rajah, 2012; Stern, 2013, pp. 228–230). Meanwhile, countries such as Egypt and the United Arab Emirates have developed legal institutions for resolving economic disputes, especially those concerning foreign investors, that far outpace the effectiveness of institutions responsible for criminal justice (Cambanis, 2007; Moustafa, 2007). Critically, one of the major insights emerging from this growing research agenda is that legal dualism "need not be a halfway house on the path to the rule of law" (Frye, 2017). Moreover, as the merging of the Russian commercial courts and criminal justice system discussed above indicates, even if legal dualism is unstable, there is no guarantee that change will be in the direction of greater rule of law. Equally possible is for the repression common in the political sphere to begin impinging on the economic realm.

It remains to be seen whether the spillover effects of private sector institutional demand will have a positive effect on society and politics more broadly, or whether other negative developments will eventually reverse firms' willingness to utilize law. The barriers to the rule of law in Russia remain severe. Yet when one considers the extensive violence and corruption of the 1990s, the fact that firms today regularly turn to courts and lawyers represents a significant step in a positive direction.

8.4 Rethinking the Role of the State

The Russian case not only illustrates the importance of institutional demand but also provides grounds to rethink the state's role in shaping property security strategies. As discussed in Chapter 2, the state plays three roles in property security: the *direct supplier* of formal legal institutions, a *predatory threat* to property security, and *indirect facilitator* of institutional demand. Existing studies of property rights focus primarily on the first two roles, emphasizing the challenge of creating a state that is sufficiently strong to protect property rights yet also sufficiently constrained to limit predation by rulers and other state officials (Weingast, 1995). From this vantage point, the state's primary influence on firm's property security strategies occurs via the effectiveness of formal legal institutions.

The state's role as a facilitator of institutional demand, however, has received much less attention. The state acts as a facilitator when its policies reduce demand-side barriers or decrease the effectiveness of illegal strategies in ways unrelated to the strengthening of formal legal institutions. Two key examples in the Russian case include tax reforms, which alleviated firms' concerns about using legal institutions by improving tax compliance, and improved financial sector regulation, which raised illegal strategies' cost by encouraging firms to reduce reliance on cash transactions.

A crucial insight is that a focus on state legal capacity's direct influence on firms' strategies produces an overly narrow scope of inquiry both for social scientists seeking to better understand property security and for policymakers seeking to build the rule of law. For example, in line with traditional supply-side theories, rule-of-law reform packages usually emphasize reform of the judiciary, law enforcement agencies, the penal system, and the legal profession (e.g., Carothers, 1998; Daniels and Trebilcock, 2004).[3] These types of reforms are undeniably critical for

---

[3] Although tax administration reform is sometimes considered in the context of rule-of-law projects, the purpose of such tax reforms is to generate revenue needed to build legal capacity, a complementary yet distinct goal from the reduction of demand-side barriers (see, e.g., Daniels and Trebilcock, 2004, p. 117).

building the rule of law. But considering the state as a facilitator of institutional demand encourages the adoption of a more holistic perspective that places the legal sphere in a broader institutional context.

One implication of this broader perspective is that improving legal institutions' effectiveness may have a minimal impact if demand-side barriers to the use of these institutions are not removed first. A more weighty implication is that a broader vantage point draws attention to potential complementarities across institutional spheres. As emphasized in Hall and Soskice's (2001) influential "varieties of capitalism" framework, institutional complementarities occur when "the presence (or efficiency) of one [institution] increases the returns from (or efficiency of) the other" (p. 17). This framework attributes the persistence of distinct institutional regimes in different types of capitalist systems to positive externalities resulting from complementary interactions among five institutional spheres: industrial relations, vocational training, corporate governance, inter-firm relations, and employee relations. A focus on institutional complementarities, however, has not gained traction in studies of property rights and legal development.[4] The integration of supply- and demand-side approaches to property security thus points to a potentially fruitful avenue for future research: the institutional complementarities among legal, tax, and financial institutions.

To be clear, key demand-side influences on property security strategies, such as improved tax compliance or reduced reliance on cash transactions, can and do in many instances occur *independently* of state reforms, spurred by changes in the economy, evolving cultural norms, or numerous other factors. In other words, the fact that the state at times acts as a facilitator of institutional demand encourages rethinking of the state's possible roles in creating property security. It does not, however, imply that institutional demand is a simple reflection of state policy or state capacity, a point reinforced by consideration of institutional demand in countries and time periods other than post-Soviet Russia.

8.5   Pathways to the Rule of Law in Comparative Perspective

The case of post-Soviet Russia serves to illustrate the key tenets of this book's argument. First, state legal capacity is necessary but insufficient to induce firms to use formal legal institutions. Second, increased use

---

[4] One partial exception is the work of Jonathan Hay and collaborators (see Hay and Shleifer, 1998; Alexeev et al., 2004).

of legal institutions frequently occurs even in the absence of heightened state legal capacity. In such cases, firm strategies for securing property are often determined by demand-side barriers and the effectiveness of illegal alternatives to formal legal institutions. More broadly, the experiences of contemporary Russia, as well as the experiences of other developing and transition countries discussed below, demonstrate that existing studies' state-centric approach encourages overly narrow analysis of the pathways to the rule of law. To be sure, developing effective formal legal institutions and constraining predatory rulers remains a fundamental prerequisite to the security of property, as made clear by the recent increase of state predation in Russia. But equally vital for understanding pathways to the rule of law is an emphasis on how societal actors come to *use* formal state institutions, rather than strategies of private or corrupt coercion.

The framework developed throughout this book offers insights into property security in a wide range of countries beyond the Russian case, particularly in countries with intermediate levels of state capacity. From Vietnam to Ghana, it is not hard to find examples of countries in which the ineffectiveness of formal institutions impedes firms' use of legal strategies.[5] But one must look no further than neighboring Ukraine to find an example of a country where restricted legal capacity combined with extensive demand-side barriers has not only limited firms' use of legal strategies, but also encouraged firms' protracted reliance on violence and corruption. Just as in Russia, Ukrainian firms in the 1990s relied extensively on coercion provided by private actors. As Åslund (2009, p. 113) observed, "every businessman [in Ukraine] was exposed to racketeering." By the end of the first post-communist decade, strategies of private and corrupt coercion coexisted. Powerful businesspeople had created "their own large armies of security guards," while state institutions such as the Security Services of Ukraine (SBU), the Ministry of Internal Affairs, and the State Tax Administration had become "centralized, commercial organizations, competing among themselves as oligarchic groups" (Åslund, 2009, p. 115). Over time, services provided by criminal groups and by illegal actors within the state became increasingly entangled. As recently as 2010, the Ukrainian version of the newspaper *Segodnya* published an extensive report detailing how organized crime groups were carrying out kidnappings on behalf of state officials

---

[5] See, respectively, McMillan and Woodruff (1999) and Fafchamps (1996).

seeking to pressure businessmen. Firms, meanwhile, were paying criminal groups to exploit their connections with state officials to obtain access
to basic government services such as the registration of new enterprises
(Zolotukhina, 2010).

Not only did strategies of private coercion persist longer in Ukraine
than in Russia and become more intertwined with strategies of corrupt
coercion, but Ukrainian firms also remained significantly more hesitant
to utilize legal strategies. Cases filed in Ukraine's commercial courts fell
dramatically in the immediate years following the Soviet collapse, from
just under 100,000 cases per year to around 50,000, a trend similar to that
found in Russia (Eremenko, 1996). In the second half of the 1990s, however, the number of cases heard in the commercial courts nearly quadru-
pled (Gavrish, 2001). In 2001 the commercial courts, which to this point
had enjoyed institutional autonomy as a distinct branch of the judiciary,
were recreated as specialized economic courts within the system of general courts (Zakhvataev, 2001). Following these reforms, annual caseloads
continued to increase at a moderate pace up through the middle of the
2000s, peaking at just under 300,000 in 2008 – before falling dramatically.
The fact that this decline occurred precisely during a worldwide financial crisis, a period of exacerbated interenterprise conflict, suggests that
firms instead turned to informal or illegal means of resolving debt disputes. Indeed, one Russian entrepreneur who operated several businesses
in Ukraine and encountered criminal thugs at the outset of the financial
crisis recounted that these *bandity* openly joked with him that "thank God
the '1990s' are back. We now have decent jobs [collecting debts again]"
(Firm 5, interview, 2009).[6] By 2013, the number of cases being heard in
the economic courts had fallen to well below 200,000 per year, a level not
seen since the late 1990s.[7] Recently, Ukrainian leaders have even called

---

[6] This trend toward renewed reliance on private coercion stands in sharp contrast to the
Russian case, where firms' use of the courts spiked sharply during the 2008–2009 financial
crisis (see Section 3.3 in Chapter 3).

[7] Caseload data are from various reports of the Supreme Commercial Court of Ukraine,
including *Kilkist rosglyanutikh sudami Ukraini sprav ta materialiv usikh kategorii* [Num-
ber of cases heard by Ukrainian courts for all categories], *Statistichnii oglyad diyalnosti
sudiv zagalnoy yurisdiktsii Ukraini* [Statistical review of the courts of general jurisdiction of Ukraine], *Oglyad danikh pro stan zdiisnennya pravosuddya* [Review of data on the
state of justice], and *Analitichni tablitsi shchodo stanu zdiisnennya pravosuddya* [Analyti-
cal tables on the state of administration of justice], available online at www.scourt.gov.ua
and http://court.gov.ua. As discussed in greater detail below, direct comparisons between
the Russian and Ukrainian commercial courts are complicated by significant institutional
differences, particularly after the year 2000.

for the abolishment of the economic courts, citing their relatively low caseloads as justification (Yasinskaya, 2014; Proskurin, 2015).

A brief survey of the development of state legal capacity in Ukraine provides insight into why Ukrainian firms have been hesitant to rely on formal legal institutions. Like Russia, Ukraine emerged from the Soviet Union's collapse lacking essential laws, regulations, and other state institutions needed for a market economy to function effectively. Unlike Russia, to this day Ukraine has struggled to establish even the rudiments of a formal legal infrastructure. Commercial courts (*arbitrazhnye sudy*) were created almost immediately, but other critical legislation lagged far behind. Until the adoption of a new Constitution in 1996, there existed only an ad hoc legal foundation for an independent judiciary. Similarly, it was not until 2004 that a new Civil Code replaced the Soviet-era Civil Code of 1963, thereby finally creating a comprehensive legal basis for private contracting. Unfortunately, whatever progress legal reformers had hoped for was largely undermined by a new Commercial Code, also adopted in in 2004, that directly contradicted the Civil Code on fundamental matters ranging from the types of businesses allowed by Ukrainian law to the regulation of securities. Equally striking was the inability of the Ukrainian legislature to pass a modern law governing joint stock companies until 2008. As a result, for nearly two decades, a modified 1991 Law on Business Associations served as the sole legal basis for the primary form of corporate ownership in the Ukrainian economy (OECD, 2004; Yefymenko, 2009).

The commercial courts themselves underwent repeated institutional changes. As noted above, Ukraine's institutionally autonomous commercial courts were transformed into a set of specialized economic courts (referred to as *khozyastvennye sudy* in Russian and *gospodarski sudy* in Ukrainian) within the broader system of general courts in 2001. Meanwhile, in 2006 some of the economics courts' jurisdiction was transferred to newly established administrative courts, and in 2010 an extensive rewriting of the laws overseeing the judiciary was undertaken once again. Yet there is little evidence that these reforms improved the legal system's performance. Even as the second post-communist decade unfolded, Yeltsov (2003), writing in the Ukrainian periodical *Biznes*, remarkably concluded: "The laws don't work effectively, the government doesn't fulfill its functions ... If everything is done according to the law, then when turning to a court, the violator of a contract can buy the judge or prolong the case. [By contrast] when turning to a criminal authority (*vorovskii avtoritet*) everything proceeds with maximum efficiency, and the failure to comply with the authority's decision is fraught not only with loss of one's whole business, but with loss of one's life." In short, Ukraine's legal institutions remained hapless to such an extent that the crudest of property security strategies continued to be appealing well into the 2000s.

Along with a dearth of state legal capacity, demand-side barriers emphasized in this book, such as low tax compliance, also contributed to the persistence of illegal property security strategies in Ukraine. Similar to Russia, byzantine tax regulations and corrupt tax officials forced many Ukrainian firms to hide significant shares of their sales revenue and payroll expenses from government authorities, making these firms hesitant to turn to formal legal institutions out of concerns that their legal violations might be unveiled in the process. Periodically, various measures, such as the anti-corruption campaigns by the government of Viktor Yushchenko following the 2004 popular uprising that came to be known as the Orange Revolution, induced firms to reduce their operations in the informal economy. As then Prime Minister Yulia Timoshenko exulted in 2005, "All of the tax rates are exactly the same, yet the revenue received is one and one-half times greater. This is simply the legalization of the economy, the legalization of profit" (cited in Reynolds, 2005). Notably, the mid-2000s were also the peak of firms' reliance on legal strategies. Improved tax compliance was short-lived, however, as changes in tax regulations for small businesses forced many small entrepreneurs to again "go underground or close down their shops" (Åslund, 2005, p. 346). By 2010, ongoing political clashes over how to improve the tax code instigated some of the largest protests since the Orange Revolution – and not without reason, given that the World Bank in that year ranked the Ukrainian tax system the third-worst in the world (Olearchyk, 2010).

If the case of Ukraine demonstrates that at least a modicum of state legal capacity is a prerequisite for firms' use of formal legal institutions, the experiences of numerous other countries illustrate the inverse: The establishment of even relatively effective legal institutions frequently is not sufficient to induce firms' adoption of legal strategies. Pistor et al. (1999), for example, offer a detailed analysis of legal development in China, India, Japan, Malaysia, South Korea, and Taiwan. They illustrate how throughout much of Asia, a relatively high-capacity formal legal infrastructure lay dormant for extended periods of time, as firms settled disputes outside of the formal legal system. Moreover, in countries in which firms eventually did turn to legal strategies, there was little evidence that changing strategies were a direct response to rising state legal capacity. Instead, Pistor et al. (1999, p. 11) refer to a "demand led evolution in law" in many Asian countries, noting that "Economic actors demanded change in aspects of the legal system that affected them. This shift was not simply a matter of those in charge of law supplying more market-allocative law on their own initiative."

The case of China is particularly illustrative of the second key argument this book puts forth: Increased reliance on formal legal institutions frequently occurs despite limited improvements in state legal capacity. As in Russia, Chinese firms at one point relied heavily on illegal strategies, but over the past several decades firms in China increasingly have come to utilize legal property security strategies. Notably, this increased reliance on law has occurred notwithstanding the persistence of significant deficiencies in formal legal institutions.

In contemporary China, private coercion in the form of criminal protection rackets and private security agencies never played the prominent role it played in post-Soviet Russia (Wank 1999, p. 270; Whiting 2010, pp. 208–209), but Chinese firms have actively employed strategies of corrupt coercion with striking resemblance to the strategies of their Russian counterparts. For example, since the 1980s, business owners have collaborated with government officials to operate private enterprises under the guise of a collective firm, a strategy that has become known as "wearing a red hat." Similar to bureaucratic patrons of private firms in Russia, Chinese firms wearing a red hat "benefit from bureaucratic protection and favors, while cadres benefit materially (or otherwise) from providing such services" (Tsai, 2007, pp. 57–58). Likewise, referring to a wide range of government and quasi-government agencies, from state-run business associations to regulatory agencies, Wank (1999, pp. 265–266) relates how Chinese firms rely on "various distributive, manufacturing, and administrative units in the government that are business partners or direct sponsors of non-state firms. Operators prevail on these units to intercede on their behalf in disputes and when harassed by other agencies," as well as to enforce contracts.

While there is no denying that Chinese firms continue to utilize strategies based on corrupt coercion, their increasing adoption of legal strategies is also quite remarkable. Commercial litigation in China increased annually by almost 19 percent between 1983 and 2001, rising from a meager 36,000 annual cases to over one million. Meanwhile, a World Bank survey of 1,500 firms in 2000 found that approximately 39 percent of respondents had resorted to litigation to resolve a dispute with at least one client, and around 30 percent had turned to the courts to resolve a dispute with a supplier (Whiting, 2010, pp. 199–202; see also Pei, 2001).[8] Chinese firms do not only directly rely on formal legal institutions, but they also increasingly employ legalistic tactics in a broader sense. As Whiting (2010, p. 206) notes, "Interviews with lawyers and enterprise managers suggest that ... [firms] make a credible threat to use the courts and then bargain within the 'shadow of law.'" An additional piece of evidence that law is coming to play a greater role in property security in China is the rapid growth in the number of Chinese law firms and lawyers, which increased by approximately 50 percent between 1997 and 2005. During this same time period, law was also the fastest growing field of study at both the undergraduate and graduate levels, indicating that Chinese youth perceive a significant demand for legal services (Whiting, 2010, pp. 202–204).[9]

Strikingly, in China, as in Russia, increasing reliance on legal strategies has occurred despite well-recognized and significant deficiencies with formal legal institutions. Over several decades, China has incrementally established the formal legal infrastructure required for a market economy to function effectively, but this has been a long and drawn out process. Although China's transition to a market economy began in 1978, the first legislation providing solid legal foundations for joint stock and limited liability companies was not passed until the 1990s. (For that matter, even legislation concerning the legal foundations for the collective township and village enterprises, which formed a large part of the Chinese economy from the late 1970s onward, was not adopted until 1996.) Only in the 2000s were constitutional amendments and related laws passed that finally recognized the legitimacy of private property. The legal framework for contracting and for the regulation of private enterprise developed in a similarly piecemeal manner. Even though an initial Economic Contract Law came into force in 1981, it was primarily a tool of economic planning

---

[8] Although annual caseloads declined following a peak in the early 2000s, the reason for this decline does not appear to be a reduced propensity to utilize law, but rather a decrease in the types of conflicts that had led to litigation in previous decades. See Whiting (2010, pp. 199–202).

[9] To some degree, Chinese firms' use of courts can be categorized as corrupt rather than legal coercion. Ang and Jia (2014), for example, find that politically connected firms are more likely than non-connected firms to turn to courts, and provide further evidence that well-connected firms' actively employ these connections to influence courts' adjudication of their disputes. Although the corrupt use of courts is a concern in Russia as well, existing evidence suggests that the vast majority of economic cases are litigated without resort to corruption. Additional research is required to assess the extent to which Chinese firms' use of courts predominantly represents an illegal or legal property security strategy.

rather than a legal foundation for exchange between private entities. It was not until 1999 that a unified Contract Law integrated the fragmented rules that had separately regulated contracting for private domestic entities, foreign firms, and individuals. Meanwhile, the first laws on issuing stock and regulating securities also did not emerge until the 1990s, while laws governing licensing and modern antimonopoly legislation did not come into being until the 2000s. More broadly, it was only in 1999 that the constitution was amended to give formal recognition to the legal system as part of the Chinese system of governance (Clarke et al., 2008, pp. 380–392).

Even with the eventual establishment of a formal legal infrastructure, the effectiveness of formal legal institutions remained very much in question, casting doubt on explanations for Chinese firms' increasing use of legal strategies that focus on heightened state legal capacity. As Wank (1999, p. 251) noted at the end of the 1990s, "Uncertainty in regard to legal rights is exacerbated by the lack of impartial courts to enforce legal rights to private property. Even after almost two decades of reform, the courts are viewed as easily influenced in any but the most petty cases." A decade later, Whiting (2010, p. 183) was not much more sanguine in her assessment of China's formal legal institutions: "Courts in the PRC are subordinate to the party, lack competent judges, and have weak enforcement powers." Given these substantial drawbacks of the Chinese legal system, she concludes that "the dramatic increase in the litigation of economic disputes appears surprising." Among other problems, Chinese courts remain relatively low in the bureaucratic hierarchy of the government, meaning that "other government agencies may ignore courts with impunity" (Clarke et al., 2008, p. 396). Moreover, many commercial laws list duties of specific actors but provide no legal remedy for those suffering a breach of these duties. For these and other reasons, Clarke et al. (2008, p. 400) conclude that "The possibility of court involvement cannot be generally assumed when a law is violated, and even if the courts became involved, their effectiveness is highly uncertain."

Reforms aimed at raising the effectiveness of China's legal infrastructure thus provided the necessary foundation for firms to use legal strategies, but rising state legal capacity does not appear to be the primary force behind Chinese firms' use of formal legal institutions. Rather, many of the factors that reduced demand-side barriers or decreased the effectiveness of illegal property security strategies in Russia have played a similar role in the Chinese case. For instance, just as operations in the formal economy due to low tax compliance created a demand-side barrier in Russia, Wank (1999, p. 266) attributed many Chinese firms' hesitancy to use law to their concern that "going to court exposes one's affairs to scrutiny by government agencies, which is risky given the ambiguity of many commercial practices." In China, such problems were exacerbated by the private sector's absolute lack of legal status, which forced many businesspeople who otherwise might have turned to law to reconsider. Although private firms would eventually emerge as even more litigious than their state-owned counterparts (Pei, 2001, pp. 201–202), until well into the 1990s it was the case that "private enterprise owners felt they had no recourse when they encountered contract disputes, since courts were unwilling to recognize their claims" (Whiting, 2010, p. 185).

Other demand-side factors influencing Russian firms' calculations about whether or not to use legal strategies can be observed in China as well. As discussed in Chapter 5, Russian firms' concerns that other firms would continue using violence or corruption contributed to a collective action problem that hindered the adoption of legal strategies – but once a critical mass of firms began using formal legal institutions, this also contributed to a virtuous cycle in which reliance on law by some firms encouraged other firms' use of law. Likewise, in the Chinese case, Pei (2001, p. 204) finds that "Court victories may also have produced positive social spillover effects by *demonstrating* to potential litigants the benefits of accessing the new legal system. The positive spillover effects may be the force driving the dramatic rise in the litigation rate since the late 1970s" (emphasis in original). Meanwhile, many factors that reduced the effectiveness of illegal alternatives in Russia have influenced property security strategies in China in a similar manner. Chapter 6 explored how Russian firms' growing use of the formal financial system and reduced reliance on cash transactions raised the transaction costs of employing illegal strategies, while the integration of Russian firms into the international economy placed new constraints on their ability and willingness to resort to violence or corruption. Although she does not specify the specific mechanism of banking sector development, Whiting (2010, p. 181) explores whether the development of the Chinese economy has reduced the effectiveness of illegal strategies, questioning whether "the informal networks in which firms are embedded and the bureaucratic structures by which firms are governed [now] fail to provide adequate information and sanctions for the resolution of disputes, making the courts an increasingly important element in the process of dispute resolution." Tsai (2007, p. 61), meanwhile, cites studies suggesting that the same types of international influences which have moderated Russian firms' behavior appear to also exist in China. These studies indicate, for instance, that the "interaction between foreign and Chinese firms increased the use of meritocratic hiring and promotion practices and enhanced respect for the rule of law."

This brief survey of the role of firms and states in the development of property security and the rule of law throughout the developing world substantiates the need for a greater focus on institutional demand to complement existing studies' emphasis on institutional supply. It also raises questions about the role of institutional demand in what today has become known as the advanced industrialized countries.

Throughout much of Western Europe and North America, state legal capacity has reached a level at which it is difficult to imagine firms reverting to widespread reliance on property security strategies that blatantly utilize violence or corruption. This does not, however, mean that in the West firms *initially* turned to formal legal institutions in response to rising state legal capacity. It is equally possible that a bottom-up, prolonged process of evolving institutional demand had to occur *first* in order for state legal capacity to reach the level it is at today. Indeed, De Soto (2003, ch. 5) catalogues numerous ways in which firms' strategies for securing property in the United States dramatically (and often violently) violated official laws until late in the 19th century. Recent work has also begun to revisit the state-centric focus of North and Weingast's (1989) seminal analysis of 17th-century England. As Markus (2015, p. 216) explains, "Even the canonical case of credible commitment by the British Crown, stressing a one-time institutionalization of the king's promises to his creditors, is undergoing a revision, suggesting that the ongoing, bottom-up, resistance-based, and informal mechanisms played a much larger role in enhancing the Crown's accountability than the narrative of top-down commitment has acknowledged."

As new research accumulates, it is possible that scholars will assign a larger role to institutional demand in the development of property rights and the rule of law in the West. But regardless of institutional demand's role in historical cases, it is clear that societal actors' willingness to utilize formal state institutions in the contemporary world's developing countries cannot be taken for granted. When demand-side barriers to the use of formal institutions are prevalent, and when illegal alternatives to formal institutions are highly effective, firms and other societal actors will face powerful incentives to rely on strategies that utilize violence or corruption. By employing such strategies, societal actors undermine or subvert formal state institutions. As a consequence, the effectiveness of state institutions – and, ultimately, the security of property and the prospects for the rule of law – suffer. Only by recognizing the importance of both institutional supply *and* institutional demand will scholars and policymakers begin to understand the foundations for developing secure property rights, the rule of law, and effective state institutions.

Appendices

Appendix A

Original Interview Data

Ninety semistructured interviews were conducted by the author throughout 2009. The breakdown across firms, lawyers, and private security agencies is presented in Table A1. Seventy-seven interviews were conducted in Moscow; the remaining interviews were conducted in Barnaul. Seventy-five of the respondents were Russian; the other 15 were expatriates with extensive business experience in Russia. Thirty-six supplementary interviews were conducted with business journalists, academics, non-governmental organizations, and business association representatives. Twenty of the original respondents were then re-interviewed in the fall of 2014. Table A2 provides additional background information for the 90 semistructured interviews.

Table A1   *Characteristics of Interview Respondents*

Total Interviews	90
Firms	56
of which	
<15 employees	15
15 to 100 employees	12
101 to 250 employees	12
>250 employees	17
Lawyers	22
Private Security Agencies	12

Table A2   *List of Interview Respondents*

	Date(s) of Interview(s)	Job Title	Approx. Age	Firm Size and Sector	Location
Firm 1	2/10/09	owner	30s	small importer and retailer	Moscow
Firm 2	2/17/09	owner	30s	small real estate investment firm	Moscow
Firm 3	2/18/09	head of legal	50s	large domestic pharmaceutical company	Moscow
Firm 4	2/20/09	owner	20s	small Internet start-up	Moscow
Firm 5	2/26/09	M&A manager	30s	large domestic financial holding	Moscow
Firm 6	2/27/09	co-owner	50s	small trading firm for valuable metals	Moscow
Firm 7	3/10/09	owner	40s	small management consulting firm	Moscow
Firm 8	3/10/09	owner	20s	small retail business	Moscow
Firm 9	3/11/09	asst. gen. director	30s	small mail order business	Moscow
Firm 10	3/14/09	finance analyst	30s	large intl. consumer goods company	Moscow
Firm 11	3/20/09	owner	40s	small management consulting firm	Moscow
Firm 12	3/20/09 10/22/14	general manager	40s	large domestic automobile retailer	Moscow
Firm 13	3/20/09	managing director	30s	large intl. automobile manufacturer	Moscow
Firm 14	3/23/09 10/10/14	chairman of board	50s	large intl. bank	Moscow
Firm 15	3/26/09	owner	40s	small regional investment consulting firm	Moscow
Firm 16	3/26/09 10/14/14	owner	50s	small importer and retailer	Moscow
Firm 17	3/27/09	exec. director	40s	large intl. automobile manufacturer	Moscow
Firm 18	4/01/09 10/14/14	co-owner	40s	small public relations firm	Moscow

Firm	Date	Role	Age	Description	City
Firm 19	4/02/09	CEO	30s	large domestic Internet firm	Moscow
	10/16/14				Kaliningrad
Firm 20	4/07/09	owner	40s	medium-sized agricultural producer	Moscow
Firm 21	4/07/09	owner	50s	small software firm	Moscow
Firm 22	5/07/09	CEO	30s	medium-sized domestic Internet firm	Moscow
Firm 23	5/25/09	owner	50s	small medical practice	Moscow
Firm 24	5/30/09	partner	50s	large intl. auditing firm	Moscow
Firm 25	6/03/09	owner	30s	small financial consultancy for start-ups	Moscow
Firm 26	6/09/09	exec. director	40s	medium-sized real estate investment firm	Moscow
Firm 27	6/10/09	director, public affairs	50s	intl. division of large domestic steel company	Moscow
Firm 28	10/13/09	owner	40s	medium-sized light manufacturing company	Moscow
Firm 29	10/22/09	co-owner	40s	medium-sized chemical company	Moscow
	10/24/14				
Firm 30	10/23/09	director	50s	medium-sized hi-tech engineering company	Taganrog
Firm 31	10/26/09	managing partner	40s	small management consulting firm	Moscow
Firm 32	10/30/09	consultant	20s	medium-sized recruiting company	Moscow
Firm 33	11/06/09	HR director	20s	medium-sized energy company	Moscow
Firm 34	11/23/09	owner	30s	small IT outsourcing company	Moscow
Firm 35	11/24/09	procurement manager	30s	large domestic cell phone retailer	Moscow
Firm 36	12/01/09	owner	20s	small tourist agency	Moscow
Firm 37	12/02/09	director, regional dev.	50s	large domestic pharmaceutical company	Moscow

Table A2   (cont.)

	Date(s) of Interview(s)	Job Title	Approx. Age	Firm Size and Sector	Location
Firm 38	12/02/09	general director	50s	small medical equipment company	Moscow
Firm 39	12/03/09	manager	20s	large construction company	Moscow
Firm 40	12/04/09	general director	50s	small medical equipment company	Moscow
Firm 41	12/08/09	finance director	50s	large intl. pharmaceutical company	Moscow
Firm 42	12/10/09	general director	40s	small auto repair service	Moscow
Firm 43	12/10/09	owner	30s	small management consulting firm	Moscow
Firm 44	12/15/09	owner	20s	small importer and retailer	Moscow
Firm 45	12/15/09	owner	20s	small Internet start-up	Moscow
Firm 46	12/16/09 10/06/14	VP, corp. affairs	30s	large intl. bank	Moscow
Firm 47	12/17/09	general director	40s	small plastics company	Moscow
Firm 48	12/17/09	owner	50s	small tourist agency	Moscow
Firm 49	12/19/09	sales manager	30s	medium-sized energy company	Moscow
Firm 50	9/24/09	owner	40s	chain of movie theaters and nightclubs	Barnaul
Firm 51	9/28/09	entrepreneur	20s	owner of digital payment terminals	Barnaul
Firm 52	9/28/09	general manager	30s	medium-sized manufacturing company	Barnaul
Firm 53	9/29/09	owner	50s	chain of gas stations	Barnaul
Firm 54	9/30/09	owner	40s	chain of retail stores	Barnaul
Firm 55	9/30/09	owner	50s	chain of grocery stores	Barnaul
Firm 56	10/01/09	owner	50s	small supplier for energy companies	Barnaul

Legal 1	3/02/09	associate	20s	large intl. law firm	Moscow
Legal 2	3/04/09	associate	20s	large intl. law firm	Moscow
Legal 3	3/04/09	managing partner	30s	large domestic law firm	Moscow
Legal 4	3/05/09	independent lawyer	40s		Moscow
Legal 5	3/06/09	independent lawyer	50s		Moscow
Legal 6	3/06/09 10/17/14	managing partner	30s	large domestic law firm	Moscow
Legal 7	3/12/09	independent lawyer	50s		Moscow
Legal 8	2/06/09 8/24/14	independent lawyer	30s		Moscow
Legal 9	2/21/09	in-house lawyer	30s	large domestic energy company	Moscow
Legal 10	3/18/09 10/09/14	in-house lawyer	30s	large domestic financial holding	Moscow
Legal 11	3/23/09	in-house lawyer	40s	large domestic steel company	Moscow
Legal 12	3/31/09 10/10/14	partner	40s	large intl. law firm	Moscow
Legal 13	3/31/09 10/08/14	associate	30s	large intl. law firm	Moscow
Legal 14	4/07/09	partner	40s	small domestic tax law firm	Moscow
Legal 15	5/07/09	in-house lawyer	20s	large intl. real estate firm	Moscow
Legal 16	5/19/09	head, dispute resolution	40s	large intl. law firm	Moscow
Legal 17	5/19/09	partner	30s	small domestic law firm	Moscow

Table A2 (cont.)

	Date(s) of Interview(s)	Job Title	Approx. Age	Firm Size and Sector	Location
Legal 18	5/21/09	associate	30s	large intl. law firm	Moscow
Legal 19	9/14/09	senior counsel	50s	large intl. law firm	Moscow
Legal 20	10/28/09	partner	30s	small domestic law firm	Moscow
Legal 21	11/05/09	partner	50s	large domestic tax law firm	Moscow
Legal 22	9/30/09	independent lawyer	40s		Barnaul
Security 1	2/14/09	owner	30s	business support agency	Moscow
Security 2	3/16/09	security consultant	50s	employer assoc. for lawyers	Moscow
Security 3	3/17/09	manager, dispute resolution	30s	large intl. auditing firm	Moscow
Security 4	9/17/09 10/23/14	co-owner	50s	private security agency	Moscow
Security 5	9/18/09	co-owner	50s	private security agency	Moscow
Security 6	10/22/09	exec. director	50s	employer assoc. for security specialists	Moscow
Security 7	11/22/09	in-house security	–	large domestic energy company	Moscow
Security 8	11/26/09	general director	40s	private security agency	Moscow
Security 9	11/30/09	ind. security consultant	30s		Moscow
Security 10	12/18/09	VP	40s	private security agency	Moscow
Security 11	4/02/10	chairman of board	40s	private security agency	Moscow
Security 12	9/30/09	director	30s	private security agency	Barnaul

Appendix B

Original Survey Data

The survey sample consists of 301 industrial and service firms from Moscow, St. Petersburg, and 6 regional cities: Ekaterinburg, Nizhniy Novgorod, Samara, Novosibirsk, Rostov-on-Don, and Kazan. Firms were selected using stratified random sampling. The stratification was conducted to ensure that the sample would include a sufficient number of micro, small, medium, and large firms, as well as a sufficient number of firms in Moscow, St. Petersburg, and regional cities. Each cell was further divided evenly between industrial and service firms.

Table B1 shows the distribution of respondents by firm size and city. One hundred and one firms (33 percent of the sample) were from Moscow, 75 (25 percent) from St. Petersburg, and 125 (42 percent) from the 6 regional cities. One hundred and five firms (35 percent of the sample) had 100 or fewer employees, 130 (43 percent) had between 101 and 500 employees, and 66 (22 percent) had 501 or more employees.

With respect to sectors, one hundred firms (33 percent of the sample) were in manufacturing. Other sectors with significant representation in the sample include 40 firms in the retail, wholesale, or repairs sector (13 percent of the sample), 27 in food and beverages (9 percent), 25 in transport and communications (8 percent), 24 in construction (8 percent), 18 in finance (6 percent), and 16 in hotels, restaurants, and tourism (5 percent). Enterprises in which

Table B1   *Distribution of Respondents by Firm Size and City*

	Micro	Small	Medium	Large	Very Large	Total
# of Employees	<15	15–100	101–250	251–500	>500	
Moscow	16	19	21	23	22	101
St. Petersburg	11	15	16	16	17	75
Regional	22	22	28	26	27	125
Total	49	56	65	65	66	301

the government holds a controlling stake were intentionally excluded from the sample.

The response rate for the survey was 41 percent. Survey-related interviews were conducted face-to-face during June and July 2010 by interviewers from the Russian survey-research firm Bashkirova and Partners with either the firm's owner, general director, deputy general director, or chief financial officer. All questions were close-ended.

Appendix C

Other Surveys Cited or Analyzed

Researcher(s)	Sample	Year
EBRD–World Bank (1999, 2002, 2006)	552 (for 1999), 506 (for 2002), and 601 (for 2005) industrial and service firms of various sizes from approximately 60 Russian cities and towns	1999, 2002, 2005
Frye (2002)	240 small retail shops from Russia (Ulyanovsk, Moscow, Smolensk) and Poland (Warsaw)	1998
Frye and Zhuravskaya (2000)	230 small retail shops from Ulyanovsk, Moscow, and Smolensk	1996
Hendley et al. (2000, 2001)	328 industrial firms of various sizes from the Moscow, Barnaul, Novosibirsk, Ekaterinburg, Voronezh, and Saratov regions	1997
INDEM-CIPE (2009)	602 industrial and service firms from 16 regions	2008
Levada Center (2010)	837 industrial and service firms from a nationally representative sample	2010
OPORA (2005, 2006)	80 regions, 50 small businesses from each with the exception of Moscow (300 firms) and St. Petersburg (150 firms)	2004 and 2005
Radaev (1999)	221 small business from 21 regions	1997
Yakovlev et al. (2004)	304 open joint stock companies from the Moscow, Tomsk, and Novgorod regions	2002
Yakovlev (2008); Frye (2004)	500 enterprises from the Moscow, Bashkortastan, Voronezh, Nizhniy Novgorod, Novgorod, Sverdlosvk, Smolensk, and Tula regions	2000 and 2007

Appendix D

Formalizing the Argument

This appendix presents a simple model that formalizes the key insights introduced in Chapter 2. Specifically, the model demonstrates that: (1) *state legal capacity* is necessary but frequently insufficient to induce firms' use of legal strategies for securing property, and (2) firms frequently adopt legal strategies even without heightened state legal capacity, due to declining *demand-side barriers* or *effectiveness of illegal strategies*. The analysis also elucidates the mechanisms whereby *coordination effects* among firms create demand-side barriers to firms' use of formal legal institutions and illustrates how these coordination effects interact with exogenous parameters of the model.

Model Setup

Consider a game in which a conflict arises between two firms drawn randomly from a large population of firms over an asset with value V. All firms are assumed to be identical. This assumption, while clearly unrealistic, facilitates analysis of the primary question of interest: How levels of state legal capacity, demand-side barriers to firms' use of formal legal institutions, and the effectiveness of illegal strategies affect firms' choices about how to secure property. Each firm i has a pure strategy space $s_i = \{l, f\}$, where l represents legal strategies and f represents illegal strategies based on force and corruption. Legal strategies include turning to courts and law enforcement agencies. Illegal strategies include reliance on criminal protection rackets or informal ties with state bureaucrats and law enforcement personnel to resolve business conflicts. An endogenous proportion λ_l of firms rely on legal strategies, while a proportion $1 - \lambda_l$ rely on illegal strategies. More realistically, but with the same implications for the model, λ_l can be interpreted as the proportion of each firm's portfolio of property security strategies based on law, and $1 - \lambda_l$ as the proportion of each firm's portfolio of property security strategies based on force and corruption.

When the conflict begins, the two firms choose their strategies simultaneously, representing firms' inability to observe the preferred strategies of other

Payoff Matrix

Firm 2

		l	f
	l	$(\alpha - \gamma)\frac{V}{2}$, $(\alpha - \gamma)\frac{V}{2}$	$q(\alpha - \gamma)V$, $(1-q)\beta V$
Firm 1	f	$(1-q)\beta V$, $q(\alpha - \gamma)V$	$(1-q)\beta \frac{V}{2}$, $(1-q)\beta \frac{V}{2}$

individual firms. After both firms choose a strategy, payoffs are realized, and the game ends.

Payoffs

The payoffs to a conflict reflect the three variables in the framework developed in Chapter 2 – state legal capacity, demand-side barriers, and the effectiveness of illegal strategies – and depend on the profile of strategies chosen by the two firms.

Legal vs. legal strategies When a conflict occurs between two firms using legal strategies, the loser receives nothing, and the winner receives $(\alpha - \gamma)V$, where $\alpha \in (0, 1)$ is a measure of the effectiveness of formal legal institutions (i.e., the lower is α, the more resources are wasted during the resolution of the conflict) and $\gamma \in (0, \alpha)$ is a measure of demand-side barriers (i.e., the higher is γ, the less effectively a firm can use formal legal institutions). Because all firms are identical, firms have an equal chance of winning when they both use the same strategies. The expected payoff for either firm in a conflict in which both sides use legal strategies therefore is $(\alpha - \gamma)\frac{V}{2}$.

Illegal vs. illegal strategies When a conflict occurs between two firms using illegal strategies, the loser receives nothing, and the winner receives βV, where $\beta \in (0, 1)$ is a measure of the effectiveness of illegal strategies. Use of illegal strategies also involves a risk that illegal activity will be detected with probability q and all assets will be confiscated by the state. Because this probability depends on the effectiveness of formal legal institutions, $q = q(\alpha)$, where $q(\cdot)$ is continuous and monotonically increasing in α. Additionally, because all firms are identical, firms again have an equal chance of winning when they both use the same strategies. The expected payoff for either firm in a conflict in which both sides use illegal strategies therefore is $(1 - q)\beta\frac{V}{2}$.

Legal vs. illegal strategies The firm using the illegal strategy wins the conflict and acquires the asset of value V, but with probability q the state detects the illegal activity, confiscates the assets, and returns them to the lawful firm.[1]

---

[1] Assuming illegal beat legal strategies simplifies analysis but does not qualitatively change results.

Accordingly, the expected payoff for a firm that uses a legal strategy against a firm using an illegal strategy is $q(\alpha - \gamma)V$, where q represents the probability the state locates and punishes the unlawful firm, α represents the effectiveness of the formal legal institutions the state uses to return the assets to the lawful firm, and γ again represents demand-side barriers. Correspondingly, the expected payoff for a firm that uses an illegal strategy against a firm using a legal strategy is $(1-q)\beta V$, where $1-q$ represents the probability the unlawful firm escapes punishment.

In summary, state legal capacity enters the model through the state's ability to adjudicate disputes (α) and punish law breakers ($q(\alpha)$). Meanwhile, demand-side barriers are represented by the parameter γ and the effectiveness of illegal strategies is represented by the parameter β. The expected payoffs for all combinations of strategies are presented in the Payoff Matrix above. I make one additional technical assumption that $q < \frac{1}{4}$. This assumption rules out regions of the parameter space that result in a game of chicken, in which illegal strategies are a best response to legal strategies and vice versa, for it is difficult to conceive of real-world scenarios represented by such a game.

Analysis: State Legal Capacity and the Use of Legal Strategies

A Nash Equilibrium (NE) in this game will be a combination of strategies for each firm such that each firm's strategy is a best response to the strategies played by all other firms in the economy. More formally, a NE in this game is a strategy profile (s_i^*, s_{-i}^*) for all firms $i \in \mathcal{I}$ such that $s_i^* \in BR_i(s_{-i}^*)$.

To examine the effects of state legal capacity on firm strategies, first consider an economy in which legal institutions (α) are ineffective to such a degree that a firm's expected payoff to using illegal strategies is greater than the payoff to using legal strategies *regardless* of other firms' strategies. In this low-capacity economy, the unique NE is for all firms to utilize illegal strategies. Consequently, a necessary condition for firms' use of legal strategies is that legal capacity must be high enough that the equilibrium in which all firms use illegal strategies is no longer unique. Now consider an economy in which formal legal institutions are effective enough that a firm's expected payoff to using legal strategies is at least as great as the payoff to using illegal strategies, but *only if* a sufficient number of other firms also employ legal strategies. In such intermediate-capacity economies, multiple equilibria exist, including equilibria in which some or all firms use legal strategies (as discussed below) but also an equilibrium in which all firms use illegal strategies. In other words, an intermediate level of legal capacity is insufficient to guarantee firms' use of legal strategies. The following proposition formalizes these intuitions:

Proposition 1 Let $\underline{\alpha} = 2\beta(1-q) + \gamma$ and $\overline{\alpha} = \frac{\beta}{2q}(1-q) + \gamma$. Then:[2]

1. For any $\alpha < \underline{\alpha}$, the unique NE for the game is $s_i^* = f$ for all firms $i \in \mathcal{I}$.
2. For any $\alpha \in [\underline{\alpha}, \overline{\alpha})$, there exists a NE in which $s_i^* = f$ for all firms $i \in \mathcal{I}$.

Proposition 1 states that $\alpha \geq \underline{\alpha}$ is a *necessary* but *insufficient condition* for the use of legal strategies. Consequently, state legal capacity plays a central role in inducing firms to rely on law, but explanations relying on state capacity alone remain incomplete.

Complete explanations require further consideration of demand-side factors, particularly in intermediate-capacity states (i.e., in states where $\alpha \in [\underline{\alpha}, \overline{\alpha}]$. For this region of the parameter space, illegal strategies yield higher payoffs than legal strategies when all firms use illegal strategies (i.e., when $\lambda_l = 0$), and legal strategies yield higher payoffs than illegal strategies when all firms use legal strategies (i.e., when $\lambda_l = 1$). Consequently, when all firms use the same strategy, no firm can increase its expected payoffs by adopting an alternative strategy. Meanwhile, a third equilibrium exists in which $\lambda_l = \lambda^*$, where λ^* is the proportion of firms using legal strategies such that the marginal firm is indifferent between legal and illegal strategies. Although such an equilibrium is "unstable," in the sense that a small perturbation of parameter values leads all firms to adopt either legal or illegal strategies, no firm has an incentive to alter its strategy given the distribution of strategies in the economy. This proportion of firms using legal strategies, λ_l^*, represents a *tipping point*, as defined more formally below:

Definition 1 The proportion of firms using legal strategies $\lambda_l^* \in (0, 1)$ is a *tipping point* if $U_j(l; \lambda_l^*, s_{-j}^*, \alpha, \beta, \gamma) = U_j(f; \lambda_l^*, s_{-j}^*, \alpha, \beta, \gamma)$ for the marginal firm j.

This tipping point is essential for analyzing transitions from one equilibrium to another.

Prior to turning to such transitions, it is worth noting that a sufficient condition for state legal capacity to induce firms' use of legal strategies is that $\alpha \geq \overline{\alpha}$. Within this region of the parameter space, legal strategies strictly dominate illegal strategies regardless of the strategies used by other firms, resulting in a unique NE in which all firms use legal strategies. Substantively, this condition corresponds to high-capacity states such as the advanced industrialized countries. However, the fact that legal capacity is sufficient to ensure a unique lawful equilibrium in high-capacity states does not necessarily mean that an increase in legal capacity induced firms to adopt legal strategies. It is equally possible that such historical transitions resulted from reduced demand-side barriers

---

[2] Formal proofs for all propositions are included in the Online Appendix.

and declining effectiveness in illegal strategies, which shifted an intermediate-capacity state from an unlawful to a lawful equilibrium, and that subsequent increases in state legal capacity occurred after firms came to use legal strategies.

For the remainder of this analysis, the focus is on intermediate-capacity states such as post-Soviet Russia, in which state legal capacity is sufficiently high to make legal strategies feasible but insufficiently high to ensure a unique lawful equilibrium.

Analysis: Demand-Side Barriers and the Effectiveness of Illegal Strategies

Many states throughout the developing world exhibit levels of state legal capacity in an intermediate range, and these states are the focus here. I model intermediate levels of legal capacity by assuming that α is within a region of the parameter space $\alpha \in [\underline{\alpha}, \overline{\alpha})$ such that legal strategies are a best response to legal strategies, but illegal strategies are a best response to illegal strategies. In other words, a firm facing another firm using legal strategies knows that it will win the dispute only half of the time, and therefore such a firm might be tempted to switch to an illegal strategy with which it would prevail with certainty against the other firm's use of law. But the risk of being caught is high enough, and legal institutions are effective enough relative to illegal property security strategies, that the firm finds it more appealing to stay within the bounds of law. However, state capacity is not high enough to warrant the use of legal strategies when the other firm resorts to illegal strategies. A firm facing another firm using illegal strategies knows that it will win the dispute only half of the time, and therefore such a firm might be tempted to switch to a legal strategy and receive some portion of the assets back from the state should law enforcement catch and punish the unlawful firm. But this probability is not high enough, and the amount of assets that will be returned to the firm are not significant enough, to make this switch to law appealing.

Under these circumstances, demand-side barriers and the effectiveness of illegal strategies play a determinative role in firm strategies. One key demand-side barrier, discussed in Section 2.2.2 of Chapter 2, pertains to *coordination effects*. As stated above, when all firms use illegal strategies (i.e., when $\lambda_l = 0$), then any individual firm is strictly better off also choosing illegal strategies. Note that this is true even though all firms would be better off using legal strategies *as long as* other firms also use legal strategies, given the payoffs defined in the Payoff Matrix above.[3]

---

[3] Formally, when $\alpha \in [\underline{\alpha}, \overline{\alpha})$, then $\alpha \geq 2\beta(1-q)+\gamma$ or, equivalently, $\alpha - \gamma \geq 2\beta(1-q)$. It follows that $U(l; \lambda_l = 1) = (\alpha - \gamma)\frac{V}{2} > (1-q)\beta\frac{V}{2} = U(f; \lambda_l = 0)$, where $U(l; \lambda_l = 1)$ is the expected payoff of a firm using legal strategies when all firms use legal strategies and

To further analyze the impact of coordination effects on firm strategies, reconsider the proportion of firms using legal strategies, λ_l^*, such that the marginal firm is indifferent between legal and illegal strategies. Defining $\lambda_f^* = 1 - \lambda_l^*$, this indifference condition can be written as:

$$U(l) = \lambda_l^* \left[(\alpha - \gamma)\frac{V}{2} \right] + \lambda_f^* \left[q(\alpha - \gamma)V \right]$$

$$= \lambda_l^* \left[(1 - q)\beta V \right] + \lambda_f^* \left[(1 - q)\beta\frac{V}{2} \right] = U(f) \qquad \text{(D.1)}$$

$$\Longleftrightarrow \lambda_l^* \left[\frac{(\alpha - \gamma)}{2} - (1 - q)\beta \right] = \lambda_f^* \left[(1 - q)\frac{\beta}{2} - q(\alpha - \gamma) \right] \qquad \text{(D.2)}$$

where the lefthand side of Equation (D.1) is the marginal firm's expected payoff for legal strategies and the righthand side is the marginal firm's expected payoff for illegal strategies, given the strategies of all other firms. Equation (D.2) rearranges this indifference condition to make it more tractable for analyses of transitions from one equilibrium to another. When the lefthand side of Equation (D.2) increases, an economy "tips" toward a lawful equilibrium in which all firms use legal strategies; when the righthand side increases, the opposite occurs.

Following Lamberson and Page (2012), I analyze both *direct* and *contextual* tipping points. A direct tip occurs when a variable of interest, in this case the proportion of firms using each strategy, tilts an economy over the tipping point. Consider an exogenous shock that induces some firms to use legal strategies. This shock could result from a number of factors: a new president with a reputation as a reformer comes to power, a country joins an international organization such as the WTO, or a state initiates an anticorruption propaganda campaign. Formally, let $\Delta_\lambda > 0$ define a shift in the number of firms using legal strategies resulting from an external shock. Then for an economy in which λ_l firms are using legal strategies, we can see from Equation (D.2) that a shock Δ_λ will initiate a direct tip as long as $(\lambda_l + \Delta_\lambda) \left[\frac{(\alpha - \gamma)}{2} - (1 - q)\beta \right] > (\lambda_f - \Delta_\lambda) \left[(1 - q)\frac{\beta}{2} - q(\alpha - \gamma) \right]$.

Meanwhile, a contextual tip occurs when a shift in a parameter of the model – such as demand-side barriers or the effectiveness of illegal strategies – tilts an economy over the tipping point. Consider, for example, a reduction in demand-side barriers resulting from firms' increased tax compliance, such that demand-side barriers fall by $\Delta_\gamma > 0$. (As discussed in Section 2.2.2, low tax compliance makes firms wary of using formal legal institutions out of concerns that their tax violations will be exposed.) Then for an economy in

---

$U(f; \lambda_l = 0)$ is the expected payoff of a firm using illegal strategies when all firms use illegal strategies.

which λ_l firms are using legal strategies, we can see from Equation (D.2) that this reduction in demand-side barriers will initiate a contextual tip as long as $\lambda_l \left[\frac{(\alpha - (\gamma - \triangle_\gamma))}{2} - (1-q)\beta \right] > \lambda_f \left[(1-q)\frac{\beta}{2} - q(\alpha - (\gamma - \triangle_\gamma)) \right]$. A shift in the effectiveness of illegal institutions, $\triangle_\beta$, can be formalized analogously.

Economies are quite sensitive to direct and contextual tips when near their tipping point. But when an economy is locked in an unlawful equilibrium, then a significant external shock to firm strategies would be needed to initiate a direct tip. Likewise, a contextual tip requires a significant parameter shift or a lesser parameter shift combined with a small exogenous shock to the number of firms using legal strategies. Equation (D.2) offers insights into the types of parameter shifts that make a tip more likely. All else equal, it becomes easier to a tip an economy toward a lawful equilibrium as state legal capacity (α) increases. But in many developing countries, legal reforms are politically or technically infeasible. Fortunately, Equation (D.2) also makes clear that even if legal capacity remains stagnant or marginally deteriorates, sufficiently large declines in demand-side barriers (γ) or the effectiveness of illegal strategies (β) can facilitate a tip toward a lawful equilibrium. Proposition 2 formalizes these intuitions:

Proposition 2 Given q, β, and γ, let $\alpha \in [\underline{\alpha}, \overline{\alpha})$, where $\underline{\alpha}$ and $\overline{\alpha}$ are as defined in Proposition 1. Suppose initially that $\lambda_l = 0$. Then:

1. For any $\hat{\alpha} \in [\underline{\alpha}, \overline{\alpha}]$ and $\hat{\gamma} \leq \gamma$, there exists a $\hat{\beta}$ such that if β declines to $\hat{\beta}$ for a portion of firms $\omega \geq \lambda^*$, then $\lambda_l = \lambda^*$ or $\lambda_l = 1$ will be an equilibrium.
2. For any $\hat{\alpha} \in [\underline{\alpha}, \overline{\alpha}]$ and $\hat{\beta} \leq \beta$, there exists a $\hat{\gamma}$ such that if γ declines to $\hat{\gamma}$ for a portion of firms $\omega \geq \lambda^*$, then $\lambda_l = \lambda^*$ or $\lambda_l = 1$ will be an equilibrium.[4]

In words, consider an intermediate-capacity economy locked in an unlawful equilibrium in which all firms use illegal strategies, and assume that improvements in state legal capacity are infeasible. Then, for a portion of firms ω, demand-side barriers and/or the effectiveness of illegal strategies declines to an extent that for these firms legal strategies dominate illegal strategies, leading them to adopt legal strategies. If the number of early adopters of legal strategies is sufficiently large (i.e., $\omega \geq \lambda^*$), then this initial shift can tip the economy and induce all other firms to also adopt legal strategies. In short, Proposition 2 states that given a necessary level of state legal capacity $\alpha \geq \underline{\alpha}$, falling demand-side barriers and/or declining effectiveness of illegal strategies can be *sufficient*

---

[4] Part 2 requires the assumption $\gamma > (\frac{1}{2q} - 2)(1 - q)\beta$. Substantively, this ensures that demand-side barriers (γ) play a sufficiently large role in firms' initial reluctance to use legal strategies, such that a reduction in barriers can induce a strategy shift even holding illegal strategies' effectiveness (β) constant.

conditions for firms to use legal strategies *even if* legal capacity is unchanged or decreasing.

Summary

The model captures the logic of the narrative detailed in this book, but in barebones form. Two issues deserve further discussion. First, because actors in the model adjust according to best-response functions, there is an immediate return to an equilibrium state following exogenous shocks to the proportion of firms using legal strategies or following parameter shifts. A more realistic setup might instead utilize an evolutionary framework, with a replicator dynamic such that the change in the share of firms using a given strategy from time t to time $t + 1$ depends on the difference between the expected payoff of a given strategy and the average payoff for all firms in the economy (see, e.g., Taylor and Jonker, 1978). Strategies with above-average payoffs become more prominent over time while strategies with below-average payoffs become less prominent over time, such that the economy *tends* toward a stable equilibrium. With such a setup, economies would be in different states of disequilibria, and parameter shifts could alter the tipping point, shifting the trend of the economy in one direction or the other. While less realistic, the model presented here offers similar insights without the additional analysis required to set up an evolutionary framework.

Second, the assumption that firms are identical produces a unique tipping point for the overall economy. By contrast, in the real world different types of firms employ certain strategies with differing degrees of effectiveness, which is likely to produce multiple tipping points unique to specific sectors, regions, or types of firms.

In summary, the model formalizes the logic underlying the theory presented in Chapter 2. It elucidates why state legal capacity is a necessary but frequently insufficient condition for firms to use legal strategies, why firms frequently adopt legal strategies even without improvements in legal capacity, and how demand-side barriers and the effectiveness of illegal strategies become determinative of firm strategies once a requisite level of state legal capacity exists. The model furthermore illustrates the interactions between coordination effects among firms and exogenous parameter shifts in demand-side barriers and the effectiveness of illegal strategies. Substantively, the model makes clear that declining demand-side barriers or effectiveness of illegal strategies have a *direct* effect on property security strategies by inducing many firms to reconsider their use of illegal strategies, as well as an *indirect* and ongoing effect as other firms adapt to the initial wave of changes that shocks set in motion.

Appendix E

Descriptive Statistics for Key Variables

Table E1   *Dependent Variables*

Respondents' likeliness of using a particular strategy to respond to a property or debt dispute on a scale of 1 to 7, where 1 means "highly unlikely" and 7 means "highly likely"

Variables	N	Mean	SD	Min	Max
	Property Disputes				
Lawyers (out of court)	297	6.04	1.50	1	7
Courts	293	5.69	1.79	1	7
Law Enforcement (official)	295	5.18	1.98	1	7
Bureaucrats (official)	290	4.57	2.11	1	7
Courts (with connections)	268	4.33	2.24	1	7
Law Enforcement (unofficial)	280	3.78	2.19	1	7
Bureaucrats (unofficial)	281	3.63	2.18	1	7
Internal Security Service	272	3.29	2.26	1	7
Private Security	278	2.21	1.77	1	7
Criminal Racket	272	1.87	1.57	1	7
	Debt Disputes				
Lawyers (out of court)	301	6.31	1.27	1	7
Courts	292	5.86	1.60	1	7
Law Enforcement (official)	298	4.83	2.24	1	7
Bureaucrats (official)	294	3.99	2.18	1	7
Courts (with connections)	268	4.19	2.25	1	7
Law Enforcement (unofficial)	288	3.65	2.19	1	7
Bureaucrats (unofficial)	286	3.37	2.16	1	7
Internal Security Service	274	3.22	2.27	1	7
Private Security	278	2.09	1.71	1	7
Criminal Racket	277	1.75	1.38	1	7

Note: See Table 3.3 in Chapter 3 for exact wording of the property and debt dispute scenarios.

Table E2 *Independent Variables*

Variables	Description	N	Mean	SD	Min	Max
Tax Violator	1 if firm reports less than 90% of sales revenue for tax purposes, 0 otherwise	167	0.32	0.47	0	1
Others Unlawful	1 if respondent disagrees that other firms seek to follow the law, 0 otherwise	299	0.34	0.47	0	1
Consolidated	1 if firm has single owner or owner with controlling packet of shares, 0 otherwise	284	0.73	0.45	0	1
Privatized	1 if privatized, 0 if created *de novo*	301	0.26	0.44	0	1
Low Cash	1 if less than 10% of transactions conducted in cash, 0 otherwise	209	0.50	0.50	0	1
Service Sector	1 if firm provides services, 0 if deals in physical products	301	0.56	0.49	0	1
Local Market	1 if firm operates in local (e.g., neighborhood, city, regional) market, 0 if operates in national market	301	0.54	0.50	0	1
SOE	1 if firm's suppliers or main clients/customers include state-owned enterprises, 0 otherwise	294	0.31	0.46	0	1
Wealthy Client	1 if firm's main clients/customers include wealthy individuals, 0 otherwise	294	0.41	0.49	0	1
Licensing Barrier	1 if firm considers business licensing an obstacle to the success of its business, 0 otherwise	298	0.40	0.49	0	1
Customs Barrier	1 if firm considers customs regulations an obstacle to the success of its business, 0 otherwise	293	0.31	0.46	0	1

Table E3 *Control Variables*

Variables	Description	N	Mean	SD	Min	Max
Firm Age	founded or privatized in 1 = the past year; 2 = last 3 years; 3 = last 5 years; 4 = last 10 years; 5 = last 15 years; 6 = more than 15 years ago	296	4.42	1.37	1	6
Gov. Owner	1 if firm has 10 or more percent government ownership stake, 0 otherwise	293	0.09	0.29	0	1
Foreign Owner	1 if firm has 10 or more percent foreign ownership stake, 0 otherwise	290	0.10	0.30	0	1
Bus. Assoc.	1 if firm is member of a business association, 0 otherwise	301	0.41	0.49	0	1
Legal Ed.	1 if respondent has legal degree, 0 otherwise	301	0.13	0.34	0	1
Rights Violated	1 if firm experienced violation of its legal rights in last 3 years, 0 otherwise	290	0.67	0.47	0	1
Litigated	1 if firm has been to court in last 3 years, 0 otherwise	292	0.47	0.50	0	1
Age	age of respondent	301	43.5	11.0	22	76
Male	1 if male, 0 if female	301	0.48	0.50	0	1
City Dummies	Ekaterinburg (excluded), Kazan, Moscow, Nizhniy Novgorod, Novosibirsk, Rostov-on-Don, Samara, St. Petersburg	301	–	–	–	–
Firm Size Dummies	< 101 employees (excluded), 101–250, 251–500, > 500	301	–	–	–	–
Firm Finances Dummies	bad (excluded), satisfactory, good, excellent	301	–	–	–	–
Job Title Dummies	owner (excluded), general director, assistant director, finance director, other	301	–	–	–	–

Appendix F

Correlations and Cluster Analysis

An important question is the extent to which firms combine legal and illegal strategies. Table F1 below presents pairwise correlations across different types of property security strategies. The correlation tables indicate that firms' propensity to use a specific strategy of private, corrupt, or legal coercion is positively correlated with propensity to use other similar strategies. In the case of debt disputes, there is also some evidence that firms' propensity to use legal strategies is negatively correlated with propensity to use private or corrupt coercion. The results of hierarchical cluster analysis in Figure F1 similarly show that strategies based on violence, corruption, or law appear to cluster together.

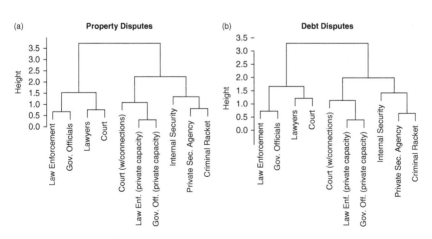

Figure F1 Hierarchical Cluster Analysis

229

Table F1 *Correlations across Firm Strategies*

(a) Property Disputes

	1	2	3	4	5	6	7	8	9	10
1. Lawyers										
2. Court	0.51									
3. Law Enforcement	0.29	0.36								
4. Gov. Officials	0.23	0.34	0.56							
5. Court (w/connections)	0.17	0.30	0.13	0.15						
6. Law Enf. (private capacity)	ns	ns	0.23	0.19	0.50					
7. Gov. Offic. (private capacity)	ns	ns	0.14	0.32	0.52	0.83				
8. Internal Security	ns	ns	ns	ns	0.19	ns	ns			
9. Private Sec. Agency	ns	ns	ns	ns	0.17	0.31	0.29	0.22		
10. Criminal Racket	ns	ns	ns	ns	0.29	0.24	0.31	0.20	0.45	

(b) Debt Disputes

	1	2	3	4	5	6	7	8	9	10
1. Lawyers										
2. Court	0.23									
3. Law Enforcement	0.25	0.29								
4. Gov. Officials	0.19	0.18	0.53							
5. Court (w/connections)	0.14	0.19	0.16	0.11						
6. Law Enf. (private capacity)	ns	−0.23	0.36	0.22	0.49					
7. Gov. Offic. (private capacity)	ns	−0.21	0.18	0.35	0.47	0.77				
8. Internal Security	ns	ns	0.10	0.20	0.20	0.11	0.11			
9. Private Sec. Agency	ns	−0.21	0.13	ns	0.21	0.40	0.38	0.22		
10. Criminal Racket	−0.13	−0.21	ns	ns	0.18	0.30	0.35	0.25	0.57	

Note: All correlations shown are statistically significant at $p < 0.05$.

Appendix G

Selected Regression Tables

Missing data were multiply imputed for all regression analyses shown in Chapters 4 through 6 using the AMELIA II package for R (Honaker et al., 2011). As King et al. (2001) have shown, when data are not missing completely at random, listwise deletion – removing all observations for which data are missing on one or more variables from analyses – is always inefficient and often can lead to biased inference. With the exception of rare circumstances, multiple imputation therefore is preferable to listwise deletion.

Multiple imputation leverages data from other observations in the dataset to impute values for missing data. To capture the uncertainty regarding how well the imputed data represent the true values of missing data, it utilizes multiple imputed datasets. In the current case, 50 sets of imputations were conducted. The imputation model used all variables included in the analyses presented in Chapters 5 through 7 as well as additional variables from the survey data. A complete list of variables used in the imputation model can be found in the replication materials. Regression coefficients displayed in the figures in Chapters 5 through 7 and in the tables below are the mean of these analyses on each of the 50 imputed datasets, while standard errors capture sample variance within each imputed dataset as well as variance across datasets.

In the supplementary analyses in the Online Appendix, I show that listwise deletion produces very similar results for bivariate regressions and regressions with the complete set of control variables. The results are less robust for the saturated model specifications, which is to be expected, given that listwise deletion in many cases removes more than half of the sample for these specifications.

The following tables present selected regression results for model specifications with control variables and for saturated models. Full regression results for each figure – including the bivariate models, the models with control variables, and the saturated models – can be found in the Online Appendix.

Regressions for Figure 5.3 *Tax Compliance and Property Security Strategies*

				Property Dispute Scenario – With Control Variables						
	Lawyers	Courts (formal)	Law Enf. (formal)	Gov. Officials (formal)	Courts (informal)	Law Enf. (informal)	Gov. Officials (informal)	Criminal Rackets	Private Sec. Agency	Internal Security
Tax Violator	−0.43†	−0.71**	−0.27	−0.26	0.61†	0.91**	1.03**	0.81***	0.30	0.07
	(0.24)	(0.26)	(0.30)	(0.31)	(0.33)	(0.33)	(0.32)	(0.23)	(0.29)	(0.29)
Firm Age	0.10	0.24*	0.08	0.13	−0.06	0.04	−0.06	0.00	0.05	0.03
	(0.08)	(0.11)	(0.10)	(0.11)	(0.13)	(0.11)	(0.11)	(0.08)	(0.09)	(0.12)
Foreign Owner	0.08	0.64†	−0.39	−0.78†	0.40	0.12	−0.06	0.39	0.30	0.13
	(0.27)	(0.33)	(0.40)	(0.45)	(0.42)	(0.42)	(0.41)	(0.33)	(0.38)	(0.40)
Gov. Owner	−0.14	0.23	−0.14	0.20	0.23	−0.41	−0.22	0.01	−0.18	−0.05
	(0.32)	(0.37)	(0.39)	(0.41)	(0.41)	(0.44)	(0.45)	(0.32)	(0.35)	(0.49)
Bus. Assoc.	0.01	−0.03	0.71**	0.89***	0.53†	0.45†	0.42	0.00	−0.02	0.57†
	(0.20)	(0.22)	(0.25)	(0.26)	(0.30)	(0.26)	(0.27)	(0.22)	(0.23)	(0.30)
Rights Violated	−0.03	0.22	0.23	0.16	0.36	0.78*	0.53†	0.25	0.27	0.37
	(0.23)	(0.27)	(0.28)	(0.30)	(0.32)	(0.32)	(0.29)	(0.22)	(0.26)	(0.30)
Litigated	0.38	0.31	0.52†	−0.33	0.23	0.16	−0.08	−0.37	−0.65*	−0.01
	(0.28)	(0.30)	(0.31)	(0.33)	(0.32)	(0.33)	(0.31)	(0.24)	(0.26)	(0.35)
Legal Ed.	−0.00	0.35	0.26	0.35	0.45	0.09	0.60	0.85**	0.42	0.44
	(0.27)	(0.30)	(0.39)	(0.40)	(0.41)	(0.36)	(0.37)	(0.31)	(0.31)	(0.38)
Age	0.00	0.03**	−0.02	−0.02	0.00	−0.01	−0.01	−0.04***	−0.02†	−0.00
	(0.01)	(0.01)	(0.01)	(0.01)	(0.01)	(0.01)	(0.01)	(0.01)	(0.01)	(0.01)
Male	−0.29	−0.28	−0.11	−0.11	−0.38	−0.13	−0.33	0.30	−0.17	0.18
	(0.20)	(0.22)	(0.24)	(0.25)	(0.28)	(0.26)	(0.25)	(0.20)	(0.23)	(0.26)
Constant	6.23***	3.63***	7.15***	6.35***	3.21**	3.26**	3.49***	3.52***	4.32***	3.88***
	(0.75)	(0.81)	(0.84)	(0.96)	(1.06)	(1.06)	(1.00)	(0.76)	(0.92)	(1.01)

	(1)	(2)	(3)	(4)	(5)	(6)	(7)	(8)	(9)	(10)
City Dummies	yes	yes	yes	yes	yes	yes	yes	yes	yes	yes
Sector Dummies	yes	yes	yes	yes	yes	yes	yes	yes	yes	yes
Firm Size Dummies	yes	yes	yes	yes	yes	yes	yes	yes	yes	yes
Firm Finances Dummies	yes	yes	yes	yes	yes	yes	yes	yes	yes	yes
Job Title Dummies	yes	yes	yes	yes	yes	yes	yes	yes	yes	yes
R-sq.	0.28	0.24	0.29	0.26	0.23	0.21	0.24	0.20	0.25	0.16
Adj. R-sq.	0.20	0.17	0.22	0.19	0.15	0.13	0.16	0.12	0.17	0.07

Debt Dispute Scenario – With Control Variables

	(1)	(2)	(3)	(4)	(5)	(6)	(7)	(8)	(9)	(10)
Tax Violator	0.22	0.37	0.66**	1.14**	1.01**	0.66†	0.06	0.07	−0.61*	0.02
	(0.31)	(0.28)	(0.21)	(0.35)	(0.36)	(0.35)	(0.33)	(0.32)	(0.24)	(0.20)
Firm Age	0.11	−0.04	0.04	−0.10	−0.07	−0.10	0.14	0.11	0.15	0.07
	(0.12)	(0.08)	(0.08)	(0.11)	(0.12)	(0.13)	(0.11)	(0.11)	(0.10)	(0.08)
Foreign Owner	0.14	0.24	0.25	−0.00	−0.17	0.32	−0.04	−0.34	0.29	−0.03
	(0.42)	(0.33)	(0.28)	(0.40)	(0.40)	(0.41)	(0.45)	(0.42)	(0.29)	(0.25)
Gov. Owner	0.32	−0.10	−0.06	0.05	−0.15	0.12	0.40	0.16	0.20	−0.02
	(0.50)	(0.27)	(0.24)	(0.42)	(0.43)	(0.45)	(0.45)	(0.43)	(0.36)	(0.30)
Bus. Assoc.	0.53†	0.13	−0.05	0.20	0.31	0.40	0.09	0.31	−0.00	−0.17
	(0.31)	(0.21)	(0.18)	(0.27)	(0.28)	(0.30)	(0.29)	(0.28)	(0.20)	(0.16)
Rights Violated	0.24	0.42	0.30	0.16	0.05	0.31	0.09	0.61*	0.28	−0.04
	(0.30)	(0.26)	(0.20)	(0.31)	(0.34)	(0.33)	(0.32)	(0.31)	(0.24)	(0.18)
Litigated	−0.23	−0.50*	−0.13	0.18	0.21	0.19	−0.16	−0.07	−0.09	0.19
	(0.34)	(0.24)	(0.21)	(0.32)	(0.34)	(0.33)	(0.33)	(0.33)	(0.25)	(0.18)
Legal Ed.	0.97**	0.59*	0.68*	0.57	0.51	0.30	0.12	0.52	0.31	−0.08
	(0.37)	(0.28)	(0.27)	(0.38)	(0.39)	(0.45)	(0.40)	(0.43)	(0.24)	(0.24)

Regressions for Figure 5.3 *(cont.)*

	Lawyers	Courts (formal)	Law Enf. (formal)	Gov. Officials (formal)	Courts (informal)	Law Enf. (informal)	Gov. Officials (informal)	Criminal Rackets	Private Sec. Agency	Internal Security
	Debt Dispute Scenario – With Control Variables									
Age	−0.00	0.01	−0.03†	−0.00	0.00	−0.02	−0.01	−0.02**	−0.01†	−0.01
	(0.01)	(0.01)	(0.01)	(0.01)	(0.01)	(0.01)	(0.01)	(0.01)	(0.01)	(0.01)
Male	−0.16	−0.27	0.09	0.06	−0.39	0.06	−0.08	0.29	0.34	0.47†
	(0.17)	(0.19)	(0.27)	(0.27)	(0.27)	(0.27)	(0.25)	(0.18)	(0.21)	(0.26)
Constant	5.70***	4.12***	5.75***	4.63***	3.16**	4.31***	3.98***	3.47***	4.63***	3.70***
	(0.70)	(0.78)	(0.98)	(1.02)	(1.11)	(1.09)	(1.09)	(0.78)	(0.83)	(1.04)
City Dummies	yes	yes	yes	yes	yes	yes	yes	yes	yes	yes
Sector Dummies	yes	yes	yes	yes	yes	yes	yes	yes	yes	yes
Firm Size Dummies	yes	yes	yes	yes	yes	yes	yes	yes	yes	yes
Firm Finances Dummies	yes	yes	yes	yes	yes	yes	yes	yes	yes	yes
Job Title Dummies	yes	yes	yes	yes	yes	yes	yes	yes	yes	yes
R-sq.	0.15	0.27	0.23	0.20	0.20	0.20	0.26	0.24	0.33	0.28
Adj. R-sq.	0.06	0.20	0.15	0.12	0.12	0.11	0.19	0.17	0.26	0.20

Note: *** $p < 0.001$, ** $p < 0.01$, * $p < 0.05$, † $p < 0.10$. Robust standard errors in parentheses. N=301.

Regressions for Figure 5.4 Collective Action and Property Security Strategies

	Property Dispute Scenario – With Control Variables									
	Lawyers	Courts (formal)	Law Enf. (formal)	Gov. Officials (formal)	Courts (informal)	Law Enf. (informal)	Gov. Officials (informal)	Criminal Rackets	Private Sec. Agency	Internal Security
Others Unlawful	−0.38†	−0.45*	−0.42†	−0.76**	0.69*	0.62*	0.41	0.63**	0.31	0.28
	(0.21)	(0.23)	(0.24)	(0.26)	(0.27)	(0.26)	(0.26)	(0.21)	(0.21)	(0.26)
Firm Age	0.12	0.27*	0.09	0.13	−0.09	0.00	−0.11	−0.03	0.03	0.02
	(0.08)	(0.11)	(0.10)	(0.10)	(0.13)	(0.11)	(0.12)	(0.08)	(0.09)	(0.12)
Foreign Owner	0.11	0.65*	−0.35	−0.69	0.34	0.10	−0.05	0.36	0.28	0.09
	(0.26)	(0.32)	(0.39)	(0.44)	(0.43)	(0.41)	(0.42)	(0.34)	(0.38)	(0.41)
Gov. Owner	−0.13	0.25	−0.13	0.21	0.21	−0.43	−0.24	−0.01	−0.18	−0.05
	(0.30)	(0.35)	(0.39)	(0.39)	(0.41)	(0.42)	(0.44)	(0.31)	(0.34)	(0.49)
Bus. Assoc.	0.04	0.02	0.74**	0.93***	0.48	0.38	0.35	−0.06	−0.05	0.56†
	(0.20)	(0.22)	(0.25)	(0.25)	(0.30)	(0.26)	(0.27)	(0.23)	(0.23)	(0.30)
Rights Violated	0.02	0.28	0.29	0.26	0.27	0.70*	0.48	0.16	0.22	0.34
	(0.24)	(0.27)	(0.28)	(0.30)	(0.32)	(0.32)	(0.30)	(0.22)	(0.26)	(0.30)
Litigated	0.41	0.36	0.54†	−0.31	0.19	0.10	−0.14	−0.43†	−0.67**	−0.02
	(0.28)	(0.30)	(0.30)	(0.31)	(0.33)	(0.34)	(0.32)	(0.23)	(0.26)	(0.34)
Legal Ed.	−0.07	0.23	0.22	0.32	0.54	0.23	0.76*	0.98**	0.46	0.45
	(0.26)	(0.29)	(0.38)	(0.38)	(0.40)	(0.34)	(0.36)	(0.32)	(0.30)	(0.37)
Age	0.00	0.03*	−0.02	−0.02†	0.01	−0.01	−0.00	−0.03***	−0.02†	−0.00
	(0.01)	(0.01)	(0.01)	(0.01)	(0.01)	(0.01)	(0.01)	(0.01)	(0.01)	(0.01)
Male	−0.19	−0.14	−0.01	0.04	−0.55*	−0.31	−0.49*	0.12	−0.25	0.13
	(0.20)	(0.22)	(0.24)	(0.25)	(0.28)	(0.26)	(0.25)	(0.21)	(0.22)	(0.26)
Constant	6.09***	3.33***	7.13***	6.45***	3.36**	3.63***	4.01***	3.82***	4.41***	3.83***
	(0.75)	(0.80)	(0.84)	(0.93)	(1.02)	(1.05)	(1.00)	(0.75)	(0.89)	(0.99)

Regressions for Figure 5.4 *(cont.)*

		Property Dispute Scenario – With Control Variables								
	Lawyers	Courts (formal)	Law Enf. (formal)	Gov. Officials (formal)	Courts (informal)	Law Enf. (informal)	Gov. Officials (informal)	Criminal Rackets	Private Sec. Agency	Internal Security
City Dummies	yes	yes	yes	yes	yes	yes	yes	yes	yes	yes
Sector Dummies	yes	yes	yes	yes	yes	yes	yes	yes	yes	yes
Firm Size Dummies	yes	yes	yes	yes	yes	yes	yes	yes	yes	yes
Firm Finances Dummies	yes	yes	yes	yes	yes	yes	yes	yes	yes	yes
Job Title Dummies	yes	yes	yes	yes	yes	yes	yes	yes	yes	yes
R-sq.	0.15	0.23	0.20	0.26	0.21	0.21	0.23	0.27	0.24	0.28
Adj. R-sq.	0.07	0.15	0.12	0.18	0.13	0.13	0.15	0.20	0.16	0.20
		Debt Dispute Scenario – With Control Variables								
Others Unlawful	−0.20	−0.27	0.01	−0.67*	0.75**	0.51†	0.18	0.47*	0.39†	0.36
	(0.17)	(0.20)	(0.27)	(0.27)	(0.29)	(0.27)	(0.25)	(0.18)	(0.20)	(0.28)
Firm Age	0.07	0.18†	0.11	0.13	−0.12	−0.12	−0.15	0.02	−0.06	0.10
	(0.07)	(0.10)	(0.11)	(0.11)	(0.13)	(0.12)	(0.11)	(0.08)	(0.08)	(0.12)
Foreign Owner	0.00	0.28	−0.34	0.06	0.26	−0.18	0.05	0.23	0.21	0.11
	(0.25)	(0.29)	(0.42)	(0.46)	(0.42)	(0.39)	(0.41)	(0.28)	(0.34)	(0.41)
Gov. Owner	−0.02	0.22	0.16	0.41	0.11	−0.17	0.04	−0.08	−0.10	0.32
	(0.30)	(0.35)	(0.43)	(0.42)	(0.47)	(0.42)	(0.43)	(0.22)	(0.26)	(0.50)

	(1)	(2)	(3)	(4)	(5)	(6)	(7)	(8)	(9)	(10)
Bus. Assoc.	-0.17	0.04	0.31	0.11	0.34	0.24	0.13	-0.10	0.10	0.51†
	(0.16)	(0.20)	(0.28)	(0.28)	(0.30)	(0.28)	(0.28)	(0.19)	(0.21)	(0.31)
Rights Violated	-0.01	0.32	0.61*	0.19	0.21	-0.02	0.13	0.23	0.37	0.19
	(0.17)	(0.24)	(0.31)	(0.32)	(0.33)	(0.35)	(0.33)	(0.20)	(0.25)	(0.31)
Litigated	0.19	-0.05	-0.08	-0.16	0.14	0.14	0.11	-0.17	-0.52*	-0.24
	(0.18)	(0.25)	(0.33)	(0.32)	(0.33)	(0.35)	(0.34)	(0.20)	(0.23)	(0.34)
Legal Ed.	-0.07	0.21	0.53	0.14	0.40	0.68†	0.76*	0.78**	0.65*	1.00**
	(0.23)	(0.24)	(0.43)	(0.39)	(0.43)	(0.37)	(0.38)	(0.29)	(0.29)	(0.36)
Age	-0.00	0.01	-0.03†	-0.01	0.00	-0.02	-0.01	-0.02*	-0.01	-0.01
	(0.01)	(0.01)	(0.01)	(0.01)	(0.01)	(0.01)	(0.01)	(0.01)	(0.01)	(0.01)
Male	-0.13	-0.17	0.08	0.16	-0.57*	-0.12	-0.22	0.15	0.24	0.39
	(0.17)	(0.20)	(0.27)	(0.27)	(0.27)	(0.27)	(0.26)	(0.18)	(0.21)	(0.26)
Constant	5.78***	3.83***	5.80***	4.92***	3.31**	4.79***	4.65***	3.73***	4.73***	3.72***
	(0.68)	(0.76)	(0.97)	(0.99)	(1.07)	(1.06)	(1.08)	(0.77)	(0.81)	(1.02)
City Dummies	yes	yes	yes	yes	yes	yes	yes	yes	yes	yes
Sector Dummies	yes	yes	yes	yes	yes	yes	yes	yes	yes	yes
Firm Size Dummies	yes	yes	yes	yes	yes	yes	yes	yes	yes	yes
Firm Finances Dummies	yes	yes	yes	yes	yes	yes	yes	yes	yes	yes
Job Title Dummies	yes	yes	yes	yes	yes	yes	yes	yes	yes	yes
R-sq.	0.16	0.25	0.23	0.22	0.21	0.16	0.21	0.22	0.32	0.28
Adj. R-sq.	0.07	0.17	0.15	0.14	0.12	0.08	0.12	0.14	0.26	0.20

Note: *** $p < 0.001$, ** $p < 0.01$, * $p < 0.05$, † $p < 0.10$. Robust standard errors in parentheses. N=301.

Regressions for Figure 6.1 *Ownership Consolidation and Property Security Strategies*

	Property Dispute Scenario – With Control Variables									
	Lawyers	Courts (formal)	Law Enf. (formal)	Gov. Officials (formal)	Courts (informal)	Law Enf. (informal)	Gov. Officials (informal)	Criminal Rackets	Private Sec. Agency	Internal Security
Privatized*Consolidated *marginal effects*	0.11	0.20	−0.41	0.23	−1.03†	−1.25*	−1.05*	0.13	−0.02	−1.04†
	(0.39)	(0.35)	(0.49)	(0.52)	(0.53)	(0.55)	(0.48)	(0.26)	(0.29)	(0.56)
Privatized	−0.32	−0.27	−1.22*	−0.36	0.40	−0.38	0.11	−0.52	−0.85*	0.60
	(0.41)	(0.42)	(0.51)	(0.54)	(0.57)	(0.59)	(0.55)	(0.38)	(0.38)	(0.57)
Consolidated	0.25	−0.02	−0.69†	−0.05	0.16	−0.69†	−0.32	0.17	−0.10	−0.12
	(0.31)	(0.34)	(0.36)	(0.41)	(0.42)	(0.40)	(0.40)	(0.28)	(0.32)	(0.35)
Privatized*Consolidated	−0.14	0.22	0.28	0.28	−1.19†	−0.56	−0.74	−0.03	0.08	−0.92
	(0.47)	(0.49)	(0.61)	(0.64)	(0.67)	(0.67)	(0.61)	(0.37)	(0.40)	(0.67)
Firm Age	0.15†	0.28*	0.14	0.14	−0.06	0.04	−0.09	−0.01	0.07	0.03
	(0.09)	(0.11)	(0.10)	(0.11)	(0.13)	(0.11)	(0.12)	(0.08)	(0.09)	(0.12)
Foreign Owner	0.06	0.59†	−0.30	−0.79†	0.46	0.29	0.06	0.47	0.38	0.15
	(0.27)	(0.31)	(0.40)	(0.44)	(0.43)	(0.42)	(0.41)	(0.33)	(0.37)	(0.39)
Gov. Owner	−0.03	0.31	−0.10	0.28	0.05	−0.62	−0.43	0.11	−0.07	−0.28
	(0.32)	(0.37)	(0.38)	(0.44)	(0.43)	(0.43)	(0.45)	(0.33)	(0.35)	(0.48)
Bus. Assoc.	0.04	0.02	0.75**	0.92***	0.47	0.39	0.35	−0.03	−0.02	0.54†
	(0.21)	(0.23)	(0.25)	(0.26)	(0.30)	(0.27)	(0.27)	(0.23)	(0.23)	(0.30)
Rights Violated	−0.02	0.21	0.27	0.15	0.42	0.84**	0.58†	0.26	0.29	0.42
	(0.23)	(0.28)	(0.28)	(0.30)	(0.31)	(0.32)	(0.30)	(0.22)	(0.26)	(0.31)

	(1)	(2)	(3)	(4)	(5)	(6)	(7)	(8)	(9)	(10)
Litigated	0.49†	0.39	0.65*	−0.28	0.21	0.13	−0.15	−0.32	−0.55*	−0.08
	(0.28)	(0.31)	(0.31)	(0.33)	(0.33)	(0.34)	(0.32)	(0.24)	(0.26)	(0.36)
Legal Ed.	−0.15	0.23	0.22	0.31	0.44	0.23	0.74*	0.91**	0.41	0.42
	(0.27)	(0.30)	(0.37)	(0.39)	(0.42)	(0.35)	(0.36)	(0.31)	(0.30)	(0.36)
Age	0.01	0.03**	−0.01	−0.02	0.00	−0.01	−0.01	−0.03***	−0.01	−0.00
	(0.01)	(0.01)	(0.01)	(0.01)	(0.01)	(0.01)	(0.01)	(0.01)	(0.01)	(0.01)
Male	−0.23	−0.22	−0.10	−0.10	−0.36	−0.19	−0.39	0.23	−0.19	0.22
	(0.20)	(0.22)	(0.24)	(0.25)	(0.28)	(0.27)	(0.26)	(0.21)	(0.22)	(0.26)
Constant	5.55***	3.15***	7.30***	6.19***	3.24**	4.23***	4.29***	3.69***	4.34***	3.99***
	(0.85)	(0.90)	(0.93)	(1.06)	(1.13)	(1.17)	(1.09)	(0.82)	(0.90)	(1.06)
City Dummies	yes	yes	yes	yes	yes	yes	yes	yes	yes	yes
Sector Dummies	yes	yes	yes	yes	yes	yes	yes	yes	yes	yes
Firm Size Dummies	yes	yes	yes	yes	yes	yes	yes	yes	yes	yes
Firm Finances Dummies	yes	yes	yes	yes	yes	yes	yes	yes	yes	yes
Job Title Dummies	yes	yes	yes	yes	yes	yes	yes	yes	yes	yes
R-sq.	0.15	0.22	0.23	0.24	0.21	0.23	0.24	0.26	0.26	0.29
Adj. R-sq.	0.06	0.14	0.15	0.15	0.12	0.14	0.15	0.18	0.18	0.21

Note: *** $p < 0.001$, ** $p < 0.01$, * $p < 0.05$, † $p < 0.10$. Robust standard errors in parentheses.

Regressions for Figure 6.1   *Ownership Consolidation and Property Security Strategies*

	Debt Dispute Scenario – With Control Variables									
	Lawyers	Courts (formal)	Law Enf. (formal)	Gov. Officials (formal)	Courts (informal)	Law Enf. (informal)	Gov. Officials (informal)	Criminal Rackets	Private Sec. Agency	Internal Security
Privatized* Consolidated	0.29 (0.35)	0.06 (0.30)	−0.37 (0.52)	−0.38 (0.52)	−1.05† (0.55)	−1.17* (0.54)	−1.30* (0.50)	0.01 (0.19)	−0.10 (0.26)	−0.57 (0.56)
marginal effects Privatized	−0.35 (0.32)	−0.40 (0.35)	−0.25 (0.56)	−0.03 (0.54)	0.14 (0.60)	0.03 (0.61)	0.34 (0.58)	−0.56† (0.29)	−0.65† (0.36)	0.27 (0.55)
Consolidated	−0.13 (0.23)	−0.46† (0.27)	−0.39 (0.41)	−0.17 (0.40)	−0.23 (0.41)	−0.81† (0.44)	−0.32 (0.40)	0.06 (0.26)	−0.27 (0.32)	−0.16 (0.34)
Privatized*	0.42 (0.40)	0.52 (0.41)	0.02 (0.67)	−0.21 (0.63)	−0.82 (0.69)	−0.36 (0.69)	−0.98 (0.62)	−0.05 (0.31)	0.17 (0.39)	−0.41 (0.66)
Consolidated	0.07 (0.07)	0.18† (0.10)	0.12 (0.11)	0.14 (0.11)	−0.10 (0.12)	−0.11 (0.12)	−0.13 (0.11)	0.04 (0.08)	−0.03 (0.08)	0.10 (0.12)
Firm Age	−0.02 (0.25)	0.28 (0.29)	−0.29 (0.43)	−0.01 (0.45)	0.42 (0.42)	−0.02 (0.40)	0.13 (0.40)	0.33 (0.28)	0.32 (0.33)	0.18 (0.41)
Foreign Owner	0.05 (0.32)	0.21 (0.36)	0.10 (0.44)	0.34 (0.45)	−0.07 (0.49)	−0.43 (0.43)	−0.22 (0.43)	0.02 (0.23)	−0.06 (0.27)	0.19 (0.49)
Gov. Owner	−0.16 (0.16)	0.04 (0.20)	0.30 (0.28)	0.08 (0.29)	0.34 (0.31)	0.23 (0.28)	0.11 (0.27)	−0.08 (0.19)	0.12 (0.21)	0.50 (0.31)

Rights Violated	−0.05	0.27	0.62*	0.11	0.36	0.09	0.21	0.31	0.43†	0.26
	(0.18)	(0.25)	(0.31)	(0.33)	(0.33)	(0.34)	(0.32)	(0.21)	(0.26)	(0.31)
Litigated	0.21	−0.06	−0.07	−0.16	0.15	0.09	0.08	−0.07	−0.45†	−0.28
	(0.18)	(0.25)	(0.34)	(0.34)	(0.33)	(0.35)	(0.34)	(0.21)	(0.24)	(0.35)
Legal Ed.	−0.04	0.28	0.56	0.12	0.36	0.75*	0.72†	0.72*	0.65*	1.01**
	(0.24)	(0.24)	(0.44)	(0.39)	(0.45)	(0.38)	(0.37)	(0.29)	(0.29)	(0.37)
Age	−0.00	0.01	−0.03†	−0.00	−0.00	−0.03†	−0.02	−0.02*	−0.01	−0.01
	(0.01)	(0.01)	(0.01)	(0.01)	(0.01)	(0.01)	(0.01)	(0.01)	(0.01)	(0.01)
Male	−0.19	−0.25	0.08	0.07	−0.41	−0.03	−0.14	0.24	0.30	0.47†
	(0.17)	(0.20)	(0.27)	(0.27)	(0.28)	(0.28)	(0.27)	(0.18)	(0.21)	(0.27)
Constant	5.84***	4.19***	6.10***	4.77***	3.61**	5.66***	4.86***	3.63***	4.95***	3.98***
	(0.76)	(0.85)	(1.09)	(1.10)	(1.16)	(1.21)	(1.18)	(0.85)	(0.85)	(1.10)
City Dummies	yes	yes	yes	yes	yes	yes	yes	yes	yes	yes
Sector Dummies	yes	yes	yes	yes	yes	yes	yes	yes	yes	yes
Firm Size Dummies	yes	yes	yes	yes	yes	yes	yes	yes	yes	yes
Firm Finances Dummies	yes	yes	yes	yes	yes	yes	yes	yes	yes	yes
Job Title Dummies	yes	yes	yes	yes	yes	yes	yes	yes	yes	yes
R-sq.	0.16	0.25	0.24	0.20	0.20	0.18	0.23	0.22	0.33	0.28
Adj. R-sq.	0.06	0.17	0.15	0.12	0.11	0.09	0.14	0.13	0.25	0.20

Note: *** $p < 0.001$, ** $p < 0.01$, * $p < 0.05$, † $p < 0.10$. Robust standard errors in parentheses. N=301.

Regressions for Figure 6.2 *Cash Transactions and Property Security Strategies*

				Property Dispute Scenario – With Control Variables						
	Lawyers	Courts (formal)	Law Enf. (formal)	Gov. Officials (formal)	Courts (informal)	Law Enf. (informal)	Gov. Officials (informal)	Criminal Rackets	Private Sec. Agency	Internal Security
Low Cash	0.01	−0.09	−0.08	0.03	−0.63†	−0.73*	−0.49	−0.16	−0.26	−0.08
	(0.22)	(0.23)	(0.28)	(0.31)	(0.34)	(0.32)	(0.33)	(0.24)	(0.27)	(0.31)
Firm Age	0.12	0.27*	0.09	0.14	−0.10	−0.01	−0.11	−0.03	0.03	0.02
	(0.08)	(0.11)	(0.10)	(0.10)	(0.13)	(0.11)	(0.12)	(0.08)	(0.09)	(0.12)
Foreign Owner	0.05	0.60†	−0.40	−0.80†	0.54	0.30	0.09	0.48	0.37	0.14
	(0.27)	(0.31)	(0.40)	(0.45)	(0.44)	(0.43)	(0.43)	(0.34)	(0.38)	(0.41)
Gov. Owner	−0.13	0.25	−0.12	0.20	0.26	−0.38	−0.21	0.01	−0.17	−0.04
	(0.31)	(0.36)	(0.39)	(0.41)	(0.41)	(0.43)	(0.45)	(0.32)	(0.34)	(0.49)
Bus. Assoc.	0.03	0.01	0.73**	0.91***	0.49	0.39	0.36	−0.04	−0.04	0.57†
	(0.21)	(0.23)	(0.25)	(0.26)	(0.30)	(0.27)	(0.27)	(0.23)	(0.23)	(0.30)
Rights Violated	−0.03	0.22	0.24	0.16	0.37	0.79*	0.54†	0.25	0.27	0.37
	(0.24)	(0.28)	(0.28)	(0.30)	(0.32)	(0.32)	(0.30)	(0.22)	(0.26)	(0.30)
Litigated	0.41	0.37	0.55†	−0.32	0.26	0.18	−0.09	−0.41†	−0.64*	−0.01
	(0.29)	(0.30)	(0.31)	(0.33)	(0.32)	(0.33)	(0.32)	(0.24)	(0.26)	(0.35)
Legal Ed.	−0.07	0.22	0.21	0.31	0.49	0.17	0.72*	0.97**	0.44	0.44
	(0.26)	(0.28)	(0.38)	(0.39)	(0.41)	(0.35)	(0.36)	(0.32)	(0.31)	(0.38)
Age	0.00	0.03**	−0.02	−0.02	0.00	−0.01	−0.00	−0.04***	−0.02†	−0.00
	(0.01)	(0.01)	(0.01)	(0.01)	(0.01)	(0.01)	(0.01)	(0.01)	(0.01)	(0.01)

	(1)	(2)	(3)	(4)	(5)	(6)	(7)	(8)	(9)	(10)
Male	−0.25	−0.19	−0.06	−0.09	−0.30	−0.06	−0.33	0.26	−0.14	0.19
	(0.20)	(0.22)	(0.24)	(0.25)	(0.28)	(0.27)	(0.25)	(0.20)	(0.23)	(0.26)
Constant	5.94***	3.20***	7.01***	6.18***	3.81***	4.09***	4.31***	4.10***	4.60***	3.95***
	(0.73)	(0.78)	(0.83)	(0.94)	(1.05)	(1.05)	(0.99)	(0.79)	(0.88)	(0.97)
City Dummies	yes	yes	yes	yes	yes	yes	yes	yes	yes	yes
Sector Dummies	yes	yes	yes	yes	yes	yes	yes	yes	yes	yes
Firm Size Dummies	yes	yes	yes	yes	yes	yes	yes	yes	yes	yes
Firm Finances Dummies	yes	yes	yes	yes	yes	yes	yes	yes	yes	yes
Job Title Dummies	yes	yes	yes	yes	yes	yes	yes	yes	yes	yes
R-sq.	0.14	0.22	0.19	0.23	0.21	0.21	0.23	0.24	0.24	0.28
Adj. R-sq.	0.05	0.14	0.11	0.16	0.13	0.13	0.15	0.17	0.16	0.20
Debt Dispute Scenario – With Control Variables										
Low Cash	−0.11	−0.16	−0.42	−0.12	−0.81*	−0.74*	−0.67*	−0.33†	−0.27	−0.21
	(0.19)	(0.23)	(0.31)	(0.33)	(0.34)	(0.34)	(0.34)	(0.20)	(0.24)	(0.32)
Firm Age	0.07	0.18†	0.11	0.13	−0.13	−0.13	−0.16	0.01	−0.06	0.10
	(0.07)	(0.10)	(0.11)	(0.11)	(0.12)	(0.12)	(0.11)	(0.08)	(0.08)	(0.12)
Foreign Owner	−0.01	0.27	−0.27	−0.02	0.49	0.01	0.18	0.35	0.31	0.19
	(0.25)	(0.29)	(0.42)	(0.45)	(0.42)	(0.40)	(0.41)	(0.29)	(0.34)	(0.42)
Gov. Owner	−0.01	0.22	0.19	0.41	0.16	−0.12	0.08	−0.06	−0.09	0.33
	(0.30)	(0.36)	(0.42)	(0.45)	(0.44)	(0.43)	(0.44)	(0.24)	(0.27)	(0.50)
Bus. Assoc.	−0.17	0.03	0.30	0.09	0.35	0.25	0.13	−0.09	0.11	0.52†
	(0.16)	(0.20)	(0.28)	(0.29)	(0.31)	(0.29)	(0.28)	(0.19)	(0.21)	(0.31)
Rights Violated	−0.04	0.28	0.61*	0.10	0.32	0.06	0.16	0.30	0.42	0.24
	(0.18)	(0.24)	(0.31)	(0.32)	(0.33)	(0.35)	(0.32)	(0.20)	(0.26)	(0.30)

Regressions for Figure 6.2 *(cont.)*

				Debt Dispute Scenario – With Control Variables					
	Lawyers	Courts (formal)	Law Enf. (formal)	Gov. Officials (formal)	Courts (informal)	Law Enf. (informal)	Gov. Officials (informal)	Criminal Rackets	Private Sec. Agency	Internal Security
Litigated	0.20	−0.03	−0.03	−0.15	0.24	0.23	0.19	−0.13	−0.49*	−0.22
	(0.18)	(0.25)	(0.33)	(0.33)	(0.33)	(0.35)	(0.34)	(0.21)	(0.24)	(0.35)
Legal Ed.	−0.09	0.19	0.49	0.11	0.34	0.61	0.70†	0.75*	0.63*	0.99**
	(0.23)	(0.24)	(0.43)	(0.39)	(0.44)	(0.38)	(0.38)	(0.29)	(0.29)	(0.37)
Age	−0.00	0.02	−0.02†	−0.00	0.00	−0.02	−0.01	−0.02**	−0.01†	−0.01
	(0.01)	(0.01)	(0.01)	(0.01)	(0.01)	(0.01)	(0.01)	(0.01)	(0.01)	(0.01)
Male	−0.14	−0.18	0.17	0.08	−0.28	0.12	−0.05	0.29	0.36†	0.49†
	(0.17)	(0.20)	(0.27)	(0.28)	(0.28)	(0.28)	(0.27)	(0.18)	(0.21)	(0.26)
Constant	5.75***	3.78***	5.95***	4.72***	3.84***	5.22***	4.94***	4.01***	4.96***	3.92***
	(0.67)	(0.75)	(0.95)	(1.01)	(1.09)	(1.06)	(1.07)	(0.81)	(0.79)	(1.04)
City Dummies	yes	yes	yes	yes	yes	yes	yes	yes	yes	yes
Sector Dummies	yes	yes	yes	yes	yes	yes	yes	yes	yes	yes
Firm Size Dummies	yes	yes	yes	yes	yes	yes	yes	yes	yes	yes
Firm Finances Dummies	yes	yes	yes	yes	yes	yes	yes	yes	yes	yes
Job Title Dummies	yes	yes	yes	yes	yes	yes	yes	yes	yes	yes
R-sq.	0.15	0.25	0.24	0.20	0.21	0.17	0.22	0.21	0.32	0.28
Adj. R-sq.	0.07	0.17	0.16	0.12	0.13	0.09	0.14	0.13	0.25	0.20

Note: *** $p < 0.001$, ** $p < 0.01$, * $p < 0.05$, † $p < 0.10$. Robust standard errors in parentheses. N=301.

Regressions for Figure 7.1a *Type of Output and Property Security Strategies*

	Lawyers	Courts (formal)	Law Enf. (formal)	Gov. Officials (formal)	Courts (informal)	Law Enf. (informal)	Gov. Officials (informal)	Criminal Rackets	Private Sec. Agency	Internal Security
	Property Dispute Scenario – With Control Variables									
Service Sector	-0.10	-0.01	-0.18	-0.40	0.14	0.74**	0.74**	0.45*	0.12	-0.45†
	(0.19)	(0.22)	(0.23)	(0.25)	(0.29)	(0.27)	(0.28)	(0.20)	(0.21)	(0.27)
Firm Age	0.12	0.27*	0.09	0.14	-0.09	-0.00	-0.11	-0.03	0.03	0.02
	(0.08)	(0.11)	(0.10)	(0.10)	(0.13)	(0.11)	(0.12)	(0.08)	(0.09)	(0.12)
Foreign Owner	0.05	0.58†	-0.42	-0.80†	0.44	0.19	0.01	0.45	0.33	0.13
	(0.27)	(0.31)	(0.40)	(0.44)	(0.42)	(0.41)	(0.41)	(0.34)	(0.38)	(0.40)
Gov. Owner	-0.13	0.25	-0.13	0.21	0.22	-0.42	-0.24	-0.00	-0.18	-0.05
	(0.31)	(0.36)	(0.39)	(0.41)	(0.41)	(0.43)	(0.44)	(0.32)	(0.34)	(0.49)
Bus. Assoc.	0.03	0.01	0.73**	0.91***	0.50	0.40	0.37	-0.04	-0.04	0.57†
	(0.20)	(0.23)	(0.25)	(0.26)	(0.30)	(0.27)	(0.27)	(0.23)	(0.23)	(0.30)
Rights Violated	-0.03	0.22	0.24	0.16	0.36	0.78*	0.53†	0.25	0.27	0.37
	(0.24)	(0.28)	(0.28)	(0.30)	(0.32)	(0.32)	(0.30)	(0.22)	(0.26)	(0.30)
Litigated	0.41	0.36	0.54†	-0.31	0.19	0.10	-0.14	-0.42†	-0.67*	-0.02
	(0.28)	(0.30)	(0.31)	(0.32)	(0.32)	(0.33)	(0.32)	(0.24)	(0.26)	(0.34)
Legal Ed.	-0.07	0.23	0.22	0.30	0.56	0.24	0.77*	0.99**	0.47	0.45
	(0.25)	(0.28)	(0.37)	(0.38)	(0.41)	(0.35)	(0.36)	(0.32)	(0.30)	(0.37)
Age	0.00	0.03**	-0.02	-0.02	0.00	-0.01	-0.01	-0.04***	-0.02†	-0.00
	(0.01)	(0.01)	(0.01)	(0.01)	(0.01)	(0.01)	(0.01)	(0.01)	(0.01)	(0.01)
Male	-0.25	-0.21	-0.08	-0.09	-0.43	-0.21	-0.43†	0.22	-0.20	0.17
	(0.20)	(0.22)	(0.24)	(0.25)	(0.28)	(0.27)	(0.25)	(0.20)	(0.22)	(0.25)

Regressions for Figure 7.1a *(cont.)*

Property Dispute Scenario – With Control Variables

	Lawyers	Courts (formal)	Law Enf. (formal)	Gov. Officials (formal)	Courts (informal)	Law Enf. (informal)	Gov. Officials (informal)	Criminal Rackets	Private Sec. Agency	Internal Security
Constant	5.95***	3.17***	6.98***	6.18***	3.61***	3.85***	4.15***	4.04***	4.52***	3.93***
	(0.73)	(0.78)	(0.82)	(0.93)	(1.05)	(1.05)	(1.00)	(0.79)	(0.88)	(0.97)
City Dummies	yes	yes	yes	yes	yes	yes	yes	yes	yes	yes
Firm Size Dummies	yes	yes	yes	yes	yes	yes	yes	yes	yes	yes
Firm Finances Dummies	yes	yes	yes	yes	yes	yes	yes	yes	yes	yes
Job Title Dummies	yes	yes	yes	yes	yes	yes	yes	yes	yes	yes
R-sq.	0.14	0.22	0.19	0.23	0.19	0.20	0.22	0.24	0.24	0.27
Adj. R-sq.	0.06	0.14	0.11	0.16	0.11	0.12	0.14	0.17	0.16	0.20

Debt Dispute Scenario – With Control Variables

	Lawyers	Courts (formal)	Law Enf. (formal)	Gov. Officials (formal)	Courts (informal)	Law Enf. (informal)	Gov. Officials (informal)	Criminal Rackets	Private Sec. Agency	Internal Security
Service Sector	-0.08	-0.12	-0.04	0.18	0.20	0.54†	0.74**	0.22	0.35†	-0.48†
	(0.15)	(0.19)	(0.26)	(0.27)	(0.31)	(0.28)	(0.27)	(0.18)	(0.19)	(0.28)
Firm Age	0.07	0.18†	0.11	0.13	-0.13	-0.12	-0.15	0.01	-0.06	0.10
	(0.07)	(0.10)	(0.11)	(0.11)	(0.12)	(0.12)	(0.11)	(0.08)	(0.08)	(0.12)
Foreign Owner	-0.03	0.24	-0.34	-0.04	0.37	-0.10	0.08	0.30	0.27	0.16
	(0.25)	(0.28)	(0.42)	(0.45)	(0.41)	(0.39)	(0.40)	(0.28)	(0.33)	(0.42)
Gov. Owner	-0.02	0.22	0.16	0.41	0.12	-0.17	0.04	-0.08	-0.10	0.32
	(0.30)	(0.36)	(0.43)	(0.45)	(0.45)	(0.42)	(0.43)	(0.23)	(0.27)	(0.50)
Bus. Assoc.	-0.17	0.03	0.31	0.09	0.36	0.25	0.13	-0.09	0.11	0.52†
	(0.16)	(0.20)	(0.28)	(0.29)	(0.31)	(0.29)	(0.28)	(0.19)	(0.21)	(0.31)

	(1)	(2)	(3)	(4)	(5)	(6)	(7)	(8)	(9)	(10)
Rights Violated	-0.04	0.28	0.61*	0.10	0.31	0.05	0.15	0.30	0.42	0.24
	(0.18)	(0.24)	(0.31)	(0.32)	(0.33)	(0.35)	(0.32)	(0.20)	(0.26)	(0.30)
Litigated	0.19	-0.05	-0.08	-0.17	0.15	0.15	0.11	-0.17	-0.52*	-0.24
	(0.18)	(0.25)	(0.33)	(0.33)	(0.33)	(0.35)	(0.33)	(0.20)	(0.24)	(0.34)
Legal Ed.	-0.07	0.20	0.53	0.12	0.42	0.69†	0.76*	0.79**	0.65*	1.01**
	(0.23)	(0.24)	(0.43)	(0.39)	(0.44)	(0.38)	(0.38)	(0.29)	(0.29)	(0.37)
Age	-0.00	0.01	-0.03†	-0.00	0.00	-0.02	-0.01	-0.02**	-0.01†	-0.01
	(0.01)	(0.01)	(0.01)	(0.01)	(0.01)	(0.01)	(0.01)	(0.01)	(0.01)	(0.01)
Male	-0.17	-0.22	0.08	0.06	-0.45	-0.04	-0.19	0.23	0.31	0.45†
	(0.17)	(0.19)	(0.27)	(0.27)	(0.27)	(0.28)	(0.26)	(0.18)	(0.21)	(0.26)
Constant	5.71***	3.73***	5.81***	4.68***	3.58**	4.97***	4.72***	3.90***	4.87***	3.85***
	(0.68)	(0.75)	(0.95)	(0.99)	(1.09)	(1.06)	(1.08)	(0.81)	(0.79)	(1.02)
City Dummies	yes	yes	yes	yes	yes	yes	yes	yes	yes	yes
Firm Size Dummies	yes	yes	yes	yes	yes	yes	yes	yes	yes	yes
Firm Finances Dummies	yes	yes	yes	yes	yes	yes	yes	yes	yes	yes
Job Title Dummies	yes	yes	yes	yes	yes	yes	yes	yes	yes	yes
R-sq.	0.15	0.24	0.23	0.20	0.18	0.15	0.20	0.20	0.31	0.27
Adj. R-sq.	0.07	0.17	0.16	0.12	0.10	0.07	0.13	0.12	0.25	0.20

Note: *** $p < 0.001$, ** $p < 0.01$, * $p < 0.05$, † $p < 0.10$. Robust standard errors in parentheses. N=301.

Regressions for Figure 7.1b *Market Size and Property Security Strategies*

				Property Dispute Scenario – With Control Variables					
	Lawyers	Courts (formal)	Law Enf. (formal)	Gov. Officials (formal)	Courts (informal)	Law Enf. (informal)	Gov. Officials (informal)	Criminal Rackets	Private Sec. Agency	Internal Security
Local Market	0.00	−0.10	0.00	−0.02	0.28	0.16	0.29	−0.16	0.19	−0.39
	(0.20)	(0.24)	(0.26)	(0.28)	(0.30)	(0.29)	(0.28)	(0.21)	(0.24)	(0.30)
Firm Age	0.12	0.27*	0.09	0.14	−0.08	0.00	−0.10	−0.04	0.04	0.01
	(0.08)	(0.11)	(0.10)	(0.11)	(0.13)	(0.11)	(0.12)	(0.08)	(0.09)	(0.12)
Foreign Owner	0.05	0.56†	−0.41	−0.80†	0.51	0.23	0.08	0.41	0.37	0.04
	(0.27)	(0.32)	(0.41)	(0.45)	(0.44)	(0.43)	(0.42)	(0.34)	(0.38)	(0.41)
Gov. Owner	−0.13	0.25	−0.13	0.20	0.23	−0.42	−0.23	−0.01	−0.18	−0.06
	(0.31)	(0.36)	(0.39)	(0.41)	(0.41)	(0.43)	(0.44)	(0.32)	(0.34)	(0.48)
Bus. Assoc.	0.03	−0.01	0.73**	0.91**	0.54†	0.43	0.41	−0.07	−0.01	0.50†
	(0.21)	(0.23)	(0.26)	(0.27)	(0.31)	(0.28)	(0.28)	(0.23)	(0.24)	(0.30)
Rights Violated	−0.03	0.22	0.24	0.16	0.36	0.78*	0.53†	0.25	0.26	0.38
	(0.24)	(0.28)	(0.28)	(0.30)	(0.32)	(0.32)	(0.30)	(0.22)	(0.26)	(0.30)
Litigated	0.41	0.35	0.54†	−0.31	0.20	0.11	−0.13	−0.43†	−0.66*	−0.03
	(0.28)	(0.30)	(0.31)	(0.33)	(0.32)	(0.33)	(0.32)	(0.24)	(0.26)	(0.34)
Legal Ed.	−0.07	0.22	0.22	0.30	0.57	0.25	0.79*	0.98**	0.48	0.43
	(0.25)	(0.28)	(0.38)	(0.38)	(0.41)	(0.36)	(0.36)	(0.32)	(0.30)	(0.38)
Age	0.00	0.03**	−0.02	−0.02	0.00	−0.01	−0.00	−0.04***	−0.02†	−0.00
	(0.01)	(0.01)	(0.01)	(0.01)	(0.01)	(0.01)	(0.01)	(0.01)	(0.01)	(0.01)

	(1)	(2)	(3)	(4)	(5)	(6)	(7)	(8)	(9)	(10)
Male	−0.25	−0.23	−0.08	−0.09	−0.39	−0.19	−0.38	0.20	−0.17	0.11
	(0.20)	(0.22)	(0.24)	(0.25)	(0.28)	(0.27)	(0.26)	(0.20)	(0.22)	(0.26)
Constant	5.95***	3.29***	6.98***	6.21***	3.25**	3.64**	3.78***	4.25***	4.28***	4.42***
	(0.76)	(0.86)	(0.88)	(0.99)	(1.12)	(1.13)	(1.08)	(0.83)	(0.92)	(1.06)
City Dummies	yes	yes	yes	yes	yes	yes	yes	yes	yes	yes
Sector Dummies	yes	yes	yes	yes	yes	yes	yes	yes	yes	yes
Firm Size Dummies	yes	yes	yes	yes	yes	yes	yes	yes	yes	yes
Firm Finances Dummies	yes	yes	yes	yes	yes	yes	yes	yes	yes	yes
Job Title Dummies	yes	yes	yes	yes	yes	yes	yes	yes	yes	yes
R-sq.	0.14	0.22	0.19	0.23	0.20	0.20	0.22	0.24	0.24	0.28
Adj. R-sq.	0.05	0.14	0.11	0.15	0.11	0.11	0.14	0.17	0.16	0.21
Debt Dispute Scenario – With Control Variables										
Local Market	−0.06	−0.64**	−0.45	0.34	0.37	0.14	0.52*	−0.06	0.07	−0.32
	(0.18)	(0.20)	(0.30)	(0.29)	(0.32)	(0.29)	(0.25)	(0.19)	(0.22)	(0.31)
Firm Age	0.07	0.16	0.09	0.15	−0.12	−0.12	−0.14	0.01	−0.06	0.09
	(0.08)	(0.10)	(0.11)	(0.11)	(0.13)	(0.12)	(0.11)	(0.08)	(0.08)	(0.12)
Foreign Owner	−0.04	0.08	−0.45	0.05	0.46	−0.07	0.21	0.28	0.29	0.08
	(0.26)	(0.29)	(0.42)	(0.46)	(0.43)	(0.40)	(0.41)	(0.29)	(0.34)	(0.42)
Gov. Owner	−0.02	0.20	0.15	0.42	0.12	−0.16	0.05	−0.08	−0.10	0.31
	(0.30)	(0.35)	(0.43)	(0.45)	(0.45)	(0.42)	(0.43)	(0.23)	(0.27)	(0.49)
Bus. Assoc.	−0.18	−0.08	0.23	0.15	0.42	0.28	0.22	−0.10	0.12	0.46
	(0.16)	(0.20)	(0.29)	(0.30)	(0.31)	(0.30)	(0.28)	(0.19)	(0.22)	(0.31)
Rights Violated	−0.04	0.29	0.61*	0.09	0.31	0.05	0.15	0.30	0.42	0.24
	(0.18)	(0.24)	(0.30)	(0.32)	(0.33)	(0.35)	(0.32)	(0.20)	(0.26)	(0.30)

Regressions for Figure 7.1b *(cont.)*

	Lawyers	Courts (formal)	Law Enf. (formal)	Gov. Officials (formal)	Courts (informal)	Law Enf. (informal)	Gov. Officials (informal)	Criminal Rackets	Private Sec. Agency	Internal Security
				Debt Dispute Scenario – With Control Variables						
Litigated	0.18	−0.07	−0.09	−0.15	0.16	0.15	0.13	−0.17	−0.52*	−0.25
	(0.18)	(0.25)	(0.33)	(0.33)	(0.33)	(0.35)	(0.34)	(0.20)	(0.24)	(0.34)
Legal Ed.	−0.08	0.17	0.51	0.14	0.44	0.69†	0.79*	0.78**	0.66*	0.99**
	(0.23)	(0.22)	(0.43)	(0.39)	(0.44)	(0.38)	(0.38)	(0.29)	(0.29)	(0.37)
Age	−0.00	0.01	−0.03†	0.00	0.00	−0.02	−0.01	−0.02**	−0.01†	−0.02
	(0.01)	(0.01)	(0.01)	(0.01)	(0.01)	(0.01)	(0.01)	(0.01)	(0.01)	(0.01)
Male	−0.18	−0.32†	0.01	0.11	−0.39	−0.01	−0.10	0.22	0.32	0.39
	(0.17)	(0.19)	(0.27)	(0.28)	(0.28)	(0.28)	(0.26)	(0.19)	(0.21)	(0.27)
Constant	5.78***	4.54***	6.38***	4.24***	3.10**	4.80***	4.05***	3.98***	4.78***	4.25***
	(0.73)	(0.81)	(1.04)	(1.05)	(1.18)	(1.14)	(1.16)	(0.85)	(0.82)	(1.08)
City Dummies	yes	yes	yes	yes	yes	yes	yes	yes	yes	yes
Sector Dummies	yes	yes	yes	yes	yes	yes	yes	yes	yes	yes
Firm Size Dummies	yes	yes	yes	yes	yes	yes	yes	yes	yes	yes
Firm Finances Dummies	yes	yes	yes	yes	yes	yes	yes	yes	yes	yes
Job Title Dummies	yes	yes	yes	yes	yes	yes	yes	yes	yes	yes
R-sq.	0.15	0.27	0.24	0.21	0.19	0.15	0.21	0.20	0.31	0.28
Adj. R-sq.	0.06	0.19	0.16	0.12	0.10	0.07	0.13	0.12	0.24	0.20

Note: *** $p < 0.001$, ** $p < 0.01$, * $p < 0.05$, † $p < 0.10$. Robust standard errors in parentheses. N=301.

Regressions for Figure 7.2 *Market Size and Property Security Strategies*

| | | | | | Property Dispute Scenario (firms with more than 250 employees) | | | | | |
	Lawyers	Courts (formal)	Law Enf. (formal)	Gov. Officials (formal)	Courts (informal)	Law Enf. (informal)	Gov. Officials (informal)	Criminal Rackets	Private Sec. Agency	Internal Security
Local Market	0.28	0.04	0.29	0.03	0.91†	1.14**	0.98*	-0.42	-0.08	-0.30
	(0.32)	(0.36)	(0.41)	(0.41)	(0.48)	(0.41)	(0.43)	(0.34)	(0.35)	(0.47)
Firm Age	0.09	0.27†	0.05	0.24	-0.21	-0.00	-0.10	-0.30†	-0.21	0.08
	(0.14)	(0.14)	(0.18)	(0.19)	(0.24)	(0.19)	(0.20)	(0.17)	(0.16)	(0.20)
Foreign Owner	-0.32	0.12	-0.72	-1.05	0.10	0.20	-0.03	0.40	0.13	-0.05
	(0.39)	(0.44)	(0.56)	(0.66)	(0.59)	(0.62)	(0.61)	(0.48)	(0.45)	(0.59)
Gov. Owner	-0.12	0.02	-0.43	-0.16	0.16	-0.61	-0.47	0.21	0.02	0.19
	(0.35)	(0.41)	(0.51)	(0.52)	(0.56)	(0.52)	(0.53)	(0.36)	(0.37)	(0.65)
Bus. Assoc.	0.77*	0.23	1.10**	0.87†	0.63	0.76†	0.71	-0.01	-0.16	0.43
	(0.33)	(0.34)	(0.41)	(0.44)	(0.48)	(0.44)	(0.45)	(0.34)	(0.30)	(0.49)
Rights Violated	0.22	-0.26	-0.08	-0.15	-0.12	0.12	-0.53	0.13	-0.08	0.70
	(0.29)	(0.39)	(0.49)	(0.49)	(0.53)	(0.52)	(0.49)	(0.41)	(0.34)	(0.51)
Litigated	0.56	0.84*	0.70	0.25	0.28	0.15	0.27	-1.01**	-0.14	-0.65
	(0.39)	(0.40)	(0.47)	(0.49)	(0.50)	(0.49)	(0.47)	(0.35)	(0.36)	(0.55)
Legal Ed.	0.06	1.00*	0.82	0.47	0.72	0.18	0.68	1.06*	0.59	0.85
	(0.44)	(0.50)	(0.71)	(0.76)	(0.65)	(0.61)	(0.64)	(0.48)	(0.43)	(0.66)
Age	-0.00	0.03*	-0.01	-0.03	0.01	-0.00	0.01	-0.04**	-0.02	-0.02
	(0.01)	(0.01)	(0.02)	(0.02)	(0.02)	(0.02)	(0.02)	(0.01)	(0.01)	(0.02)

Regressions for Figure 7.2 (cont.)

	Property Dispute Scenario (firms with more than 250 employees)									
	Lawyers	Courts (formal)	Law Enf. (formal)	Gov. Officials (formal)	Courts (informal)	Law Enf. (informal)	Gov. Officials (informal)	Criminal Rackets	Private Sec. Agency	Internal Security
Male	−0.30	−0.26	−0.23	−0.05	−0.53	−0.44	−0.54	0.28	−0.03	−0.31
	(0.30)	(0.31)	(0.39)	(0.40)	(0.44)	(0.41)	(0.40)	(0.30)	(0.30)	(0.41)
Constant	4.38***	1.36	5.51**	4.56*	3.87*	4.31**	4.89**	5.25***	6.25***	6.17***
	(1.20)	(1.35)	(1.92)	(1.97)	(1.88)	(1.55)	(1.51)	(1.32)	(1.45)	(1.71)
City Dummies	yes	yes	yes	yes	yes	yes	yes	yes	yes	yes
Sector Dummies	yes	yes	yes	yes	yes	yes	yes	yes	yes	yes
Firm Size Dummies	yes	yes	yes	yes	yes	yes	yes	yes	yes	yes
Firm Finances Dummies	yes	yes	yes	yes	yes	yes	yes	yes	yes	yes
Job Title Dummies	yes	yes	yes	yes	yes	yes	yes	yes	yes	yes
R-sq.	0.28	0.34	0.26	0.35	0.32	0.33	0.35	0.47	0.37	0.30
Adj. R-sq.	0.10	0.18	0.08	0.19	0.15	0.17	0.19	0.34	0.21	0.12
	Debt Dispute Scenario (firms with more than 250 employees)									
Local Market	0.21	−0.29	−0.34	0.57	0.98*	0.61	0.78†	−0.17	−0.17	−0.55
	(0.31)	(0.29)	(0.51)	(0.47)	(0.44)	(0.42)	(0.41)	(0.26)	(0.31)	(0.47)
Firm Age	0.21	0.21	0.14	0.46*	−0.20	0.04	−0.07	−0.08	−0.07	0.22
	(0.13)	(0.14)	(0.20)	(0.19)	(0.21)	(0.20)	(0.20)	(0.11)	(0.13)	(0.21)
Foreign Owner	−0.64	−0.47	−0.90	−0.51	0.13	−0.17	0.19	0.14	0.27	−0.04
	(0.41)	(0.39)	(0.59)	(0.59)	(0.53)	(0.52)	(0.52)	(0.36)	(0.48)	(0.49)
Gov. Owner	−0.22	−0.02	−0.35	−0.12	0.06	−0.31	−0.04	0.12	0.02	0.49
	(0.35)	(0.37)	(0.61)	(0.58)	(0.56)	(0.54)	(0.56)	(0.28)	(0.31)	(0.64)

	(1)	(2)	(3)	(4)	(5)	(6)	(7)	(8)	(9)	(10)
Bus. Assoc.	0.02	0.12	0.37	0.18	0.55	0.48	0.32	−0.04	−0.25	0.13
	(0.27)	(0.28)	(0.49)	(0.48)	(0.49)	(0.46)	(0.43)	(0.23)	(0.26)	(0.50)
Rights Violated	0.23	−0.24	0.07	−0.26	−0.31	−0.05	0.37	0.14	0.15	0.24
	(0.30)	(0.31)	(0.51)	(0.44)	(0.55)	(0.56)	(0.51)	(0.29)	(0.36)	(0.53)
Litigated	0.22	0.48	0.47	0.16	0.11	0.02	0.01	−0.57*	−0.33	−0.71
	(0.30)	(0.31)	(0.53)	(0.46)	(0.52)	(0.52)	(0.48)	(0.23)	(0.33)	(0.51)
Legal Ed.	−0.33	0.31	0.91	0.57	0.30	0.19	0.27	0.58†	0.41	1.47*
	(0.41)	(0.35)	(0.81)	(0.68)	(0.67)	(0.58)	(0.60)	(0.32)	(0.38)	(0.57)
Age	−0.00	0.01	−0.01	−0.00	0.02	−0.01	−0.00	−0.03**	−0.02†	−0.03
	(0.01)	(0.01)	(0.02)	(0.02)	(0.02)	(0.02)	(0.02)	(0.01)	(0.01)	(0.02)
Male	−0.17	−0.39	−0.63	−0.09	−0.81†	−0.63	−0.76†	0.22	0.12	0.05
	(0.29)	(0.26)	(0.44)	(0.43)	(0.41)	(0.41)	(0.40)	(0.23)	(0.28)	(0.41)
Constant	2.52†	1.63	6.17***	1.36	3.35†	6.69***	4.58**	5.27**	6.05***	5.32**
	(1.39)	(1.41)	(1.72)	(1.73)	(1.78)	(1.45)	(1.71)	(1.66)	(1.31)	(1.68)
City Dummies	yes	yes	yes	yes	yes	yes	yes	yes	yes	yes
Sector Dummies	yes	yes	yes	yes	yes	yes	yes	yes	yes	yes
Firm Size Dummies	yes	yes	yes	yes	yes	yes	yes	yes	yes	yes
Firm Finances Dummies	yes	yes	yes	yes	yes	yes	yes	yes	yes	yes
Job Title Dummies	yes	yes	yes	yes	yes	yes	yes	yes	yes	yes
R-sq.	0.25	0.34	0.27	0.31	0.34	0.32	0.37	0.42	0.45	0.33
Adj. R-sq.	0.07	0.17	0.08	0.14	0.17	0.15	0.21	0.27	0.31	0.17

Note: *** $p < 0.001$, ** $p < 0.01$, * $p < 0.05$, † $p < 0.10$. Robust standard errors in parentheses. N=131.

Regressions for Figure 7.3a   *Ties to SOEs and Property Security Strategies*

		Property Dispute Scenario – With Control Variables								
	Lawyers	Courts (formal)	Law Enf. (formal)	Gov. Officials (formal)	Courts (informal)	Law Enf. (informal)	Gov. Officials (informal)	Criminal Rackets	Private Sec. Agency	Internal Security
SOE	0.08	-0.07	-0.15	0.37	0.71*	0.51†	0.61*	0.20	-0.04	-0.17
	(0.19)	(0.22)	(0.28)	(0.28)	(0.31)	(0.31)	(0.29)	(0.22)	(0.23)	(0.31)
Firm Age	0.12	0.27*	0.09	0.14	-0.09	-0.00	-0.11	-0.03	0.03	0.02
	(0.08)	(0.11)	(0.10)	(0.10)	(0.13)	(0.11)	(0.11)	(0.08)	(0.09)	(0.12)
Foreign Owner	0.06	0.57†	-0.44	-0.75†	0.54	0.26	0.09	0.48	0.32	0.11
	(0.27)	(0.31)	(0.40)	(0.44)	(0.42)	(0.40)	(0.40)	(0.34)	(0.38)	(0.41)
Gov. Owner	-0.13	0.25	-0.13	0.20	0.21	-0.43	-0.25	-0.01	-0.18	-0.04
	(0.31)	(0.36)	(0.39)	(0.41)	(0.40)	(0.43)	(0.44)	(0.32)	(0.34)	(0.49)
Bus. Assoc.	0.03	0.01	0.73**	0.92***	0.51†	0.41	0.38	-0.04	-0.04	0.56†
	(0.20)	(0.23)	(0.25)	(0.26)	(0.30)	(0.27)	(0.27)	(0.23)	(0.23)	(0.30)
Rights Violated	-0.03	0.21	0.23	0.18	0.40	0.81*	0.57†	0.26	0.26	0.36
	(0.24)	(0.28)	(0.28)	(0.30)	(0.31)	(0.32)	(0.29)	(0.22)	(0.26)	(0.30)
Litigated	0.41	0.36	0.55†	-0.34	0.15	0.07	-0.18	-0.44†	-0.66*	-0.01
	(0.28)	(0.30)	(0.31)	(0.33)	(0.32)	(0.33)	(0.31)	(0.24)	(0.26)	(0.35)
Legal Ed.	-0.08	0.23	0.22	0.30	0.55	0.24	0.77*	0.99**	0.47	0.45
	(0.25)	(0.28)	(0.37)	(0.38)	(0.40)	(0.36)	(0.36)	(0.32)	(0.30)	(0.38)
Age	0.00	0.03**	-0.02	-0.02	0.00	-0.02	-0.01	-0.04***	-0.02†	-0.00
	(0.01)	(0.01)	(0.01)	(0.01)	(0.01)	(0.01)	(0.01)	(0.01)	(0.01)	(0.01)
Male	-0.26	-0.20	-0.06	-0.13	-0.52†	-0.27	-0.50*	0.20	-0.19	0.19
	(0.20)	(0.22)	(0.24)	(0.25)	(0.28)	(0.27)	(0.25)	(0.20)	(0.22)	(0.25)

Constant	5.94***	3.17***	6.99***	6.15***	3.53***	3.80***	4.09***	4.03***	4.52***	3.94***
	(0.73)	(0.78)	(0.82)	(0.94)	(1.04)	(1.05)	(1.00)	(0.79)	(0.88)	(0.98)
City Dummies	yes	yes	yes	yes	yes	yes	yes	yes	yes	yes
Sector Dummies	yes	yes	yes	yes	yes	yes	yes	yes	yes	yes
Firm Size Dummies	yes	yes	yes	yes	yes	yes	yes	yes	yes	yes
Firm Finances Dummies	yes	yes	yes	yes	yes	yes	yes	yes	yes	yes
Job Title Dummies	yes	yes	yes	yes	yes	yes	yes	yes	yes	yes
R-sq.	0.14	0.22	0.20	0.24	0.21	0.20	0.23	0.24	0.24	0.28
Adj. R-sq.	0.05	0.14	0.11	0.16	0.13	0.12	0.15	0.17	0.16	0.20
Debt Dispute Scenario – With Control Variables										
SOE	0.10	0.15	0.25	0.36	0.91**	0.49	0.51†	−0.02	0.08	0.23
	(0.19)	(0.20)	(0.29)	(0.28)	(0.30)	(0.30)	(0.30)	(0.17)	(0.20)	(0.32)
Firm Age	0.07	0.18†	0.11	0.13	−0.13	−0.12	−0.16	0.01	−0.06	0.10
	(0.07)	(0.10)	(0.11)	(0.11)	(0.12)	(0.12)	(0.11)	(0.08)	(0.08)	(0.12)
Foreign Owner	−0.01	0.26	−0.30	0.01	0.50	−0.03	0.15	0.30	0.28	0.20
	(0.25)	(0.29)	(0.42)	(0.45)	(0.41)	(0.38)	(0.40)	(0.29)	(0.34)	(0.42)
Gov. Owner	−0.02	0.21	0.16	0.40	0.10	−0.17	0.03	−0.08	−0.10	0.32
	(0.30)	(0.36)	(0.43)	(0.45)	(0.44)	(0.42)	(0.43)	(0.23)	(0.27)	(0.50)
Bus. Assoc.	−0.17	0.04	0.31	0.09	0.38	0.27	0.15	−0.09	0.11	0.52†
	(0.16)	(0.20)	(0.28)	(0.28)	(0.30)	(0.29)	(0.28)	(0.19)	(0.21)	(0.30)
Rights Violated	−0.03	0.29	0.62*	0.12	0.36	0.08	0.18	0.29	0.42†	0.26
	(0.17)	(0.24)	(0.31)	(0.32)	(0.32)	(0.34)	(0.32)	(0.20)	(0.26)	(0.30)

Regressions for Figure 7.3a   (cont.)

					Debt Dispute Scenario – With Control Variables					
	Lawyers	Courts (formal)	Law Enf. (formal)	Gov. Officials (formal)	Courts (informal)	Law Enf. (informal)	Gov. Officials (informal)	Criminal Rackets	Private Sec. Agency	Internal Security
Litigated	0.18	-0.06	-0.09	-0.19	0.10	0.12	0.08	-0.17	-0.53*	-0.26
	(0.18)	(0.25)	(0.33)	(0.33)	(0.33)	(0.34)	(0.33)	(0.20)	(0.24)	(0.34)
Legal Ed.	-0.08	0.20	0.53	0.12	0.41	0.68†	0.76*	0.79**	0.65*	1.01**
	(0.23)	(0.24)	(0.43)	(0.39)	(0.43)	(0.38)	(0.38)	(0.29)	(0.29)	(0.37)
Age	-0.00	0.01	-0.03†	-0.00	-0.00	-0.02	-0.02	-0.02**	-0.01†	-0.01
	(0.01)	(0.01)	(0.01)	(0.01)	(0.01)	(0.01)	(0.01)	(0.01)	(0.01)	(0.01)
Male	-0.18	-0.23	0.06	0.01	-0.56*	-0.09	-0.25	0.23	0.30	0.42
	(0.16)	(0.19)	(0.27)	(0.27)	(0.27)	(0.28)	(0.26)	(0.18)	(0.21)	(0.26)
Constant	5.70***	3.72***	5.78***	4.65***	3.49**	4.92***	4.67***	3.90***	4.86***	3.83***
	(0.68)	(0.75)	(0.96)	(1.00)	(1.07)	(1.06)	(1.08)	(0.81)	(0.79)	(1.02)
City Dummies	yes	yes	yes	yes	yes	yes	yes	yes	yes	yes
Sector Dummies	yes	yes	yes	yes	yes	yes	yes	yes	yes	yes
Firm Size Dummies	yes	yes	yes	yes	yes	yes	yes	yes	yes	yes
Firm Finances Dummies	yes	yes	yes	yes	yes	yes	yes	yes	yes	yes
Job Title Dummies	yes	yes	yes	yes	yes	yes	yes	yes	yes	yes
R-sq.	0.15	0.24	0.23	0.21	0.21	0.16	0.21	0.20	0.31	0.28
Adj. R-sq.	0.06	0.17	0.15	0.12	0.13	0.07	0.13	0.12	0.24	0.20

Note: *** $p < 0.001$, ** $p < 0.01$, * $p < 0.05$, † $p < 0.10$. Robust standard errors in parentheses. N=301.

Regressions for Figure 7.3b *Wealthy Clients and Property Security Strategies*

					Property Dispute Scenario – With Control Variables					
	Lawyers	Courts (formal)	Law Enf. (formal)	Gov. Officials (formal)	Courts (informal)	Law Enf. (informal)	Gov. Officials (informal)	Criminal Rackets	Private Sec. Agency	Internal Security
Wealthy Clients	0.07	0.00	0.29	0.25	0.38	0.39	0.22	−0.06	0.12	0.18
	(0.19)	(0.22)	(0.24)	(0.25)	(0.28)	(0.27)	(0.26)	(0.20)	(0.21)	(0.26)
Firm Age	0.12	0.27*	0.10	0.14	−0.09	0.00	−0.11	−0.03	0.03	0.02
	(0.08)	(0.11)	(0.10)	(0.10)	(0.13)	(0.11)	(0.12)	(0.08)	(0.09)	(0.12)
Foreign Owner	0.06	0.58†	−0.39	−0.77†	0.48	0.22	0.03	0.45	0.34	0.15
	(0.27)	(0.31)	(0.39)	(0.44)	(0.43)	(0.41)	(0.41)	(0.34)	(0.38)	(0.41)
Gov. Owner	−0.12	0.25	−0.09	0.24	0.27	−0.37	−0.21	−0.01	−0.16	−0.02
	(0.31)	(0.36)	(0.38)	(0.41)	(0.42)	(0.44)	(0.45)	(0.32)	(0.35)	(0.50)
Bus. Assoc.	0.03	0.01	0.73**	0.91***	0.50	0.40	0.37	−0.04	−0.04	0.57†
	(0.20)	(0.23)	(0.25)	(0.26)	(0.30)	(0.27)	(0.28)	(0.23)	(0.23)	(0.30)
Rights Violated	−0.04	0.22	0.20	0.13	0.32	0.74*	0.51†	0.25	0.25	0.36
	(0.24)	(0.28)	(0.28)	(0.30)	(0.32)	(0.32)	(0.30)	(0.22)	(0.26)	(0.30)
Litigated	0.42	0.36	0.57†	−0.29	0.23	0.14	−0.12	−0.43†	−0.66*	−0.00
	(0.28)	(0.30)	(0.31)	(0.33)	(0.32)	(0.33)	(0.32)	(0.24)	(0.26)	(0.34)
Legal Ed.	−0.07	0.23	0.22	0.30	0.56	0.24	0.77*	0.99**	0.47	0.45
	(0.25)	(0.28)	(0.38)	(0.38)	(0.41)	(0.35)	(0.36)	(0.32)	(0.31)	(0.38)
Age	0.00	0.03**	−0.02	−0.02	0.01	−0.01	−0.00	−0.04***	−0.02†	−0.00
	(0.01)	(0.01)	(0.01)	(0.01)	(0.01)	(0.01)	(0.01)	(0.01)	(0.01)	(0.01)
Male	−0.24	−0.21	−0.06	−0.07	−0.41	−0.19	−0.41†	0.22	−0.19	0.18
	(0.20)	(0.22)	(0.24)	(0.25)	(0.28)	(0.26)	(0.25)	(0.20)	(0.22)	(0.25)

Regressions for Figure 7.3b   (cont.)

	Property Dispute Scenario – With Control Variables									
	Lawyers	Courts (formal)	Law Enf. (formal)	Gov. Officials (formal)	Courts (informal)	Law Enf. (informal)	Gov. Officials (informal)	Criminal Rackets	Private Sec. Agency	Internal Security
Constant	5.91***	3.16***	6.81***	6.04***	3.38**	3.62***	4.02***	4.08***	4.45***	3.82***
	(0.73)	(0.79)	(0.83)	(0.93)	(1.06)	(1.06)	(1.02)	(0.79)	(0.90)	(1.00)
City Dummies	yes	yes	yes	yes	yes	yes	yes	yes	yes	yes
Sector Dummies	yes	yes	yes	yes	yes	yes	yes	yes	yes	yes
Firm Size Dummies	yes	yes	yes	yes	yes	yes	yes	yes	yes	yes
Firm Finances Dummies	yes	yes	yes	yes	yes	yes	yes	yes	yes	yes
Job Title Dummies	yes	yes	yes	yes	yes	yes	yes	yes	yes	yes
R-sq.	0.14	0.22	0.20	0.24	0.20	0.20	0.22	0.24	0.24	0.28
Adj. R-sq.	0.05	0.14	0.12	0.16	0.12	0.12	0.14	0.16	0.16	0.20
	Debt Dispute Scenario – With Control Variables									
Wealthy Clients	0.22	−0.06	0.70**	0.49†	0.26	0.54†	0.61*	0.06	0.10	0.14
	(0.16)	(0.21)	(0.26)	(0.27)	(0.28)	(0.28)	(0.26)	(0.18)	(0.19)	(0.26)
Firm Age	0.07	0.18†	0.11	0.14	−0.13	−0.12	−0.15	0.01	−0.06	0.10
	(0.07)	(0.10)	(0.11)	(0.10)	(0.13)	(0.12)	(0.11)	(0.08)	(0.08)	(0.12)
Foreign Owner	−0.01	0.24	−0.27	0.01	0.40	−0.05	0.14	0.30	0.28	0.18
	(0.26)	(0.29)	(0.41)	(0.44)	(0.42)	(0.39)	(0.40)	(0.28)	(0.33)	(0.42)
Gov. Owner	0.01	0.21	0.26	0.47	0.15	−0.09	0.12	−0.07	−0.09	0.34
	(0.31)	(0.36)	(0.41)	(0.44)	(0.46)	(0.43)	(0.44)	(0.24)	(0.27)	(0.50)

	(1)	(2)	(3)	(4)	(5)	(6)	(7)	(8)	(9)	(10)
Bus. Assoc.	−0.17	0.03	0.31	0.09	0.36	0.25	0.13	−0.09	0.11	0.52†
	(0.16)	(0.20)	(0.28)	(0.29)	(0.31)	(0.29)	(0.28)	(0.19)	(0.21)	(0.31)
Rights Violated	−0.06	0.29	0.53†	0.04	0.28	−0.01	0.09	0.29	0.41	0.23
	(0.18)	(0.25)	(0.30)	(0.32)	(0.33)	(0.34)	(0.32)	(0.20)	(0.26)	(0.30)
Litigated	0.21	−0.06	−0.01	−0.12	0.17	0.20	0.17	−0.16	−0.51*	−0.23
	(0.18)	(0.25)	(0.33)	(0.33)	(0.33)	(0.34)	(0.33)	(0.20)	(0.24)	(0.34)
Legal Ed.	−0.07	0.20	0.53	0.13	0.42	0.69†	0.77*	0.79**	0.65*	1.01**
	(0.23)	(0.24)	(0.43)	(0.39)	(0.44)	(0.37)	(0.37)	(0.29)	(0.29)	(0.37)
Age	0.00	0.01	−0.02	0.00	0.00	−0.02	−0.01	−0.02**	−0.01†	−0.01
	(0.01)	(0.01)	(0.01)	(0.01)	(0.01)	(0.01)	(0.01)	(0.01)	(0.01)	(0.01)
Male	−0.15	−0.22	0.13	0.09	−0.43	−0.00	−0.15	0.23	0.31	0.46†
	(0.16)	(0.19)	(0.26)	(0.27)	(0.28)	(0.27)	(0.26)	(0.18)	(0.21)	(0.26)
Constant	5.58***	3.77***	5.39***	4.39***	3.43**	4.65***	4.35***	3.86***	4.81***	3.76***
	(0.66)	(0.75)	(0.93)	(1.01)	(1.10)	(1.07)	(1.10)	(0.79)	(0.81)	(1.04)
City Dummies	yes	yes	yes	yes	yes	yes	yes	yes	yes	yes
Sector Dummies	yes	yes	yes	yes	yes	yes	yes	yes	yes	yes
Firm Size Dummies	yes	yes	yes	yes	yes	yes	yes	yes	yes	yes
Firm Finances Dummies	yes	yes	yes	yes	yes	yes	yes	yes	yes	yes
Job Title Dummies	yes	yes	yes	yes	yes	yes	yes	yes	yes	yes
R-sq.	0.16	0.24	0.25	0.21	0.19	0.16	0.22	0.20	0.32	0.27
Adj. R-sq.	0.07	0.17	0.17	0.13	0.10	0.08	0.14	0.12	0.24	0.20

Note: *** $p < 0.001$, ** $p < 0.01$, * $p < 0.05$, † $p < 0.10$. Robust standard errors in parentheses. N=301.

Regressions for Figure 7.4   Wealthy Clients and Property Security Strategies

		Property Dispute Scenario (firms with 250 or fewer employees)								
	Lawyers	Courts (formal)	Law Enf. (formal)	Gov. Officials (formal)	Courts (informal)	Law Enf. (informal)	Gov. Officials (informal)	Criminal Rackets	Private Sec. Agency	Internal Security
Wealthy Clients	-0.03	-0.00	0.01	0.12	0.66†	0.55	0.53	-0.10	0.13	0.06
	(0.28)	(0.32)	(0.33)	(0.34)	(0.37)	(0.37)	(0.35)	(0.27)	(0.30)	(0.33)
Firm Age	0.14	0.26†	0.14	0.04	0.05	0.09	-0.09	0.05	0.17	0.03
	(0.11)	(0.16)	(0.13)	(0.14)	(0.17)	(0.16)	(0.16)	(0.11)	(0.11)	(0.16)
Foreign Owner	0.69	1.33*	0.21	-0.41	1.20	0.53	0.56	0.40	0.58	0.35
	(0.43)	(0.53)	(0.61)	(0.66)	(0.78)	(0.69)	(0.64)	(0.46)	(0.72)	(0.65)
Gov. Owner	0.30	0.56	-0.01	0.55	0.12	-0.03	-0.07	-1.21*	-1.76*	-0.73
	(0.59)	(0.85)	(0.77)	(0.76)	(0.94)	(0.85)	(0.92)	(0.49)	(0.69)	(0.92)
Bus. Assoc.	-0.46	-0.14	0.43	0.73*	0.68	0.28	0.11	-0.00	0.04	0.77†
	(0.29)	(0.32)	(0.34)	(0.36)	(0.42)	(0.37)	(0.38)	(0.32)	(0.36)	(0.41)
Rights Violated	-0.13	0.32	0.33	0.31	0.51	1.16*	1.19**	0.42	0.60	0.16
	(0.36)	(0.42)	(0.36)	(0.41)	(0.47)	(0.49)	(0.42)	(0.28)	(0.38)	(0.39)
Litigated	0.17	-0.04	0.61	-0.62	0.15	-0.04	-0.37	0.02	-1.00**	0.43
	(0.42)	(0.44)	(0.43)	(0.43)	(0.51)	(0.53)	(0.46)	(0.32)	(0.38)	(0.46)
Legal Ed.	-0.03	-0.24	-0.33	0.05	0.36	0.12	0.76†	0.74†	0.23	-0.01
	(0.35)	(0.37)	(0.46)	(0.43)	(0.57)	(0.42)	(0.43)	(0.38)	(0.42)	(0.46)
Age	0.00	0.04†	-0.02	-0.00	0.01	-0.03	-0.01	-0.04**	-0.01	0.00
	(0.02)	(0.02)	(0.02)	(0.02)	(0.02)	(0.02)	(0.02)	(0.01)	(0.01)	(0.02)
Male	-0.15	-0.11	0.24	-0.12	-0.06	0.27	-0.11	0.18	-0.29	0.58†
	(0.28)	(0.33)	(0.33)	(0.36)	(0.40)	(0.36)	(0.34)	(0.28)	(0.35)	(0.34)

Constant	6.85***	3.78**	8.12***	6.64***	2.99*	3.26*	3.52*	3.98***	3.29*	3.17*
	(0.95)	(1.17)	(1.09)	(1.25)	(1.35)	(1.49)	(1.44)	(1.02)	(1.28)	(1.29)
City Dummies	yes	yes	yes	yes	yes	yes	yes	yes	yes	yes
Sector Dummies	yes	yes	yes	yes	yes	yes	yes	yes	yes	yes
Firm Size Dummies	yes	yes	yes	yes	yes	yes	yes	yes	yes	yes
Firm Finances Dummies	yes	yes	yes	yes	yes	yes	yes	yes	yes	yes
Job Title Dummies	yes	yes	yes	yes	yes	yes	yes	yes	yes	yes
R-sq.	0.21	0.27	0.26	0.22	0.23	0.22	0.25	0.24	0.28	0.39
Adj. R-sq.	0.06	0.14	0.12	0.08	0.09	0.08	0.11	0.10	0.15	0.28
Debt Dispute Scenario (firms with 250 or fewer employees)										
Wealthy Clients	0.43*	0.16	0.60†	0.10	0.81*	0.74†	0.72*	0.01	0.10	0.08
	(0.20)	(0.30)	(0.35)	(0.35)	(0.37)	(0.38)	(0.35)	(0.27)	(0.26)	(0.35)
Firm Age	0.01	0.15	0.11	-0.03	0.03	-0.08	-0.08	0.05	-0.06	0.09
	(0.10)	(0.14)	(0.14)	(0.15)	(0.17)	(0.17)	(0.15)	(0.13)	(0.12)	(0.15)
Foreign Owner	0.76*	1.16*	0.57	0.90	1.25	0.07	0.32	0.52	0.42	0.12
	(0.31)	(0.46)	(0.56)	(0.69)	(0.84)	(0.67)	(0.66)	(0.53)	(0.60)	(0.75)
Gov. Owner	-0.05	0.34	0.53	0.78	-0.08	0.18	0.27	-0.84*	-1.21*	-0.54
	(0.54)	(0.90)	(0.56)	(1.00)	(1.15)	(0.92)	(0.87)	(0.40)	(0.51)	(0.87)
Bus. Assoc.	-0.43†	-0.20	0.03	-0.16	0.41	0.09	0.06	-0.12	0.32	0.78†
	(0.22)	(0.29)	(0.37)	(0.39)	(0.42)	(0.41)	(0.39)	(0.32)	(0.35)	(0.42)
Rights Violated	-0.20	0.48	0.86*	0.28	0.60	0.12	0.02	0.45	0.66†	0.24
	(0.23)	(0.35)	(0.40)	(0.45)	(0.48)	(0.50)	(0.46)	(0.29)	(0.37)	(0.38)

Regressions for Figure 7.4 *(cont.)*

	Lawyers	Courts (formal)	Law Enf. (formal)	Gov. Officials (formal)	Courts (informal)	Law Enf. (informal)	Gov. Officials (informal)	Criminal Rackets	Private Sec. Agency	Internal Security
	Debt Dispute Scenario – With Control Variables									
Litigated	0.18	−0.49	−0.12	−0.31	0.22	0.12	0.15	0.13	−0.68†	−0.05
	(0.22)	(0.39)	(0.43)	(0.46)	(0.52)	(0.53)	(0.49)	(0.32)	(0.35)	(0.49)
Legal Ed.	0.00	0.06	−0.10	−0.22	0.26	0.75†	0.84†	0.80†	0.56	0.35
	(0.29)	(0.30)	(0.53)	(0.54)	(0.59)	(0.44)	(0.48)	(0.42)	(0.42)	(0.47)
Age	−0.00	0.02	−0.03	0.00	−0.02	−0.04	−0.03	−0.02	−0.02	−0.01
	(0.01)	(0.02)	(0.02)	(0.02)	(0.02)	(0.02)	(0.02)	(0.02)	(0.01)	(0.02)
Male	−0.19	−0.11	0.82*	0.40	0.23	0.56	0.49	0.24	0.53	0.71*
	(0.20)	(0.28)	(0.37)	(0.40)	(0.40)	(0.38)	(0.35)	(0.29)	(0.32)	(0.33)
Constant	6.66***	4.55***	6.22***	6.19***	3.47*	4.22**	4.66**	3.44**	4.28***	3.32*
	(0.77)	(1.06)	(1.21)	(1.33)	(1.46)	(1.61)	(1.58)	(1.16)	(1.18)	(1.41)
City Dummies	yes	yes	yes	yes	yes	yes	yes	yes	yes	yes
Sector Dummies	yes	yes	yes	yes	yes	yes	yes	yes	yes	yes
Firm Size Dummies	yes	yes	yes	yes	yes	yes	yes	yes	yes	yes
Firm Finances Dummies	yes	yes	yes	yes	yes	yes	yes	yes	yes	yes
Job Title Dummies	yes	yes	yes	yes	yes	yes	yes	yes	yes	yes
R-sq.	0.23	0.32	0.33	0.25	0.23	0.19	0.23	0.20	0.33	0.37
Adj. R-sq.	0.09	0.20	0.21	0.12	0.09	0.04	0.09	0.05	0.21	0.26

Note: *** $p < 0.001$, ** $p < 0.01$, * $p < 0.05$, † $p < 0.10$. Robust standard errors in parentheses. N= 170.

Regressions for Figure 7.5a *Licensing Barriers and Property Security Strategies*

				Property Dispute Scenario – With Control Variables					
	Lawyers	Courts (formal)	Law Enf. (formal)	Gov. Officials (formal)	Courts (informal)	Law Enf. (informal)	Gov. Officials (informal)	Criminal Rackets	Private Sec. Agency	Internal Security
Licensing Burden	0.11	−0.25	−0.08	−0.09	0.58*	0.88**	0.63*	−0.05	0.23	−0.09
	(0.20)	(0.23)	(0.26)	(0.27)	(0.28)	(0.28)	(0.29)	(0.21)	(0.21)	(0.27)
Firm Age	0.12	0.28**	0.10	0.14	−0.11	−0.03	−0.13	−0.03	0.03	0.03
	(0.08)	(0.11)	(0.10)	(0.11)	(0.13)	(0.11)	(0.12)	(0.08)	(0.09)	(0.12)
Foreign Owner	0.07	0.53†	−0.43	−0.81†	0.55	0.36	0.13	0.44	0.37	0.12
	(0.27)	(0.32)	(0.40)	(0.45)	(0.43)	(0.42)	(0.41)	(0.33)	(0.38)	(0.41)
Gov. Owner	−0.12	0.23	−0.13	0.20	0.26	−0.36	−0.20	−0.01	−0.17	−0.05
	(0.31)	(0.36)	(0.39)	(0.41)	(0.40)	(0.41)	(0.43)	(0.32)	(0.34)	(0.49)
Bus. Assoc.	0.04	−0.01	0.72**	0.90***	0.55†	0.48†	0.42	−0.05	−0.02	0.56†
	(0.21)	(0.23)	(0.25)	(0.26)	(0.30)	(0.27)	(0.28)	(0.23)	(0.23)	(0.30)
Rights Violated	−0.03	0.22	0.24	0.16	0.35	0.76*	0.52†	0.25	0.26	0.38
	(0.24)	(0.28)	(0.28)	(0.30)	(0.32)	(0.31)	(0.29)	(0.22)	(0.26)	(0.30)
Litigated	0.42	0.34	0.53†	−0.32	0.22	0.15	−0.10	−0.43†	−0.65*	−0.02
	(0.28)	(0.30)	(0.31)	(0.33)	(0.32)	(0.32)	(0.31)	(0.24)	(0.26)	(0.35)
Legal Ed.	−0.07	0.21	0.21	0.30	0.60	0.31	0.82*	0.99**	0.49	0.44
	(0.25)	(0.28)	(0.38)	(0.38)	(0.41)	(0.36)	(0.37)	(0.32)	(0.31)	(0.38)
Age	0.00	0.03**	−0.02	−0.02	0.00	−0.02	−0.01	−0.04***	−0.02†	−0.00
	(0.01)	(0.01)	(0.01)	(0.01)	(0.01)	(0.01)	(0.01)	(0.01)	(0.01)	(0.01)
Male	−0.23	−0.25	−0.09	−0.10	−0.34	−0.07	−0.33	0.21	−0.16	0.16
	(0.21)	(0.23)	(0.25)	(0.25)	(0.28)	(0.27)	(0.26)	(0.20)	(0.23)	(0.25)

Regressions for Figure 7.5a   *(cont.)*

			Property Dispute Scenario – With Control Variables							
	Lawyers	Courts (formal)	Law Enf. (formal)	Gov. Officials (formal)	Courts (informal)	Law Enf. (informal)	Gov. Officials (informal)	Criminal Rackets	Private Sec. Agency	Internal Security
Constant	5.89***	3.31***	7.03***	6.24***	3.27**	3.33**	3.79***	4.07***	4.39***	3.98***
	(0.75)	(0.79)	(0.85)	(0.96)	(1.07)	(1.05)	(0.99)	(0.79)	(0.90)	(0.99)
City Dummies	yes	yes	yes	yes	yes	yes	yes	yes	yes	yes
Sector Dummies	yes	yes	yes	yes	yes	yes	yes	yes	yes	yes
Firm Size Dummies	yes	yes	yes	yes	yes	yes	yes	yes	yes	yes
Firm Finances Dummies	yes	yes	yes	yes	yes	yes	yes	yes	yes	yes
Job Title Dummies	yes	yes	yes	yes	yes	yes	yes	yes	yes	yes
R-sq.	0.14	0.22	0.19	0.23	0.21	0.23	0.24	0.24	0.24	0.27
Adj. R-sq.	0.05	0.14	0.11	0.15	0.13	0.15	0.16	0.16	0.16	0.20
			Debt Dispute Scenario – With Control Variables							
Licensing Burden	0.36*	$-0.40^{\dagger}$	-0.01	-0.12	$0.56^{\dagger}$	1.08***	0.75**	-0.18	0.13	-0.37
	(0.15)	(0.20)	(0.28)	(0.28)	(0.30)	(0.28)	(0.28)	(0.18)	(0.20)	(0.26)
Firm Age	0.06	$0.19^{\dagger}$	0.11	0.14	-0.15	-0.16	-0.18	0.02	-0.06	0.11
	(0.07)	(0.10)	(0.11)	(0.11)	(0.13)	(0.12)	(0.11)	(0.08)	(0.08)	(0.12)
Foreign Owner	0.04	0.17	-0.34	-0.06	0.48	0.11	0.23	0.26	0.29	0.09
	(0.25)	(0.29)	(0.42)	(0.46)	(0.42)	(0.39)	(0.40)	(0.29)	(0.33)	(0.42)
Gov. Owner	0.01	0.19	0.16	0.40	0.15	-0.09	0.09	-0.09	-0.09	0.30
	(0.31)	(0.36)	(0.43)	(0.45)	(0.45)	(0.40)	(0.41)	(0.23)	(0.27)	(0.49)

	(1)	(2)	(3)	(4)	(5)	(6)	(7)	(8)	(9)	(10)
Bus. Assoc.	-0.14	-0.00	0.30	0.08	0.41	0.35	0.20	-0.10	0.12	0.48
	(0.16)	(0.20)	(0.28)	(0.29)	(0.31)	(0.28)	(0.27)	(0.19)	(0.21)	(0.31)
Rights Violated	-0.04	0.29	0.61*	0.10	0.30	0.03	0.14	0.30	0.42	0.25
	(0.17)	(0.24)	(0.31)	(0.32)	(0.33)	(0.33)	(0.32)	(0.20)	(0.26)	(0.30)
Litigated	0.21	-0.07	-0.08	-0.17	0.18	0.21	0.16	-0.18	-0.51*	-0.26
	(0.18)	(0.25)	(0.33)	(0.33)	(0.33)	(0.32)	(0.32)	(0.20)	(0.24)	(0.34)
Legal Ed.	-0.05	0.17	0.53	0.12	0.46	0.77*	0.82*	0.77**	0.66*	0.98**
	(0.23)	(0.24)	(0.43)	(0.39)	(0.45)	(0.38)	(0.38)	(0.28)	(0.29)	(0.37)
Age	-0.00	0.02	-0.03†	-0.00	-0.00	-0.02†	-0.02	-0.02**	-0.01†	-0.01
	(0.01)	(0.01)	(0.01)	(0.01)	(0.01)	(0.01)	(0.01)	(0.01)	(0.01)	(0.01)
Male	-0.11	-0.28	0.08	0.04	-0.36	0.14	-0.07	0.20	0.33	0.39
	(0.16)	(0.20)	(0.28)	(0.28)	(0.28)	(0.28)	(0.26)	(0.18)	(0.21)	(0.26)
Constant	5.50***	3.96***	5.81***	4.75***	3.26**	4.34***	4.28***	4.00***	4.79***	4.06***
	(0.69)	(0.76)	(0.97)	(1.03)	(1.11)	(1.03)	(1.08)	(0.81)	(0.82)	(1.01)
City Dummies	yes	yes	yes	yes	yes	yes	yes	yes	yes	yes
Sector Dummies	yes	yes	yes	yes	yes	yes	yes	yes	yes	yes
Firm Size Dummies	yes	yes	yes	yes	yes	yes	yes	yes	yes	yes
Firm Finances Dummies	yes	yes	yes	yes	yes	yes	yes	yes	yes	yes
Job Title Dummies	yes	yes	yes	yes	yes	yes	yes	yes	yes	yes
R-sq.	0.17	0.26	0.23	0.20	0.20	0.20	0.23	0.20	0.32	0.28
Adj. R-sq.	0.08	0.18	0.15	0.12	0.11	0.12	0.15	0.12	0.25	0.20

Note: *** $p < 0.001$, ** $p < 0.01$, * $p < 0.05$, † $p < 0.10$. Robust standard errors in parentheses. N=301.

Regressions for Figure 7.5b *Customs Barriers and Property Security Strategies*

					Property Dispute Scenario – With Control Variables					
	Lawyers	Courts (formal)	Law Enf. (formal)	Gov. Officials (formal)	Courts (informal)	Law Enf. (informal)	Gov. Officials (informal)	Criminal Rackets	Private Sec. Agency	Internal Security
Customs Burden	−0.17	−0.37	−0.38	−0.76**	0.60*	0.64*	0.42	0.13	0.44†	−0.06
	(0.21)	(0.24)	(0.27)	(0.28)	(0.29)	(0.31)	(0.29)	(0.22)	(0.24)	(0.28)
Firm Age	0.13	0.28**	0.10	0.15	−0.10	−0.02	−0.12	−0.03	0.02	0.03
	(0.09)	(0.11)	(0.10)	(0.10)	(0.13)	(0.11)	(0.12)	(0.08)	(0.09)	(0.12)
Foreign Owner	0.04	0.55†	−0.45	−0.85†	0.49	0.24	0.04	0.46	0.36	0.13
	(0.27)	(0.31)	(0.40)	(0.45)	(0.43)	(0.42)	(0.41)	(0.34)	(0.39)	(0.41)
Gov. Owner	−0.14	0.21	−0.17	0.13	0.28	−0.36	−0.20	0.01	−0.14	−0.05
	(0.31)	(0.36)	(0.39)	(0.40)	(0.41)	(0.42)	(0.43)	(0.32)	(0.34)	(0.50)
Bus. Assoc.	0.02	−0.01	0.70**	0.86**	0.54†	0.44†	0.39	−0.03	−0.01	0.56†
	(0.20)	(0.23)	(0.25)	(0.26)	(0.30)	(0.26)	(0.27)	(0.23)	(0.23)	(0.30)
Rights Violated	−0.02	0.24	0.25	0.20	0.33	0.75*	0.51†	0.24	0.25	0.38
	(0.24)	(0.28)	(0.28)	(0.29)	(0.31)	(0.32)	(0.30)	(0.22)	(0.26)	(0.30)
Litigated	0.42	0.38	0.56†	−0.27	0.15	0.06	−0.17	−0.43†	−0.69**	−0.01
	(0.28)	(0.30)	(0.31)	(0.33)	(0.32)	(0.33)	(0.31)	(0.24)	(0.26)	(0.35)
Legal Ed.	−0.09	0.19	0.18	0.22	0.62	0.31	0.82*	1.00**	0.52†	0.44
	(0.26)	(0.29)	(0.37)	(0.38)	(0.41)	(0.35)	(0.36)	(0.32)	(0.30)	(0.38)
Age	0.00	0.03*	−0.02	−0.02†	0.01	−0.01	−0.00	−0.04***	−0.01	−0.00
	(0.01)	(0.01)	(0.01)	(0.01)	(0.01)	(0.01)	(0.01)	(0.01)	(0.01)	(0.01)
Male	−0.26	−0.25	−0.12	−0.16	−0.37	−0.15	−0.39	0.24	−0.15	0.16
	(0.20)	(0.22)	(0.24)	(0.24)	(0.27)	(0.27)	(0.25)	(0.20)	(0.22)	(0.25)

Constant	6.07***	3.44***	7.26***	6.74***	3.17**	3.38**	3.84***	3.95***	4.19***	3.97***
	(0.73)	(0.81)	(0.85)	(0.96)	(1.07)	(1.09)	(1.01)	(0.79)	(0.92)	(0.99)
City Dummies	yes	yes	yes	yes	yes	yes	yes	yes	yes	yes
Sector Dummies	yes	yes	yes	yes	yes	yes	yes	yes	yes	yes
Firm Size Dummies	yes	yes	yes	yes	yes	yes	yes	yes	yes	yes
Firm Finances Dummies	yes	yes	yes	yes	yes	yes	yes	yes	yes	yes
Job Title Dummies	yes	yes	yes	yes	yes	yes	yes	yes	yes	yes
R-sq.	0.14	0.23	0.20	0.26	0.21	0.21	0.23	0.24	0.25	0.27
Adj. R-sq.	0.05	0.15	0.12	0.18	0.13	0.13	0.15	0.17	0.17	0.20
Debt Dispute Scenario – With Control Variables										
Customs Burden	0.10	−0.38†	−0.47	−0.78**	0.76*	1.06***	0.58*	0.10	0.54*	0.02
	(0.17)	(0.23)	(0.29)	(0.29)	(0.31)	(0.30)	(0.28)	(0.18)	(0.23)	(0.28)
Firm Age	0.07	0.19†	0.12	0.15	−0.14	−0.14	−0.17	0.01	−0.07	0.10
	(0.07)	(0.10)	(0.11)	(0.11)	(0.12)	(0.12)	(0.11)	(0.08)	(0.08)	(0.12)
Foreign Owner	−0.02	0.21	−0.37	−0.10	0.43	−0.02	0.13	0.31	0.31	0.16
	(0.25)	(0.28)	(0.42)	(0.46)	(0.42)	(0.39)	(0.41)	(0.29)	(0.34)	(0.41)
Gov. Owner	−0.01	0.18	0.11	0.33	0.19	−0.06	0.10	−0.07	−0.05	0.32
	(0.30)	(0.35)	(0.43)	(0.45)	(0.47)	(0.42)	(0.42)	(0.23)	(0.27)	(0.50)
Bus. Assoc.	−0.17	0.01	0.27	0.04	0.41	0.32	0.17	−0.08	0.15	0.52†
	(0.16)	(0.20)	(0.28)	(0.28)	(0.30)	(0.28)	(0.27)	(0.19)	(0.21)	(0.31)
Rights Violated	−0.04	0.30	0.63*	0.13	0.28	0.00	0.13	0.29	0.39	0.24
	(0.18)	(0.24)	(0.31)	(0.32)	(0.32)	(0.33)	(0.32)	(0.20)	(0.25)	(0.30)

Regressions for Figure 7.5b (*cont.*)

	Property Dispute Scenario – With Control Variables									
	Lawyers	Courts (formal)	Law Enf. (formal)	Gov. Officials (formal)	Courts (informal)	Law Enf. (informal)	Gov. Officials (informal)	Criminal Rackets	Private Sec. Agency	Internal Security
Litigated	0.18	−0.03	−0.05	−0.12	0.10	0.08	0.08	−0.17	−0.55*	−0.24
	(0.18)	(0.25)	(0.33)	(0.34)	(0.33)	(0.33)	(0.33)	(0.21)	(0.24)	(0.34)
Legal Ed.	−0.06	0.16	0.48	0.04	0.50	0.80*	0.83*	0.80**	0.71*	1.01**
	(0.23)	(0.24)	(0.42)	(0.38)	(0.45)	(0.38)	(0.39)	(0.29)	(0.28)	(0.37)
Age	−0.00	0.01	−0.03*	−0.01	0.01	−0.02	−0.01	−0.02*	−0.01	−0.01
	(0.01)	(0.01)	(0.01)	(0.01)	(0.01)	(0.02)	(0.01)	(0.01)	(0.01)	(0.01)
Male	−0.16	−0.25	0.04	−0.02	−0.37	0.07	−0.13	0.24	0.36†	0.45†
	(0.17)	(0.19)	(0.27)	(0.27)	(0.27)	(0.27)	(0.26)	(0.18)	(0.20)	(0.26)
Constant	5.64***	4.01***	6.15***	5.25***	3.02**	4.19***	4.29***	3.83***	4.48***	3.83***
	(0.70)	(0.80)	(0.99)	(1.03)	(1.13)	(1.08)	(1.09)	(0.80)	(0.84)	(1.02)
City Dummies	yes	yes	yes	yes	yes	yes	yes	yes	yes	yes
Sector Dummies	yes	yes	yes	yes	yes	yes	yes	yes	yes	yes
Firm Size Dummies	yes	yes	yes	yes	yes	yes	yes	yes	yes	yes
Firm Finances Dummies	yes	yes	yes	yes	yes	yes	yes	yes	yes	yes
Job Title Dummies	yes	yes	yes	yes	yes	yes	yes	yes	yes	yes
R-sq.	0.15	0.25	0.24	0.22	0.20	0.19	0.22	0.20	0.33	0.27
Adj. R-sq.	0.06	0.18	0.16	0.15	0.12	0.11	0.14	0.12	0.26	0.20

Note: *** $p < 0.001$, ** $p < 0.01$, * $p < 0.05$, † $p < 0.10$. Robust standard errors in parentheses. N=301.

Regression Results *Property Dispute Scenario (Saturated Models)*

		Lawyers	Courts (formal)	Law Enf. (formal)	Gov. Officials (formal)	Courts (informal)	Law Enf. (informal)	Gov. Officials (informal)	Criminal Rackets	Private Sec. Agency	Internal Security
Fig. 5.3:	Tax Violator	$-0.42^{\dagger}$	-0.65^{*}	-0.14	-0.03	0.39	0.78^{*}	0.96^{**}	0.78^{***}	0.17	0.12
		(0.25)	(0.28)	(0.31)	(0.32)	(0.34)	(0.32)	(0.33)	(0.23)	(0.30)	(0.31)
Fig. 5.4:	Others Unlawful	-0.30	-0.35	-0.29	-0.64^{*}	0.64^{*}	0.55^{*}	0.33	0.51^{*}	0.24	0.32
		(0.23)	(0.24)	(0.25)	(0.28)	(0.29)	(0.27)	(0.27)	(0.21)	(0.22)	(0.28)
Fig. 6.1:	Priv.*Cons. marginal effects	0.20	0.17	-0.43	0.26	$-1.00^{\dagger}$	-1.09^{*}	-0.98^{*}	-0.05	0.04	-1.18^{*}
		(0.44)	(0.39)	(0.51)	(0.53)	(0.52)	(0.53)	(0.49)	(0.27)	(0.32)	(0.58)
Fig. 6.2:	Low Cash	0.04	-0.23	-0.03	-0.01	-0.35	-0.45	-0.27	-0.04	-0.07	-0.08
		(0.24)	(0.25)	(0.30)	(0.33)	(0.35)	(0.34)	(0.35)	(0.24)	(0.29)	(0.33)
Fig. 7.1a:	Service Sector	-0.16	-0.03	$-0.48^{\dagger}$	-0.59^{*}	-0.05	0.42	$0.52^{\dagger}$	0.29	-0.04	$-0.50^{\dagger}$
		(0.21)	(0.25)	(0.25)	(0.27)	(0.29)	(0.28)	(0.28)	(0.22)	(0.23)	(0.28)
Fig. 7.1b:	Local Market	0.04	-0.05	0.02	-0.06	0.23	0.06	0.15	-0.26	0.17	-0.40
		(0.20)	(0.24)	(0.27)	(0.28)	(0.31)	(0.28)	(0.28)	(0.21)	(0.25)	(0.31)
Fig. 7.3a:	SOE	0.08	-0.11	-0.06	0.34	0.84^{**}	0.74^{**}	0.77^{**}	0.23	0.05	-0.15
		(0.19)	(0.22)	(0.28)	(0.27)	(0.30)	(0.29)	(0.27)	(0.21)	(0.23)	(0.31)
Fig. 7.3b:	Wealthy Clients	0.01	-0.05	0.18	0.21	0.19	0.15	0.07	-0.11	0.03	0.15
		(0.21)	(0.24)	(0.25)	(0.26)	(0.29)	(0.28)	(0.28)	(0.21)	(0.23)	(0.28)
Fig. 7.5a:	Licensing Burden	0.26	-0.13	0.06	0.33	0.32	0.68^{*}	0.48	-0.09	0.04	-0.21
		(0.25)	(0.26)	(0.29)	(0.31)	(0.32)	(0.32)	(0.33)	(0.21)	(0.25)	(0.32)

Regression Results (*cont.*)

	Lawyers	Courts (formal)	Law Enf. (formal)	Gov. Officials (formal)	Courts (informal)	Law Enf. (informal)	Gov. Officials (informal)	Criminal Rackets	Private Sec. Agency	Internal Security
Fig. 7.5b: Customs Burden	−0.19	−0.14	−0.48	−0.79*	0.15	−0.12	−0.16	−0.11	0.27	−0.14
	(0.25)	(0.28)	(0.31)	(0.33)	(0.34)	(0.34)	(0.32)	(0.23)	(0.29)	(0.33)
Privatized	−0.38	−0.21	−1.24*	−0.51	0.30	−0.57	−0.09	−0.53	−0.84*	0.70
	(0.43)	(0.43)	(0.52)	(0.54)	(0.56)	(0.59)	(0.56)	(0.38)	(0.39)	(0.58)
Consolidated	0.30	0.07	−0.69†	−0.09	−0.05	−0.96*	−0.59	0.04	−0.15	−0.12
	(0.31)	(0.34)	(0.37)	(0.40)	(0.42)	(0.42)	(0.42)	(0.29)	(0.32)	(0.37)
Priv.*Cons.	−0.10	0.10	0.26	0.35	−0.95	−0.13	−0.39	−0.09	0.18	−1.06
	(0.52)	(0.51)	(0.63)	(0.65)	(0.66)	(0.68)	(0.63)	(0.39)	(0.42)	(0.69)
	(0.09)	(0.11)	(0.10)	(0.11)	(0.13)	(0.11)	(0.12)	(0.08)	(0.09)	(0.12)
Foreign Owner	0.18	0.65†	−0.26	−0.63	0.67	0.49	0.24	0.29	0.43	−0.05
	(0.28)	(0.33)	(0.42)	(0.44)	(0.46)	(0.43)	(0.42)	(0.33)	(0.39)	(0.43)
Gov. Owner	−0.01	0.28	−0.12	0.27	0.12	−0.53	−0.39	0.05	−0.03	−0.33
	(0.33)	(0.36)	(0.38)	(0.42)	(0.42)	(0.42)	(0.45)	(0.32)	(0.35)	(0.47)
Bus. Assoc.	0.05	−0.05	0.72**	0.91**	0.57†	0.50†	0.47†	−0.06	0.03	0.43
	(0.21)	(0.23)	(0.26)	(0.28)	(0.30)	(0.26)	(0.27)	(0.23)	(0.24)	(0.31)
Rights Violated	0.02	0.27	0.30	0.26	0.34	0.77*	0.57†	0.24	0.23	0.37
	(0.24)	(0.28)	(0.29)	(0.30)	(0.31)	(0.31)	(0.29)	(0.22)	(0.25)	(0.31)
Litigated	0.50†	0.38	0.71*	−0.19	0.24	0.23	−0.07	−0.31	−0.55*	−0.06
	(0.29)	(0.31)	(0.32)	(0.33)	(0.33)	(0.32)	(0.31)	(0.24)	(0.26)	(0.36)

	(1)	(2)	(3)	(4)	(5)	(6)	(7)	(8)	(9)	(10)
Legal Ed.	-0.08	0.28	0.20	0.27	0.42	0.15	$0.62^{\dagger}$	0.74*	0.43	0.32
	(0.29)	(0.32)	(0.39)	(0.40)	(0.41)	(0.35)	(0.37)	(0.30)	(0.31)	(0.37)
Age	0.00	0.03*	-0.02	-0.03*	0.01	-0.01	-0.01	-0.04***	-0.01	-0.00
	(0.01)	(0.01)	(0.01)	(0.01)	(0.01)	(0.01)	(0.01)	(0.01)	(0.01)	(0.01)
Male	-0.21	-0.20	-0.07	-0.06	-0.36	-0.11	-0.32	0.13	-0.15	0.11
	(0.21)	(0.24)	(0.26)	(0.26)	(0.28)	(0.27)	(0.27)	(0.21)	(0.23)	(0.28)
Constant	5.78***	3.95***	7.68***	6.76***	$2.33^{\dagger}$	3.45**	3.46**	3.63***	3.78***	4.47***
	(0.89)	(1.06)	(1.01)	(1.20)	(1.22)	(1.26)	(1.22)	(0.84)	(1.01)	(1.26)
City Dummies	yes	yes	yes	yes	yes	yes	yes	yes	yes	yes
Sector Dummies	yes	yes	yes	yes	yes	yes	yes	yes	yes	yes
Firm Size Dummies	yes	yes	yes	yes	yes	yes	yes	yes	yes	yes
Firm Fin. Dummies	yes	yes	yes	yes	yes	yes	yes	yes	yes	yes
Job Title Dummies	yes	yes	yes	yes	yes	yes	yes	yes	yes	yes
R-sq.	0.19	0.27	0.25	0.29	0.28	0.33	0.32	0.34	0.28	0.30
Adj. R-sq.	0.07	0.16	0.15	0.19	0.18	0.23	0.22	0.24	0.17	0.20

Note: *** $p < 0.001$, ** $p < 0.01$, * $p < 0.05$, † $p < 0.10$. Robust standard errors in parentheses. N=301.

Regression Results *Debt Dispute Scenario (Saturated Models)*

		Lawyers	Courts (formal)	Law Enf. (formal)	Gov. Officials (formal)	Courts (informal)	Law Enf. (informal)	Gov. Officials (informal)	Criminal Rackets	Private Sec. Agency	Internal Security
Fig. 5.3:	Tax Violator	0.05	−0.45†	0.26	0.26	0.40	0.88*	1.06**	0.63**	0.25	0.26
		(0.21)	(0.25)	(0.34)	(0.35)	(0.34)	(0.35)	(0.35)	(0.21)	(0.28)	(0.33)
Fig. 5.4:	Others Unlawful	−0.25	−0.22	0.05	−0.53†	0.67*	0.30	0.04	0.35†	0.28	0.31
		(0.18)	(0.21)	(0.29)	(0.28)	(0.30)	(0.27)	(0.26)	(0.18)	(0.20)	(0.29)
Fig. 6.1:	Priv.*Cons. *marginal effects*	0.53	−0.10	−0.40	−0.39	−1.06*	−0.78	−1.04*	−0.16	−0.09	−0.83
		(0.37)	(0.31)	(0.55)	(0.52)	(0.53)	(0.50)	(0.49)	(0.22)	(0.29)	(0.60)
Fig. 6.2:	Low Cash	−0.05	−0.42†	−0.36	−0.05	−0.59†	−0.47	−0.34	−0.23	−0.15	−0.25
		(0.23)	(0.24)	(0.33)	(0.35)	(0.35)	(0.36)	(0.35)	(0.21)	(0.26)	(0.33)
Fig. 7.1a:	Service Sector	−0.12	−0.12	−0.34	−0.12	0.01	0.39	0.46†	0.02	0.26	−0.53†
		(0.17)	(0.21)	(0.28)	(0.29)	(0.31)	(0.29)	(0.26)	(0.19)	(0.21)	(0.30)
Fig. 7.1b:	Local Market	−0.09	−0.60**	−0.54†	0.25	0.33	−0.00	0.32	−0.18	0.05	−0.35
		(0.19)	(0.20)	(0.31)	(0.30)	(0.32)	(0.29)	(0.25)	(0.19)	(0.22)	(0.32)
Fig. 7.3a:	SOE	0.12	0.12	0.27	0.37	1.08***	0.69*	0.67*	0.01	0.16	0.24
		(0.19)	(0.20)	(0.29)	(0.28)	(0.29)	(0.28)	(0.28)	(0.17)	(0.21)	(0.32)
Fig. 7.3b:	Wealthy Clients	0.20	−0.13	0.60*	0.43	0.03	0.39	0.47†	−0.01	0.05	0.13
		(0.17)	(0.21)	(0.27)	(0.27)	(0.29)	(0.28)	(0.27)	(0.18)	(0.21)	(0.28)
Fig. 7.5a:	Licensing Burden	0.43*	−0.31	0.16	0.20	0.19	0.65†	0.44	−0.31	−0.16	−0.60†
		(0.18)	(0.22)	(0.32)	(0.32)	(0.34)	(0.34)	(0.33)	(0.21)	(0.25)	(0.31)

Fig. 7.5b:

Customs Burden	−0.05 (0.20)	−0.15 (0.26)	−0.68† (0.35)	−0.86* (0.35)	0.35 (0.35)	0.44 (0.36)	0.06 (0.33)	−0.01 (0.22)	0.47† (0.28)	0.15 (0.32)
Privatized	−0.45 (0.34)	−0.29 (0.35)	−0.25 (0.59)	−0.18 (0.52)	0.04 (0.58)	−0.14 (0.58)	0.15 (0.56)	−0.49† (0.29)	−0.60 (0.36)	0.42 (0.56)
Consolidated	−0.15 (0.22)	−0.40 (0.27)	−0.49 (0.41)	−0.30 (0.39)	−0.49 (0.41)	−1.06* (0.44)	−0.61 (0.40)	−0.04 (0.26)	−0.32 (0.31)	−0.22 (0.36)
Priv.*Cons.	0.68 (0.42)	0.30 (0.42)	0.09 (0.71)	−0.09 (0.65)	−0.57 (0.67)	0.28 (0.66)	−0.43 (0.62)	−0.12 (0.33)	0.23 (0.41)	−0.61 (0.69)
Firm Age	0.05 (0.08)	0.15 (0.10)	0.12 (0.11)	0.18 (0.11)	−0.10 (0.12)	−0.12 (0.12)	−0.10 (0.11)	0.08 (0.08)	−0.03 (0.09)	0.12 (0.12)
Foreign Owner	0.11 (0.27)	0.19 (0.30)	−0.32 (0.44)	0.19 (0.46)	0.70 (0.46)	0.23 (0.41)	0.42 (0.40)	0.17 (0.29)	0.32 (0.34)	0.01 (0.43)
Gov. Owner	0.14 (0.33)	0.13 (0.34)	0.10 (0.44)	0.34 (0.43)	−0.01 (0.48)	−0.23 (0.41)	−0.07 (0.43)	−0.04 (0.23)	−0.02 (0.26)	0.12 (0.47)
Bus. Assoc.	−0.12 (0.17)	−0.13 (0.19)	0.20 (0.29)	0.12 (0.30)	0.46 (0.30)	0.38 (0.28)	0.28 (0.27)	−0.12 (0.19)	0.16 (0.22)	0.40 (0.31)
Rights Violated	−0.06 (0.18)	0.35 (0.24)	0.60* (0.30)	0.19 (0.32)	0.31 (0.31)	−0.01 (0.32)	0.16 (0.31)	0.29 (0.21)	0.38 (0.25)	0.24 (0.31)
Litigated	0.25 (0.18)	−0.09 (0.26)	0.05 (0.35)	−0.04 (0.34)	0.16 (0.33)	0.17 (0.32)	0.20 (0.31)	−0.05 (0.21)	−0.48† (0.25)	−0.31 (0.36)
Legal Ed.	−0.00 (0.25)	0.23 (0.24)	0.41 (0.45)	0.04 (0.39)	0.34 (0.43)	0.73† (0.38)	0.64† (0.36)	0.56* (0.28)	0.64* (0.29)	0.88* (0.37)

Regression Results *(cont.)*

	Lawyers	Courts (formal)	Law Enf. (formal)	Gov. Officials (formal)	Courts (informal)	Law Enf. (informal)	Gov. Officials (informal)	Criminal Rackets	Private Sec. Agency	Internal Security
Age	−0.00	0.01	−0.03*	−0.01	0.00	−0.02	−0.01	−0.02*	−0.01	−0.01
	(0.01)	(0.01)	(0.01)	(0.01)	(0.02)	(0.02)	(0.01)	(0.01)	(0.01)	(0.01)
Male	−0.10	−0.34	0.04	0.15	−0.38	0.15	0.07	0.20	0.31	0.34
	(0.17)	(0.21)	(0.28)	(0.29)	(0.28)	(0.27)	(0.27)	(0.19)	(0.22)	(0.28)
Constant	5.74***	5.72***	6.85***	4.81***	2.69*	4.52***	3.59**	3.70***	4.47***	4.41***
	(0.79)	(0.93)	(1.21)	(1.26)	(1.27)	(1.30)	(1.23)	(0.87)	(0.95)	(1.24)
City Dummies	yes	yes	yes	yes	yes	yes	yes	yes	yes	yes
Sector Dummies	yes	yes	yes	yes	yes	yes	yes	yes	yes	yes
Firm Size Dummies	yes	yes	yes	yes	yes	yes	yes	yes	yes	yes
Firm Fin. Dummies	yes	yes	yes	yes	yes	yes	yes	yes	yes	yes
Job Title Dummies	yes	yes	yes	yes	yes	yes	yes	yes	yes	yes
R-sq.	0.19	0.32	0.28	0.26	0.30	0.31	0.33	0.29	0.36	0.31
Adj. R-sq.	0.08	0.22	0.18	0.16	0.20	0.21	0.24	0.19	0.27	0.21

Note: *** $p < 0.001$, ** $p < 0.01$, * $p < 0.05$, † $p < 0.10$. Robust standard errors in parentheses. N=301.

REFERENCES

Acemoglu, D., Johnson, S., and Robinson, J. (2001). The colonial origins of comparative development: An empirical investigation. *American Economic Review*, 91(5):1369–1401.

Acemoglu, D., and Robinson, J. (2006). Economic backwardness in political perspective. *American Political Science Review*, 100(1):115–131.

Albats, Y. (2004). Bureaucrats and the Russian Transition: The Politics of Accommodation, 1991–2003. Doctoral Dissertation, Department of Government, Harvard University. Cambridge, MA.

Alexeev, M., Conrad, R., and Hay, J. (2004). Nalogoblozhenie i pravovaya reforma v perekhodnoi ekonomike: predvaritelnyi analiz [The tax burden and legal reform in transition economies: Preliminary analysis]. *Beyond Transition: World Bank Newsletter on Reforming Economies (Russian Version)*. No. 3.

Allina-Pisano, J. (2008). *The Post-Soviet Potemkin Village: Politics and Property Rights in the Black Earth*. Cambridge and New York: Cambridge University Press.

American Chamber of Commerce in Russia (2007). Impact of American Business Practice Values in Russia: Preliminary results. Unpublished report.

Andreoni, J., Erard, B., and Feinstein, J. (1998). Tax compliance. *Journal of Economic Literature*, 36(2):818–860.

Ang, Y. Y., and Jia, N. (2014). Perverse complementarity: Political connections and the use of courts among private firms in China. *Journal of Politics*, 76(2):318–332.

Åslund, A. (1995). *How Russia Became a Market Economy*. Washington, DC: Brookings Institution Press.

Åslund, A. (2005). The economic policy of Ukraine after the Orange Revolution. *Eurasian Geography and Economics*, 46(5):327–353.

Åslund, A. (2009). *How Ukraine Became a Market Economy and Democracy*. Washington, DC: Peterson Institute for International Economics.

Åslund, A., and Johnson, S. (2003). Small Enterprises and Economic Policy. Carnegie Paper No. 43.

Avdasheva, S., and Shastitko, A. (2011). Russian anti-trust policy: Power of enforcement versus quality of rules. *Post-Communist Economies*, 23(4):493–505.

275

Backer, P. (July 31, 2008). Survival Guide to Russia: Business, Law, Regulations and Compliance (Part 5). Johnson's Russia List. JRL 2008-140.

Barisitz, S. (2009). Russian banking in recent years: Gaining depth in a fragile environment. In Balling, M., editor, *Current Trends in the Russian Financial System*. Vienna: SUERF, The European Money and Finance Forum.

Barnes, A. (2006). *Owning Russia: The Struggle over Factories, Farms, and Power*. Ithaca, NY: Cornell University Press.

Barzel, Y. (1997). *Economic Analysis of Property Rights*. Cambridge and New York: Cambridge University Press.

Belokurova, G. (2013). When Does Business Turn Violent? Elections and Business-Related Violence in Russia. Working Paper, University of Wisconsin, Madison, Department of Political Science.

Belton, C. (May 20, 2008). BP office raid raises fears over Russia venture. *Financial Times*.

Benson, B. (1989). The spontaneous evolution of commercial law. *Southern Economic Journal*, 55(3):644–661.

Berman, H. (1983). *Law and Revolution*. Cambridge: Harvard University Press.

Bernstein, L. (1992). Opting out of the legal system: Extralegal contractual relations in the diamond industry. *Journal of Legal Studies*, 21(1):115–157.

Bigsten, A., Collier, P., Dercon, S., Fafchamps, M., Gauthier, B., Gunning, J. W., Oduro, A., Oostendorp, R., Patillo, C., Soderbom, M., Teal, F., and Zeufack, A. (2000). Contract flexibility and dispute resolution in African manufacturing. *Journal of Development Studies*, 36(4):1–37.

Black, B., Kraakman, R., and Tarassova, A. (2000). Russian privatization and corporate governance: What went wrong? *Stanford Law Review*, 52:1731–1808.

Black, D. (1976). *The Behavior of Law*. New York: Academic.

Blasi, J., Kroumova, M., and Kruse, D. (1997). *Kremlin Capitalism: The Privatization of the Russian Economy*. Ithaca, NY: Cornell University Press.

Boone, P., and Rodionov, D. (August 23, 2002). Reformed rent-seekers promoting reform? *Moscow Times*.

Borodkin, A. (November 24, 2008). Razoruzhennaya okhrana [Disarmed guards]. *Dengi*.

Braguinsky, S. (2009). Postcommunist oligarchs in Russia: Quantitative analysis. *Journal of Law and Economics*, 52(2):307–349.

Brambor, T., Clark, W. R., and Golder, M. (2006). Understanding interaction models: Improving empirical analyses. *Political Analysis*, 14(1):63–82.

Brautigam, D. (1997). Substituting for the state: Institutions and industrial development in Eastern Nigeria. *World Development*, 25(7):1063–1080.

Browder, W. (July 6, 2009). Russian sharks are feeding on their own blood. *Financial Times*.

Bruce, J., Garcia-Bolivar, O., Roth, M., Knox, A., and Schmid, J. (2007). Land and Business Formalization for Legal Empowerment of the Poor. Strategic Overview Paper prepared by ARD Inc. for USAID.

Buckley, N. (January 16, 2014). Amnesty will do little to improve Russia business climate. *Financial Times*.

Burger, E., and Holland, M. (2008). Law as politics: The Russian procuracy and its investigative committee. *Columbia Journal of East European Law*, 2(2):143–194.

Cambanis, T. (November 1, 2007). In rape case, a French youth takes on Dubai. *New York Times*.

Carey, J. (2000). Parchment, equilibria, and institutions. *Comparative Political Studies*, 33(6–7):735–761.

Carothers, T. (1998). The rule of law revival. *Foreign Affairs*, 77(2):95–106.

Center for International Private Enterprise (CIPE) (2006). Strengthening Local Democracy in Russia: The Case for Business Associations. Economic Reform Case Study No. 0505.

Chivers, C. (December 1, 2010). Below surface, US has dim view of Putin and Russia. *New York Times*.

Chowdhury, A. (2003). Banking Reform in Russia: A Window of Opportunity? William Davidson Institute Working Papers Series.

Clarke, D., Murrell, P., and Whiting, S. (2008). The role of law in China's economic development. In Rawski, T. and Brandt, L., editors, *China's Great Economic Transformation*. Cambridge and New York: Cambridge University Press.

Cole, D., and Grossman, P. (2002). The meaning of property rights: Law versus economics? *Land Economics*, 78(3):317–330.

Cooter, R., and Schaefer, H. (2009). Law and the poverty of nations. Unpublished manuscript, UC Berkeley.

Dam, K. (2006). *The Law-Growth Nexus: The Rule of Law and Economic Development*. Washington, DC: Brookings Institution Press.

Daniels, R., and Trebilcock, M. (2004). The political economy of rule of law reform in developing countries. *Michigan Journal of International Law*, 26:99–139.

Danilov, Y. and Yakushin, A. (2008). IPO v Rossii: Itogi 2007 [IPOs in Russia: Summary of 2007]. Center for Capital Market Development Foundation Working Paper.

De Soto, H. (2003). *The Mystery of Capital: Why Capitalism Triumphs in the West and Fails Everywhere Else*. New York: Basic Books.

Demsetz, H. (1967). Toward a theory of property rights. *American Economic Review*, 57(2):347–359.

Dolgopyatova, T. (2005). Evolution of corporate control models in Russian companies: New trends and factors. Higher School of Economics Problems of Institutional Economics Working Paper.

Dolgopyatova, T. (2010). Kontsentratsiya sobstvennosti v rossiiskoy promyshlennosti: evolyutsionnye izmeneniya na mikrourovne [Concentration of ownership in Russian industry: Evolutionary change on the micro-level]. *Dzhurnal novoy ekonomicheskoy assotsiatsii [Journal of the New Economic Association]*, (8):80–100.

Dolgova, A. (2005). Organizovannaya prestupnost, terrorizm i korruptsiya: ten-dentsii i sovershenstvovanie borby s nim [Organized crime, terrorism and corruption: Trends and perfection of the fight against them]. In Dol-gova, A., editor, *Organizovannaya prestupnost, terrorizm i korruptsiya v ikh proyavleniyakh i borba s nimi*. Moscow: Russian Criminological Association.

Dubova, A., and Kosals, L. (2013). Russian police involvement in the shadow economy. *Russian Politics and Law*, 51(4):48–58.

Duvanova, D. (2013). *Building Business in Post-Communist Russia, Eastern Europe, and Eurasia: Collective Goods, Selective Incentives, and Predatory States*. Cambridge and New York: Cambridge University Press.

Easter, G. (2002a). Politics of revenue extraction in post-communist states: Poland and Russia compared. *Political Theory*, 30(4):599–627.

Easter, G. (2002b). The Russian tax police. *Post-Soviet Affairs*, 18(4):332–362.

Edwards, L. (July 1, 2009). Russia claws at the rule of law. *ABA Journal*.

Ellickson, R. (1991). *Order without Law: How Neighbors Settle Disputes*. Cambridge: Harvard University Press.

Eremenko, A. (October 18, 1996). Arbitrazhi kak pokazateli razvitiya ekonomiki [Commercial courts as an indicator of economic development]. *Zerkalo nedeli*.

Evans, P. (1995). *Embedded Autonomy: States and Industrial Transformation*. Princeton, NJ: Princeton University Press.

Evans, P., Rueschemeyer, D., and Skocpol, T. (1985). *Bringing the State Back In*. Cambridge and New York: Cambridge University Press.

Fafchamps, M. (1996). The enforcement of commercial contracts in Ghana. *World Development*, 24(3):427–448.

Fafchamps, M., and Minten, B. (2001). Property rights in a flea market economy. *Economic Development and Cultural Change*, 49(2):229–267.

Faulconbridge, J., Beaverstock, J., Muzio, D., and Taylor, P. (2008). Global law firms: Globalization and organizational spaces of cross-border legal work. *Northwestern Journal of International Law and Business*, 28(3):455–488.

Favarel-Garrigues, G. (2011). *Policing Economic Crime in Russia: From Soviet Planned Economy to Privatization*. New York: Columbia University Press.

Filippov, S. (2010). Russian companies: The rise of new multinationals. *International Journal of Emerging Markets*, 5(3-4):307–332.

Firestone, T. (2008). Criminal corporate raiding in Russia. *International Lawyer*, 42(4):1207–1230.

Fish, M. (2005). *Democracy Derailed in Russia: The Failure of Open Politics*. Cambridge and New York: Cambridge University Press.

Fraenkel, E. (1941). *The Dual State: A Contribution to the Theory of Dictatorship*. Oxford: Oxford University Press.

Freeland, C. (2000). *Sale of the Century: Russia's Wild Ride from Communism to Capitalism*. New York: Crown Business.

Frye, T. (2000). *Brokers and Bureaucrats: Building Market Institutions in Russia*. Ann Arbor: University of Michigan Press.

Frye, T. (2002). Private protection in Russia and Poland. *American Journal of Political Science*, 46(3):572–584.

Frye, T. (2003). Markets, democracy, and new private business in Russia. *Post-Soviet Affairs*, 19(1):24–45.

Frye, T. (2004). Credible commitment and property rights: Evidence from Russia. *American Political Science Review*, 98(3):453–466.

Frye, T. (2010). Corruption and the rule of law. In Åslund, A., Guriev, S., and Kuchins, A., editors, *Russia after the Global Economic Crisis*. Washington, DC: Peter G. Peterson Institute for International Economics.

Frye, T. (2017). *Property Rights and Property Wrongs: How Power, Institutions, and Norms Shape Economic Conflict in Russia*. Cambridge and New York: Cambridge University Press.

Frye, T., and Zhuravskaya, E. (2000). Rackets, regulation, and the rule of law. *Journal of Law, Economics, and Organization*, 16(2):478–502.

Gaddy, C., and Partlett, W. (July 19, 2013). Russia's Financial Police State. *The National Interest*.

Galanter, M. (1974). Why the "haves" come out ahead: Speculations on the limits of legal change. *Law and Society Review*, 9(1):95–160.

Gambetta, D. (1996). *The Sicilian Mafia: The Business of Private Protection*. Cambridge: Harvard University Press.

Gans-Morse, J. (2012). Threats to property rights in Russia: From private coercion to state aggression. *Post-Soviet Affairs*, 28(3):263–295.

Gavrish, O. (June 20, 2001). D. Prityka: V proshlom godu v arbitrazhnye sudy postupilo rekordnoe kolichestvo del [Interview with D. Prityka: Last year a record number of cases filed in commercial courts]. News release from the Supreme Commercial Court of Ukraine (http://vgsu.arbitr.gov.ua/news/print/130).

Geddes, B. (1994). *The Politician's Dilemma: Building State Capacity in Latin America*. Berkeley and Los Angeles: University of California Press.

Gehlbach, S. (2007). Revenue traps. *Economics & Politics*, 19(1):73–96.

Gehlbach, S. (2008). *Representation through Taxation: Revenue, Politics, and Development in Postcommunist States*. Cambridge and New York: Cambridge University Press.

Gerber, T., and Mendelson, S. (2008). Public experiences of police violence and corruption in contemporary Russia: A case of predatory policing? *Law & Society Review*, 42(1):1–44.

Ginsburg, T., and Hoetker, G. (2006). The unreluctant litigant? An empirical analysis of Japan's turn to litigation. *The Journal of Legal Studies*, 35(1):31–59.

Goble, P. (June 25, 2008). Crime Continues to Increase in Russia, Especially in Mid-Sized Cities. *Window on Eurasia*.

Goldman, M. (2003). *The Piratization of Russia: Russian Reform Goes Awry*. New York: Routledge.

Goldman, M. (2004). Putin and the oligarchs. *Foreign Affairs*, 83(6):33–44.

Greif, A. (1993). Contract enforceability and economic institutions in early trade: The Maghribi traders' coalition. *The American Economic Review*, 83(3):525–548.

Grzymala-Busse, A. (2007). *Rebuilding Leviathan: Party Competition and State Exploitation in Post-Communist Democracies*. Cambridge and New York: Cambridge University Press.

Grzymala-Busse, A. (2010). The Best Laid Plans: The Impact of Informal Rules on Formal Institutions in Transitional Regimes. *Studies in Comparative International Development*, 45(3):1–23.

Guriev, S., and Rachinsky, A. (2005). The role of oligarchs in Russian capitalism. *Journal of Economic Perspectives*, 19(1):131–150.

Haber, S., Maurer, N., and Razo, A. (2003). *The Politics of Property Rights: Political Instability, Credible Commitments, and Economic Growth in Mexico, 1876–1929*. Cambridge and New York: Cambridge University Press.

Haggard, S., MacIntyre, A., and Tiede, L. (2008). The rule of law and economic development. *Annual Review Political Science*, 11:205–234.

Hall, P., and Soskice, D. (2001). *Varieties of Capitalism: The Institutional Foundations of Comparative Advantage*. New York: Oxford University Press.

Hall, P. and Thelen, K. (2009). Institutional change in varieties of capitalism. *Socio-Economic Review*, 7(1):7–34.

Handelman, S. (1994). The Russian Mafiya. *Foreign Affairs*, 73(2):83–96.

Hanson, P., and Teague, E. (2005). Big business and the state in Russia. *Europe-Asia Studies*, 57(5):657–680.

Hanson, S. (2007). The uncertain future of Russia's weak state authoritarianism. *East European Politics & Societies*, 21(1):67–81.

Hay, J., and Shleifer, A. (1998). Private enforcement of public laws: A theory of legal reform. *The American Economic Review*, 88(2):398–403.

Hellman, J. (1998). Winners take all: The politics of partial reform in postcommunist transitions. *World Politics*, 50(2):203–234.

Hellman, J., Jones, G., and Kaufmann, D. (2002). Far from home: Do foreign investors import higher standards of governance in transition economies? Available at SSRN 386900.

Hendley, K. (1996). *Trying to Make Law Matter: Legal Reform and Labor Law in the Soviet Union*. Ann Arbor: University of Michigan Press.

Hendley, K. (1997). Legal development in post-Soviet Russia. *Post-Soviet Affairs*, 13(3):228–251.

Hendley, K. (1998). Remaking an Institution: The Transition in Russia from State *Arbitrazh* to *Arbitrazh* Courts. *American Journal of Comparative Law*, 46(1):93–127.

Hendley, K. (1999). Rewriting the rules of the game in Russia: The neglected issue of demand for law. *East European Constitutional Review*, 8(4):89–95.

Hendley, K. (2001a). Beyond the tip of the iceberg: Business disputes in Russia. In Murrell, P., editor, *Assessing the Value of Law in Transition Economies*. Ann Arbor: University of Michigan Press.

Hendley, K. (2001b). Demand for law in Russia: A mixed picture. *East European Constitutional Review*, 10(4):72–78.

Hendley, K. (2002). Suing the state in Russia. *Post-Soviet Affairs*, 18(2):122–147.

Hendley, K. (2003). Reforming the procedural rules for business litigation in Russia: To what end? *Demokratizatsiya: Journal of Post-Soviet Democratization*, 11(3):363–380.

Hendley, K. (2004). Business litigation in the transition: A portrait of debt collection in Russia. *Law & Society Review*, 38(2):305–348.

Hendley, K. (2005). Accelerated procedure in the Russian *arbitrazh* courts: A case study of unintended consequences. *Problems of Post-Communism*, 52(6): 21–31.

Hendley, K. (2006). Assessing the rule of law in Russia. *Cardozo Journal International and Comparative Law*, 14(2):347–391.

Hendley, K. (2007a). Are Russian judges still Soviet? *Post-Soviet Affairs*, 23(3): 240–274.

Hendley, K. (2007b). Putin and the law. In Herspring, D., editor, *Putin's Russia: Past Imperfect, Future Uncertain*. Lanham, MD: Routledge, 3rd edition.

Hendley, K. (2009). "Telephone law" and the "rule of law": The Russian case. *Hague Journal on the Rule of Law*, 1(2):241–262.

Hendley, K. (2010). The role of in-house counsel in post-Soviet Russia in the wake of privatization. *International Journal of the Legal Profession*, 17(1):5–34.

Hendley, K. (2011). Varieties of legal dualism: Making sense of the role of law in contemporary Russia. *Wisconsin International Law Journal*, 29:233–262.

Hendley, K. (2012). The puzzling non-consequences of societal distrust of courts: Explaining the use of Russian courts. *Cornell International Law Journal*, 45:517–567.

Hendley, K., Murrell, P., and Ryterman, R. (2000). Law, relationships and private enforcement: Transactional strategies of Russian enterprises. *Europe-Asia Studies*, 52(4):627–656.

Hendley, K., Murrell, P., and Ryterman, R. (2001a). Agents of change or unchanging agents? The role of lawyers within Russian industrial enterprises. *Law & Social Inquiry*, 26(3):685–715.

Hendley, K., Murrell, P., and Ryterman, R. (2001b). Law works in Russia: The role of law in interenterprise transactions. In Murrell, P., editor, *Assessing the*

Value of Law in Transition Economies. Ann Arbor, MI: University of Michigan Press.

Hersh, S. (1994). The wild east. *The Atlantic Monthly*, 273(6):61–75.

Hill, F. and Gaddy, C. (2013). *Mr. Putin: Operative in the Kremlin*. Washington, DC: Brookings Institution Press.

Himes, S., and Milliet-Einbinder, M. (1999). Russia's tax reform. *OECD Observer*, 26–30.

Hoff, K., and Stiglitz, J. (2004). After the big bang? Obstacles to the emergence of the rule of law in post-communist societies. *American Economic Review*, 94(3):753–763.

Hoffman, D. (May 12, 1997). Banditry threatens the New Russia. *Washington Post*.

Hoffman, D. (2002). *The Oligarchs: Wealth and Power in the New Russia*. New York, NY: Public Affairs.

Hohfeld, W. (1913). Some fundamental legal conceptions as applied in judicial reasoning. *The Yale Law Journal*, 23(1):16–59.

Honaker, J., King, G., and Blackwell, M. (2011). Amelia II: A program for missing data. *Journal of Statistical Software*, 45(7):1–47.

INDEM-CIPE (2009). *Sudebnaya vlast i predprinimateli: rezultaty sotsiologicheskogo analiza [The judiciary and entrepreneurs: Results of Sociological Analysis]*. Summary report of joint project conducted by INDEM Foundation and the Center for International Private Enterprise (CIPE).

Institute for Economic Transition (2006). Russian Economy in 2006: Trends and Outlooks.

Jackson, J., Klich, J., and Poznanska, K. (2003). Democratic institutions and economic reform: The Polish case. *British Journal of Political Science*, 33(1):85–108.

Jensen, M., and Meckling, W. (1976). Theory of the firm: Managerial behavior, agency costs and ownership structure. *Journal of Financial Economics*, 3(4):305–360.

Johns, K., Kromann, J., and McLinden, G. (2011). Russian federation customs development project: Measurable progress. *World Bank Europe & Central Asia Knowledge Brief*, 41.

Johnson, S., Kaufmann, D., McMillan, J., and Woodruff, C. (2000). Why do firms hide? Bribes and unofficial activity after communism. *Journal of Public Economics*, 76(3):495–520.

Johnson, S., Kaufmann, D., Shleifer, A., Goldman, M., and Weitzman, M. (1997). The unofficial economy in transition. *Brookings Papers on Economic Activity*, (2):159–239.

Johnson, S., McMillan, J., and Woodruff, C. (2002a). Courts and relational contracts. *Journal of Law, Economics, & Organization*, 18(1):221–277.

Johnson, S., McMillan, J., and Woodruff, C. (2002b). Property rights and finance. *American Economic Review*, 92(5):1335–1356.

Joireman, S. (2011). *Where There Is No Government: Enforcing Property Rights in Common Law Africa*. Oxford and New York: Oxford University Press.

Jones Luong, P., and Weinthal, E. (2004). Contra coercion: Russian tax reform, exogenous shocks, and negotiated institutional change. *American Political Science Review*, 98(1):139–152.

Kahn, P. (2002). The Russian bailiffs service and the enforcement of civil judgments. *Post-Soviet Affairs*, 18(2):148–181.

Kaufmann, D., Pradhan, S., and Ryterman, R. (2001). World Bank finds new ways to diagnose corruption symptoms. *Beyond Transition: The Newsletter about Transforming Economies*, 10(1):10–11.

Khodorych, A. (April 17, 2002). Poslednii dovod zashchity [The defense's last argument]. *Dengi*.

King, G., Honaker, J., Joseph, A., and Scheve, K. (2001). Analyzing incomplete political science data: An alternative algorithm for multiple imputation. *American Political Science Review*, 94(1):49–69.

Knack, S., and Keefer, P. (1995). Institutions and economic performance: Cross-country tests using alternative institutional measures. *Economics and Politics*, 7(3):207–227.

Kommersant (December 1, 2008). Bureaucrats are mostly the victims of contract killing in Russia.

Kornai, J. (1992). *The Soviet System: The Political Economy of Communism*. Oxford and New York: Oxford University Press.

Kramer, A. (September 29, 2005). $13 billion Sibneft deal fulfills Gazprom quest. *New York Times*.

Kramer, A. (December 21, 2006). Shell cedes control of Sakhalin-2 to Gazprom. *New York Times*.

Kramer, A. (July 25, 2008). Vladimir Putin's comments drive a company's stock down $6 billion. *New York Times*.

Kramer, A. (February 2, 2010). Russia's evolution, seen through golden arches. *New York Times*.

Kramer, A. (August 8, 2013). Russia's Stimulus Plan: Open the Gulag Gates. *New York Times*.

Krylov, A., Krylov, G., and Sidorov, V. (2008). *Bankir pod pritselom [Banker in the Crosshairs]*. Moscow: Novaya Yustitsiya.

Kuran, T. (1989). Sparks and prairie fires: A theory of unanticipated political revolution. *Public Choice*, 61(1):41–74.

Kwok, C. C., and Tadesse, S. (2006). The MNC as an agent of change for host-country institutions: FDI and corruption. *Journal of International Business Studies*, 37(6):767–785.

Lafontaine, F., and Slade, M. (2007). Vertical integration and firm boundaries: The evidence. *Journal of Economic Literature*, 45(3): 629–685.

Laitin, D. (1998). *Identity in Formation: The Russian-Speaking Populations in the Near Abroad*. Ithaca, NY: Cornell University Press.

Lamberson, P., and Page, S. (2012). Tipping points. *Quarterly Journal of Political Science*, 7(2):175–208.

Larraín, F. and Tavares, J. (2004). Does foreign direct investment decrease corruption? *Cuadernos de economía*, 41(123):199–215.

Lashkina, E. (November 9, 2007). Chopnutie: Chastnie okhrannie predpriyatiya postavili pod kontrol [Private security agencies have been brought under control]. *Rossiiskaya gazeta*.

Lazareva, O., Rachinsky, A., and Stepanov, S. (2007). A survey of corporate governance in Russia. CEFIR/NES Working Paper No. 103.

Ledeneva, A. (2006). *How Russia Really Works: The Informal Practices That Shaped Post-Soviet Politics and Business*. Ithaca, NY: Cornell University Press.

Levada Center (2010). *Otnoshenie predpriyatii k sudebnoy sisteme [Enterprises' relations with the court system]*.

Levi, M. (1989). *Of Rule and Revenue*. Berkeley, CA: University of California Press.

Levine, R. (2005). Finance and growth: Theory and evidence. In Aghion, P. and Durlauf, S., editors, *Handbook of Economic Growth*. Amsterdam: Elsevier.

Levitsky, S., and Slater, D. (2013). Ruling Politics: The Formal and Informal Foundations of Institutional Reform. Unpublished Manuscript, Harvard University and University of Chicago.

Libecap, G. (1993). *Contracting for Property Rights*. Cambridge and New York: Cambridge University Press.

Libman, A., and Feld, L. (2007). Strategic tax collection and fiscal decentralization: The case of Russian regions. CESIFO Working Paper No. 2031.

Lysova, A., Shchitov, N., and Pridemore, W. (2012). Homicide in Russia, Ukraine, and Belarus. In Liem, M. and Pridemore, A., editors, *Handbook of European Homicide Research: Patterns, Explanations, and Country Studies*. Springer Science Business Media, LLC.

Macaulay, S. (1963). Non-contractual relations and business: A preliminary study. *American Sociological Review*, 28:55–69.

Markus, S. (2007). Capitalists of all Russia, unite! Business mobilization under debilitated dirigisme. *Polity*, 39(3):277–304.

Markus, S. (2012). Secure property as a bottom-up process: Firms, stakeholders, and predators in weak states. *World Politics*, 64(2):242–277.

Markus, S. (2015). *Property, Predation, and Protection: Piranha Capitalism in Russia and Ukraine*. Cambridge and New York: Cambridge University Press.

Matveeva, N. (2007). Kriminologicheskiy analiz sostoyaniya zashchishchennosti predprinimatelei ot tyazhkogo nasiliya v Tsentralnom Federalnom okruge [Criminological analysis of the entrepreneurs' degree of protection from harmful violence in the Central Federal District]. In Dolgova, A.,

editor, *Kriminalnaya ekonimika i organizovannaya prestupnost [The Criminal Economy and Organized Crime]*. Moscow: The Russian Criminological
Association and the Nizhgovorod Academy of the MVD.

McFaul, M., and Stoner-Weiss, K. (2008). The myth of the authoritarian model:
How Putin's crackdown holds Russia back. *Foreign Affairs*, 87(1):68–84.

McMillan, J., and Woodruff, C. (1999). Dispute prevention without courts in
Vietnam. *Journal of Law, Economics, and Organization*, 15(3):637–658.

McMillan, J., and Woodruff, C. (2000). Private order under dysfunctional public
order. *Michigan Law Review*, 98(8):2421–2458.

Mendras, M. (2012). *Russian Politics: The Paradox of a Weak State*. New York:
Columbia University Press.

Mereminskaya, Y. (September 29, 2016). Russian Anti-Monopoly Service: State
Doubles Presence over Past Decade. *Moscow Times*.

Mereu, F. (June 20, 2008). Everyone pays, few want to stop. *Moscow Times*.

Merrill, T., and Smith, H. (2001). The property/contract interface. *Columbia Law
Review*, 101(4):773–852.

Migdal, J. (1988). *Strong Societies and Weak States: State-Society Relations and State
Capabilities in the Third World*. Princeton, NJ: Princeton University Press.

Migdal, J. (2001). *State in Society: Studying How States and Societies Transform and
Constitute One Another*. Cambridge and New York: Cambridge University
Press.

Milhaupt, C., and Pistor, K. (2008). *Law & Capitalism: What Corporate Crises
Reveal about Legal Systems and Economic Development around the World*.
Chicago: University of Chicago Press.

Milhaupt, C., and West, M. (2000). The dark side of private ordering: An institutional and empirical analysis of organized crime. *University of Chicago Law
Review*, 67(1):41–98.

Mnookin, R., and Kornhauser, L. (1978). Bargaining in the shadow of the law: The
case of divorce. *Yale Law Journal*, 88(5):950–997.

Modestov, N. (1996). *Moskva banditskaya [Criminal Moscow]*. Moscow: Tsentr-
poligraf.

Moustafa, T. (2007). *The Struggle for Constitutional Power: Law, politics, and
economic development in Egypt*. Cambridge and New York: Cambridge University Press.

Murrell, P. (2003). Firms facing new institutions: Transactional governance in
Romania. *Journal of Comparative Economics*, 31:695–714.

Myers, S., and Becker, J. (December 25, 2014). Even loyalty no guarantee against
Putin. *New York Times*.

Nazrullaeva, E., Baranov, A., and Yakovlev, A. (2013). Criminal persecution of busi-
ness in Russia's regions: Private interests vs. "stick" system. Working Paper.
International Center for the Study of Institutions and Development at the
Higher School of Economics.

Noel, M., Kantur, Z., and Krasnov, Y. (2006). Development of capital markets and institutional investors in Russia: Recent achievements and policy challenges ahead. World Bank Working Paper No. 87.

North, D. (1981). *Structure and Change in Economic History*. New York: Norton.

North, D. (1990). *Institutions, Institutional Change, and Economic Performance*. Cambridge and New York: Cambridge University Press.

North, D., and Weingast, B. (1989). Constitutions and commitment: The evolution of institutional governing public choice in seventeenth-century England. *Journal of Economic history*, 49(4):803–832.

OECD (2004). *Legal Issues with Regard to Business Operations and Investment in Ukraine*. OECD Publishing.

OECD (2005). Regulatory Reform in Russia: Enhancing Market Openness through Regulatory Reform. OECD Reviews of Regulatory Reform.

OECD (2009). *OECD Economic Surveys: Russian Federation*. Organization for Economic Cooperation and Development.

Olearchyk, R. (November 16, 2010). Big protest at Ukraine tax reforms. *Financial Times*.

Olson, M. (1965). *The Logic of Collective Action: Public Goods and the Theory of Groups*. Cambridge: Harvard University Press.

Olson, M. (1993). Dictatorship, democracy, and development. *American Political Science Review*, 87(3):567–576.

OPORA (2005). *Usloviya i faktory razvitiya malogo predprinimatelstva v regionakh Rossii [Conditions and Factors of Small Business Development in the Russian Regions]*.

OPORA (2006). *Usloviya i faktory razvitiya malogo predprinimatelstva v regionakh Rossii [Conditions and Factors of Small Business Development in the Russian Regions]*.

Orlov, B. (2008a). My investiryuem v cheloveka i tekhnologii! [We are investing in people and technology!]. *kp.ru*. December 9.

Orlov, B. (2008b). My okhranyaem vse – ot kvartiry do gidro elektrostantsii [We guard everything – from an apartment to a hydroelectric station]. *kp.ru*. September 8.

Panibratov, A., and Kalotay, K. (2009). Russian outward FDI and its policy context. Columbia FDI Files, Vale Columbia Center on Sustainable International Investment.

Pappe, Y., and Galukhina, Y. (2009). *Rossiiskii krupnyi biznes: pervyi 15 let, 1993-2008 [Russian Big Business: The First 15 Years, 1993–2008]*. Moscow: Higher School of Economics.

Peerenboom, R. (2002). *China's Long March toward Rule of Law*. Cambridge and New York: Cambridge University Press.

Pei, M. (2001). Does legal reform protect economic transactions? Commercial disputes in China. In Murrell, P., editor, *Assessing the Value of Law in Transition Economies*. Ann Arbor: University of Michigan Press.

Pinto, P., and Zhu, B. (2009). Fortune or evil? The effect of inward foreign direct investment on corruption. Available at SSRN 1324750.

Pistor, K. (1996). Supply and demand for contract enforcement in Russia: Courts, arbitration, and private enforcement. *Review of Central and East European Law*, 22(1):55–87.

Pistor, K., Wellons, P., and Sachs, J. (1999). *The Role of Law and Legal Institutions in Asian Economic Development: 1960–1995*. Oxford and New York: Oxford University Press.

Polishchuk, L., and Savvateev, A. (2004). Spontaneous (non)emergence of property rights. *Economics of Transition*, 12(1):103–127.

Pomeranz, W. (October 28, 2013). Russia's fading judiciary. *The National Interest*.

Portes, A., and Hoffman, K. (2003). Latin American class structures: Their composition and change during the neoliberal era. *Latin American Research Review*, 38(1):41–82.

Poser, J. (1998). Monetary disruptions and the emergence of barter in FSU economies. *Communist Economies and Economic Transformation*, 10(2): 157–177.

Posner, R. (1998). Creating a legal framework for economic development. *The World Bank Research Observer*, 13(1):1–11.

Potanin, V. (2003). Corporate governance: "Russian Model" in progress. *Journal on Foreign Affairs and International Relations*.

Pravotorov, M. (October 4, 2006). Proshchay, "krysha"! [Goodbye rackets!]. *Profil*.

Proskurin, S. (January 14, 2015). Khozyastvennye sudy: stoit li rubit s plecha? [The commercial courts: Pulling no punches?]. *Vlasti.net*.

Pryadilnikov, M. (2009). The state and markets in Russia: Understanding the development of bureaucratic implementation capacities through the study of regulatory reform, 2001–2008. Doctoral Dissertation, Department of Government, Harvard University.

Putnam, R. (1994). *Making Democracy Work: Civic Traditions in Modern Italy*. Princeton, NJ: Princeton University Press.

Pyle, W. (2005a). Collective action and post-communist enterprise: The economic logic of Russia's business associations. William Davidson Institute Working Paper No. 794.

Pyle, W. (2005b). Contractual disputes and the channels for interfirm communication. *Journal of Law, Economics, and Organization*, 21(2):547–575.

Pyle, W. (2011). Organized business, political competition, and property rights: Evidence from the Russian Federation. *Journal of Law, Economics, and Organization*, 27(1):2–31.

Radaev, V. (1999). The role of violence in Russian business relations. *Problems of Economic Transition*, 41(12):34–61.

Radaev, V. (2002). Institutsionalnaya dinamika rynkov i formirovanie novych konseptsii kontrolya [Institutional market dynamics and the formation of new concepts of control]. Higher School of Economics working paper.

Radygin, A., and Arkhipov, S. (2001). Tendentsii v structure sobstvennosti, intensivnost korporativnykh konfliktov i finansovoe sostoyanie predpriyatii: Empiricheskii analiz i problemy gosudarstvennogo regulirovaniya [Trends in ownership structure, the intensity of corporate conflicts, and the financial condition of enterprises: Empirical analysis and problems for government regulation]. Working Paper of the Russian-European Center for Economic Policy.

Radygin, A., Entov, R., Gontmakher, A., and Mezheraups, I. (2004). Ekonomiko-pravovye faktory i ogranicheniya v stanovlenii modeley korporativnogo upravleniya [Economic-legal factors and limitations for the creation of a corporate governance model]. Working Paper of the Russian-European Center for Economic Policy.

Rajah, J. (2012). *Authoritarian Rule of Law: Legislation, Discourse and Legitimacy in Singapore*. Cambridge and New York: Cambridge University Press.

Ram, V. (March 12, 2009). Why you should still be worried about Russia. *Forbes*.

Reynolds, G. (August 19, 2005). Ukraine revenue up as tax dodging falls, premier says. *Bloomberg.com*.

Riker, W., and Sened, I. (1991). A political theory of the origin of property rights: Airport slots. *American Journal of Political Science*, 35(4):951–969.

Rimskii, V. (2009). Vzaimodeistvie s sudami predprinimateley po delam ikh biznesov [Entrepreneurs' use of the courts in relation to their business activities]. Unpublished report. INDEM Foundation.

Root, H. (1989). Tying the king's hands: Credible commitments and royal fiscal policy during the Old Regime. *Rationality and Society*, 1(2):240–258.

Rutland, P. (2009). Putin and the oligarchs. In Wegren, S. and Herspring, D., editors, *After Putin's Russia: Past Imperfect, Future Uncertain*. Lanham, MD: Rowman and Littlefield.

Sakwa, R. (2014). *Putin and the Oligarch: The Khodorkovsky-Yukos Affair*. London: I.B. Tauris & Co. Ltd.

Sborov, A. (July 21, 2003). Oborotni v pogonakh [Were wolves in Epaulets]. *Vlast.*

Schelling, T. (1971). Dynamic models of segregation. *Journal of Mathematical Sociology*, 1(2):143–186.

Sevastyanov, G., and Tsyplenkova, A. (2007). Tendentsii razvitiya institutsional-nykh nachal alternativnogo razresheniya sporov [Trends in the Development of Institutional Foundations for Alternative Dispute Resolution]. *Vestnik VAS*, 63(4).

Shebaldin, Y. (October 2007). Na grani fola [Almost a foul]. *Ogyenok*, 43.

Shelley, L. (2007). The government bureaucracy, corruption, and organized crime: Impact on the business community. In Hendley, K., editor, *Remaking the Role of Law: Commercial Law in Russia and the CIS*. Huntington, NY: Juris.

Shetinin, O., Zamulin, O., Zhuravskaya, E., and Yakovlev, E. (2005). Monitoring the administrative barriers to small business development in Russia. 5th Round. CEFIR Policy Paper series No. 22.

Shim, D. C., and Eom, T. H. (2008). E-government and anti-corruption: Empirical analysis of international data. *International Journal of Public Administration*, 31(3):298–316.

Shleifer, A., and Treisman, D. (2001). *Without a Map: Political Tactics and Economic Reform in Russia*. Cambridge: The MIT Press.

Shleifer, A., and Vishny, R. (1998). *The Grabbing Hand: Government Pathologies and Their Cures*. Cambridge: Harvard University Press.

Silverstein, G. (2003). Globalization and the rule of law: A machine that runs itself? *International Journal of Comparative Law*, 1(3):427–445.

Silverstein, G. (2008). Singapore: The exception that proves rules matter. In Ginsburg, T. and Moustafa, T., editors, *Rule by Law: The Politics of Courts in Authoritarian Regimes*. Cambridge and New York: Cambridge University Press.

Skoblikov, P. (1997). *Istrebovanie dolgov i organizovannaya prestupnost [Debt Collection and Organized Crime]*. Moscow: Yurist.

Skoblikov, P. (2001). *Imushchestvennye spory i kriminal v sovremennoy Rossii [Property Disputes and Criminals in Modern Russia]*. Moscow: Publishing House DELO.

Skvortsova, E. (July 14, 2000). Gromkie zakaznie ubiistva [Bold contract killings]. *Agenstvo federalnykh ressledovanii*.

Solomon, P. (1997). The persistence of judicial reform in contemporary Russia. *East European Constitutional Review*, 6:50–56.

Solomon, P. (2004). Judicial power in Russia: Through the prism of administrative justice. *Law & Society Review*, 38(3):549–582.

Solomon, P. (2005). The reform of policing in the Russian Federation. *Australian & New Zealand Journal of Criminology*, 38(2):230–240.

Solomon, P. (2008). Assessing the courts in Russia: Parameters of progress under Putin. *Demokratizatsiya: Journal of Post-Soviet Democratization*, 16(1):63–73.

Sonin, K. (2003). Why the rich may favor protection of property rights. *Journal of Comparative Economics*, 31(4):715–731.

Spector, R. (2008). Securing property in contemporary Kyrgyzstan. *Post-Soviet Affairs*, 24(2):149–176.

Sprenger, C. (2010). State ownership in the russian economy: Its magnitude, structure and governance problems. *Journal of Institute of Public Enterprise*, 33(1–2):63–110.

Statkus, V. (1998). Raskrytie prestuplenii – vazhneishee sredtsvo borby s prestupnostyu [Solving crimes – the most important tool for the struggle against criminality]. *Gosudarstvo i pravo*, (4):66–73.

Stern, R. (2013). *Environmental Litigation in China: A Study in Political Ambivalence*. Cambridge and New York: Cambridge University Press.

Taylor, B. (2007). *Russia's Power Ministries: Coercion and Commerce*. Syracuse, NY: Institute for National Security and Counterterrorism, Syracuse University.

Taylor, B. (2011). *State Building in Putin's Russia: Policing and Coercion after Communism*. Cambridge and New York: Cambridge University Press.

Taylor, B. (2014). Police reform in Russia: The policy process in a hybrid regime. *Post-Soviet Affairs*, 30(2-3):226–255.

Taylor, P., and Jonker, L. (1978). Evolutionary stable strategies and game dynamics. *Mathematical Biosciences*, 40(1-2):145–156.

Tolstych, P. (June 2, 2005). Administrativnye sudy i rynok sudebnykh posrednikov [Administrative courts and the market for judicial intermediaries]. *Polit.ru*.

Tompson, W. (1999). The price of everything and the value of nothing? Unravelling the workings of Russia's "virtual economy." *Economy and Society*, 28(2): 256–280.

Tompson, W. (2004). Banking reform in Russia: Problems and prospects. OECD Economics Working Paper No. 410.

Tovkailo, M. (August 18, 2011). Medvedev orders customs service reforms. *Moscow Times*.

Treisman, D. (1999). Russia's tax crisis: Explaining falling revenues in a transitional economy. *Economics & Politics*, 11(2):145–169.

Treisman, D. (2002). Russia renewed? *Foreign Affairs*, 81(6):58–72.

Treisman, D. (2003). Fiscal pathologies and federal politics: Understanding tax arrears in Russia's regions. In McClaren, J., editor, *Institutional Elements of Tax Design and Reform*. World Bank Publications.

Treshchev, S. (December 17, 2013). Obedinenie sudov [Merging of the Courts]. *lawfirm.ru*.

Tsai, K. (2007). *Capitalism without Democracy: The Private Sector in Contemporary China*. Ithaca, NY: Cornell University Press.

Tyler, T. (1990). *Why People Obey the Law*. New Haven, CT: Yale University Press.

Umbeck, J. (1981). *A Theory of Property Rights: With Application to the California Gold Rush*. Ames, IA: Iowa State University Press.

Uzzi, B. (1996). The sources and consequences of embeddedness for the economic performance of organizations: The network effect. *American Sociological Review*, 61(4):674–698.

Varese, F. (2001). *The Russian Mafia*. Oxford and New York: Oxford University Press.

Vestnik federalnoy palaty advokatov rossiiskoi federatsii (2010). Informatsionnaya spravka o sostoyanii advokatury i advokatskoy deyatelnosti v 2009 [Report on the State of the Bar and the Legal Profession's Activity in 2009]. 28(2):32.

Volkov, V. (2002). *Violent Entrepreneurs: The Use of Force in the Making of Russian Capitalism*. Ithaca, NY: Cornell University Press.

Volkov, V. (2004). The selective use of state capacity in Russia's economy: Property disputes and enterprise takeovers, 1998–2002. *Review of Central and East European Law*, (4):527–548.

Volkov, V. (2005). Po tu storonu sudebnoy sistemy, ili Pochemu zakony rabotayut ne tak, kak dolzhny [The other side of the court system, or, Why laws don't work like they are supposed to]. *Niprikosnovennii zapas*, (42).

Volkov, V., Paneyakh, E., and Titaev, K. (2010). Proizvolnaya aktivnost pravookhranitelnykh organov v sfere borby s ekonomicheskoy prestupnostyu [Arbitrary activity of law enforcement agencies in the sphere of the struggle with economic crime]. Analytical Paper. Institute for the Rule of Law.

Vysshyi arbitrazhnyi sud (VAS) [High commercial court] (2011). *Osnovnye pokazateli raboty arbitrazhniykh sudov RF [Basic Indicators of the Work of the Commercial Courts of the RF]*. www.arbitr.ru.

Wall Street Journal (June 15, 2011). Khodorkovksy unabridged.

Wang, Y. (2015). *Tying the Autocrat's Hands: The Rise of the Rule of Law in China*. Cambridge and New York: Cambridge University Press.

Wank, D. (1999). Producing Property Rights: Strategies, Networks, and Efficiency in Urban China's Nonstate Firms. In Oi, J. and Walder, A., editors, *Property Rights and Economic Reform in China*. Palo Alto, CA: Stanford University Press.

Wank, D. (2004). Business-state clientelism in China: Decline or evolution. In Gold, T., Guthrie, D., and Wank, D., editors, *Social Connections in China: Institutions, Culture, and the Changing Nature of* Guanxi. Cambridge and New York: Cambridge University Press.

Webster, W. (1997). *Russian Organized Crime: Global Organized Crime Project*. Washington, DC: Center for Strategic and International Studies.

Weingast, B. (1995). The economic role of political institutions: Market-preserving federalism and economic development. *Journal of Law, Economics, and Organization*, 11(1):1–31.

Weingast, B. (1997). The political foundations of democracy and the rule of law. *American Political Science Review*, 91(2):245–263.

Whiting, S. (2010). Contracting and dispute resolution among Chinese firms: Law and its substitutes. In Leng, T.-K. and Chu, Y.-h., editors, *Dynamics of Local Governance in China during the Reform Era*. Lanham, MD: Lexington Books.

Williamson, O. (1985). *The Economic Institutions of Capitalism*. New York: Macmillan, Inc.

Wilson, I. (2010). Reconfiguring rackets: Racket regimes, protection and the state in post-New Order Jakarta. In Aspinall, E. and van Klinken, G., editors, *The State and Illegality in Indonesia*. Lanham, MD: Lexington Books.

Winn, J. K. (1994). Relational practices and the marginalization of law: Informal financial practices of small businesses in Taiwan. *Law and Society Review*, 193–232.

Winters, J. (2011). *Oligarchy*. Cambridge and New York: Cambridge University Press.

Woodruff, D. (2002). The end of "primitive capitalist accumulation"? The new bankruptcy law and the political assertiveness of Russian big business. PONARS Policy Memo No. 274.

Yaffa, J. (December 28, 2013). Signs of a Russian thaw (toward business). *New York Times.*

Yakovlev, A. (2001). "Black cash" tax evasion in Russia: Its forms, incentives and consequences at firm level. *Europe-Asia Studies,* 53(1):33–55.

Yakovlev, A. (2008). Pravo i pravoprimenenie v Rossii glazami biznesa: Chto izmenilos za sem let [Law and law enforcement in Russia through the eyes of business: What has changed in the last seven years]. In Tikhomirov, Y., editor, *Pravoprimenenie: teoriya i praktika [Law Enforcment: Theory and Practice].* Moscow: Formula prava.

Yakovlev, A., Golikova, V., Dolgopyatova, T., Kuznetsov, B., and Simachev, Y. (2004). *Spros na pravo v sfere korporativnogo upravleniya: ekonomichekie aspekty [Demand for Law in the Sphere of Corporate Governance: Economic Aspects].* Moscow: Higher School of Economics.

Yakovlev, A., Sobolev, A., and Kazun, A. (2014). Means of production versus means of coercion: Can Russian business limit the violence of a predatory state? *Post-Soviet Affairs,* 30(2–3):171–194.

Yasinskaya, M. (September 19, 2014). Byt li khozyaistvennym sudam v Ukraine? [Will there be commercial courts in Ukraine?]. *Yurliga.ligazakon.ua.*

Yefymenko, A. (2009). Corporate governance under Ukraine's new Joint Stock Company Law. Working paper, Institute of International Relations of Kyiv Taras Shevchenko University.

Yeltsov, O. (September 11, 2003). Reket: vglyad iz proshlogo [The racket: View from the past]. *Biznes.*

Yudaeva, K., Kozlov, K., Melentieva, N., and Ponomareva, N. (2003). Does foreign ownership matter?: The Russian Experience. *Economics of Transition,* 11(3):383–409.

Zakhvataev, V. (2001). Ukraine tackles court reform with unification. *International Financial Law Review,* 20:46.

Zarakhovich, Y. (2009). Mikhail Gutseriyev and the expediency of Russian justice. *Eurasia Daily Monitor,* 6(206).

Zhdanova, N. (January 19, 2012). Nuzhno reshat bazovye problemy, togda dolya nalichnykh deneg v obrashchenii umenshitsya [It's necessary to resolve fundamental problems to reduce the share of cash in circulation]. *Kommersant.*

Zhuravskaya, E. (2007). Whither Russia? A review of Andrei Shleifer's "A Normal Country". *Journal of Economic Literature,* 45(1):127–146.

Zolotukhina, I. (January 5, 2010). V ukrainu vernulsya reket [The racket has returned to Ukraine]. *Segodnya.ua.*

Zysman, J. (1983). *Governments, Markets, and Growth: Financial Systems and the Politics of Industrial Change.* Ithaca, NY: Cornell University Press.

INDEX

Note: "*fig*" after a locator refers to a figure, while tables are indicated by "t" after the locator.

CPSIA information can be obtained
at www.ICGtesting.com
Printed in the USA
LVHW050919290419
615923LV00010B/165/P